# Secure Edge Computing

# Secure Edge Computing

## Applications, Techniques and Challenges

*Edited by*
Mohiuddin Ahmed and Paul Haskell-Dowland

## CRC Press
Taylor & Francis Group
Boca Raton  London  New York

CRC Press is an imprint of the
Taylor & Francis Group, an **informa** business

First edition published 2022
by CRC Press
6000 Broken Sound Parkway NW, Suite 300, Boca Raton, FL 33487-2742

and by CRC Press
2 Park Square, Milton Park, Abingdon, Oxon, OX14 4RN

CRC Press is an imprint of Taylor & Francis Group, LLC

ISBN: 978-0-367-46414-1 (hbk)
ISBN: 978-1-032-05632-6 (pbk)
ISBN: 978-1-003-02863-5 (ebk)

Typeset in Sabon
by SPi Technologies India Pvt Ltd (Straive)

Dedicated to

*'My Loving Siblings: Farid and Nizam'*

**Mohiuddin Ahmed**

# Contents

# Preface

The Internet is making our daily life increasingly digital, introducing a new era – the Internet of Everything (IoE). Edge computing is an emerging data analytics concept to address the challenges associated with IoE. More specifically, edge computing facilitates data analysis at the edge of the network instead of interacting with cloud-based servers. The consequence of this is that more devices will be added in remote locations without any overarching monitoring strategy. The increased connectivity and devices used for edge computing will create more opportunity for cyber criminals to exploit the system and its vulnerabilities.

Ensuring cyber security at the edge is a significant challenge and addressing it should not be an afterthought. The devices used for edge computing are not designed with traditional IT hardware protocols. There are diverse use cases in the context of edge computing and Internet of Things (IoT) devices in remote locations. However, cyber security configuration and software updates are often overlooked when it is most needed to fight cyber-crime and ensure data privacy. Therefore, the threat landscape in the context of edge computing becomes wider and far more challenging. There is a clear need for collaborative work throughout the entire value chain of the network.

In this context, this book addresses the cyber security challenges associated with edge computing, and will provide a bigger picture on the concepts, techniques, applications and open research directions in this area. In addition, this book will serve as a single source of reference for acquiring knowledge on the technology, process and people involved in the next generation of computing and security.

### Section I
Chapter 1: Secure Fog-Cloud of Things: Architectures, Opportunities and Challenges
Chapter 2: Collaborative and Integrated Edge Security Architecture
Chapter 3: A Systemic IoT–Fog–Cloud Architecture for Big-Data Analytics and Cyber Security Systems: A Review of Fog Computing
Chapter 4: Security and Organizational Strategy: A Cloud and Edge Computing Perspective
Chapter 5: An Overview of Cognitive Internet of Things: Cloud and Fog Computing
Chapter 6: Privacy of Edge Computing and IoT

### Section II
Chapter 7: Reducing the Attack Surface of Edge Computing IoT Networks via Hybrid Routing Using Dedicated Nodes
Chapter 8: Early Identification of Mental Health Disorder Employing Machine Learning-based Secure Edge Analytics: A Real-time Monitoring System
Chapter 9: Harnessing Artificial Intelligence for Secure ECG Analytics at the Edge for Cardiac Arrhythmia Classification

The first section contains six chapters which cover the fundamental concepts of edge computing architecture and security aspects. These chapters reflect important knowledge areas such as security architecture, big data and organizational strategies. The second section has five chapters that cover the usage of edge computing in different applications, with a specific focus on healthcare applications (an emerging trend for edge computing with commensurate opportunities for future research). The third section is dedicated to the application domain of Internet-connected vehicles while the final section contains two chapters relating to edge computing applications for blockchain.

Mohiuddin Ahmed
Paul Haskell-Dowland

# Acknowledgments

It is another incredible book editing experience and our sincere gratitude goes to the publisher for facilitating the process. This book editing journey enhanced our patience, communication and tenacity. We are thankful to all the contributors, reviewers and publishing team. Last but not least, our thanks to our family members whose support and encouragement contributed significantly to completing this book.

# Editors

**Dr Mohiuddin Ahmed** is currently working as lecturer of Computing and Security in the School of Science at Edith Cowan University. Mohiuddin has been working in the areas of data analytic and cyber security, in particular false data injection attacks in Internet of Health Things (IoHT) and Internet of Flying Things (IoFT). His research projects are funded by different external agencies. He has edited books on data analytics, security analytics, blockchain and other contemporary issues. He has also engaged with media outlets such as newspapers, magazines, *The Conversation*, etc. He is also an ACM Distinguished Speaker, Australian Computer Society certified professional and a senior member of IEEE.

**Associate Professor Paul Haskell-Dowland** is the associate dean for Computing and Security in the School of Science at Edith Cowan University. Paul has delivered keynotes, invited presentations, workshops, professional development/training and seminars across the world for audiences including RSA Security, ITU and IEEE. He has appeared on local and national media (newspaper, radio and TV) commenting on current cyber issues as well as contributions through articles published in *The Conversation*. Paul has more than 20 years of experience in cyber security research and education in both the UK and Australia.

# Contributors

**Monjur Ahmed** is senior lecturer and research leader at the Centre for Information Technology (CfIT), Waikato Institute of Technology, New Zealand. Monjur's research areas include Cyber Leadership, Information Security & Privacy, Securing computing environment through Decentralized Computing, Cloud Computing, edge computing, fog computing and Internet-of-Things. He has contributed in research events and conference in New Zealand and internationally with different roles as organizing/committee member. Monjur is a member (MIITP) of IT Professionals New Zealand (ITPNZ). He is certified in cybersecurity leadership and holds GIAC Strategic Planning, Policy and Leadership (GSTRT).

**Sabbir Ahmed is** currently working as a PhD researcher student at the UniSA STEM, University of South Australia. Prior to joining University of South Australia, he worked as an assistant professor in the Department of Computer Science, American International University–Bangladesh (AIUB), Dhaka, Bangladesh. He earned his BSc and MSc in computer science from the same university. His research work focuses on the cyber security but is not limited to that field. At present, his research plan and study concentrates on big data analytics for the distributed system.

**Mehmet Ali Eken** is an MSc student of Computer Engineering at Middle East Technical University, Turkey. He got his BS in Electrical and Electronics Engineering at Middle East Technical University in 2019. He is currently among the student members of the Wireless Systems, Networks and Cybersecurity Laboratory at METU. He is also a scholar within the 5G and Beyond Joint Graduate Support Program coordinated by Information and Communication Technologies Authority in Turkey, where he is conducting research in collaboration with Vodafone Turkey. His current research interests lie in the fields of vehicular edge computing, cybersecurity and fifth-generation wireless networks.

**Adam A. Alli** is a PhD fellow in computer science and engineering fellow at Islamic University of Technology (IUT), Board Bazar, Gazipur-1704, Bangladesh. He received his MSc in computer science (2008) at the University of Mysore, India, BSc in computer science (2002) at Islamic University in Uganda. He also received a postgraduate diploma in management and teaching at Higher Education (2015) at Islamic University in Uganda, and a graduate diploma in ICT Leadership and Knowledge Society (2013) at Dublin City University through the GeSCI program. He was dean Faculty of Science at Islamic University in Uganda from 2011 to 2016. He is a lecturer of computer science and Engineering at both Islamic University in Uganda and Uganda Technical College (UTC) Bushenyi. He is a lead researcher for Islamic University in Uganda ICT4D group.

**Shahriar Arnab** was born in Khulna, Bangladesh. In 2013, he completed his Secondary School Certificate (SSC) examination from Foylahat Kamal Uddin Secondary School in Science group. After that from Digraj Degree College he earned his higher Secondary School Certificate in 2016 from Science. At present, he has been doing his undergraduate in Electrical and Electronic Engineering in Brac University since 2017. He has also been working there as a student tutor since 2019. As his area of interests are electronics and communication, specifically microelectronics and wireless communication, he has done a major in Electronics as well as he has done some core courses in communication. He has earned some skills like leadership, communication, time management, interpersonal relationship by scouting, sports Olympiad and debating. His areas of interest include IOT, smart grid, MATLAB® and Python. Now, he is trying to do research in these areas.

**Pelin Angin** is an assistant professor of Computer Engineering at Middle East Technical University, Turkey. She completed her BS in Computer Engineering at Bilkent University in 2007 and her PhD in computer science at Purdue University, USA in 2013. Between 2014 and 2016, she worked as a visiting assistant professor and postdoctoral researcher at Purdue University. Her research interests lie in the fields of cloud computing and IoT security, distributed systems, 5G networks and blockchain. She is among the founding members of the Systems Security Research Laboratory and an affiliate of the Wireless Systems, Networks and Cybersecurity Laboratory at METU. She serves on the editorial boards of multiple journals on IoT and mobile computing. She has over 12 years of experience in cybersecurity with over 40 publications at high impact journals and conferences.

**Rachel Cardell-Oliver** studies distributed sensor networks, designing systems that integrate data measurement using environmental sensors, data collection with wireless communication systems and data analysis using data mining techniques. Working with multidisciplinary teams, she has researched environmental challenges such as understanding public transport use, reducing household water consumption, measuring water use by native Australian plants and the performance of rammed earth for sustainable buildings in outback Australia. Rachel was introduced to distributed systems during her Honours and Master's degrees in computer science at UWA, leading to a PhD on formal methods for distributed systems at the University of Cambridge. She has worked at the University of Essex in the UK and the University of Western Australia, where she is now head of Department of Computer Science and Software Engineering.

**Shivani Chaskar** has received her MSc degree in computer science from Lakehead University. Her research interests are in smart health and IoT.

**Salimur Choudhury is** an associate professor in the Department of Computer Science and leads the Optimization Research Group at Lakehead University. He received the PhD degree in computing from Queen's University, Kingston, Ontario, Canada, in 2012. The primary research focus of Dr Choudhury is network optimization, wireless communication, cellular automata, approximation algorithms and so on. He has published more than 40 peer reviewed publications and received grants from various government sectors and industries as well. He is the co-founder of the conference, SGIoT. He has been serving as an editor for the Parallel Processing Letters and the International Journal of Computers and Applications.

**Sumit Chowdhury** was born and raised in Dhaka, Bangladesh. He is currently pursuing BSc in Electrical and Electronic Engineering from Brac University in 2020. He majored in both Electronics and Computer. Winning first prize for showcasing the project titled 'Smart Street Light' in the 2019 International Conference on Energy and Power Engineering organized by IEEE Power and Energy Society was one of his best achievements in recent times. His research interests include the IoT, edge computing and wireless communication. Upon completion of his undergraduate studies, he intends to apply for the higher studies to further his knowledge of nanotechnology and progress toward a career as a researcher.

**Dhruvi Desai** has received her MSc degree in computer science from Lakehead University. Her research interests are in health informatics, security and IoT. Before immigrating to Canada in 2018, she worked as an Application Development Analyst for two years with Accenture Solutions Pvt LTD. She has pursued her BE in Computer Engineering in 2016. She is adventurous and likes to hike in new places.

**Abebe Diro** received PhD degree in Cybersecurity from La Trobe University, Australia, 2019. He received his MSc degree in computer science from Addis Ababa University, Ethiopia, in 2010. He also completed BSc degree at Haramaya University, Ethiopia, 2007. Abebe worked at Wollega University from 2007 to 2013 as a director of ICT Development and lecturer in computer science. He is currently a Postdoctoral fellow at Optus La Trobe Cyber Security Innovation Hub. He is a member of Australian Information Security Association (AISA). His research interests include machine learning based cybersecurity, IoT security, cryptography, fog security, cloud security and software-defined networking.

**Mahzabeen Emu** is a graduate research assistant at the Department of Computer Science, Lakehead University. She was awarded a BSc degree in computer science and engineering from Ahsanullah University of Science and Technology (AUST) in 2017. She is currently pursuing her MSc in computer science at Lakehead University. Her research interests include optimization, IoT and artificial intelligence in the field of networking. She was awarded with Gold Medal award at the 10th convocation of Ahsanullah University of Science and Technology (AUST) by the Education Minister of Bangladesh. She is the recipient of Vector Institute AI Masters Scholarship (2019), MITACS accelerate research award (2020), Ontario Graduate Scholarship-OGS 2020-21.

**Fariha Eusufzai** was born and raised in Dhaka, Bangladesh. She is currently pursuing BSc in Electrical and Electronics Engineering from Brac University in 2020. She has done her major in the Communication sector. She currently occupies the job of an intern in the Brac University Research and Development Lab as a content writer. She has received the 'VICE Chancellor Award' for maintaining discipline and devotion to duties during a Residential Semester at Brac University. Her research interests include MIMO-OFDM/NOMA, Wireless Communication, IoT and smart city. After finishing her graduation, she plans to proceed to pursue higher education to advance her understanding of cognitive IoT and smart city and to advance her career in research.

**Mostafa M. Fouda** received the BS (Hons.) and MS degrees in electrical engineering from Benha University, Egypt, in 2002 and 2007, respectively, and the PhD degree in information sciences from Tohoku University, Japan, in 2011. He is currently an assistant professor with the Department of Electrical and Computer Engineering, Idaho State University, ID, USA. He also holds the position of associate professor with Benha University, Egypt. He has served as an assistant professor with Tohoku University, Japan. He was a Postdoctoral research associate with Tennessee Technological University, USA. He has published over 30 articles in IEEE conference proceedings and journals. His research interests include cyber security, machine learning, blockchain, the IoT, 5G networks, smart healthcare, and smart grid communications. He has served on the technical committees of several IEEE conferences. He is also a reviewer in several IEEE Transactions and Magazines and an associate editor of IEEE Access.

**David G. Glance** is the director of the UWA Centre for Software and Security Practice, a UWA research and development center. Dr Glance worked in the finance and software industry for over 20 years before spending the last 18 years at UWA. The UWA CSSP provides training and research opportunities for students and has developed commercial software in the health and education sectors that is being used across Australia in hospitals, GP clinics and aboriginal medical services. Dr Glance has consulted with the OECD on reviewing national cybersecurity strategies and assessments of cybersecurity maturity in national SMEs. Dr Glance has written monographs, chapters and numerous research papers and has published over 500 articles working as a columnist for The Conversation. Dr Glance regularly appears on radio and TV discussing cybersecurity and other topics.

**Habiba Hamid** is a PhD candidate at the Department of Computer System & Technology, Faculty of Computer Science & Information Technology, Universiti Malaya (UM), Kuala Lumpur, Malaysia. She holds a master's degree in Information Technology from International Islamic University Malaysia (IIUM) and a bachelor's degree in Information Technology from the Islamic University in Uganda (IUIU), Mbale. Her research interests include IoT Security, Wireless Sensor Networks, big data and Machine Learning. She is a researcher with the Department of Computer System & Technology, Faculty of Computer Science & Information Technology, Universiti Malaya (UM).

**Tahmidul Haq** is currently pursuing the BSc degree in Electronic and Communication Engineering from Brac University, Dhaka, Bangladesh. His research interests include NOMA, cognitive radio, IoT and wireless communication.

**Lwembawo Ibrahim** is a Master's student of Technical Education with specialization in computer science engineering at the Islamic University of Technology (IUT), Board Bazar, Gazipur-1074, Dhaka, Bangladesh. He completed his bachelor's degree in Information Technology (2018) at the Islamic University in Uganda (IUIU) and he also works as a computer Lab Officer at the same University. His main research interests include cloud computing, IoT, design thinking, digital learning, mobile computing and machine learning.

**James Jin Kang** has worked in areas including telecommunication networks, health informatics, IoHT (Internet of Health Things) and sensor networks, cybersecurity and disaster recovery using smart sensors in low-power wide area networks. He has worked in the telecommunications industry for over 25 years with projects in Spark NZ, Nokia (Alcatel-Lucent), NBN Co., Telstra, Siemens and Vodafone, Australia. He specialized in network intelligence for wired and mobile networks during the earlier stages of his career and later worked on career networks such as IP/MPLS, IMS, NGN, NBN and VoIP technologies. He recently went to Ethiopia as a volunteer IT advisor sponsored by the Australian Government (DFAT) to help NGOs and plans to teach in developing countries as a volunteer in the future.

**Kalinaki Kassim** is a technology enthusiast, researcher and a lecturer with more than 5 years teaching experience. He completed both his bachelor's and master's degrees in Technical Education with specialization in computer science and engineering from the Islamic University of Technology (IUT) in Dhaka, Bangladesh. Currently he serves both as a lecturer and the head of computer science department at Islamic University in Uganda.

His main research interests include Cybersecurity, IoT, Machine Learning, Data Science and Educational Technologies.

**Sarthak Kothari**, born in Mumbai, India, in 1993, moved to Canada in 2018. He obtained his master's degree in computer science in 2020. He graduated with a bachelor's degree in computer engineering in 2015 and worked in the information technology industry for 3 years after graduation. He also coauthored technical papers 'Managing Data Provenance in the Semantic Web' in 2019 and 'Android Suburban Railway Ticketing with GPS as Ticket Checker' in 2015 are considered to be his other significant works. he actively volunteers for projects aimed at uplifting the community. People can find him exploring nature or doodling in a coffee shop during his spare time.

**Zubair Md Fadlullah** is currently an associate professor with the Computer Science Department, Lakehead University and a Research Chair of the Thunder Bay Regional Health Research Institute (TBRHRI), Thunder Bay, Ontario, Canada. He was an associate professor at the Graduate School of Information Sciences (GSIS), Tohoku University, Japan, from 2017 to 2019. His main research interests are in the areas of emerging communication systems, such as 5G New Radio and beyond, deep learning applications on solving computer science and communication system problems, UAV-based systems, smart health technology, cyber security, game theory, smart grid and emerging communication systems. He received several best paper awards at conferences including IEEE/ACM IWCMC, IEEE GLOBECOM and IEEE IC-NIDC. He is currently editor of *IEEE Transactions on Vehicular Technology* (TVT), *IEEE Network Magazine, IEEE Access, IEEE Open Journal of the Communications Society* and *Ad Hoc & Sensor Wireless Networks* (AHSWN) journal. Dr Fadlullah is a senior member of the Institute of Electrical and Electronics Engineers (IEEE) and IEEE Communications Society (ComSoc).

**A B M Mehedi Hasan** is working as a Lecturer at Australian Institute of Higher Education, NSW, Australia. He completed his Master of Information Technology (Software Development) from University of Technology Sydney, Australia. He also completed MBA (Finance and Banking) from Jahangirnagar University, Bangladesh and Bachelor of Science in computer science from American International University, Bangladesh. His research interests are data mining, big data, business analytics and user experience design.

**Amit Kumar** received the MSc degree in computer science from Lakehead University, Thunder Bay, Canada. Prior to Master's, he worked as a software engineer at Hyderabad, India. He has filed a patent with India Patent Organization in January 2017 (current status: Published). He is also a certified ethical hacker and security analyst from Ec – Council. He has served as a cyber security trainer for over 7 years and shared his knowledge with students and working professionals across pan India. He has received critical appreciation toward his work and training programs from various colleges and universities. His current main interests are in the IoT, cyber security and machine learning.

**Dr Andrew Levula** is the director of Academic Program and acting academic dean at Sydney International School of Technology and Commerce. He completed his PhD in the Faculty of Engineering and IT at The University of Sydney and he holds a Master's of Information Communication Technology with Distinction from the University of Wollongong. He has over 8 years of program development and academic teaching experience in Information Systems. He has published many journals, book chapters, conference papers and industry reports. Additionally, He has over 7 years of industry experience having worked in Telecommunication and for the Fijian Government. In Government, he oversaw the Business Solutions Department which managed the whole of Government critical and non-critical applications. He was instrumental in the development of new Government department websites and the development of critical e-Government application systems.

**Nour Moustafa** is postgraduate discipline coordinator (Cyber) and lecturer in Cyber Security at the School of Engineering and Information Technology (SEIT), University of New South Wales (UNSW)'s UNSW Canberra Australia. He was a postdoctoral fellow in Cybersecurity at UNSW Canberra from June 2017 till February 2019. He received his PhD degree in the field of Cyber Security from UNSW in 2017. He obtained his bachelor's and master's degrees in Information Systems in 2009 and 2014, respectively, from the Faculty of Computer and Information, Helwan University, Egypt. His areas of interest include cyber security and AI, in particular, network security, AI-enabled cyber defenses, microservices, intrusion detection systems, statistics, deep learning and machine learning techniques. He is interested in designing and developing threat detection and forensic mechanisms to the Industry 4.0 technology for identifying malicious activities from cloud computing, fog computing, IoT and industrial control systems over virtual machines and physical systems. He has several research grants with totaling over AUD 1.5 Million. He has been awarded the 2020 prestigious Australian Spitfire Memorial Defence Fellowship award. He is also a senior IEEE Member, ACM distinguished speaker, as well as CSCRC and Spitfire fellow. He has served his academic community, as the guest associate editor of IEEE transactions journals, including *IEEE Transactions on Artificial Intelligence, IEEE IoT Journal, IEEE Communications Magazine, IEEE Access, Electronics, Future Internet and journal of Information Security Journal: A Global Perspective.* He has also served over seven conferences in leadership roles, involving vice-chair, session chair, Technical Program Committee (TPC) member and proceedings chair, including 2020 IEEE TrustCom and 2020 33rd Australasian Joint Conference on Artificial Intelligence.

**Nambobi Mutwalibi** is a research assistant at Motion Analysis Research Lab, Islamic University in Uganda. He is also working as the Head of Science and Technology, Labour College of East Africa. He was a research assistant in Technical and Vocational Education

(TVE) department at Islamic University of Technology, Bangladesh (IUT, 2018). He holds MBA (Nexus International University Formally Virtual University of Uganda, Muyenga, Kampala), BSc Technical Education (Islamic University of Technology, Dhaka, Bangladesh) specializing in computer science and engineering. His research interests include Disruptive Innovations, JTBD, Wargaming Strategy, Game theory, Blue Ocean Strategy, Blended learning, Green Skills, TVET and ICTs in a developing country.

**Naveen Kumar Oburi** has received his MSc degree in computer science from Lakehead University. His research interests are in health informatics and IoT. He graduated in Bachelor of Computer Science in Mallareddy Institute of Technology, Hyderabad, India in 2017 and did Microsoft .Net Course in Naresh IT Hyderabad, India. He created many web-based applications and projects on healthcare and developed Android applications and is currently doing projects and research on Data Science Technologies.

**Anam Parveen** completed her bachelor's in computer science from Dr A.P.J. Abdul Kalam Technical University, India, and master's in computer science from Lakehead University, Thunder Bay, in 2020. Her final year project was on Securing Healthcare Records Using Hyperledger Fabric Across the Network Edge. She was an excellent student, who performed to the best of her abilities in each subject and completed her curriculum with a percentile of 81. She currently resides in Toronto, Ontario, Canada and is pursuing her career as a software tester at FDM.

**Krassie Petrova** is a senior research lecturer and director of Postgraduate Studies at the School of Engineering, Computer and Mathematical Sciences (SECMS), Auckland University of Technology, New Zealand. She has over 10 years of international experience of consulting in information systems development and management, and over 15 years of university teaching in information systems, programming, data communications and networks. She has published and presented in New Zealand and internationally. Her research areas include digital service and application adoption and business models, information security, AI/ML applications, mobile- and eLearning, and IS/IT education, curriculum development and student skill and capability building. Her current research is focused on developing security solutions for cloud computing including mobile cloud and cloud-based computing environments, and on the study of the role of human factors in information security. She is the managing co-editor of Quality Assurance in Education (QAE), and an accepting editor at the *Journal of Information Technology and Education* (JITE). Professional memberships: Association for Information Systems (AIS), ATNAC New Zealand (Vice-chair).

**Md Shamsur Rahim** is currently a working as a lecturer at the Australian Institute of Higher Education. He completed his BSc in computer science and software engineering and MSc in computer science from American International University, Bangladesh. His research interests include data science, big data, data mining and machine learning.

**Leeyana Farheen Rahman** was born on May 13, 1997 in Bangladesh. She is currently a final year student pursuing her BSc in Electronic and Communication Engineering at Brac University in Dhaka. She is also appointed by BRACU as a teacher's assistant in the EEE Department for her meritorious record. She took her primary and secondary education in Playpen School where she was awarded with the Certificate of Excellence in all academic years. After completing her Cambridge International O level in 2014 and A level in 2016 with outstanding results, she started her own tutoring business to teach mathematics, physics and chemistry to O-level students. Her research interests include telecommunications, mobile networks, IoT, smart grids and network security. Apart from studies, she has keen interest in apparel designing and event planning.

**Akshai Ramesh** has received his MSc degree in computer science from Lakehead University. His research interests are in smart health and IoT. Currently, he is working as a web designer at Digital Main Street, Toronto, Ontario, Canada. He is always eager to learn more about the current technological advances and the developments that can change this fast-growing world. He enjoys being challenged in areas that require him to work outside his comfort and knowledge set. He is extremely motivated and enthusiastic by new challenges and looks forward to being as innovative as ever.

**Saifur Rahman Sabuj** was born in Bangladesh. He is currently working with the Electronics and Control Engineering Department as a Postdoctoral research fellow at Hanbat National University, South Korea. He has held the position of an assistant professor in the Department of Electrical and Electronic Engineering at Brac University, Bangladesh, since September 2017. From 2008 to 2013, he was a faculty member of Green University of Bangladesh, Metropolitan University, Sylhet and Bangladesh University. He received a BSc in Electrical, Electronics and Communication Engineering from Dhaka University, Bangladesh in 2007, an MSc Engineering from the Institute of Information and Communication Technology, Bangladesh University of Engineering and Technology, Bangladesh, in 2011 and a PhD degree in the Graduate School of Engineering, Kochi University of Technology, Japan, in 2017. His research interests include MIMO-OFDM/NOMA, cooperative communication, cognitive radio, IoT and machine-to-machine for wireless communications.

**Prem Sagar** has received his MSc degree in computer science from Lakehead University. His research interests are in smart health informatics and IoT. He completed his bachelor's degree in computer science & Engineering at Kakatiya University, India, in 2016. Later in the same year he started working as a software engineer in IBM Private Limited, India for almost 2 years. During his master's he has worked on different projects related to web-based applications, android applications, text analysis and interactive interfaces which resulted in the publication of a book chapter. He is currently applying for the developer positions in IT companies.

**Shohani Sahren** was born in Bangladesh. She is currently a fourth-year Electrical and Electronics Engineering (EEE) student at Brac University. She will be graduating in 2020 with a BSc degree in Electrical and Electronics Engineering, with a concentration in Electronics and Computer Studies. Her research interests include cyber security, smart city, IoT, industrial IoT and wireless communication. She plans to apply for higher studies after completing her undergraduate studies to enhance her knowledge of industrial cloud IoT & big data analytics and research. She hopes to create innovations that will not only make life easier for people but will also inspire the next generation of engineers.

**Sadman Sakib** has completed his BSc in CSE from Ahsanullah University of Science and Technology, Dhaka, Bangladesh, in 2017. He has been with the Department of Computer Science, Lakehead University, Thunder Bay, Ontario, Canada, as a graduate student since 2019. His research interests are in the field of intelligent computing/communication systems for mobile health (mHealth) applications for providing better health outcomes in northern Ontario and beyond. He was the winner of the best student's poster award of the Canadian Institutes of Health Research (CIHR) category in the graduate conference held at the Graduate Student Conference - Poster Presentation, Research and Innovation Week, Lakehead University, 2020. He also received an internship opportunity through the Mitacs Accelerate research grant in 2020.

**Arti Sharma** has received her MSc degree in computer science from Lakehead University. Her research interests are in smart health and IoT. She is a full stack developer with technology and management skills and works for a software company. The company develops and designs as per the user requirement to provide solutions that enable for high-quality service. She inherently understands that the customers are the single most valuable asset an organization can have and is driven by the ideals and user experience. As a full stack developer, she is responsible for design, developing and maintaining the frontend and backend of websites. She has a bachelor's degree in information technology from Nagpur Institute of Technology.

**Mosarrat Jahan Siddika** was born and raised in Bangladesh. She is currently pursuing Bachelor of Science in Electrical and Electronics Engineering under Brac University in Dhaka. In 2013, she completed her O level and graduated in 2016, completing her International A level from Pearson Edexcel. She has provided tutoring assistance to children of all ages, specializing in mathematics and science. Her research interests include wireless communications, IoT, edge computing and artificial intelligence in MEC. She was also involved in her respective club, IEEE as well as a business club to further enrich and diversify her knowledge. Furthermore, she has also indulged herself in activities to test her potential in fields beyond her expertise.

**Leslie F. Sikos**, PhD, is a computer scientist specializing in network forensics and cybersecurity applications powered by artificial intelligence and data science. He has worked both in academia and the industry, and has 20+ industry certificates. He is an active member of the research community as an author, editor, reviewer, conference organizer and speaker. His community engagement includes public talks, media appearances and articles in professional magazines. He is a reviewer at flagship journals in cybersecurity, such as *Computers & Security, Crime Science* and *IEEE Transactions on Dependable and Secure Computing*. He is a volume editor of Springer's Advanced Information & Knowledge Processing and Intelligent Systems Reference Library book series. As an invited expert, he reviews book proposals in computer science for Springer. Dr Sikos published more than 20 books, including *AI in Cybersecurity* and *Data Science in Cybersecurity and Cyberthreat Intelligence*.

**Aniqa Tasnim Oishi** was born in Bangladesh. She is currently completing her BSc degree from Brac University, Bangladesh, in Electrical and Electronic Engineering. She completed her O level and International A level under Pearson Edexcel in 2014 and 2016, respectively, with exceptional grades. Since then, she has been a private tutor for A-level students. She has also worked as a student tutor in her department since 2019. She is a trained Rabindra-sangeet singer and has worked in Shurer Dhara Music School from 2016 to 2018. She was also associated with Brac University Cultural Club and has performed on several occasions. Moreover, she has actively volunteered in Bangladesh Red Crescent Society. Her research interests include electronics and communication, particularly Wireless Communication, 5G networks, IoT and Photonics.

**Tahrat Tazrin** has been with the Department of Computer Science with Artificial Intelligence Specialization, Lakehead University, Thunder Bay, Ontario, Canada, since 2019. She is currently serving as a graduate and research assistant at Lakehead University. She completed her BSc in computer science and engineering from Brac University, Dhaka, Bangladesh, in 2018. Her research interests are in smart health analytics with a particular focus on developing logic-in-sensor EEG headsets, IoT and edge computing. She has reviewed several papers in IEEE journals, and magazines including *IEEE IoT Magazine, IEEE Communications Magazine* and *IEEE Access.*

**Wencheng Yang** is a postdoctoral researcher at the Security Research Institute in the School of Science, Edith Cowan University. His major research interests are biometric security, biometric recognition, network security. He has authored a number of papers published in high-ranking journals, including, *IEEE Transactions on Information Forensics* and *Security, Pattern Recognition.*

# Section 1

Chapter 1

# Secure Fog-Cloud of Things
## Architectures, Opportunities and Challenges

*Adam A. Alli*
Uganda Technical College Bushenyi, Uganda

*Kalinaki Kassim and Nambobi Mutwalibi*
Islamic University in Uganda, Uganda

*Habiba Hamid*
University of Malaya, Malaysia

*Lwembawo Ibrahim*
Islamic University of Technology Dhaka, Bangladesh

## CONTENTS

## 1.1 INTRODUCTION

The paradigm of Internet of Things (IoT) has emerged due to recent advances in computer hardware, software, embedded computing technologies, communication together with reduced costs and a drastic improvement in the performance of interacting devices. IoT has become a formal means of connecting people, things and information systems to the Internet through cyber-physical devices. This has resulted in a new breed of systems that allow real-world solutions to be implemented across countless Internet infrastructure and services such as cities, health and agriculture [1].

The challenges associated with the swarm of IoT devices encourage Fog computing, and its related edge computing models (MEC, cloudlets, Dew and Mist) to intelligently distribute processes and data along the physical boundaries of a network (radio access networks,

3

routers and switches), resulting in a complex distributed cloud system over the Internet that is seen to improve the performance and Quality of Services (QoS) among IoT systems [2].

Performance is improved through approving the application of mobility support, latency minimization, location awareness and ensuring the security of processes, infrastructure and data [3]. With the considerable increase in the number of applications that attract the use of fog-cloud of things infrastructure, platforms and services, security and privacy concerns have prevailed over the IoT infrastructure starting from the end device to the core networks. Studies in [4] note that the success of applications of IoT systems depends on the ecosystem characteristics with emphasis to security. It is apparent that efficient security mechanisms that fit the behavior of IoT devices must be thought of. Secondly, it has become important to think of mechanisms that mimic intelligent behavior [3] such as self-healing besides considerable use of computing power.

Fog-cloud of things involves a Fog computing paradigm that allows computing, networking and storage that could not otherwise happen at the IoT device level. With fogging, the cloud is extended closer to the user where data is generated. A node is characterized as a Fog node if it has ability to connect to the Internet, is rich in resources and has the ability to outsource its resources to clients. Fog devices may include embedded servers, wireless routers, switches, edge routers and access points. Resources constrained devices are often installed at the IoT points which may include controllers, sensors and actuators that utilize the fog facility for latency-sensitive, mobile and response-sensitive applications. Thus, Fog computing benefits organizations by allowing conservation of network resources, reducing expenses of using powerful computing only when needed, providing better analysis of local data, repositioning processing closer to the edge of a network, hence increasing ownership and privacy. Lastly, it provides a range of security options on data and computing devices.

Security concerns in IoT–Fog systems are aggravated by the nature of outsourced computing from either lower or upper levels of the network infrastructure. The placement of devices on the network infrastructure may aggravate confidentiality, authenticity, integrity, trust and data protection [5, 6]. For example, in smart homes users connect to each IoT device using wireless connectivity most of which may use Bluetooth or Wi-Fi. Through listening to the network, a Bluetooth id or Wi-Fi password may be obtained. This may give full access to a home network through which security breaches such as controlling devices and locating other devices of the same kind across the whole network to expand attack areas can be achieved. Using such access holding facilities at ransom can become very easy. Other forms of attack on the home facility may include the use of leaky video cameras or social media attacks. Each of the above kinds of attack requires users to fix their device identification numbers, personal identification numbers, passwords and proof of security of the devices. Another important consideration is to separate home/enterprise networks from public networks by the use of secured Edge device.

Authors in [7] explain the complications that arise when data is stored or computation is transferred to be performed in the fog. Among them is the loss of control over either data or computation. Fog nodes are resource constrained and therefore may choose to initiate a deletion, modification or a destruction without leaving a trace to reserve its resources. In [8], authors illustrate security concerns that arise when a Fog node reclaims its computational resources by discarding data. Authors in [9] and [10] ascertain the effect of big data generated at the lower level in the IoT–Fog–Cloud hierarchy as a security concern. The difficulty of classifying big data as an attack or not increases the complexity of handling complex data at the fog [3]. These concerns make security in fog-cloud of things [2] is a crucial area of study. This chapter discusses some of the important aspects of security in the fog-cloud of things domain.

In this work, we address security issues in the fog-cloud of things environment by providing fog-cloud of things security architecture, key features of attack in fog-cloud environment and new methods of detecting the growing grounds of cyberattack in the IoT–Fog–Cloud arrangement. Further we offer material on application and challenges in secure fog-cloud of things systems. Our contributions in this regard are as follows:

- The authors provide a comprehensive discussion about the secure fog-cloud of things architecture.
- Secondly, we describe the characteristics of attacks and perform cybercrime classifications.
- Thirdly, we provide an appropriate machine learning (ML) kit for secure fog-cloud of things architecture that may enable detection of new strains of attacks in fog framework.
- Lastly, we provide guidance to the readers about fog-cloud of things by presenting applications and future research direction into security aspects in Fog computing.

### 1.1.1 Chapter Road Map

In this chapter, we address security aspects in the building block of fog-cloud of things infrastructure. In Section 1.1, we present an introduction to secure fog of things. In Section 1.2, we discuss the secure fog-cloud of things environment and architecture, whereas in Section 1.3, threats vulnerabilities and exploits in fog-cloud of things ecosystem are discussed. In Section 1.4, ML kits that are necessary to enable the architecture to adapt to new arising threats are presented. Key applications that attract the use of secure fog-cloud of things are presented in Section 1.5. In Section 1.6, we present opportunities and challenges in improving security in the fog-cloud of things ecosystems. In Section 1.7, we present future trends, and conclusion is drawn in Section 1.8.

## 1.2 SECURE FOG-CLOUD OF THINGS

The next generation of smart infrastructure that links the information and communication technologies(ICT), the industry and sustainable development will be achieved by leveraging advances in information services that optimize operational cost, preserve energy consumption and allow service provision even in times of crisis will be powered mainly by IoT [9, 10]. The IoT networks are characterized by a wide range of users, heterogeneity, production of a massive amount of data, and some applications that require high-speed networks. The above features of IoT have encouraged the use of cloud computing, Fog computing, and other related extended cloud paradigms. The fog-cloud of things extends the services of the cloud in a distributed fashion, encouraging efficiency and robustness in latency-sensitive applications that can be deployed with ease [11, 12].

The distributed nature of fog-cloud of things architectures is organized in hierarchical nature, with the lower layers hosting IoT devices, the middle layers hosting the Fog devices and the upper layers hosting the cloud. These applications hosted at each layer are susceptible to security threats and attacks which may result from the distributed design flaws, misconfigurations and implementation bugs, and sometimes less attention paid to security requirement of IoT devices by both the users and designers of IoT systems. New forms of attacks have been discovered to include on and off attacks [13], Distributed Denial of Service (DDoS) [14], flooding attacks [15], side-channel attacks and malware injection. These attacks have potential to disrupt fog services, compromise a user's security and privacy using any publicly accessible information or create a rogue Fog node to compromise the fog-cloud of things infrastructure [16]–[17]. In totality, the means of autonomously provisioning application resources to respond to changes in load on a given platform without any central enterprise infrastructure causes numerous challenges. These challenges include sandboxing for security, secure distributed load balancing, resource management and hardware-based defense against malware and ransoms. In a bid to mitigate security concerns in the fog-cloud of things frameworks that are viewed to mitigate several challenges have been discussed in [4, 18]–[19]. The general arrangements of the frameworks are constructed on securing the IoT devices, services and applications at the tiered planes of the fog-cloud infrastructure.

### 1.2.1  Environment

Recently, there has been a continuous transformation of ICT systems toward multi-domain architectures. These architectures create ecosystems that encourage the use of different forms of cloud services internally on the edge devices and externally via the Internet on cloud services. The progressive use of IoT, the edge, the fog and the cloud extends the boundaries between private ICT zones and public domains. The extension of these boundaries allows employees to work off premises while accessing the ICT resources of the enterprise. The off-premise employment model forces enterprise cyber-security to adopt security mechanisms that assume safe isolation of enterprise ICT assets. This is done by creating a virtual private network (VPN). VPN is used as a mechanism to segment enterprises network resources and denying remote access by unauthorized. Such security models is unproductive.

Some of the common security breaches that have rendered such a mechanism ineffective include externalization and offloading, demand for hosting sensitive and complex data on third parties' infrastructures, multiplicity and heterogeneity of abundant data collected by sensors and delivered in floods to the clouds for service. Secondly, most IoT devices have limited processing capabilities, which makes them more exposed to compromise than other IT assets in enterprise networks [2]. Thirdly, most organizations encourage their employees to use personal and mobile devices (smartphones, tablets and removable media) in the enterprise ICT assets. These devices brought in the enterprises can be compromised at different stages. Fourthly, inflexible defense toward DDoS and busty data traffic is a situation that is tricky to resolve, often the ICT administration may choose to 'turn open' allowing traffic to pass without inspection in a struggle to maintain availability until the problem is resolved, or 'to fail closed' blocking all traffic in application of a lockdown until the problem is fixed. All the choices may not leave business undisrupted.

Fog-cloud of things ecosystem in Figure 1.1 encompasses a myriad of IT resources (IoT devices, the edge, network, Fog devices, the cloud, services and applications) spanning several geographical locations to catch up with increased demand for flexibility in enterprise models. The models enable fog-cloud of things resources to be distributed across multiple networks – sometimes across publicly available networks. This makes fog systems candidate to attacks at the cyberspace level, computing resources level or even at the physical level. Resources like processors, storage devices, networks can physically be compromised because of ease to reach. Therefore, securing individual resources in such heterogeneous distributed systems created by fog-cloud of things requires new forms of pervasive security techniques that can ably deal with network threats, correlate events in both time and space dimensions, provide timely operational information to feed novel disruptive approaches capable of estimating the risk in real-time and carry out focused and effective defensive and mitigation actions [4].

Observing the ecosystem in Figure 1.1, security ought to be maintained at the IoT devices level, at the edge level, at the multi-tier fog level and multi-tier cloud level. IoT security takes care of security issues at the IoT devices level, whereas the edge security takes care of security

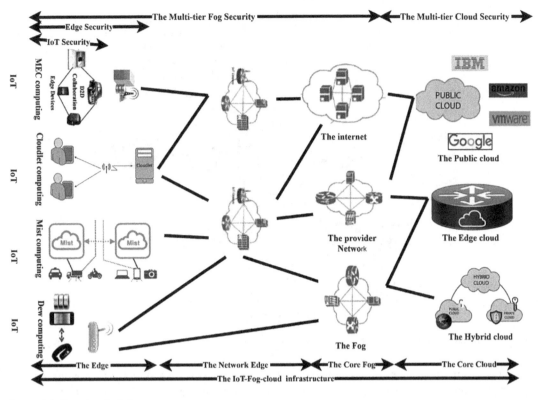

*Figure 1.1* Fog-cloud of things ecosystem.

issues at the edge of the network. Beyond the edge issues of security at the multi-tier fog level are taken care of by the Fog security and lastly issues of security at the cloud level are taken care of by the cloud security.

## 1.2.2 Architecture

Figure 1.2 is a graphical representation of the secure fog of things architecture. This architecture is motivated to protect individual devices, data and processes in the IoT ecosystem. This is achieved through the implementation of end-to-end solutions that achieve protection through intelligent policy management, enforcement and continuous monitoring through aggregation. In addition, correlation of data is used to encourage the use of insights to enable automated functions of security in the IoT ecosystem. Automation of security function requires that the end-to-end solutions provide the following: i) Access control to users and devices based on security policy – these policies include issues of authentication, authorization, determination of security requirements, identification and inventorization of non-authenticated devices such as printers, scanners, etc.; ii) opportunities for context-aware policies that define security based on the full context of the situation – context-awareness may be defined in terms of sender/recipient information, size of information sent and received, reliability and the complexity of data. Context-awareness aligns closely with the business logic of the company; therefore, the context-aware solution is easy to implement and administer. With context-aware secure solutions, organizations can craft autonomous security policies that allow them to have effective security plan that gives them huge operational efficiency and control; iii) flexible deployment which includes options such as secure fog services and

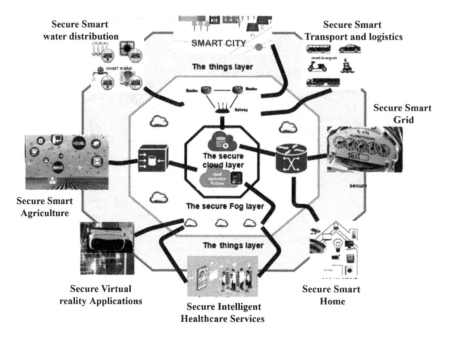

*Figure 1.2* The secure fog-cloud of things architecture.

integrated security services across all the level of the network infrastructure to bring protection at the edge of the network; iv) support to reasonable insights into the network activities, transactions and threats. This allows enhanced protection and fast detection of anomalies.

The framework considered in the secure fog of things architecture is a layered architecture consisting of three layers. The framework is aimed at protecting things, processes and data in the fog-cloud of things ecosystems. The lower layers protect things (sensors and actuators), the second layer protects the network, the fog systems, data, processes and services, whereas the upper layer protects the cloud layer. Below we describe the functions of each layer.

i. **The secure things layer**

The things layer protects all types of cyber-physical objects that can connect to the Internet. These objects have embedded technologies that allow them to interact with the environment, collect a vast amount of data, send the data for processing over the network and then receive results of computation for further decision-making. The embedded technologies consist of sensors and actuators.

At this level, attacks mainly occur on IoT hardware (sensors, actuators and controllers) and produced data. One way by which hardware can be compromised is by placing an attack that increases the activities on the processors, memory, etc. forcing an overload, which in turn leads to poor resource utilization. On a poor resource utilization, the system performance is compromised leading to processor slow down and overuse of battery at IoT devices. These activities reduce the efficiency of the system as a whole. The second way of attacking devices at the IoT layers is forcing unauthorized access. This results in the misuse of data, jamming the device, privacy concerns, etc. To mitigate issues of security at the IoT layer, authentication mechanism, intrusion detection systems (IDS), lightweight encryption and anti-jamming mechanisms are applied.

At the things layer attacks are viewed in terms of being local or foreign. Local attacks originate from inside the network, whereas the foreign attacks originate from public networks. Inside attacks are launched from devices to physical objects, controllers and gateways. Some instances involve controllers' devices (e.g. gateways, switches, access points and routers) and users' devices. These attacks are triggered by rogue controllers, which pretend to be genuine on the network to serve as authentication point. Inside attacks affect controllers, IP and non-IP devices. The foreign attacks are launched from outside the network through gateways and routers. The foreign attacker formulates their attack in such a way that they disrupt services, applications and corrupt data used by the IoT devices. These attacks include denial of services, on and off attacks and botnets.

ii. **The secure fog layers**

The secure fog layer is responsible for protecting network resources, fog resources, applications and services. This layer protects not only attacks that are targeted toward gateways, routers, firewalls, etc. but also protocol services and application served at the fog. It prevents foreign attacks that are meant to disrupt the IoT services.

The secure fog layer host intelligent mechanisms that address network access concerns, information leakages and service attacks. Authentication, encryption, authorization and confidentiality are important considerations of the fog layer. Machine Learning(ML) plays a critical role in this layer as a means of advancing solutions that detect data disruption and distortion, intrusion and session breaches. The use of ML at this layer allows the network to adapt to changing dynamics to predict the behavior of applications and services. Further, the network can adjust to new forms of attack without compromising the robustness of the system. ML is used to advance recovery in form of self-healing.

iii. **The secure cloud layer**

The secure cloud is the upper layer of the architecture that provides a set of technologies, policies, software and applications that protect the cloud infrastructure as well as related data. The cloud security protects sensitive data, compliments data privacy, users' authentication and access control mechanisms to grant access and maintain security activities.

At this layer, security solutions are maintained on either public cloud, private cloud or hybrid cloud. Secure public cloud solutions offer both accessibility and security to data. Data in the public cloud is most often unstructured and attention is not given to customization. Security solutions at this level are cheap and affordable. On the other hand, the private cloud provides expensive security solutions but gives users security policies that allow them to manage their data. Secure hybrid cloud solutions are those that possess characteristics of both private and public cloud. In this setting, private secure policies apply to sensitive and complex data whereas, non-sensitive data are guided by public policy. The secure hybrid environment offers users with an alternative that strikes a balance between affordability and customization.

At the cloud, layer data is secured using advanced firewalls, intelligent intrusion detection systems, event logging, encryption and biometric physical security. Firewalls inspect data packets, verify the integrity of the packets and monitor behavior of the source and destination of the packets. Firewalls through inspection, verification and monitoring process can grant autonomous access and detect security breaches. Intelligent intrusion systems can detect intruders based on event log analysis. Proper analysis of event logs provides narratives that enable detection, prediction and prevention of new threats, attempted intrusion and other security breaches. This layer also provides advanced encryption and tight physical security normally based on biometric authentication systems.

## 1.3 THREATS, VULNERABILITIES AND EXPLOITS IN FOG-CLOUD OF THINGS ECOSYSTEMS

Threats, vulnerabilities and exploits in the IoT systems have continued to increase due to continuous desire to interconnect all things to the Internet. The increase in security threats in IT systems is motivated by the increase in value of information on the Internet, monitory resources on the Internet such as bank accounts that translate in monitory gains, complexity of the systems that attract satisfaction when compromised, alerts about security concerns reported by the users about the company information assets and lastly, increased interest in hacking as a profession.

In Figure 1.3, we group fog-cloud attacks in two basic categories: i) service disruption and ii) privacy breaches as discussed below.

Service disruption cybercrimes are intended to interrupt services provided by IoT systems, applications and processes. These attacks include but are not limited to

a. Ransomware: These are becoming the most public way of attacks accomplished through encryption of data. When successful hackers take control of services and processes provided by the IoT ecosystem using ransomware, they pursue for ransom from the service provider or the users [20]. Ransomware are of two kinds: i) those that encrypt valuable files on a computer and ii) those that lock the victim out of their device. Two interesting examples in these regards are WannaCry that appeared in 2017 and Ryuk that first

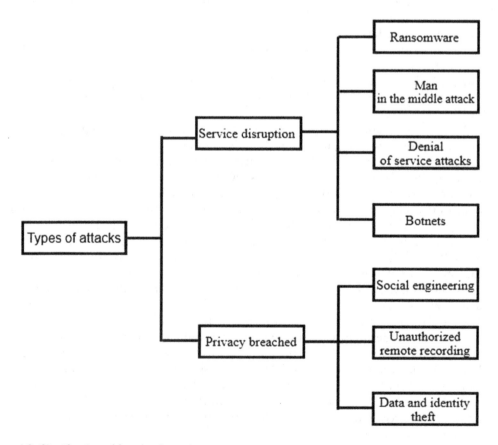

*Figure 1.3* Classification of fog-cloud attacks.

appeared in 2018. WannaCry affected over 200,000 devices over the globe. Mainly its target was windows systems and locked its users out. A ransom was requested in bitcoin to gain access to your files or devices, whereas, Ryuk disabled windows restore, encrypted files and network drives. It affected many organizations in the USA. Ryuk is observed to be one of the most expensive ransomware attacks in history. Other examples include locky, jigsaw trodesh, cryptolocker and recently wastelocker.

b. Man-in-the-Middle attack: This is when a hacker positions himself in the middle of the individual communication system with an objective of intercepting and gaining access. On gaining access they can create harm to a fine working system [21]. Examples of Man-in-the-Middle attacks are IP, DNS, HTTPS spoofing and email hijacking.

c. Denial of service attacks (DoS): These are motivated to upset services by deliberately overloading the system. Overloading systems sets efficiency and reliability of systems to question. By downplaying the system reliability, users feel uncomfortable and frustrated about the system. In the critical system DoS can cause serious accidents. For example, delays in response in autonomous vehicle system can cause the autonomous vehicle to lose course. Normally DoS does not result in theft of data or identity [22, 23].

d. Botnets: With this kind of attack, a hacker creates a network in association with many systems to take control of the target system. The aim of botnets is normally to compromise confidentiality of a stable system, obtain data and access that would enable them to launch attacks on systems that use IoT devices and services [23]. Botnets can be very effective in launching a successful attack on a vulnerable IoT system. Examples of botnets include Mirai which targeted smart devices that run on ARC processors to launch DDoS attacks. Other Botnets are 3ve, Methbot, mariposa and Grum.

On the other hand, privacy breach attacks are motivated to withdraw freedom from users to use services, application and data provided by IoT systems. These types of attacks include the following:

a. Social engineering: Social engineering attacks involve manipulating users so that they can give up information that can grant hackers access to the system without question by posing as legitimate users. An example of social engineering could be a received mail fooling the user to change his password through a provided link. When the user chooses to update his email through the false link, his information is captured and used to have access and compromise the system [24]. Another related example is to compel users to click a link sent to the emails so that an automatic malware or spyware that continues collecting information about the system can be used to sidetrack the network on which the system is connected. Social engineering tricks can range from simply posing as a helper on call to sophisticated tricks that attackers attract user curiosity to share very important information about them and the systems they use on a daily basis. Social engineering can be avoided if the users verify the persons from whom they seek help in regard to their information, changing login information occasionally, setting security instruments such as anti-spamware and filters, and keeping information about their transaction as private as possible [25].

b. Unauthorized remote recording: This involves either audio, text or video surveillance of users so as to temper with their privacy. This is common with gadgets that are installed in places of work or homes such as surveillance cameras, TV and nanny dolls. Hackers find means through which they can take control of these gadgets and record activities around the environment and can use it to misrepresent person's character of interest. As a result of leaked information, the person of interest is forced to give up his career or buy out to save his integrity. This kind of attack can be avoided by ensuring that one installs security and surveillance equipment from legitimate providers and a well-stipulated user contract is signed. Secondly, the user should have the knowledge on how privacy can be breached. In addition, all the default security setting should be changed before use. To avoid physical tempering, the surveillance equipment must be installed in secure hard to reach places around the users' location.

c. Data and identity theft happens when hackers steal user's personal information that may include bank accounts, social security details, billing details, passwords or email details. With the rise in the use of smart devices, gaining access to information about a user is becoming easier. They use this information to impersonate a genuine user resulting in loss of credibility or property through using the stolen information to gain access to user's digital life. Along with this information, hackers may gain access to sensitive information about users' family, belongings and health. This information can be used to harm the user in numerous ways, which may include reputation obliteration, covering security crimes, public humiliation and financial loss. Data and identity theft can be avoided by proper management of user accounts starting with device access accounts by creating strong passwords that cannot easily be cracked. A strong password is that which is long enough to remember, consists of a combination of text, numbers and special symbols. Finally, users should avoid unlimited social media exposure, opening suspicious emails and also learn about site privacy and security policies [25].

In Table 1.1 below, we present types of attacks and their attack vectors. These vectors may be engineered in many ways to allow the hacker hurt the organizational ICT resources with ease.

Table 1.1 Showing types of attacks and their attack vectors.

| Articles | Attack Type | Attack Vector |
| --- | --- | --- |
| [5, 8, 9] | Ransomware | • Remote desktop protocol (RDP)<br>• Email phishing<br>• Software vulnerabilities |
| [5, 13, 15] | Man-in-the-Middle | • Rouge Fog nodes<br>• Vulnerabilities in web browsers<br>• SQL injection<br>• Trojan Horses, worms<br>• Public networks |
| [5, 13, 26] | DDoS | • **DNS Amplification**<br>• **UDP flood**<br>• IP fragmentation<br>• SNMP Reflection<br>• SYN flood |
| [5, 20, 27] | Botnet | • **DNS Amplification**<br>• **UDP flood**<br>• IP fragmentation<br>• SNMP Reflection<br>• SYN flood |
| [24, 28] | Social engineering | • **Rouge websites**<br>• **Fake emails**<br>• posing as a helper on call |
| [5, 8] | Unauthorized remote recording | • surveillance cameras<br>• **Television**<br>• **Nanny dolls**<br>• **Personal assistant devices** |
| [28, 29] | Data and identity theft | • Social media<br>• Emails<br>• Rogue websites |

## 1.4 KEY MACHINE LEARNING KITS FOR SECURE FOG-CLOUD OF THINGS ARCHITECTURE

Fog computing is a source of big data. Observing the emerging trends in Fog computing technology and applications of ML has been explored in many places such as improving efficient resource management, modeling traffic in fog-cloud environment, improving security, etc. The importance of ML kits is threefold: i) improving security techniques in terms of security models, handling security in systems in order to manage large volumes and varied data, flexibility in handling attacks and issues of cryptography; ii) developing security architectures that are able to autonomously detect and handle future security vulnerabilities with little human intervention; iii) improving issues of reliability, trust and privacy in the fog-cloud of things at all levels.

ML approaches provide useful mechanisms that have been used for data analytics to engineering pattern, extract useful features and predict values from massive amounts of data [30, 31]. ML approaches at the fog allow development of autonomous security systems at the fog of things that are distributed, can manage and update security credentials at a local level, scan for security vulnerabilities such as malware and distribute timely software patches on large scale [3]. In this section, we highlight some important aspects of ML kits for authentication, access control, etc.

  a. ML-based authentication.
     Hackers have recently developed a mechanism that bypasses the utmost complicated authentication mechanisms. These authentication mechanisms may include password-enabled authentication [32], two-factor authentications [25], biometric authentication or by the use of extensible authentication protocols. The superlative way to keep unwanted users' authentication is to combine ML with n-factor authentication where n defines many or multiple factors. This would enable security systems to learn and prevent attacks based on behavior.
     The ML-based authentication at the fog level enables identification of high-risk users at the local level and gives them different treatment other than those given to trustworthy users. For example, resident users (those logging in from the inside) are treated differently from the off-premise users. This is accomplished through authentication-related data of the users over time to establish baseline normal behavior putting numerous factors to check. These factors may include time-based login activities, location and IP address used to log in, successful and failed log in frequencies, analysis of the login done on premises and off premises, frequencies of application-level authentication, analysis of risky authentication, etc. Generally, machine authentication is capable of keeping authentication procedures local and private, keeping track of users and guarantee authentication at both the IoT level and cloud.
  b. ML-based access control
     Hackers dedicate most of their time crafting complicated mechanisms to realize an attack on ICT infrastructure of organizations no matter how intricate the security is. Most of the time security breaches in a network system are traced back to the inadequate access control mechanism especially during this period of the IoT that has brought up new working habits and policies. Such habits may include but are not limited to working anywhere at any time, bring your own device, etc. Due to requirements of working off-premise companies most often relax or completely neglect access policies creating security loopholes.
     ML access control could help bridge access control gaps by enabling systems to autonomously learn how to adjust privileges to include write or read access, isolating

access according to roles, duties and functions let alone enabling the system to group users devices according to behavior then applying policies such as no sharing among groups, locking down some groups based on IP or working time. On the other hand, auditing and monitoring of accounts is important such that devices can take care of sensitive information for i) local processing, ii) prompt users to renew their passcode locally or iii) update policies on accessing information regularly. Secure fog of things ensures well-structured access control mechanisms for both local and cloud infrastructure.

c. ML botnet detection

Botnet detection involves spotting attacks caused by controlled network environment. The botnet systems are used to create DDoS attacks, floods and sometimes used to spread the virus. Attackers often recruit an army of computers and IoT systems to allow them to fulfill their mission. These recruited systems are known as bots. The bots are usually unaware that they are used as attack agents. The way botnets work is by the use of botnet master to initiate, manage, coordinate and recruit attack systems as many as possible for destructive mission. The botnets then send instructions to the bots to launch an attack. With the increase in computing capacities of ICT devices mobilizing smart devices, computers and IoT into a botnet can launch a pretty powerful and disruptive attack.

The primary purpose of ML techniques for botnet detection is to identify, learn, and collapse the botnet server including all its assets. The kits used for botnet detection collect information and find out what technology is used in the botnets, analyze the risk and intensity of attack and identify botnet server for disabling action. Furthermore, the kits are equipped with the ability to observe network traffic, responses, loads and link status. This information is used in different ways to monitor sleepers, sniffers and trojans. These kits can be used to accomplish both passive and active monitoring of the IoT ecosystem for the intrusion. We note that the botnet detection systems can be loosely characterized as intrusion detection systems [26] and HoneyNets [27].

d. ML-based Malware detection and classification

Overtime the number of malwares, their complexity and dynamicity in signatures have increased rendering the traditional methods ineffective in detecting and classifying malware files [33]. Their intricacy increases more in the era of big data whose velocity, size and variability plays important role in identifying the underlying signatures of attacking malware.

ML toolkits at the fog are useful mechanisms to obtain statistics and reports about the malware activities, explore them, select features important for their identification, train and retrain on datasets using different kinds of suitable ML algorithms [33, 34], and then deploy the machine at the Secure fog of things to monitor traffic. The toolkit deployed here would help identify and classify malware on both entry and exit of IoT network.

Secondly, these toolkits are getting considerable attention among the anomaly detection scholars to address the weaknesses of knowledge base detection techniques [34]. This is due to the fact that anomaly detection can effectively help in catching fraud while discovering strange activity in large and complex big data sets, thus proving to be useful in areas such as banking security, natural sciences, medicine and marketing, which are prone to malicious activities [14]. Moreover, anomaly detection can be a key for solving intrusions [35], while detecting anomalies. Worries of abnormal behavior indicate a presence of intended induced attacks, defects and faults.

ML algorithms installed at the fog have the ability to learn from data and make predictions based on that data. ML for anomaly detection includes techniques that provide a promising alternative for detection and classification of anomalies based on an initially large set of features. Generally, secure fog of things frameworks will allow businesses to be provided with a simple yet effective approach for detecting and classifying anomalies.

e. Offloading

Critical infrastructures that are powered by IoT such as health facilities, industries, utilities and cities may be compromised thus lowering the Quality of Service (QoS) and experience. To maintain the QoS of these systems, offloading is encouraged [36]. The emergency of Fog computing combines IoT and ML to facilitate the moving of services near to the devices at the edge, offloading minimizes delay, improves performance and balances traffic load in the network. Besides load balancing, offloading can be done to save IoT devices that under attack. Secondly, offloading sensitive data can be localized on the fog or private cloud to preserve confidentiality and trustworthy computing. Further, offloading combined with technologies such as blockchain may yield excellent security mechanism [28]

## 1.5 APPLICATIONS

The core objective of enterprises is improving productivity using IoT systems, at the same time maintaining quality of service and experiences. Securing devices is critical for business environments, utility industry, factories and other infrastructures such as health facilities, cities, and environment that host services that are delay-sensitive. The following applications attract the use of secure fog-cloud of things:

Secure Intelligent healthcare services

Numerous wearable smart devices are being used by health workers to monitor the user's general health condition and keep the records of the patients [37]. During the use of these IoT devices to monitor the health status of the patients by harvesting data which is sensitive and private. Securing confidential information of the patients and processing them on local or the fog is the best use of extended cloud framework [29]. Thus, secure Fog computing can be employed to minimize issues related to detecting, predicting and preventing a breach of patients' devices and data to cause harm to their health or attacking their privacy by sending warning signals to the patients, doctors and caretakers. This increases issues of trust, reliability and prevention of data and information in the secure Fog-cloud infrastructure for smart health [38].

Intelligent traffic lights

Smart traffic regulator systems may assume some functionality of Fog devices to coordinate traffic signals as well as send a warning signal to an approaching vehicle [29]. Moreover, the intelligent traffic lights are also capable of identifying the flashing lights of an ambulance or a police car at crossroads using video cameras and immediately change traffic lights accordingly [38]. Similarly, the smart traffic systems may communicate locally with sensors to identify the occurrence of the person on foot and cyclists thereby evaluating the distance and speed of approaching vehicles thus preventing accidents while maintaining a stable flow of traffic [29]. Such a system requires robust intelligent security applied to it.

Intelligent Grid

In many of power generation and distribution systems, IoT have been deployed to be used in different ways starting from power generation, optimized distribution and consumption. The intelligent grid technology is made up of a two-way smart and intelligent flow of information between the consumer and supplier. The IoT fixed at consumers' premise gather data and forward it to the nearest Fog. At the Fog near real-time analytics is performed to discover issues related to electricity supply, consumption patterns, metering and pricing among other particulars. This next-generation application of IoT and related fog infrastructure requires to be safe, secure and trustworthy. Explicit security and privacy solutions at the fog-cloud of things should be able to maintain data confidentiality, handle big data and serve intelligent meters fixed at both the supplier and consumer households without being compromised.

Other applications related to secure Fog computing are industrial IoT, smart agriculture, Augmented reality, smart water metering among others. Each of these applications require robust, scalable, trustworthy security mechanisms that allow them to handle complex, sensitive and big data.

## 1.6 OPPORTUNITIES AND CHALLENGES IN IMPROVING SECURITY IN FOG-CLOUD OF THINGS

The use of smartphones and other cyber-physical devices has opened a Pandora's box in the areas of security, privacy and trust in the IoT ecosystems. Most of the concerns fall in three broad areas: a) the ever-increasing number of IoT-based attacks launched from heterogeneous platforms of smart devices (smartphones, cameras, printers, etc.). Hackers use these platforms to exploit enterprise ICT default systems, bringing the critical system in the organization down and affect many applications around enterprise daily operations. b) The second concern is the interoperability in IoT–Fog systems. The IoT–Fog architectures are fairly new and have not been dealt with before. Therefore, issues that involve handling heterogeneous protocols, operating procedures, communication resources and constrained resource utilization in a secure fog environment are still at large. c) In addition to the novelty of IoT–Fog, the upcoming of the new multi-tier IoT–Fog–Cloud paradigms defined by multiple customers and tenants, exposed hardware, software and distributed infrastructure present new concerns in their way.

### 1.6.1 Opportunities

The secure fog of things provides security opportunities in mainly two ways:

i. Boosting security services: This is done by improving the security function of the Fog device through provision of service and support functions. The fog may be used to process, store and transmit sensitive data locally along the edge protecting the users' privacy. Secondly, the fog software backplane may be improved to supply IoT devices with the necessary security updates and patches to keep them secure. Updating billions of IoT devices is a challenging undertaking; therefore, management functions that include new policy-based access control models may be used to overcome the limitations of updating IoT security functions.

ii. Provision of SECurity as a Service (SECaaS): Secure fog may also offer SECaaS along with the ability to solve many other fog challenges such as Latency Constraints, Network Bandwidth Constraints, Resource-Constrained Devices, Uninterrupted Services with Intermittent Connectivity to the Cloud [3].

Generally, the secure fog of things provides opportunity for secure and trusted computing to be available to IoT devices. They are capable of making IoT systems more robust and trustworthy.

## 1.6.2 Challenges

Challenges associated with security in the next-generation IoT systems include the following:

i. Interoperability of security systems. Perhaps the most complex phenomena arising in computing today. Interoperability cuts along many dimensions specifically the diversity of devices (surveillance, wearables, smart appliance, etc.), interfaces (wireless, vehicular, powerline, etc.) and operating paradigms. Each of these may need a diverse security mechanism to communicate first among themselves and the longstanding network-based use of TCP/IP and its related security mechanisms.

ii. Unlike in the cloud or enterprise data centers setting where important ICT resources are protected by physical security mechanisms such as key and lock, physical security breach in Fog computing has not been completely resolved yet. Most IoT devices in the fog environment are formed within the reach of any unauthorized person. Therefore, anybody with the intention of attacking the systems can physically reach the sensors, actuators and the Fog devices. This gives opportunity to malicious person to physically manipulate the systems. An example of such attack is planting a trojan on a flash disk and dropping it in parking yard. If a person picks and plugs it in the organization system, then a Trojan horse is automatically transferred to a computer on the systems without the user's knowledge. Another example is tempering with fog by physically resetting them without the knowledge of the administrator with the intention of creating backchannels to access the system. It is easy to initiate a physical security breach in the Fog working environment which results in a complex attack. Due to probable physical reach to the fog, it is easy to compromise the system and make it available to attackers who will gain control. Therefore, ensuring physical security and privacy becomes a serious concern in the security of fog systems.

iii. Trust, security tracking and monitoring is another serious challenge. Trust plays a two-way role in a fog network. The first role is that the Fog nodes offer services to IoT devices. In this case the fog should be in position to corroborate whether the devices requesting services are genuine. Secondly, since IoT networks are expected to provide secure and reliable services to the end-users, it becomes a requirement for all devices that form part of the fog network to have a certain level of trust.

iv. The Fog networks are complex distributed systems. Complexity of fog systems increases vulnerabilities which in turn creates loop holes. This makes it easy for hackers to find a way of connecting to the network from many unauthorized points without notice. This provides grounds for attackers to deploy attack mechanisms such as DDoS, Jamming, Eavesdropping, Man-in-the-Middle attacks, Active impersonation, Message replay attacks, Data breach, Sniffing and Illegal resource consumption.

## 1.7 FUTURE TRENDS

Recently, there has been a renewed effort to boost security of complex IoT systems. The complexity arises from the need for mobility, diversity in applications and hardware, and the demand of distributed powerful computing closer to the user. This nature of computing encouraged by IoT devices and networks does not only provide rich ground for hackers but also simulate large transactions over the network which is an ingredient to poor quality of service (QoS). Adopting secure Fog computing is a means of improving quality of service at the same time stopping intruders from conducting their business. Fog computing eliminates vulnerabilities as a result of decentralized architecture. Secondly, they localize computing, which in turn reduces the target of cyberattack. It is hoped that advances in ML and blockchain in the fog will eliminate new threats and single point of failure created by centralized architectures. Hence the future will see a) secure and trusted service and b) SECaaS provided at the edge of the network.

a. Secure and trusted computing services
   The beauty embedded in future of secure Fog computing is trustworthy computing. The ability to create an accurate defense system built upon pillars of different security domains such that when an anomaly is detected, a policy or behavior-based decision is taken. Using such in-depth strategy, a responsive security system that is always available is built. Additionally, such kind of a system shall exhibit survivability given that it can respond to new threats without difficulties. Secure Fog of things enables distributed data processing and storage near the data source, and affordable high-performance trusted computing anywhere any time. This shall enable adoption of new technologies (5G and beyond) with considerable ease.

b. SECurity as a Service
   The secure fog of things is seen to be a great enabler of SECaaS on the edge of a network. The edge SECaaS shall provide protection to both the lower and the upper layer IoT systems. In addition, it shall facilitate secure transaction between the local networks and the cloud. This will be realized through fog-based intrusion detection systems and secure data repositories. Moreover, the secure fog shall provide coordinated and distributed defense in a way that the fog systems shall be integrated with dynamic centralized response to any form of attack, threat and vulnerabilities.

## 1.8 CONCLUSION

This chapter covered content related to secure fog architecture. We provided a discussion on fog-cloud infrastructure, ML kits that may enable autonomous detection of new strains of attack in Fog. We noted that ML is usable in many fog applications, and security is one of them. ML methods are capable of adapting to new threats, vulnerabilities and exploits. As part of Fog computing we have included fog-cloud of things and their applications. The challenging aspects of fog-cloud of things include interoperability of security issues, easy physical access that enables easy compromise, complexity in motoring attacks due to mobility of devices, vast amount of data generated, traffic bust along the infrastructure which may not necessarily mean an attack and scalability in network devices. Lastly, the future prospects of secure fog shall be based on trusted services and SECaaS. Therefore, readers may consider various ML kits in fog-cloud architecture to develop secure fog systems and address diverse challenges. In future we intend to study methodologies that may be used to enhance intelligent security at the Fog.

# REFERENCES

1. H. Ren, H. Li, Y. Dai, K. Yang, and X. Lin, "Querying in internet of things with privacy preserving: Challenges, solutions and opportunities," *IEEE Netw.*, vol. 32, no. 6, pp. 144–151, Nov. 2018.

2. A. A. Alli and M. M. Alam, "The fog cloud of things: A survey on concepts, architecture, standards, tools, and applications," *Internet of Things*, vol. 9, p. 100177, Feb. 2020.

3. A. A. Alli and M. M. Alam, "SecOFF-FCIoT: Machine learning based secure offloading in Fog-Cloud of things for smart city applications," *Internet of Things*, vol. 7, p. 100070, Sep. 2019.

4. M. Ammar, G. Russello, and B. Crispo, "Internet of things: A survey on the security of IoT frameworks," *J. Inf. Secur. Appl.*, vol. 38, pp. 8–27, Feb. 2018.

5. S. Yi, Z. Qin, and Q. Li, "Security and privacy issues of fog computing: A survey," *In International conference on wireless algorithms, systems, and applications* 2015 Aug 10, pp. 685–695.

6. M.-H. Maras, "Internet of things: Security and privacy implications," *Int. Data Priv. Law*, vol. 5, no. 2, pp. 99–104, May 2015.

7. M. R. Anawar, S. Wang, M. Azam Zia, A. K. Jadoon, U. Akram, and S. Raza, "Fog computing: An overview of big IoT data analytics," *Wirel. Commun. Mob. Comput.*, vol. 2018, Article ID 7157192, p. 22, 2018. doi:10.1155/2018/715719.

8. J. Yakubu, H. A. Christopher, H. Chiroma, M. Abdullahi, and others, "Security challenges in fog-computing environment: A systematic appraisal of current developments," *J. Reliab. Intell. Environ.*, vol. 5, no. 4, pp. 209–233, 2019.

9. E. K. Markakis et al., "Efficient next generation emergency communications over multi-access edge computing," *IEEE Commun. Mag.*, vol. 55, no. 11, pp. 92–97, 2017.

10. J. Gubbi, R. Buyya, S. Marusic, and M. Palaniswami, "Internet of things (IoT): A vision, architectural elements, and future directions," *Futur. Gener. Comput. Syst.*, vol. 29, no. 7, pp. 1645–1660, 2013.

11. E. Ahmed and M. H. Rehmani, "Mobile edge computing: Opportunities, solutions, and challenges," *Futur. Gener. Comput. Syst.*, vol. 70, pp. 59–63, 2017.

12. O. Salman, I. Elhajj, A. Kayssi, and A. Chehab, "Edge computing enabling the internet of things," in *IEEE World Forum on Internet of Things, WF-IoT 2015 - Proceedings*, Milan, Italy, 2015.

13. C. V. L. Mendoza and J. H. Kleinschmidt, "Mitigating on-off attacks in the internet of things using a distributed trust management scheme," *Int. J. Distrib. Sens. Networks*, vol. 11, no. 11, p. 859731, Nov. 2015.

14. R. Doshi, N. Apthorpe, and N. Feamster, "Machine learning DDoS detection for consumer internet of things devisces," *Proc. - 2018 IEEE Symp. Secur. Priv. Work. SPW 2018*, no. Ml, pp. 29–35, 2018.

15. S. T. Zargar, J. Joshi, and D. Tipper, "A survey of defense mechanisms against distributed denial of service (DDoS) flooding attacks," *IEEE Commun. Surv. Tutorials*, vol. 15, no. 4, pp. 2046–2069, 2013.

16. W. Zhou, Y. Jia, A. Peng, Y. Zhang, and P. Liu, "The effect of IoT new features on security and privacy: New threats, existing solutions, and challenges yet to be solved," *IEEE Internet Things J.*, vol. 6, pp. 1606–1616, 2018.

17. E. Alemneh, S.-M. Senouci, P. Brunet, and T. Tegegne, "A two-way trust management system for fog computing," *Futur. Gener. Comput. Syst.*, vol. 106, pp. 206–220, 2020.

18. N. Djedjig, D. Tandjaoui, F. Medjek, and I. Romdhani, "Trust-aware and cooperative routing protocol for IoT security," *J. Inf. Secur. Appl.*, vol. 52, 2020.

19. X. Huang, P. Craig, H. Lin, and Z. Yan, "SecIoT: A security framework for the Internet of Things," *Secur. Commun. Networks*, vol. 9, no. 16, pp. 3083–3094, Nov. 2016.

20. A. Namavar Jahromi et al., "An improved two-hidden-layer extreme learning machine for malware hunting," *Comput. Secur.*, vol. 89, 2020.

21. I. Stojmenovic and S. Wen, "The Fog computing paradigm: Scenarios and security issues," *2014 Federated Conference on Computer Science and Information Systems*, Warsaw, Poland, 2014, pp. 1–8, doi: 10.15439/2014F503.

22. C. Douligeris and A. Mitrokotsa, "DDoS attacks and defense mechanisms: classification and state-of-the-art", *Computer Networks*, vol. 44, no. 5, 2004, pp. 643–666, ISSN 1389-1286, doi:10.1016/j.comnet.2003.10.003. https://www.sciencedirect.com/science/article/pii/S1389128603004250

23. M. Alauthman, N. Aslam, M. Al-Kasassbeh, S. Khan, A. Al-Qerem, and K.-K. Raymond Choo, "An efficient reinforcement learning-based Botnet detection approach," *J. Netw. Comput. Appl.*, vol. 150, p. 102479, 2020.

24. K. Krombholz, H. Hobel, M. Huber, and E. Weippl, "Advanced social engineering attacks," *J. Inf. Secur. Appl.*, vol. 22, pp. 113–122, Jun. 2015.

25. S. Abraham and I. Chengalur-Smith, "An overview of social engineering malware: Trends, tactics, and implications," *Technol. Soc.*, vol. 32, no. 3, pp. 183–196, Aug. 2010.

26. W. Li, W. Meng, and M. H. Au, "Enhancing collaborative intrusion detection via disagreement-based semi-supervised learning in IoT environments," *J. Netw. Comput. Appl.*, vol. 161, 2020.

27. Z. Li, A. Goyal, and Y. Chen, "Honeynet-based Botnet Scan Traffic Analysis," *Botnet Detection*, in Lee, W., Wang, C., & Dagon, D. Ed. Boston, MA: Springer US, 2008, pp. 25–44.

28. A. A. Alli, M. Fahadi, and C. Atebeni, "Blockchain and fog computing: Fog-blockchain concept, opportunities, and challenges," in *Blockchain in Data Analytics*, Mohiuddin Ahmed, Ed. Cambridge: Cambridge Scholars Publishing, 2020, p. 75.

29. G. Rahman and C. C. Wen, "Fog computing, applications, security and challenges, review," *Int. J. Eng. Technol.*, vol. 7, no. 3, pp. 1615–1621, 2018.

30. S. Abu-Nimeh, D. Nappa, X. Wang, and S. Nair, "A comparison of machine learning techniques for phishing detection," in *Proceedings of the Anti-phishing Working Groups 2nd Annual eCrime Researchers Summit on - eCrime '07*, Pittsburgh, PA, USA, 2007, pp. 60–69.

31. S. M. A. Karim and J. J. Prevost, "*A machine learning based approach to mobile cloud offloading*," *2017 Computing Conference*, no. July, pp. 675–680, 2017.

32. K. M. Renuka, S. Kumari, D. Zhao, and L. Li, "Design of a Secure Password-Based Authentication Scheme for M2M Networks in IoT Enabled Cyber-Physical Systems," *IEEE Access*, vol. 7, pp. 51014–51027, 2019.

33. S. Joshi, H. Upadhyay, L. Lagos, N. S. Akkipeddi, and V. Guerra, "Machine learning approach for malware detection using random forest classifier on process list data structure," in *Proceedings of the 2nd International Conference on Information System and Data Mining - ICISDM '18*, Lakeland, FL, USA, 2018, pp. 98–102.

34. D. Raposo, A. Rodrigues, S. Sinche, J. S. Silva and F. Boavida, "Securing wirelessHART: monitoring, exploring and detecting new vulnerabilities," *2018 IEEE 17th International Symposium on Network Computing and Applications (NCA)*, Cambridge, MA, USA, 2018, pp. 1–9, doi: 10.1109/NCA.2018.8548060

35. R. U. Khan, X. Zhang, R. Kumar, A. Sharif, N. A. Golilarz, and M. Alazab, "An adaptive multilayer botnet detection technique using machine learning classifiers," *Appl. Sci.*, vol. 9, no. 11, 2019.

36. P. Patil, A. Hakiri, and A. Gokhale, "Cyber foraging and offloading framework for internet of things cyber foraging and offloading framework for internet of things," no. September, 2016.

37. N. Tariq *et al.*, "The security of big data in fog-enabled IoT applications including blockchain: A survey," pp. 1–33, 2019.

38. J. Ni, S. Member, K. Zhang, X. Lin, and X. S. Shen, "Securing fog computing for internet of things applications: Challenges and solutions," *IEEE Commun. Surv. Tutorials*, vol. 20, no. 1, pp. 601–628, 2020.

39. A. Kumari, S. Tanwar, S. Tyagi, N. Kumar, R. M. Parizi, and K.-K. R. Choo, "Fog data analytics: A taxonomy and process model," *J. Netw. Comput. Appl.*, vol. 128, pp. 90–104, 2019.

40. A. V. Dastjerdi and R. Buyya, "Fog computing: Helping the internet of things realize its potential," *Computer (Long. Beach. Calif.)*, vol. 49, pp. 112–1162016.

41. P. Hu, S. Dhelim, H. Ning, and T. Qiu, "Survey on fog computing: Architecture, key technologies, applications and open issues," *J. Netw. Comput. Appl.*, vol. 98, pp. 27–42, 2017.

42. K. Sethi, R. Kumar, L. Sethi, P. Bera, and P. K. Patra, "*A novel machine learning based malware detection and classification framework*," in *2019 International Conference on Cyber Security and Protection of Digital Services (Cyber Security)*, Oxford, UK, 2019, pp. 1–4.

Chapter 2

# Collaborative and Integrated Edge Security Architecture

*Abebe Diro*

La Trobe University, Australia

## CONTENTS

## 2.1 BACKGROUND

Modern societies depend on cyberspace for daily lives as it plays a key role in the way people learn, interact and do businesses [1], [2]. It has been a robust, efficient and cost-effective means of communication by eliminating geographical barriers between communicating parties. As one of the main cyberspace services, the Internet has undergone several evolutions since its inception in the late 1960s as an outcome of the ARPANET [3] project. This evolution has brought about an explosion of online services and applications, and consequently, an exponential increment in the number of Internet users. The continuously evolving pace of the Internet as a result of embracing new technologies such as wireless sensor networks (WSNs) and cyber physical systems (CPSs) has given birth to the Internet of Things (IoT). The term IoT was first coined in 2009 by Kevin Ashton to refer to the combination of radio-frequency identification (RFID) and the Internet [4]. It was envisioned that it would enable the interaction and cooperation between cyber and physical domains as the main enabler of Industry 4.0. The current horizon of the IoT, however, includes a wide range of technologies and connectivity, such as human-to-machine interactions, lab-on-a-chip (LOC) sensors, location-based services and augmented reality [5]. Figure 2.1 shows the evolution of various technologies to shape the IoT. Thus, the evolution of the Internet has been a stepping-stone for the emergence of the IoT and other edge computing technologies.

The IoT is an evolving pervasive and ubiquitous edge network that enables the monitoring and control of the physical environment. The pervasiveness of IoT applications has been supported by the technological advancements of IPv6, low-power WLANs and lightweight

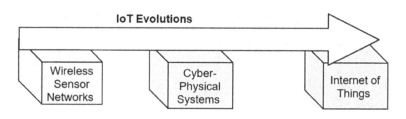

*Figure 2.1* Evolution of the IoT.

OSs [6]. First, the continuous production and development of new IoT devices call for large IP address space. In this regard, the legacy addressing scheme of IPv4 has already failed to meet the massive connectivity requirements of the IoT. As a result, IPv6 has been adopted for Internet services as it can accommodate wider address spaces. Furthermore, ubiquitous connectivity requires battery sources, especially in remote areas where a power supply is out of reach. In the absence of low-power wireless systems, IoT devices such as sensors cannot operate for long hours on battery power. Finally, light operating systems have enabled these small devices to deploy smart applications with limited processing and storage systems [7]. To sum up, the advancement of IoT systems has been backed by various technological enablers.

The potential of IoT technologies and services has prompted wide interest across the globe in the adoption of IoT applications. IoT technologies have been applied to applications, in particular, to smart cities and factories [8]. For instance, as of 2008, the number of connected IoT devices had already surpassed the world population. This figure will exponentially increase to 50 million by 2025 and elevates the number of connected users to about 4.1 billion in the world [9]. Consequently, the popularity of IoT devices has increased the demand for smart applications as a key component of the smart world.

The deployment rate of smart devices is about fivefold that of electricity and telephony in total. The accumulative effect of this massive connectivity and wide applicability is the surge of data in edge and fog networks. The explosion of data accounts for about 9 trillion USD economic impacts [10]. The big data generated from IoT devices can have a potential influence on people's day-to-day activities such as offering huge profitability and improving quality of life. At the same time, the surge in the traffic from IoT applications increases the potential danger of cyber-attacks as the IoT comes with unseen protocols, workflows, interfaces and applications [11]. Hence, it follows that IoT devices, which are the main source of data, can have both positive and negative effects on the daily lives of citizens, and so safeguarding a network edge has become critical for security and safety.

## 2.2 EDGE SECURITY CHALLENGES

The massive-scale deployment and the associated generation of big data by the edge network have a profound effect in bringing about cyber risks at the edge of the network in several critical applications. The security of edge devices is challenged by several factors such as *resource constraints, heterogeneity, massive-scale distribution and lack of supportive architecture [12].*

Unlike IT environment, edge devices lack the necessary resources of processing, storage and communication to support complex and resource-hungry security solutions [13]. It is almost impossible to deploy strong security controls on the devices due to resource limitations. Despite its huge elasticity of resources, the cloud is also not effective to mitigate cyber-attacks from the IoT due to its remoteness and centralized architecture [14]. Though the security architecture of the cloud has already been proved to be successful for IT security, the lack of scalability and the low delay requirements of IoT applications make this solution infeasible. On the other hand, the traditional perimeter security architectures in IT are no longer the appropriate solutions for the massively large-scale deployment of distributed and heterogeneous edge devices [15]. These indicate that edge security challenges can be compensated using efficient security architectural solutions.

Edge devices can be secured by a geographically nearby and distributed architecture that can deploy security parameters and operations in proximity [16]. This kind of architecture is a holistic design approach that can solve the fundamental security implementation problems related to resource constraints in the edge devices such as the IoT by offloading processing, storage and communication overheads from the devices. It also handles the scalability and high-delay bottlenecks reflected in the centralized cloud by hosting security functions closer to the devices. Finally, it solves the heterogeneity of devices in protocols and communication technologies by deploying a common platform that can optimize resources [17]. Thus, this distributed architectural arrangement gives a tremendous opportunity to provide a collaborative security platform that is scalable, highly responsive and resource-efficient for edge computing.

## 2.3 PERSPECTIVES OF EDGE SECURITY ARCHITECTURE

The edge platforms such as fog nodes provide novel architectural support for security controls that can take various forms to mitigate security breaches. As shown in Figure 2.2, the architectural support aimed at alleviating resource-constraints in the edge can be seen from three perspectives [18], [19]: edge devices, users and end-to-end security provision.

Edge device-centric security architecture enables to deploy security solutions based on specific needs of edge devices, for instance, resource requirements and critical applications

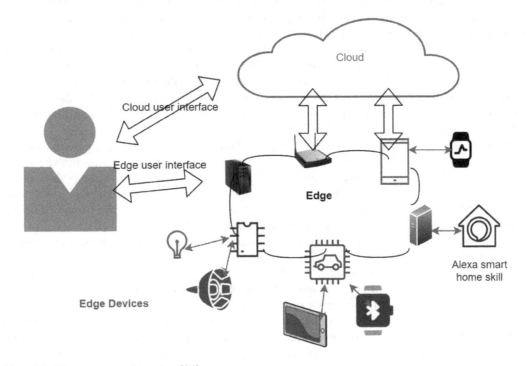

*Figure 2.2* Edge-centric architecture [14].

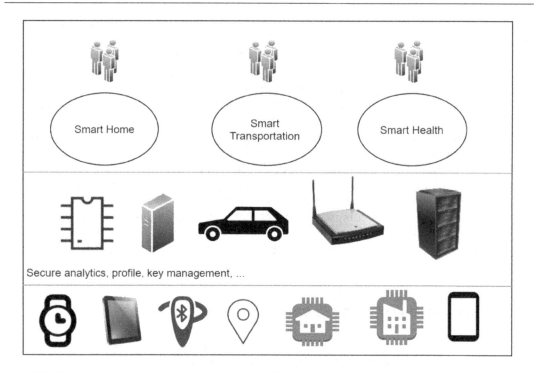

*Figure 2.3* Device-centric edge security architecture [14].

in control. The main goal of this approach is to offload resources such as memory, processor and communications from devices to edge servers [20]. This architecture is appealing as it doesn't change the underlying network architecture and protocols, rather it complements the existing security solutions. In this approach, as shown in Figure 2.3, device-specific behaviors can profile at edge sever for security requirements such as anomaly detection [21]. From the profile, the edge nodes such as fog nodes can be applied for edge devices' security analysis, protocol mapping, heterogeneity monitoring and security dependence among devices. By offloading complex computations such as cryptographic functions from edge devices, it is also essential that edge nodes implement customized security controls such as authentication, authorization and accounting (AAA) [22].

With the abundance and pervasiveness of edge applications, end-users such as smart home users are vulnerable and attractive targets to security breaches. Figure 2.4 shows the architecture of user-centric edge security solutions [23]. This is since most of the edge devices are unprotected, and end-users lack the awareness and skills of security management. Due to this, edge-based security design making use of fog architecture such as edge virtualization is a novel design for securing personal information by offloading security operations and credentials. For instance, a trusted domain can be established at the edge of network as a virtual container to enable end-users to securely connect edge applications [24].

Integrated in the daily lives of citizens, edge devices are involved in the collection, storage, processing and dissemination of sensitive data which can be personally identifiable information (PII) [25]. Leakage of information or compromise of the device at network edge brings about privacy violations. Data is better secured if it is kept at the edge nodes than on the device itself or on the cloud, as edge nodes act as a protective shield in distributing controls. Using cryptographic solutions such as differential privacy and k-anonymity, it is possible to provide stringent privacy control for edge networks, specifically for the IoT applications involved in

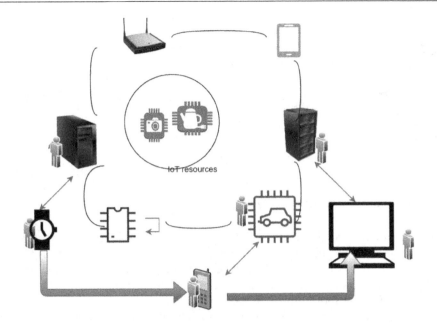

*Figure 2.4* User-centric edge security architecture [14].

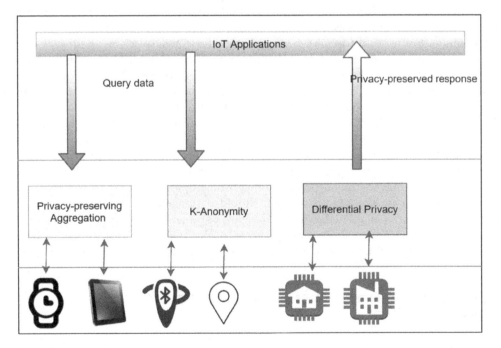

*Figure 2.5* Privacy-centric edge security architecture [14].

sensitive data manipulations [26]. The anonymity provision of blockchain technology can be leveraged to provide privacy-preserving data exchange among the IoT and mobile devices. As depicted in Figure 2.5, techniques such as proxy-encryption and searchable encryptions can be implemented at fog-level nodes to realize end-to-end security, especially for privacy-preserving edge applications [27]. Apart from offloading operations, the container helps in

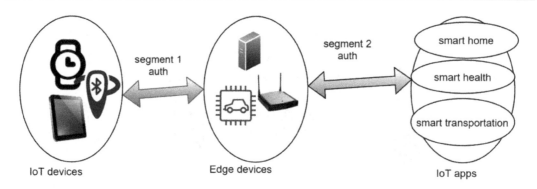

*Figure 2.6* Access control-centric edge security architecture [14].

translating user policy specifications into policy language to implement controls such as firewall, anti-malware and inspection tools. In mobile systems, network function virtualization (NFV) can be employed to contain applications, enforce network, migrate and orchestrate resources by hosting security controls such as firewalls and anti-malware that are customized according to specific user requirements [28].

In the plethora of edge devices communications with themselves, with edge nodes and the cloud, satisfying security for end-to-end architecture is challenging mainly due to device level heterogeneities and massive-scale communications [29]. To bridge these communications and heterogeneity gaps, edge/fog nodes can act as a middleware to enable secure end-to-end message exchange for edge devices. As in IT systems, access control mechanisms such as AAA form a foundation for end-to-end security of edge devices despite the challenges of realizing these goals for various factors [30]. However, traditional AAA controls fail to meet the resource requirements of the edge ecosystem. For this reason, it is of paramount importance to outsource computation, storage and communications of access controls to nearby edge nodes that have enough resources, as shown in Figure 2.6. This architecture, for instance, can provide end-to-end authentication systems that enable to communicate edge devices to edge nodes, the cloud or other edge devices. In this case, lightweight cryptographic solutions such as ECC can be carefully designed to be used with techniques such as proxy re-encryption and searchable encryption to provide end-to-end security for edge devices [31]. Due to massive connectivity, multi-factor authentication can be employed for smart applications. The communication among the edge ecosystem should be logged for accounting and anomaly detection purposes. To enable edge nodes to share parameters among themselves in mobile applications that support mobile users or devices, a blockchain technology can be leveraged to provide an additional layer of security without leveraging third-party providers [32].

## 2.4 EMERGING TRENDS AND ENABLERS FOR EDGE SECURITY ARCHITECTURE

This section discusses the background and theories of emerging schemes or technologies and concepts that play a significant role in securing the edge network.

### 2.4.1 The Edge Computing Architecture

In the edge-to-cloud continuum, the edge computing architecture varies significantly based on applications. It consists of three-tiers: edge device, fog and cloud. Tier-1 is a layer in

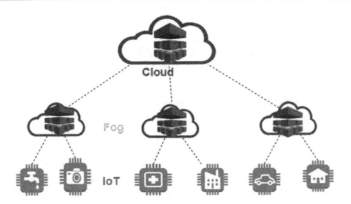

*Figure 2.7* Typical fog architecture.

which sensors and actuators interact with environments. The fog tier consists of intermediary devices such as gateways and access points. The cloud is located at the extreme end of the tier [33]. Figure 2.7 shows the typical edge architecture consisting of the three fundamental components.

Distributed and embedded intelligence is a core architectural element of edge network systems. This has emanated from the fact that centralized systems have a scalability problem for data collection, a lack of bandwidth for communication and high reaction time for edge systems [34]. This distributed intelligence capability known as fog computing is an architecture specifically designed to process data and events from edge devices closer to the source as opposed to a central cloud. This means the fog computing architecture extends the cloud into the physical environment, where events are processed in a local and distributed way. The evolving adoption of fog network, however, is not to substitute the architecture of the cloud, but it complements the cloud by bringing distributed intelligence into distributed edge nodes [35]. This reinforces that the fog platform is an ideal architectural element in the application of edge devices. Thus, this architecture is ideal in deploying security solutions for latency-intolerant critical edge applications.

## 2.4.2  Leveraging Fog-Based Security Architecture for Edge Networks

The lack of scalable architecture is one of the challenges in securing edge components. Fog platform can be adopted for the security of edge devices in three fundamental architectures: **Fog-to-Cloud, devices-fog-cloud and devices-to-fog.** The summary of the architectural efficiencies in scalability and resources usage is shown in Table 2.1.

*Fog-to-Cloud Security Architecture*: In this architecture, edge devices are an integral part of fog computing rather than considering both as separate layers. The security parameters,

*Table 2.1* Resource provisions, latency, scalability and visibility of edge security architectures.

| Architecture | Computation | Storage | Latency | Scalability | Visibility |
|---|---|---|---|---|---|
| Fog-to-Cloud | High | High | Medium | Medium | High |
| Devices-to-Fog-to-Cloud | High | High | High | Low | High |
| Devices-to-Fog | Medium | Medium | Low | High | Medium |
| Traditional Device-to-Cloud | High | High | Very high | Very low | High |

credentials and functions can be distributed across fog and cloud levels [36]. For instance, as a lightweight mechanism, fog nodes can be leveraged to detect anomalies based on lightweight machine learning models such as autoencoders (AEs). This can be adopted as a first layer defense by detecting suspicious events before propagating to critical infrastructures. Apart from offloading overheads from resource-constrained devices [37], fog nodes can horizontally scale to share local models and parameters. As the fog nodes are relatively less in computing and storage resources than cloud, heavyweight tasks such as intrusion classification or clustering can be performed separately at the cloud level. This architecture provides better computing and storage resources and global network visibility than devices-to-fog architecture. While it provides tremendous resources to mitigate complex cyber-attacks, Fog-to-Cloud offers relatively higher response time and latency, and lower scalability than devices-to-fog architecture. However, the architecture is slightly better than traditional device-to-cloud and device-to-Fog-to-Cloud architectures in providing lower latency and higher scalability while the resource provisions are almost similar. This indicates that Fog-to-Cloud architecture is slightly more scalable and provides better response time than any architecture involving the communication of edge devices directly to the cloud.

*Devices-to-Fog-to-Cloud Security Architecture*: Security solutions and controls can be distributed on three nodes [38]: *cloud, fog and edge*. Like Fog-to-Cloud architecture, heavyweight functions such as cryptographic functions, clustering and machine learning training can be performed by the cloud while the fog nodes provide functions such as cryptographic key generation and alerting functions based on anomaly detection. However, edge devices can be leveraged to host primitive functions such as storage of keys and pre-trained models. The resource efficiency and performance, reliability and global network visibility of this architecture seems reasonably acceptable while the latency and design complexity can be problems to be introduced by the architecture [39]. However, the architecture seems more scalable than the traditional device-to-cloud architecture since some of the security functions are served at the fog level. Hence, this architecture can be leveraged to applications that employ heavy security functions at the expense of scalability.

*Devices-to-Fog Security Architecture*: As fog computing provides richer resources than edge devices, the *devices-to-fog architecture* supplements edge devices by offloading some of their storage, processing and communication functions [39]. For instance, IoT devices can store and process lightweight activities such as cryptographic keys while fog nodes handle proxy re-encryption in machine-to-machine or machine-to-cloud communications, as shown in Figure 2.8.

In intrusion detection scenarios, this architecture also brings about efficient cyber threat detection coverage for massive-scale IoT devices as IoT devices have host-level visibility while the fog nodes have subnetwork-level control and visibility. Apart from locally detecting malicious events for IoT devices under control, a fog node can share cyber threat intelligence with its neighborhoods. This brings about accurate threat hunting and detection if, specifically, detection systems can exchange AI models and parameters.

Figure 2.9 shows an example of devices-to-fog security architecture for smart cities where each fog node learns from local edge traffic and exchange parameters via the coordinator server. However, it is computationally complex to perform training machine learning models for massive-scale IoT devices. This inculcates that pre-trained models should be deployed on fog nodes or the number of IoT devices monitored under a single fog node should be optimized. Nonetheless, with the advancement of hardware technologies such as GPU, this architecture will reasonably enable efficient use of computing, processing and communication resources at the edge of the network [13]. On the other hand, the lack of global network

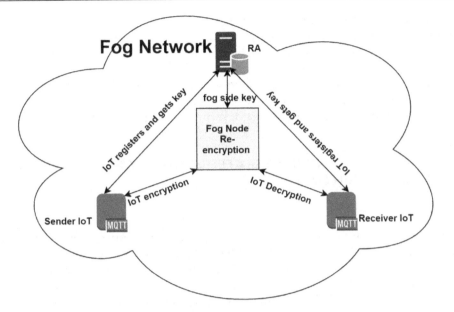

*Figure 2.8* Typical devices-to-fog access control architecture.

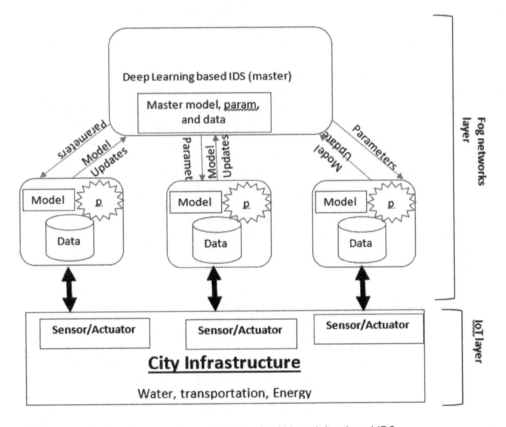

*Figure 2.9* An example of a devices-to-fog architecture for AI-based distributed IDSs.

visibility by the fog nodes devices-to-fog architecture can significantly decrease the accuracy of the detector. For this, devices-to-fog architecture could enhance security control efficiency and robustness at the edge, specifically if there is a mechanism of horizontal co-operation among fog nodes. Finally, machine learning models can be a subject of adversarial attacks such as training or detection poisoning, and insider attacks. Thus, collaborative architectures such as blockchain can alleviate the drawbacks of devices-to-fog security architecture by providing a secure and auditable exchange of security parameters at the edge [19].

## 2.5 COLLABORATIVE AND INTEGRATED SECURITY ARCHITECTURE FOR EDGE COMPUTING

### 2.5.1 Overview

Collaborative cyber defense mechanisms such as cooperative authentications and intrusion detection systems (IDSs) have been in the literature for several decades though the actual implementation has been hindered by several requirements such as accountability, integrity, resilience, consensus, scalability, resource efficiency and privacy. For instance, collaborative IDSs for the massive-scale IoT (scalability) must log suspicious events (accountability) by ensuring that records in each IDS cannot be altered by a malicious attacker (integrity) in collaborative decision-making (consensus).

Distributed ledger technology can be leveraged to satisfy the essential requirements of collaborative cyber defense [15]. Federated learning models can be implemented on relatively resource-rich devices such as gateways for intrusion detection in IoT devices using blockchain [40], [41]. The adoption of blockchain can mitigate the poisoning of nodes, as blockchain provides immutability for every transaction.

The state-of-the-art distributed architectures are victims of integrity cyber-attacks such as man-in-the-middle and adversarial attacks [41]. The emerging distributed ledger-based technology such as the blockchain has been successful in securing financial applications [42], [43]. This technological architecture can significantly boost the robustness of edge network if it is adopted for edge security architecture that can leverage AI algorithms. In this section, we explore the architectures of edge security, specifically, blockchain-based edge architecture which is fueled with the power of AI algorithms for firewall and IDS applications. The general architecture of collaborative and integrated security architecture is depicted in Figure 2.10.

With the emergence of ledger technologies such as fog computing and distributed ledge technologies such as blockchain, an integrated approach to security architecture is viably essential. This design and architectural scheme provides comprehensive security controls, specifically distributed virtual firewalls (DFWs), IDSs, access controls and privacy-preserving schemes.

### 2.5.2 Distributed Virtual Firewall (DFWs)

Firewalls are essential components of the first layer defense for on-premises networks or the cloud. They filter inbound or outbound network traffic based on manually crafted policy rules, which are error-prone and inefficient for the ever-growing need of modern networks [44]. Specifically, the firewall rules managed manually for edge networks firewall rules are ineffective and costly due to large-scale deployments of edge devices. To reflect the underlying traffic, the formation of firewall rules needs to be automated for edge devices. In edge computing, edge devices can be clustered according to their application similarity to be assigned to the same security group. The automated rules govern application connectivity between

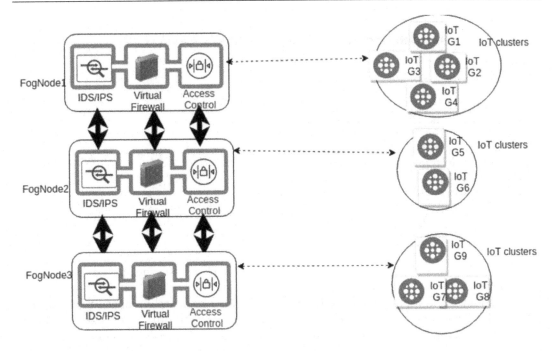

*Figure 2.10* The General Architecture of Collaborative and Integrated Security Architecture.

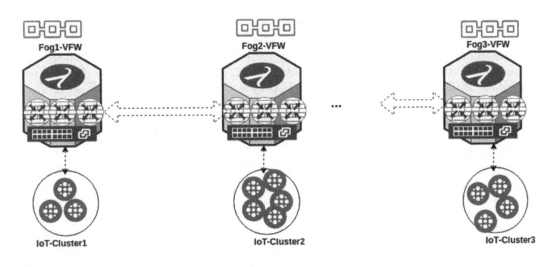

*Figure 2.11* The distributed virtual firewall architecture.

various security groups. NFV can be applied at each fog node to logically separate various edge security groups, as shown in Table 2.1. However, to orchestrate the communication of various edge devices under the control of the different network, blockchain concepts can be leveraged between various fog nodes. Figure 2.11 shows a general distributed edge firewall architecture.

Algorithm 2.1 inputs logs of various edge devices communications to perform clustering for each mini-batches. The final clustering is achieved by aggregating the clusters of mini-batches. This enables to capture asset signatures by grouping similar IoT applications into a

## ALGORITHM 2.1: LOCAL PARALLEL CLUSTERING

```
Input: K, batch_size, logs
Pre-process logs
Init Batch_queue #shared by threads
Init Centroids[] #shared by threads
While (not end of logs ) do
new_batch←load_next_batch(logs,batach_size)
enqueue(new_batch,Batch_queue)
if (Batch_queue is full) then
wait(Batch_queue) #wait dequeue
While (clustering is in progress) do
wait(Batch_queue) # wait until all clustered
C←Cluster using K-means
```

single group, known as micro-segmentation mechanism. This clustering approach is an input to the formation of homogeneous group namely the security group, which is governed by similar inbound and outbound rules. The approach can significantly reduce attack surfaces for the edge devices and prevent the spread of attack impacts to other networks by containing the intra-communication with small groups. Figure 2.12 shows the clustering output for the formation of security groups from the industry dataset. As clearly shown in the figure, K-means algorithm outperformed the other algorithms by differentiating clear security groups.

As shown in Algorithm 2.2, for each cluster or security group of IoT devices, the corresponding flows are fetched from the logs file to be used as initial input for rules formation. The fetched flows are then fed to the decision tree for rules generalization for each security group, and the anomalies flow are discarded from the tree. The output of the decision tree for the formation of the rule in each security group is depicted in Table 2.2. These rules can be leveraged in creating connectivity rules that govern the communication of different security as shown in Table 2.1. The automation security groups and connectivity rules eliminate manual and error-prone tasks by leveraging machine learning models that can learn automatic patterns from network traffic logs.

NFV has been proposed to provide reconfigurability of firewall rules, mobility and tracking of users, as shown in Table 2.1. Supported by NFV, virtual switch of a fog node provides a platform to host multiple virtual firewalls to enable the communication of each IoT security group with a corresponding virtual firewall on the fog node. Due to resource-constraints and the scale of edge devices, it is impossible to deploy individual firewalls for each mobile and IoT device. This is when relatively powerful edge nodes can be brought onboard to be adopted as segment-based DFWs that filter inbound and outbound traffic closer to the smart devices. This provides a mechanism of computation and storage offloading from resource-limited devices and supports mobility of edge users across multiple firewall nodes. The fog network environment enables to monitor IoT traffic to automatically recognize traffic, application and protocol patterns for device categorization and classification using AI algorithms. This means devices in the same cluster use similar communication and interactivity rules, and hence, similar firewall/security group rules. The connectivity rules and the AI model for application category prediction are stored in the fog nodes for references. The interactions among or across IoT–IoT, IoT–Fog and Fog–Fog interactions are based on security group rules that act as a virtual filtering mechanism. As Fog–Fog communications are regulated by security groups based on resource ownership or trust relationships, IoT device mobility

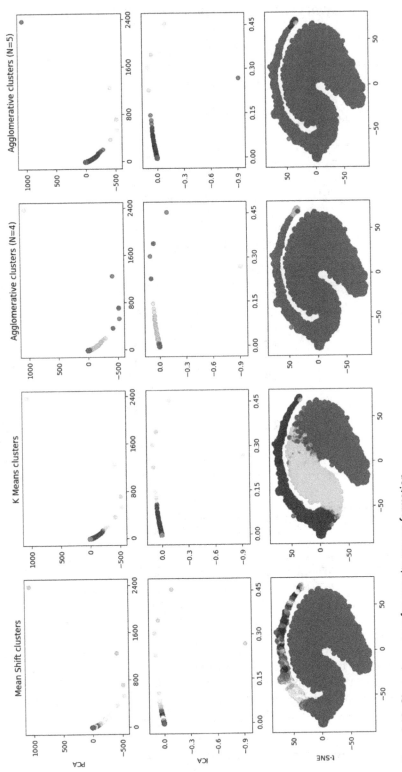

*Figure 2.12* Clustering output for security groups formation.

## ALGORITHM 2.2:  AGGREGARED CLUSTERING

```
Input: Batch_queue, centroids[], K
while queue is not empty & main thread is alive do:
batch_instances←Dequeue(queue)
C=Cluster
centroids[]=centroids[]UC
if (queue is empty) then
wait(queue) #wait dequeue
for each c in C
select log traffic rules
Construct rules Tree
Prune anomalies rules
Get Generalized Rules
```

Table 2.2 Security groups' interaction with NFV-enabled switch.

| Source Group | Service | Port | Handler Vswitch |
| --- | --- | --- | --- |
| IoT-cluster1-SG1 | TCP | 1883 | Fog1-VFW-VF1 |
| IoT-cluster1-SG2 | TCP | 1883 | Fog1-VFW-VF2 |
| IoT-cluster1-SG3 | TCP | 1883 | Fog1-VFW-VF3 |
| Fog2-VFW | TCP | 8883 | Fog1-VFW |
| IoT-cluster2-SG1 | TCP | 1883 | Fog2-VFW-VF21 |
| IoT-cluster2-SG2 | TCP | 1883 | Fog2-VFW-VF22 |
| IoT-cluster2-SG3 | TCP | 1883 | Fog2-VFW-VF23 |
| IoT-cluster2-SG4 | TCP | 1883 | Fog2-VFW-VF24 |
| IoT-cluster2-SG5 | TCP | 1883 | Fog2-VFW-VF25 |
| Fog1-VFW | TCP | 8883 | Fog2-VFW |
| Fog3-VFW | TCP | 8883 | Fog2-VFW |

Table 2.3 Security Group Rules.

| Rule | SRC | DST | SRC_PORT | DST_PORT | Direction | Protocol | Action |
| --- | --- | --- | --- | --- | --- | --- | --- |
| 1 | IoT-cluster1-SG1 | IoT-cluster1-SG2 | 8080 | 22 | Inbound | TCP | Allow |
| 2 | IoT-cluster1-SG2 | IoT-cluster1-SG3 | All | All | Inbound | TCP | Allow |
| 3 | IoT-cluster1-SG1 | IoT-cluster2-SG1 | 8080 | All | Outbound | TCP | Allow |
| 4 | IoT-cluster1-SG2 | IoT-cluster2-SG2 | 8080 | All | Outbound | TCP | Allow |

involves security group migration or joining a new security group. In this design scheme, the firewall rules are easily updated for a group of edge devices under the control of an edge server/node. To provide firewall rules and associated logs integrity, the distributed edge firewalls are assisted by distributed architectures such as blockchain. A distributed ledger is adopted as a secure mechanism of sharing parameters and rules.

### 2.5.3 Distributed Intrusion Detection Systems (IDSs)

The damage happened because of the absence of IDS was manifested from the cyber-attack caused by IoT botnet, MIRAI, on DNS servers of Dye Inc. Edge devices such as mobile and the IoT can be massively benefited from the design of edge-based IDS in resource efficiency, availability of multiple information sources and adaptability. Powerful Edge nodes can offload monitoring, data collection and pattern-learning aspects of IDS from edge devices, which is essential for resource savings and scalability. In this regard, machine learning algorithms can be applied at fog level to aggregate device network traffic to learn normal and abnormal patterns of the devices under a given fog node. Though it seems prohibitable and expensive in computations and communications as the fog nodes and their corresponding edge devices increase, patterns exchange can be taken place at the fog node level to enhance the performance of machine learning models by introducing local experience at each device level. However, with the introduction of powerful hardware, this approach can be implemented using blockchain technology using lightweight algorithms. As shown in Figure 2.13, distributed ledgers such as blockchain can be leveraged to enhance the privacy and security of machine learning models, which can be otherwise subjected to training and detection poison attacks by adversarial manipulations [45].

Each IDS forms a chain of blocks that are stored in communicating fog nodes using blockchain concept for preserving transaction integrity [46]. Fog nodes Fog1…N, have been virtualized using NFV to support distributed intrusion detection functionalities. The fog nodes agree on consensus algorithms to build a trust relationship using smart contracts and can specify the node groups they wish to join. To accept a new attack signature or ML parameters shared by an IDS as a permanent record, a consensus algorithm is issued by each fog node to keep the integrity of the transaction. To ensure more security and confidentiality in public networks, a registration authority (RA) is integrated with a blockchain-based IDS. Specifically, the off-chain RA is used to register the participating IDS entities in the contract-making process and supplies them with security keys to enhance trust relationship. Besides, the RA stores event logs, histories of transactions, permanent parameters and models of IDSs for long-term analysis and compliance. Each IDS exchange machine learning parameters with neighbor nodes using blockchain to integrity and validity through blockchain consensus algorithms. Each IDS maintains local ML models and parameters that can be exchanged among participant fog nodes to gain neighbor experience for collaborated cyber threat detection. This can significantly improve the detection rate for advanced attacks such as a denial of service attack (DoS) and its variants, and zero-day vulnerabilities. Furthermore, the architecture provides a collaborated way of guaranteeing maximum authentication, confidentiality and integrity of shared parameters using a distributed ledger. Hence, a significant operations and storages are offloaded to off-chain block, this arrangement can tremendously boost the application of distributed IDS at fog computing levels.

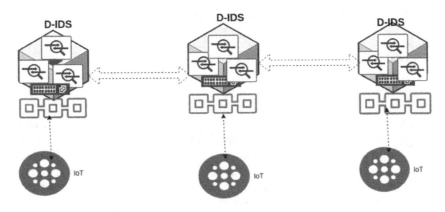

*Figure 2.13* Distributed IDS structure.

## ALGORITHM 2.3: LOCAL TRAINING ON EACH EDGE NODE

```
Get global parameters from smart contract
B ← Batches from dataset D
E ← Epochs
For each epoch e from 1 to E:
For each batch b in B:
```

$$W_{ji} := W_{ji} - \alpha \frac{\partial L\left(W, b \mid j\right)}{\partial W_{ji}}$$

$$b_{ji} := W_{ji} - \alpha \frac{\partial L\left(W, b \mid j\right)}{\partial b_{ji}}$$

```
Return ∇Wji , ∇bji to RA for bidding
```

## ALGORITHM 2.4: SMART CONTRACT ON THE AGGREGATOR NODE

```
Initialize w₀, b₀
For each round r in 1, 2, r:
Accept model bids
Score model bids
For each IDS node n in N whose bid accepted in parallel:
LocalTraining(n, wᵣ)
```

$$w_{r+1} := \sum_{n=1}^{N} \frac{d_n}{d} w^n_{r+1}, \text{ where } d_n \text{ is the size of data partition of IDS n}$$

$$\text{such that } \sum_n d_n$$

```
Push updated model to blockchain
```

In Algorithm 2.3, each IDS begins with pulling initial parameters from RA. For round r, in epochs, the training process utilizes current $w_t$ to calculate the change in gradient $\nabla w$ on local data in mini-batch using learning rate $\alpha$. The smart contractor RA opens a bid every round to accept and process bids from local IDSs where bids get score-based on matching criteria. For accepted bids, as shown in Algorithm 2.4, the RA aggregates gradients to produce an updated model which is disseminated to participants.

## 2.6 CONCLUSION AND FUTURE RESEARCH

In this chapter, existing edge security solutions have been reviewed, the gaps have been analyzed and potential solutions have been forwarded.

While investigating edge security architectures, it has been observed that there are several overall security challenges for edge computing: limitations of resources, lack of scalability, heterogeneity, distribution, lack of standard architectural support, etc. Various research works have been conducted to solve the problems of resource-constraints [11]; however, the lack of scalable and standard security architecture at the edge is a fundamental security issue in the edge at the network. While it has been found out that fog platform can answer this problem, the issue of trust relationship formation has stood out as an obstacle to security edge devices. For instance, the horizontal communications of fog nodes for roaming edge devices need the trust of one fog node for the other in the chain of communications. This chapter has introduced the adoption of distributed ledger technology such as blockchain to enable edge nodes to trust relationship formation for secure and auditable communication; however, the proposed concept should be well tested using extensive experimentation and evaluations. In the future, we will implement this architecture using the proposed blockchain-based machine learning algorithms.

## REFERENCES

1. M. Bafandehkar, S. M. Yasin, R. Mahmod, and Z. M. Hanapi, "Comparison of ECC and RSA algorithms in resource constrained devices," in *2013 International Conference on IT Convergence and Security (ICITCS)*, pp. 1–3, IEEE, 2013.
2. Y. Qin, Q. Z. Sheng, N. J. Falkner, S. Dustdar, H. Wang, and A. V. Vasilakos, "When things matter: A survey on data-centric internet of things," *Journal of Network and Computer Appli-cations*, vol. 64, pp. 137–153, 2016.
3. J. McQuillan, I. Richer, and E. Rosen, "The new routing algorithm for the ARPANET," *IEEE Transactions on Communications*, vol. 28, no. 5, pp. 711–719, 1980.
4. F. Mattern and C. Floerkemeier, "From the internet of computers to the internet of things," in *Lecture Notes in Computer Science*, Berlin, Heidelberg: Springer, 2010, pp. 242–259.
5. J. Lin, W. Yu, N. Zhang, X. Yang, H. Zhang, and W. Zhao, "A survey on internet of things: Architecture, enabling technologies, security and privacy, and applications," *IEEE Internet of Things Journal*, vol. 4, no. 5, pp. 1125–1142, 2017.
6. A. Diro, N. Chilamkurti, and N. Kumar. "Lightweight cybersecurity schemes using elliptic curve cryptography in publish-subscribe fog computing." *Mobile Networks and Applications*, vol. 22, pp. 1–11, 2017.
7. J. Frahim, P. Carlos, A. Jeff, and M. Monique, "Securing the internet of things: A proposed framework," Cisco White Paper. 2015.
8. A. Diro and N. Chilamkurti, "Distributed attack detection scheme using deep learning approach for internet of things," *Journal of Future Generation Computer Systems*, vol. 82, pp. 761–768, 2018
9. A. Diro, N. Chilamkurti, and P. Veeraraghavan, "Elliptic curve based cybersecurity schemes for publish-subscribe internet of things," in *International Conference on Heterogeneous Networking for Quality, Reliability, Security and Robustness*, pp. 258–268, Springer, 2016.
10. X. Caron, R. Bosua, S. B. Maynard, and A. Ahmad, "The internet of things (IoT) and its impact on individual privacy: An Australian perspective," *Computer Law and Security Review*, vol. 32, no. 1, pp. 4–15, 2016.
11. N. Chaabouni, M. Mosbah, A. Zemmari, C. Sauvignac and P. Faruki, "Network intrusion detection for IoT security based on learning techniques," *IEEE Communication Surveys and Tutorials*, vol. 21, no. 3, pp. 2671–2701, third quarter, 2019.
12. A. Diro, "Distributed Lightweight Security Schemes for Fog-to-Things Computing," PhD Dissertation, La Trobe University, Victoria, Australia, 2019.
13. A. Diro, et al. "Lightweight authenticated-encryption scheme for internet of things based on publish-subscribe communication." *IEEE Access*, vol. 8, pp. 60539–60551, 2020.
14. D.S. Berman, L.B. Anna, S.C. Jeffrey, and L.C. Cherita. "A survey of deep learning methods for cyber security." *Information*, vol. 10, no. 4, pp. 122, 2019.
15. D. Puthal, L.T. Yang, S. Dustdar, Z. Wen, S. Jun, A.V. Moorsel, & R. Ranjan, "A user-centric security solution for internet of things and edge convergence," *ACM Transactions on Cyber-Physical Systems*, vol. 4 no. 3, 1–19, 2020.
16. F. Bonomi, R. Milito, J. Zhu, and S. Addepalli, "Fog computing and its role in the internet of things," in *Proceedings of the first edition of the MCC workshop on Mobile cloud computing*, pp. 13–16, ACM, 2012.

17. Z. Ning, P. Dong, X. Kong, and F. Xia, "A cooperative partial computation offloading scheme for mobile edge computing enabled Internet of Things," *IEEE Internet of Things Journal*, vol. 6, no. 3, pp. 4804–4814, 2020.

18. B. Tang, Z. Chen, G. Hefferman, T. Wei, H. He, and Q. Yang, "A hierarchical distributed fog computing architecture for big data analysis in smart cities," in *Proceedings of the ASEBigData & Social Informatics 2015* , p. 28, ACM, 2015.

19. K. Sha, et al. "A survey of edge computing based designs for IoT security." Digital Communications and Networks, 2019.

20. R. Errabelly, K. Sha, W. Wei, T.A. Yang, Z. Wang Edgesec, "Design of an edge layer security service to enhance internet of things security," in *Proceedings of the First IEEE International Conference on Fog and Edge Computing (ICFEC 2017)*, 2017.

21. D. Montero, R. Serral-Gracia "Offloading personal security applications to the network edge: A mobile user case scenario," in *Proceedings of IEEE 2016 International Conference on Wireless Communications and Mobile computing*, 2016.

22. Z. Ali, M.S. Hossain, G. Muhammad, I. Ullah, H. Abachi, A. Alamri "Edge-centric multimodal authentication system using encrypted biometric templates," *Future Generation Computer Systems*, vol. 85, pp. 76–87, 2018.

23. X. Chen, L. Jiao, W. Li, X. Fu "Efficient multi-user computation offloading for mobile-edge cloud computing," *IEEE/ACM Transactions on Networking*, vol. 5, pp. 2795–2808, 2016.

24. D. Montero, et al. "Virtualized security at the network edge: A user-centric approach," *IEEE Communications Magazine*, vol. 53, no. 4), pp. 176–186, 2015.

25. P. Gope, R. Amin, S.H. Islam, N. Kumar, V.K. Bhalla "Lightweight and privacy-preserving RFID authentication scheme for distributed IoT infrastructure with secure localization services for smart city environment," *Future Generation Computer Systems*, vol. 83, pp. 629–637, 2018.

26. M. Du, et al. "Big data privacy preserving in multi-access edge computing for heterogeneous internet of things," *IEEE Communications Magazine*, vol. 56 no. 8, pp. 62–67, 2018.

27. R. Lu, K. Heung, A. Lashkari, A.A. Ghorbani "A lightweight privacy-preserving data aggregation scheme for fog computing-enhanced IoT," *IEEE Access*, vol. 5, pp. 3302–3312, 2017.

28. H. Hu, W. Han, G. Ahn, Z. Zhao Flowguard, "Building robust firewalls for software-defined networks," in *Proceedings of the Third Workshop on Hot Topics in Software Defined Networking*, 2014.

29. S. Ravidas, A. Lekidis, F. Paci, & A. Zannone, "Access control in Internet-of-Things: A survey," *Journal of Network and Computer Applications*, vol. 144, 79–101, 2019.

30. A. Molina Zarca, D. Garcia-Carrillo, J. Bernal Bernabe, J. Ortiz, R. Marin-Perez, & A. Skarmeta, "Enabling virtual AAA management in SDN-based IoT networks," *Sensors*, vol. 19, no. 2, pp. 295, 2019.

31. A. Lohachab, "ECC based inter-device authentication and authorization scheme using MQTT for IoT networks," *Journal of Information Security and Applications*, vol. 46, pp. 1–12, 2019.

32. O. Alkadi, et al. "A deep blockchain framework-enabled collaborative intrusion detection for protecting iot and cloud networks," *IEEE Internet of Things Journal*,pp. 1–1, 22 May 2020. doi:10.1109/JIOT.2020.2996590

33. G. I. Klas, "Fog computing and mobile edge cloud gain momentum open fog con-sortium, etsimec and cloudlets," 2015.

34. A. Diro and N. Chilamkurti, "Deep learning: The frontier for distributed attack detection in fog-to-things computing," *IEEE Communications Magazine*, vol. 56, no. 2, pp. 169–175, 2018

35. I. Stojmenovic and S. Wen, "The fog computing paradigm: Scenarios and security issues," in *Computer Science and Information Systems (FedCSIS), 2014 Federated Conference on*, pp. 1–8, IEEE, 2014.

36. P. Illy, G. Kaddoum, C. M. Moreira, K. Kaur, and S. Garg, "Securing Fog-to-things environment using intrusion detection system based on ensemble learn-ing,"arXiv preprint: 1901.10933, 2019.34.

37. S. Prabavathy, K. Sundarakantham and S. M. Shalinie, "Design of cognitive fog computing for intrusion detection in Internet of Things," *Journal of Communi-cations and Networks*, vol. 20, no. 3, pp. 291–298, 2018.

38. F. Hosseinpour, P. Vahdani Amoli, J. Plosila, T. Hamalainen and H. Tenhunen, "An intrusion detection system for fog computing and IoT based logistic systems using a smart data approach," *International Journal of Digital Content Technology and its Applications*, vol. 10, no. 5, pp. 34–46, 2016.

39. A. Diro, N. Chilamkurti & Y. Nam, "Analysis of lightweight encryption scheme for fog-to-things communication," *IEEE Access*, vol. 6, pp. 26820–26830, 2018 (Q1 SCmigo ranking).

40. T. Nguyen, S. Marchal, M. Miettinen, H. Fereidooni, N. Asokan and A. Sadeghi, "DÏoT: A Federated Self-learning Anomaly Detection System for IoT," *2019 IEEE 39th International Conference on Distributed Computing Systems (ICDCS)*, 2019. doi:10.1109/icdcs.2019.00080.

41. D. Preuveneers, V. Rimmer, I. Tsingenopoulos, J. Spooren, W. Joosen and E. Ilie-Zudor, "Chained anomaly detection models for federated learning: An intrusion detection case study," *Applied Sciences*, vol. 8, no. 12, p. 2663, 2018. doi:10.3390/app8122663.

42. P. Ramanan, K. Nakayama and R. Sharma, "BAFFLE: Blockchain based aggregator free federated learning," arXiv: 1909.07452v1, 2019, [online] Available: http://arxiv.org/abs/1909.07452v1.

43. V. Kanth, "Blockchain for use in collaborative intrusion detection systems," Hdl.handle.net, 2020. [Online]. Available: http://hdl.handle.net/10945/63465.

44. M. Yousefi-Azar, K. Mohamed-Ali, and A. Walker. "Unsupervised learning for security of Enterprise networks by micro-segmentation," arXiv preprint arXiv:2003.11231, 2020.

45. T. Nguyen, P. Rieger, M. Miettinen, and A. Sadeghi. "Poisoning attacks on federated learning-based IoT intrusion detection system," 2020, [online] Available: https://www.ndsssymposium.org/wp-content/uploads/2020/04/diss2020-23003-paper.pdf.

46. W. Meng, E. Tischhauser, Q. Wang, Y. Wang and J. Han, "When intrusion detection meets blockchain technology: A review," *IEEE Access*, vol. 6, pp. 10179–10188, 2018. Available: 10.1109/access.2018.2799854.

# Chapter 3

# A Systemic IoT–Fog–Cloud Architecture for Big-Data Analytics and Cyber Security Systems

## A Review of Fog Computing

Nour Moustafa

University of New South Wales-Canberra @ ADFA University
of New South Australia

## CONTENTS

## 3.1 INTRODUCTION

The Internet of Things (IoT) has emerged to digitalize our daily tasks in various systems, for example, smart homes, smart cities, smart factories, smart grids and smart healthcare [1]. Since Cloud systems offer high computational infrastructure, power, bandwidth, software, platforms and storage, IoT applications integrate with Cloud systems across network systems [2, 3]. IoT networks include the communications of sensors, actuators and services, which require high computing resources for executing big-data analytics and cyber security applications. They still suffer from the drawbacks of scalability and operability, where heterogeneous data sources are collected and analyzed from the three layers of IoT, Fog and Cloud systems [1, 4, 5].

Cloud systems, in forms of software, platforms and infrastructure, would address the challenges of scalability and operability by providing services to users and organizations. However, Cloud systems suffer from lack of mobility support, latency, location-awareness and geo-distribution [1, 6]. The Fog/Edge paradigms have been proposed to tackle the demerits of Cloud systems and enable big-data analytics at the network's edge [4]. The term 'Fog computing' was coined by the OpenFog Consortium [1, 5], which is an architecture that extends the main functions of the Cloud to provide services at the edge of a network and is an extremely virtualized architecture of the resource pool. The Fog is a decentralized infrastructure, where data is logged and analyzed between the clients and Cloud data centers. It is well located to apply real-time and big-data analysis techniques, which considerably supports distributed data management systems [1, 3, 4, 6].

Current research studies [4–9] proposed that the Fog technology will be designed in the future to offer an enhanced and trustworthy architecture for handling the ever-increasing use of interconnected appliances and services. The authors in [1, 3, 4, 6, 10, 11] suggested different methods for deploying security solutions, involving encryption, access control, firewall, authentication and intrusion detection and prevention systems at the Fog layer. Since the Fog depends on distributed architectures, which connect IoT and Cloud systems, Advanced Persistent Threats (APT) [12] could exploit Fog appliances and services if security systems are not well designed to effectively monitor and protect the Fog nodes [1, 5].

Azam et al. [13] developed a technique for connecting a smart communication and pre-processing data module in Cloud-IoT networks. The technique integrated a smart gateway with a Fog computing technique to reduce the computation overhead at the Cloud side. Alrawais et al. [14] proposed a Fog computing scheme to handle the authentication issues in IoT networks. The Fog computing device acts as a gateway to IoT devices for allocating the certificate revocation. Almadhor [15] used a Fog computing paradigm to secure Cloud-IoT platforms. Yassen et al. [16] utilized some Fog computing capabilities to develop an intrusion detection system for recognizing cyber attacks in wireless sensor networks. Dsouza et al. [17] proposed policy-based management to protect collaboration and interoperability between various customer requirements in the Fog nodes. In [18], the authors proposed a physical security framework for integrating the functions of IoT, Fog and Cloud systems. Sandhu et al. [19] proposed a framework to identify malicious activities from network edges.

In this chapter, a systemic IoT–Fog–Cloud architecture is proposed for improving the execution of big-data analytics and cyber security applications. Security threats, challenges, existing security solutions and future research directions in the Fog paradigm are also discussed. The description of the Fog architecture is described in Section 3.2. Section 3.3 explains security challenges and threats in the Fog. Security challenges and future directions of research are introduced in Section 3.4. Finally, the chapter is summarized in Section 3.5.

## 3.2 FOG COMPUTING SYSTEMS

### 3.2.1 Description of Fog

The Fog paradigm was initially proposed by Cisco to become an extension architecture of Cloud systems that provide computation, storage and communication services between Cloud servers and client systems [1, 5, 10]. It enables computations and data processing at the network edge. This means that the Fog is a complementing layer of Cloud systems, which offers the design of a distributed architecture. The architecture can handle heterogeneous data sources of IoT wireless access networks. Big-data analytics can be implemented at the network edges faster than the centralized Cloud systems [1, 17].

The OpenFog Consortium started in 2016 for designing standardized open Fog computing frameworks [20]. For instance, an Open-Machine-to-Machine (OpenM2M) framework was suggested for linking the Fog and IoT devices and services [21]. In the framework, Fog nodes were deployed at edge infrastructures with several M2M applications. In [22], another Fog architecture was proposed, where a set of application interfaces were designed for enabling virtual machines (VMs) to gain access for gathering information at Fog nodes.

Sang et al. [23] proposed a Fog framework, which is a context-aware infrastructure. The framework supports different edge technologies, including Wi-Fi and Bluetooth capabilities, which support Software Defined Networks (SDN) and virtualization tools. It is also suggested to deploy Airborne Fog systems, where air devices like drones can perform as Fog nodes for facilitating various applications and services to end-users [6].

## 3.2.2 Characteristics of Fog

Fog computing is relatively similar to Mobile-Edge Computing (MEC) and Mobile Cloud Computing (MCC) [4, 24, 25]. The MEC concentrates on Fog servers such as cloudlets that are implemented at the edge of mobile networks [25], while the MCC is an infrastructure in which both data processing and storage are executed outside of the mobile appliances [24]. The Fog has several properties that allow its integration with IoT and Cloud systems [4, 24, 25] as listed below:

- It locates at the network's edge and handles location-awareness and low latency, as Fog nodes offer a localization (i.e., a single hop from the device to Fog node) and support end-points with rich services at the edge of a network.
- It enables dense and sparse geographical distribution, where the Fog services and application require distributed deployments.
- It can use large-scale sensor networks to monitor Cloud and IoT systems.
- It has a large number of nodes for demonstrating its capability of large-scale geographical distribution.
- It facilitates the mobility use which assists Fog's users to access information for improving the quality of services.
- It enables real-time interaction for handling important Fog applications.
- It supports the M2M wireless connectivity that consumes low power for supporting scalability and mobility.
- It handles different dynamic and heterogeneous sources at various levels of the network hierarchy.
- It provides flexible, inexpensive and portable deployment of hardware and software.
- It can easily integrate IoT and Cloud applications for online big-data analytics.

## 3.2.3 Systemic Architecture of IoT–Fog–Cloud

Fog computing is mainly a virtualization technology that offers storage, computing and communication services between end devices and Cloud data centers [6, 26]. In Figure 3.1, a systemic architecture is proposed to show the connections of IoT, Fog and Cloud layers. An example of integrating IoT smart cities and smart factories, along with the Fog and Cloud elements, is presented. A set of IoT devices and sensors, such as green gas IoT and industrial IoT (IIoT) actuators, is connected to Message Queuing Telemetry Transport (MQTT) gateways to publish and subscribe to various topics, such as measuring temperature and humidity. As, in the near future, smart cities could be linked with smart factories to measure green gas emissions via IoT hubs. Therefore, it is expected that message services between various topics will be available to serve the community.

This architecture allows monitoring, filtering, inspecting, aggregating and exchanging data, resulting in saving time and computation resources for deploying and running big-data analytics and cyber security applications [1]. Fog offers Software-as-a-Service (SaaS), Platform-as-a-Service (PaaS), Infrastructure-as-a-Service (IaaS) like Cloud systems, as defined in Table 3.1, to end-user appliances [3, 4]. In the Fog, network edge infrastructures, such as routers, access points, set-top boxes and switches, should have high capabilities of CPU and GPU processors and storage [1, 3, 6]. Such infrastructures can offer computing resources as services near to customers, named Fog nodes. Edge devices are considered as

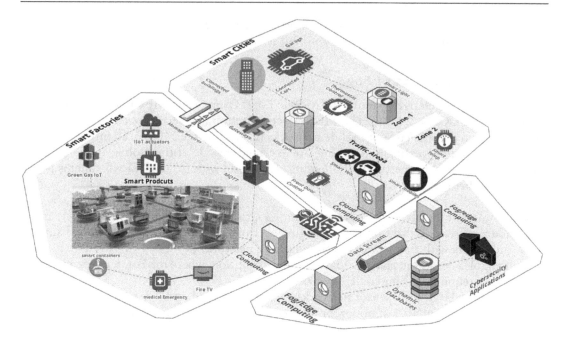

*Figure 3.1* Architecture of Fog computing and its interaction with Cloud and IoT.

*Table 3.1* Services Provided By Fog/Cloud Systems.

| Fog/Cloud services | Description |
| --- | --- |
| SaaS | Offers to a user or organization on-demand applications and software services via a Cloud infrastructure, excluding the cost of buying and maintaining these applications. Currently, Google, Amazon and Salesforce companies are the dominators of Cloud service |
| PaaS | Delivers to a user or organization an application development and host client applications using libraries, services and tools, which are supported by a PaaS provider's infrastructure |
| IaaS | Offers storage, processing units, network capabilities and other fundamental computing resources via virtual machines (VMs) to service subscribers |

Fog nodes, as they have computing, storage and network communications. The nodes are connected by a master–slave architecture, clustering or Peer-to-Peer networks [1, 4], such as the cloudlet [6].

An example of the technical Fog architecture was proposed by Cisco shown in Figure 3.2 [1] to design the Fog architecture as IaaS. The Cisco IOx platform operates by hosting programs in an operating system that runs a hypervisor on a grid router. The IOx APIs allow the Fog to connect with IoT and Cloud systems by a user-identified protocol. For designing the Fog as PaaS or SaaS, the Cisco DSX was designed to establish a bridge between SaaS and different IoT devices for managing applications. This enables processing big-data at the Fog and Cloud layers for improving the computational resources of big-data analytics and cyber security applications such as firewalls, intrusion detection and prevention systems and access control systems [1, 6].

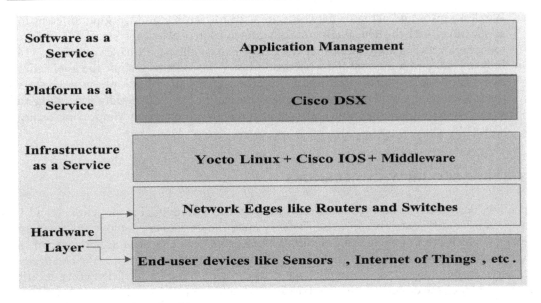

*Figure 3.2* Cisco's Fog technical architecture.

Although the distributed architecture of the Fog can improve the computational resources of big-data analytics and cyber security applications, the architecture could be breached by sophisticated cyber attacks, such as Distributed Denial of Service (DDoS) and ransomware, because the Fog nodes could be connected with unsecured and non-standard IoT sensors-based IP addresses. Therefore, different security systems should be deployed at the Fog nodes to mitigate the risk impacts of cyber threats.

### 3.2.4 Applications of IoT, Fog and Cloud Systems

The advantages of the Fog can be applied to different IoT and Cloud systems [4, 25]. This demonstrates how the Fog paradigms can be implemented in real-time and large-scale systems, as explained in the following applications:

- **Smart grid** includes smart meters and micro-grids implemented at the edge of a network as energy load balancing services. The Fog can support processing smart grid nodes at the network edges. Data generated from IoT networks are stored at Fog nodes for running big-data analytics and cyber security applications [27].
- **Software-Defined Networks (SDN)** is promising computing and network architecture. The Fog can be used for designing an SDN architecture to manage and control the SDN communication layers. The control unit is executed at a centralized server, where the nodes of SDN can execute a communication path specified by a server that requires distributed executions [25].
- **Linked vehicles and smart traffic systems** are improved by the connection with the Fog nodes, such as a vehicle to access points or vice versa. The smart traffic systems interact with different sensors at the network edge to send warning lights to the coming cars for avoiding possible accidents. Connecting these smart grids with the Fog could address the drawbacks of low latency, low mobility support and geographical distributions [4, 13].

- **Wireless sensor and actuator networks** are used for sensing and tracking different IoT applications, with the dependency on actuators to control physical systems. When actuators operate as Fog appliances, they can easily manage the performance of systems [16].
- **Industry 4.0 and Industrial IoT systems:** Industry 4.0 systems include the applications of cyber-physical systems, IIoT and IoT. These systems aim to link physical devices to the Internet and Cloud systems. These systems can be used for rapidly processing and storing different heterogeneous sources at the network edges and improving security issues [28, 29].

## 3.3 CYBER SECURITY CHALLENGES

Since Fog devices are connected with the Cloud and IoT systems, IoT networks could be exploited using different cyber threats. This is because the devices are deployed at unsecured locations which are not accurately monitored and protected. The open architecture of the Fog leads to loopholes and vulnerabilities that allow attackers to compromise the Fog devices and services, in addition to threatening the privacy of its big-data [30]. Different security issues could face the design of effective Fog–IoT–Cloud architecture as discussed below.

- **Authentication and authorization** – Fog devices could be connected with the Cloud servers via a distributing authentication system, but this connection is relatively slow in smart grids [27]. The execution of authentication protocols, for example, directory access and remote authentication, are improper due to the limitation of connections. Moreover, using Cloud servers for authentication is not the right solution as they would be penetrated by brute-force and dictionary attacks for stealing user credentials [4].
- **Advanced Persistent Threats** – Fog systems face various sophisticated attack types, such as botnets and ransomware, inherited from Cloud and IoT systems. These cyber attacks would expose Fog nodes, due to its distributed architecture [1, 4, 5, 13], as summarized in Table 3.2.

*Table 3.2* Attack Types That Could Exploit Elements Of IoT–Fog–Cloud.

| Attack types | Description |
|---|---|
| Insider intruders | Refer to authorized Cloud users who attempt to gain unauthorized rights, penetrating Cloud resources with no privileges |
| Attacks on virtual machines (VMs) or hypervisor | When the virtual layer of hypervisor is compromised using zero-day attacks, attackers can control the installed VMs and physical hosts |
| Flooding attacks | An attacker attempts to flood a victim by sending a lot of packets via DoS and DDoS from a computer host in a network (i.e., zombie) to breach VMs |
| Service abuses | Can be hijacked by malicious activities, for example, using Cloud/Fog computing resources to violate an encryption key to launch an attack |
| Advanced Persistent Threats (APT) | Penetrate systems to launch a footprint attack, then stealthily infiltrate data and intellectual property continually |
| Port scanning | Finds a list of all open ports, closed ports and filtered ports in a network. Attackers searching for finding open ports to get access to a particular system |
| Backdoor attacks | Are passive attacks in which a hacker bypasses a stealthy normal authentication mechanism to protect unauthorized remote access to a device. An attacker could control a victim's resources and make it as a zombie to initiate DoS/DDoS attacks |

- **Suspicious Fog nodes** – Since Fog nodes handle big-data collected from IoT devices, dividing workloads between the nodes is often heavy. In this sense, if an attacker compromises any of the nodes, it is hard to assert data integrity and privacy. Trust mechanisms should be deployed to ensure data transfer between Fog and Cloud systems [31].
- **Fog data management** – Since Fog nodes are geographically distributed, it is difficult to know the location of data gathered from Cloud systems. It is hard for customers to identify either the node offers the same service or not [32]. Some Fog nodes often contain duplicated data with other nodes that consume resources, and attack events may be injected into this data using data poisoning techniques.
- **Privacy issues** – Deal with concealing confidential information, such as what device was used in a particular time while enabling data summarizations to be exchanged between Fog nodes. Privacy preservation techniques should hide details of sensitive information about Fog devices and services, for example, what devices are used at a certain time. Existing Fog appliances cannot encrypt and decrypt the readings of smart meters. Therefore, those appliances could expose sensitive information while transmitting and receiving data flows across network nodes [4, 33].

## 3.4 SECURITY SOLUTIONS AND FUTURE DIRECTIONS

Various security solutions have been employed, for example, authentication, access control, encryption, firewall, as well as intrusion detection and prevention systems, for addressing different security and privacy challenges at the IoT–Fog–Cloud architecture. Each security tool can be utilized for handling a specific security challenge described in Table 3.3 and explained below:

*Table 3.3* Threats, Advantages and Disadvantages of Existing Security Solutions.

| Solutions | Threats | Advantages | Disadvantages |
|---|---|---|---|
| Authentication techniques [34] | Insider attacks, including brute force and dictionary attacks | - Are easy to use and reduce operational costs <br> - Enhance customer experience | - Cannot be reset once exploited <br> - Demand integration with different Fog devices |
| Access control systems [31] | Birthday, sniffer, spoofing and phishing attacks | - Are capable of achieving accessibility and optimal control using several options like biometrics and federated identify keys <br> - Are easy to integrate with other security controls and manage their database | - Are expensive to install, as they include an upfront financial investment <br> - Demand regular updates to reduce the chances of hacking |
| Intrusion detection systems [35, 36] | Insider attacks, flooding, VM attacks, APT, U2R attacks, backdoor and port scanning attacks | - Can be adapted to a particular <br> - content in a network for boosting the efficiency <br> - Make it easier to continue with regulation | - Do not process encrypted packets and handle header packets only <br> Produce high false alarm rates |
| Privacy and encryption techniques [31] | Flooding attacks and service abuses | - Improve security, as private keys do not transmit over networks - can offer a mechanism for digital signatures | - When attackers collect enough information, they can violate keys - the key methods have to be regularly updated |

- **Authentication technique** is the process of identifying users with different methods. Fog computing should include biometric authentication that involves face, fingerprint, balm, touch-based or keystroke-based methods. They are promising solutions compared with traditional methods, such as password-based authentication [34]. In [4], the authors stated that one of the key security challenges for Fog computing is authentication mechanisms at various levels of Fog nodes using public-key techniques. In [31, 37], the trusted execution mechanism should have its potential in Fog computing to decrease the complexity of authentication.

- **Access control** is a trustworthy mechanism installed at IoT and Cloud devices that guarantee authentication and authorization to end-users and workstations, along with servers [31]. In Fog, a policy-based control was proposed to protect the cooperation between heterogeneous sources [38]. There is still a challenge of how to design an effective access control system for clients in IoT networks to protect systems at different levels.

- **An intrusion detection system (IDS)** can be installed in the Fog layer to recognize suspicious events by inspecting audit traces of the client-side. It can also be installed at the Fog side to identify suspicious attacks by analyzing network traffic [35, 36]. In [39], the authors suggested a cloudlet mesh based on a security framework that can identify attacks from Cloud and Fog systems. There are still the challenges of implementing scalable and adaptive intrusion detection at the Fog layer to achieve the low latency requirements [31].

- **Privacy and encryption techniques** – Various privacy-preserving mechanisms have been suggested in the Cloud, smart grids and wireless networks for protecting user information which is one of the biggest issues in IoT, Fog and Cloud systems . These mechanisms could be implemented between the Cloud and Fog layers to prohibit tampering big-data transmitted between the two layers. Encryption techniques should be applied to obfuscate data exchange between different network nodes [31]. However, because of the distributions of network nodes, privacy techniques need further research for protecting the sensitive information of users.

## 3.5 CONCLUSION

This chapter has introduced an architecture to illustrate the interactions of IoT, Cloud and Fog layers for effectively running big-data analytics and cyber security applications. Since the devices and services in the three layers generate heterogeneous data sources, the Cloud systems have been used to process, compute and store such data at centralized locations. However, the mobility support, location-awareness, low latency and geographical location are still the key challenges in the Cloud layer that could be tackled using the Fog paradigms by processing computational tasks at the edge of the network. The use of Fog technology still faces security and privacy challenges that originate from the connection with the open architecture of IoT and Cloud systems. The security problems in existing security tools and future research directions are introduced to improve the security of the IoT–Fog–Cloud architecture.

## REFERENCES

1. S. Khan, S. Parkinson, and Y. Qin, "Fog computing security: a review of current applications and security solutions," *Journal of Cloud Computing*, vol. 6, no. 1, p. 19, 2017.

2. N. Moustafa, K.-K. R. Choo, I. Radwan, and S. Camtepe, "Outlier dirichlet mixture mechanism: Adversarial statistical learning for anomaly detection in the fog," *IEEE Transactions on Information Forensics and Security*, 2019.

3. A. V. Dastjerdi, H. Gupta, R. N. Calheiros, S. K. Ghosh, and R. Buyya, "Fog computing: Principles, architectures, and applications," *arXiv preprint arXiv:1601.02752*, 2016.

4. I. Stojmenovic and S. Wen, "The fog computing paradigm: Scenarios and security issues," in *Computer Science and Information Systems (FedCSIS), 2014 Federated Conference on*. IEEE, 2014, pp. 1–8.

5. G. Kurikala, K. G. Gupta, and A. Swapna, "Fog computing: Implementation of security and privacy to comprehensive approach for avoiding knowledge thieving attack exploitation decoy technology," 2017.

6. S. Yi, C. Li, and Q. Li, "A survey of fog computing: concepts, applications and issues," in *Proceedings of the 2015 Workshop on Mobile Big Data*. ACM, 2015, pp. 37–42.

7. M. Chiang, S. Ha, I. Chih-Lin, F. Risso, and T. Zhang, "Clarifying fog computing and networking: 10 questions and answers," *IEEE Communications Magazine*, vol. 55, no. 4, pp. 18–20, 2017.

8. Y. Guan, J. Shao, G. Wei, and M. Xie, "Data security and privacy in fog computing," *IEEE Network*, 2018.

9. G. Premsankar, M. Di Francesco, and T. Taleb, "Edge computing for the internet of things: A case study," *IEEE Internet of Things Journal*, 2018.

10. R. Roman, J. Lopez, and M. Mambo, "Mobile edge computing, fog et al.: A survey and analysis of security threats and challenges," *Future Generation Computer Systems*, vol. 78, pp. 680–698, 2016.

11. K.-K. R. Choo, R. Lu, L. Chen, and X. Yi, "A foggy research future: Advances and future opportunities in fog computing research," *Future Generation Computer Systems*, vol. 78, pp. 677–6792018.

12. N. Moustafa, G. Misra, and J. Slay, "Generalized outlier gaussian mixture technique based on automated association features for simulating and detecting web application attacks," *IEEE Transactions on Sustainable Computing*, 2018.

13. M. Aazam and E.-N. Huh, "Fog computing and smart gateway based communication for cloud of things," in *Future Internet of Things and Cloud (FiCloud), 2014 International Conference on*. IEEE, 2014, pp. 464–470.

14. A. Alrawais, A. Alhothaily, C. Hu, and X. Cheng, "Fog computing for the internet of things: Security and privacy issues," *IEEE Internet Computing*, vol. 21, no. 2, pp. 34–42, 2017.

15. F. Y. Okay and S. Ozdemir, "A fog computing based smart grid model," in *Networks, Computers and Communications (ISNCC), 2016 International Symposium on*. IEEE, 2016, pp. 1–6.

16. Q. Yaseen, F. AlBalas, Y. Jararweh, and M. Al-Ayyoub, "A fog computing based system for selective forwarding detection in mobile wireless sensor networks," in *Foundations and Applications of Self\* Systems, IEEE International Workshops on*. IEEE, 2016, pp. 256–262.

17. N. I. M. Enzai and M. Tang, "A taxonomy of computation offloading in mobile cloud computing," in *Mobile Cloud Computing, Services, and Engineering (MobileCloud), 2014 2nd IEEE International Conference on*. IEEE, 2014, pp. 19–28.

18. V. K. Sehgal, A. Patrick, A. Soni, and L. Rajput, "Smart human security framework using internet of things, cloud and fog computing," in *Intelligent distributed computing*. Springer, 2015, pp. 251–263.

19. R. Sandhu, A. S. Sohal, and S. K. Sood, "Identification of malicious edge devices in fog computing environments," *Information Security Journal: A Global Perspective*, pp. 1–16, 2017.

20. "Open fog consortium," Aug. 2018. [Online]. Available: http://www.openfogconsortium.org/,

21. S. K. Datta, C. Bonnet, and J. Haerri, "Fog computing architecture to enable consumer centric internet of things services," in *Consumer Electronics (ISCE), 2015 IEEE International Symposium on*. IEEE, 2015, pp. 1–2.

22. M. Zhanikeev, "A cloud 19 platform to facilitate cloud federation and fog computing," *Computer*, vol. 48, no. 5, pp. 80–83, 2015.

23. W. S. Chin, H.-s. Kim, Y. J. Heo, and J. W. Jang, "A context-based future network infrastructure for IoT services," *Procedia Computer Science*, vol. 56, pp. 266–270, 2015.

24. H. T. Dinh, C. Lee, D. Niyato, and P. Wang, "A survey of mobile cloud computing: architecture, applications, and approaches," *Wireless communications and mobile computing*, vol. 13, no. 18, pp. 1587–1611, 2013.

25. "Etsi: Mobile-edge computing," 2014. [Online]. Available: http://goo.gl/7NwTLE

26. M. Mukherjee, R. Matam, L. Shu, L. Maglaras, M. A. Ferrag, N. Choudhury, and V. Kumar, "Security and privacy in fog computing: Challenges," *IEEE Access*, vol. 5, pp. 19293–19304, 2017.

27. "Nist. guidelines for smart grid cyber security (nist 7628)," Aug. 2018. [Online]. Available: Http://csrc.nist.gov/publications/PubsNISTIRs.html

28. G. Peralta, M. Iglesias-Urkia, M. Barcelo, R. Gomez, A. Moran, and J. Bilbao, "Fog computing based efficient IoT scheme for the industry 4.0," in *Electronics, Control, Measurement, Signals and their Application to Mechatronics (ECMSM), 2017 IEEE International Workshop of*. IEEE, 2017, pp. 1–6.

29. N. Moustafa, E. Adi, B. Turnbull, and J. Hu, "A new threat intelligence scheme for safeguarding industry 4.0 systems," *IEEE Access*, vol. 6, pp. 32910–32924, 2018.

30. H. Dubey, J. Yang, N. Constant, A. M. Amiri, Q. Yang, and K. Makodiya, "Fog data: Enhancing telehealth big data through fog computing," in *Proceedings of the ASE BigData & SocialInformatics 2015*. ACM, 2015, p. 14.

31. K. Lee, D. Kim, D. Ha, U. Rajput, and H. Oh, "On security and privacy issues of fog computing supported internet of things environment," in *Network of the Future (NOF), 2015 6th International Conference on the*. IEEE, 2015, pp. 1–3.

32. A. Sinaeepourfard, J. Garcia, X. Masip-Bruin, and E. Marin-Tordera, "A novel architecture for efficient fog to cloud data management in smart cities," in *Distributed Computing Systems (ICDCS), 2017 IEEE 37th International Conference on*. IEEE, 2017, pp. 2622–2623.

33. M. Keshk, E. Sitnikova, N. Moustafa, J. Hu, and I. Khalil, "An integrated framework for privacy-preserving based anomaly detection for cyberphysical systems," *IEEE Transactions on Sustainable Computing*, 2019.

34. F. Bonomi, R. Milito, J. Zhu, and S. Addepalli, "Fog computing and its role in the internet of things," in *Proceedings of the first edition of the MCC workshop on Mobile cloud computing*. ACM, 2012, pp. 13–16.

35. N. Moustafa, J. Slay, and G. Creech, "Novel geometric area analysis technique for anomaly detection using trapezoidal area estimation on large-scale networks," *IEEE Transactions on Big Data*, 2017.

36. N. Moustafa, G. Creech, and J. Slay, "Big data analytics for intrusion detection system: Statistical decision-making using finite dirichlet mixture models," in *Data Analytics and Decision Support for Cybersecurity*. Springer, 2017, pp. 127–156.

37. C. Chen, H. Raj, S. Saroiu, and A. Wolman, "cTPM: A cloud TPM for cross-device trusted applications," *NSDI*, 2014, pp. 187–201.

38. C. Dsouza, G.-J. Ahn, and M. Taguinod, "Policy-driven security management for fog computing: Preliminary framework and a case study," in *Information Reuse and Integration (IRI), 2014 IEEE 15th International Conference on*. IEEE, 2014, pp. 16–23.

39. C. Modi, D. Patel, B. Borisaniya, H. Patel, A. Patel, and M. Rajarajan, "A survey of intrusion detection techniques in cloud," *Journal of Network and Computer Applications*, vol. 36, no. 1, pp. 42–57, 2013.

Chapter 4

# Security and Organizational Strategy
## A Cloud and Edge Computing Perspective

*Monjur Ahmed*
Waikato Institute of Technology (Wintec), New Zealand

*Krassie Petrova*
Auckland University of Technology (AUT), New Zealand

**CONTENTS**

## 4.1 INTRODUCTION

The computing paradigms are changing more rapidly than ever, with the number of new computing approaches that have been implemented in recent years. One such computing approach is cloud computing (CC). CC offers remote computing resources that are normally not owned or managed by cloud users. CC variants such as edge computing and fog computing exhibit the same fundamental characteristics as CC with no major conceptual change. Given that the term cloud-based computing (CbC) refers to any computing architecture that uses CC to a larger or a lesser degree, a variant of CC is essentially a CbC platform.

Although the concept of CC is not a new one, the rising popularity of CC is a current phenomenon. CC is changing the aspects of how and where computing is carried out (Arora & Parashar, 2013). The CC paradigm is a revolutionary one; however, it comes with its own security challenges and concerns (Dillon, Wu, & Chang, 2010).

While the exponentially rising popularity of CC/CbC ascertains the advantages of its characteristics for cloud users, the other side of the coin exists too. CC is laden with an incredibly high level of issues and its complexity is high in terms of security and privacy (Khan & Alam, 2017; Rad, Diaby & Rana, 2017; Singh & Chatterjee, 2017; Narang & Gupta, 2018; Yami & Schaefer, 2019). For organizations, the privacy- and security-related concerns to CC/CbC can be addressed at the strategic planning and policy levels. A proper strategy and policy development approach toward information security that is aimed at preventing CC/CbC security loopholes is an unavoidable must for organizations which want to embrace CC/CbC.

We are probably past the point of deciding whether an organization should adopt CC/CbC. To be on the competitive edge and just to survive, businesses nowadays are required to espouse CC/CbC. The question is probably more about how to safely survive on the CC/CbC plane than whether to adopt or adapt to CC/CbC. Being on the CC/CbC plane may emerge as either a rewarding or a threatening move, depending on how well an organization is prepared for CC or for a CC variant. This chapter presents the aspects and factors that an organization should consider as part of its strategy and policy development process, in order to adapt itself to CC/CbC. The chapter focuses on the protection of the privacy and security of the organization's digital assets. It explores organizational, human and technological factors associated with information security, privacy and compliance from a CC/CbC perspective.

The chapter is organized as follows: The Section 4.2 provides an overview of CC/CbC. The three subsequent sections discuss various organizational factors that have strategic importance from a cybersecurity perspective. Section 4.3 focuses on how CC/CbC may impact business operation and management while Section 4.4 discusses human and technological factors within the security context of CC/CbC and from a strategy standpoint. Trust (or lack of trust thereof) is considerably an influential factor in CC/CbC security; it is addressed in Section 4.5. Finally, Section 4.6 highlights the role of geographic location as a key factor in organizational strategy development in the case of an organization adopting CC/CbC.

## 4.2 CLOUD COMPUTING AND CLOUD-BASED COMPUTING

There are a number of CC definitions, see for example the ones found in Hurwitz and Kirsch (2020), Almasi and Pratx (2019), Basto, Villalobos, Cruz, Hernández, and Lezama (2019), Kumar, Laghari, Karim, Shakir, and Brohi (2019). These CC definitions refer to a computing architecture where computing resources (i.e., the cloud infrastructure) are situated at a remote location, normally under a third party's ownership and management and offered as a service to other third parties (customers) who use them for their own needs. A third-party entity that offers cloud services is known as a cloud service provider (CSP). Customers must transfer to the cloud infrastructure the data that are to be processed by the remote computing service. Depending on the specific requirement, customers' digital assets may be either transferred to the cloud infrastructure and returned to the customer once the requested computing operation is carried out, or (as an additional service) customers' digital assets may reside in cloud servers (cloud storage). Customers access the cloud resources through communication networks (via the Internet, to be precise). Furthermore, a CSP's infrastructure may not necessarily reside at a single location. A CSP's own distributed multi-location infrastructure may span different regions/countries/continents. Thus, the CSP's customers may not necessarily know the geographical location of the cloud infrastructure where their digital assets are being processed or stored.

The physical distance between a customer's premises and the cloud infrastructure is an influential performance factor. Adding an intermediary cloud infrastructure is a way to solve (at least partially) the issue of potential performance loss. This is the motivation behind the introduction of CC variants such as edge computing and fog computing which aim to improve performance by locating the infrastructure physically closer to the customer. Edge computing and fog computing are very similar to CC but have some added advantages (and disadvantages) when compared to CC. Edge computing and fog computing are explained in more detail in De Donno, Tange and Dragoni (2019), Shih (2018), Gusev and Dustdar (2018), Wang et al., (2017), Varghese, Wang, Barbhuiya, Kilpatrick, and Nikolopoulos (2016), Shi et al. (2016), and in Prasad, Bhavsar, and Tanwar (2019).

Figure 4.1 illustrates the concepts of CC, edge computing and fog computing. Since the focus of this chapter is on the privacy and security aspects of CC/CbC, the location of cloud infrastructure in these computing approaches is of importance. As shown, fog computing represents an intermediate layer in the infrastructure of a global CSP. Compared to the location of the main CC infrastructure, fog computing may be closer to the customer's premises. As a result, the response time and the overall performance of fog computing may be better compared to CC. However, using fog infrastructure may present additional security challenges (Khan, Parkinson, & Qin, 2017).

Edge computing moves the infrastructure even closer to the customer's geographical location and may be even situated at the customer's premises. Still, edge infrastructure is part of the overall cloud infrastructure. Like fog computing, edge computing is also an intermediary layer or an extension of CC. Edge computing cannot be thought of as an independent architectural entity; rather it complements the associated cloud architecture. However, if there is no associated CC infrastructure, there will be no edge infrastructure either. Both fog computing and edge computing are types of CbC which may be considered as a means of extending the services of the main CSP.

The privacy and security concerns related to CC/CbC are fully applicable to edge computing. For example, the edge infrastructure may be provisioned by a sub-CSP. A sub-CSP can be thought of as a CSP that provides infrastructure to other CSPs. Thus, a sub-CSP can be

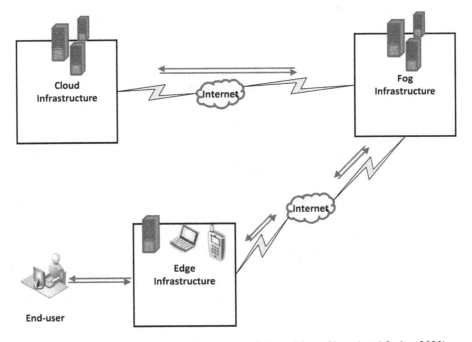

*Figure 4.1*  Cloud, Edge and Fog Computing Infrastructure (adapted from Ahmed and Sarkar, 2020).

viewed as a sub-contractor of the main CSP; the sub-CSP may also manage and maintain the provided infrastructure on behalf of the main CSP. Consider an edge infrastructure that is rented by a CSP and provided to this CSP's customers (i.e., a customer may use, for their remote data storage and computational needs, infrastructure provided by a CSP other than their 'main' CSP). In this scenario, multiple CSPs are providing infrastructure to the customer who may be under contractual obligations with only one CSP (the main CSP). While edge computing provides an intermediary cloud to the customers with the purpose to improve response time and performance (compared to the response time and performance of the cloud of the main CSP), it also adds complexity to the overall service due to the added edge infrastructure and its maintenance and management.

The distributed nature of the CC/CbC infrastructure across multiple locations results in moving (temporarily or permanently) a customer's digital assets to a location outside the customer's premises. From a privacy and security point of view this is critical factor, with a significant impact on digital asset protection. In the following sections, we focus on the implications of the above for the organization in terms of business processes, human and technological aspects, and addressing CC/CbC associated privacy and security concerns.

## 4.3 BUSINESS OPERATIONS AND MANAGEMENT

The implications of adapting the organization's business processes to the use of CC/CbC must be considered at an early stage. CC/CbC introduces a computing platform that connects the organization to the world outside. Since using the cloud refers to using remote resources, computers inside the organization would require a connection to the outside world in order to use CC/CbC. Therefore, CC/CbC may change the way an organization operates. Strategic planning and policy development are required in order to deal with the changes that would be introduced as a result of the move to CC/CbC. Business processes, business continuity, risk management, disaster recovery is just a few of the items in the list of processes that may be influenced by CC/CbC (not always positively). Consequently, there may be positive or adverse implications for these business areas depending on how CC/CbC adoption affects (directly or indirectly) the privacy and security of the digital assets of the organization.

The implications of using CC/CbC in the organization would depend on the type of the organization and on its current business processes, including the organization's strategic decision-making process. The latter is organization-specific and may differ from one organization to another. It is not feasible to create an exhaustive list of business scenarios where adopting a CC/CbC platform may cause changes or may have otter implications. However, there is a commonality between them: in any given case of an organization using CC/CbC, at least some of the organization's digital assets are either moved to a CSP's premises or are transitioned back and forth between the company's and the CSP's premises.

This use of CC/CbC by organizations as a computing approach raises concerns about how the security and the privacy of the digital assets are protected. Figure 4.2 shows a broad view of the organizational dimensions and the associated processes and factors that need to be considered from a security and privacy point of view.

The introduction of CC/CbC affects or influences the organization's business operations and the management of its day-to-day activities. As CC/CbC brings changes to the digital culture of an organization, this may have implications for the people working there. Furthermore, the introduction of new technologies may result in changing perceptions of and attitudes about the use of the CC/CbC computing and storage resources. Since multiple entities may be involved in CC/CbC service provision and use, developing trust relationships among the

*Figure 4.2* Organizational dimensions, processes and factors affected by CC/CbC adoption.

parties is critical to the successful implementation of the CC/CbC platform. Another important aspect to consider is the impact of the geographically dispersed architectures that a particular CC/CbC scenario may be comprised of. In the following sections, we discuss in more detail the aspects of business operations and management presented in Figure 4.2.

### 4.3.1 Business Process

The introduction of CC/CbC creates a new working environment where the organization becomes strongly reliant on digital technologies and on networked digital communication facilitated by the Internet. The development, distribution and implementation of enterprise systems are also influenced (Nieuwenhuis, Ehrenhard, & Prause, 2018). Though it is a common belief that moving to CC/CbC reduces information technology (IT) infrastructural costs, the resulting return-on-investment (ROI) may not be as beneficial as expected as the on-going costs related to CC/CbC usage may be significant. In addition, relying on external infrastructure for all (or most) of the organization's business operations leads to increased investment in security enhancing controls.

To adapt to CC/CbC, the organization may need to introduce new workflow or new business processes where knowledge of IT operations and general IT skills will be required at all workforce levels, and not just from IT personnel. This will require employee training. Besides, new types of employees may be required for the changing environment. While new roles may be created due to changed digital infrastructure, existing employees may face redundancy. For example, the local IT infrastructure may practically dissolve thus requiring less staff in the IT department. But at the same time, a new frontier opens that requires safeguarding: the interface with the cloud infrastructure and the seamless transfer of digital assets between the organization's premises and the cloud requires an ongoing 'gatekeeping' effort. Even assuming that the organization's CSP is trustworthy, using public network and communications infrastructures for the transfer of digital assets is still a challenge as the public network channel is highly prone to cyber-attacks.

As part of the adaptation to CC/CbC, the organization requires proper strategic planning about how to address the retrospective changes required for such adaption. Employee training, creation of new roles and hiring new personnel needs to be carried out competently and needs to consider carefully the security challenges associated with CC/CbC in order to avoid creating security loopholes. For example, inadequate training of the existing workforce may leave the organization vulnerable to social engineering that adversaries may use to compromise the systems residing on a CC/CbC plane. The recruitment process, if incompetent, may open loopholes for corporate sabotage: the organization's rival corporations may try to use the CC/CbC recruitment requirements to 'push in' people who will eventually serve as malicious insiders. This means that regardless of moving to the CC/CbC plane, the organization may be at risk of being affected by an individual malicious insider or malicious insiders planted as part of corporate sabotage. Therefore, the integrity of human resource related processes plays a crucial role in ensuring the strategic soundness of the privacy and security policies in the organization.

### 4.3.2 Business Continuity

Cloud-based services make the customer dependent on the CSP (Velzen, Jong & Jansen, 2019). Apart from moving digital assets to the cloud, CC/CbC implies a reliance on the CSP with respect to data privacy and security, as well as the continuity and the operational efficiency of day-to-day business activities. For example, Bo (2018) agrees that CC/CbC has implications for business continuity and that a remedial approach such as a hybrid cloud may be appropriate. However, our concern is not so much about the smoothness of business operations rather we focus on the disclosure of the organizations' data to third parties as a necessary requirement for processing the data in the cloud. As already discussed, an organization's CSP may use other cloud services in order to provision its own service. The emerging 'vendor of vendors' scenario is not uncommon in a CC/CbC context. Similarly, for reasons of their own, the CSP's CSP may in turn rely on their own third parties. This creates a chain (or multiple chains) of parties to whom the organization's data may be disclosed. In other words, in addition to becoming reliant on the CC/CbC platform for its business continuity, the organization must allow the distribution of its digital assets to a complex web of third parties. There may be any number of loopholes in the distributed environment through which security breaches may occur. Most importantly, a breach may go unnoticed forever.

Therefore, the decision about moving to CC/CbC requires of the organization to fully comprehend the implications of the move with respect to business continuity. It is crucial for organizations to have a clear understanding of their particular CC/CbC environment and a clear picture about how their digital assets may be handled and distributed for processing on cloud platforms. It may be disastrous for an organization not to carry out an in-depth feasibility study into the issues highlighted above.

### 4.3.3 Risk Management and Disaster Recovery

In CC/CbC, the remote infrastructure is managed and owned by CSPs; the customer may know little about how things are managed in the cloud infrastructure. Normally, a CSP serves multiple customers. Even though customer organizations use virtual infrastructure provided by the CSP as 'Infrastructure-as-a-Service (IaaS)', customer organizations must not have any access rights to the CSPs infrastructure level as not to pose additional risks to customer data security and privacy. In other words, individual CSP customers have no access privileges and no means of managing the CSP infrastructure that underlies the virtual infrastructure (IaaS) they use. Therefore, in the case of a disaster the customer must rely on the CSP and may not be able to take any other action except seeking CSP's help.

A simple example to illustrate the issue is to compare a server hosted on a physical computer and a virtual server in the cloud. Even in extreme cases such as the customer losing access to the physical server because of the server being compromised, the customer at least has the power to physically disconnect the physical server's power cord from the mains. If the same happens on the cloud platform, the only option for the customer organization is to alert the CSP and then (helplessly) wait. This metaphorical example shows that compared to having on-premise infrastructure, cloud customers have far less control and options when disaster strikes on their cyber plane.

In a CC/CbC context, the organization's disaster recovery plan also becomes largely CSP-oriented. Security program and policy around risk management may require significant changes once an organization moves to CC/CbC. Depending on the type of business, the reliance on CSP may be either a blessing or a curse. Most importantly, a feasibility study of the security and risk program must be undertaken, before moving to CC/CbC. It is required to ascertain, for each safety-critical operational scenario, what it would mean to expose itself to the outside world and to hand digital assets over to third parties. In cases such as a healthcare organization which involves operations and computerized equipment critical to patient safety, bypassing the feasibility study is simply not an option.

In addition to the privacy concerns already discussed, moving to CC/CbC may be disastrous for a safety-critical business. A cybersecurity breach may not just be limited to the privacy and security of digital assets, it may very well extend to extreme levels such as threats to the organization's physical structures or to the environment. In our opinion, moving to CC/CbC in safety-critical contexts is a high-risk factor and should be avoided; the organization must not lose sight of the potential for significant and irretrievable loss due to the inherent CC/CbC risks while considering the apparent advantages of the cloud platforms.

Since risk management deals with identifying and managing risks (Hopkin, 2018), all factors in Figure 4.2 should be considered when investigating the implications of moving to the cloud. For gaining competitive advantage, the organization may be forced to adopt CC/CbC; however, clear strategies are required to deal with the CC/CbC-related risk factors. Disaster recovery for a CC/CbC-reliant organization has the potential to bring further disaster instead of recovering from the current one. And, if we consider unauthorized disclosure of digital information as a disaster, it is irrecoverable: no disaster recovery plan may help the organization recover from it or obtain compensation for the loss. In fact, CC/CbC adds fuel to the fire as the probability of unauthorized disclosure of digital assets significantly increases with the use of CC/CbC services.

Developing cybersecurity program and policies by using/tailoring existing industry standards, approaches or frameworks may be beneficial to the organization that wishes to embrace CC/CbC. Two examples of frameworks/approaches that can be used to manage security are the National Institute of Standards and Technology (NIST) framework (Santos, 2019) and MITRE ATT&CK (Strom, Applebaum, Miller, Nickels, Pennington, & Thomas, 2018).

## 4.4 HUMAN AND TECHNOLOGICAL FACTORS

In this section, we focus on human and technological factors, and the complexities of copyright in a CC/CbC use context. The human participant is often termed 'the weakest link' in security defense systems as human-related factors are a challenge to security (Ani, He, and

Tiwari, 2019; Ghafir et al., 2018; Platsis, 2019), with threat vectors emerging from people in a number of different ways. Likewise, the technologies used in a computing architecture may also contain security loopholes. Finally, the use of technologies in CC/CbC and the Service level Agreement (SLA) (or lack of SLA thereof) may affect copyright associated with digital assets.

### 4.4.1 Human Factors

Human factors always play a role in cybersecurity breaches, and CC/CbC is no exception. For example, in edge computing, the infrastructure moves closer to the customer and may even be located within the customer's premises. If the edge infrastructure resides in the customer's premises and the ownership and management of the edge infrastructure is in the customer's hands, the customer's organizational strategies related to digital assets need to take into account factors such as staff competency levels, the possibility of having malicious insiders and the potential for social engineering.

In the case of edge computing specifically, information ownership may be also transferred back to the customer organization. This may lead to improved privacy and security protection of some of the organization's data. At the same time, the resultant use case scenario may have an overall adverse effect on the privacy and security of the organization's digital assets due to the impact of the human factors discussed above. It must be noted that in a CC/CbC context including edge computing operating in a trust-based model, security compromises are very likely to occur (Sha, Yang, Wei, & Davani, 2020).

### 4.4.2 Technological Factors

Edge infrastructure is closely tied with its 'mother' CC architecture. Infrastructure interoperability is supported by the software (including operating system platforms) and the hardware installed in both infrastructures. Any security loophole across the gamut of technologies used by edge infrastructure may pose a security threat. Furthermore, technology-related loopholes in the interconnected CC/CbC infrastructures may have a flow on effect. In other words, an edge infrastructure may be affected or compromised through the insecure technology provision of its associated CC infrastructure and vice versa. If an edge infrastructure interacts with multiple clouds, then the security concerns multiply accordingly.

In addition, edge infrastructure is relatively less powerful compared to its CC counterpart. Being part of the cloud where computing and storage capacity are highly distributed, the edge infrastructure may be subject to security breaches or attacks that the infrastructure is incapable of handling due to its limited computing capability.

Organizations need to understand well the tools and technologies that are used at the edge (and in the corresponding cloud or clouds) including the security vulnerabilities and potential for security breaches associated with the tools and technologies used in these infrastructures. In summary, the organization must not ignore this issue; rather it needs to fully realize the need to prioritize the security and privacy protection of its digital assets.

Another concerning factor for the edge infrastructure is the use of different smart gadgets (e.g., smart phone, tablet, smart watches), for example, by arranging a 'bring your own device' (BYOD) provision. A smart gadget may have an application (app) that the owner/user of the smart gadget have installed without realizing that the acceptance of the license agreement includes giving the app access rights such as reading the information residing in the gadget's memory, taking pictures or recording video- and audio data at any time. If an app installed on a smart gadget is given the above permissions and the gadget is connected to some part of an edge infrastructure (or to any CC/CbC environment), this may create a security loophole and facilitate a security breach. The organization needs to have a clear understanding of and clear policy about how to ensure that the features of the smart gadgets used under the BYOD provision are not a threat to the privacy and security of the tangible or intangible organizational processes and assets.

### 4.4.3 Copyright and SLAs

Let us start with a simple example. A cloud user wants to store a document on a cloud server. The user inadvertently accepts the terms and condition of using the service which mentions that storing any data on the cloud server comes under the condition that the CSP reserves the right to keep a copy of the document and may use the information for 'harmless' purposes (e.g., marketing). Whether information theft would take place in the above scenario is debatable, but it's certain that the CSP is able to 'read' the document uploaded. Referring to our earlier discussion, while it is quite possible for a theft of digital assets to occur, in the CC/CbC environment it is quite likely that the theft will not be detected. Without having a proper zero-trust computing mechanism and an unbreakable audit trail, it is impossible to guarantee that the CSP in the example above will not be stealing information. Besides, the information in the uploaded document may be used in such a way that the creator's (i.e., the cloud user's) copyright is violated. The irony is that the creator has agreed to let the copyright be violated (by accepting the service terms and conditions without properly understanding them).

CC/CbC deployment may lead to the creation of an extremely confusing and complex scenario around copyright and the retention of copyright. CSPs use numerous software systems in order to provision their architecture. The software, firmware, hardware, operating systems and other tools may come from many different vendors and from different countries and continents. If the firmware, software and hardware used are not open source based, there is a theoretical possibility of information being stolen (since one cannot ascertain what the software or hardware is doing behind the scene), let alone the concerns associated with the vulnerabilities (including zero-day vulnerabilities) and security loopholes that those software and firmware may come with. It is important for an organization to comprehend how their digital assets will be treated and used by these different software, hardware and firmware platforms. The organization needs to decide whether the above may pose threats to their digital assets such as being stolen or being maliciously disclosed to unauthorized parties. This is a painstaking job that comes with no alternative unless the organization is ready to accept the potential of compromising the security and privacy of their digital assets.

One of the ways to address the concerns outlined above is through the use of SLAs. Here, it is important to note that the SLA needs to consider the third parties involved with the CSP, since the operational and processing context in the cloud extends beyond a single CSP's context. Therefore, organizations need to carefully consider how SLAs may help avoid scenarios where mere unauthorized disclosure of information can cause irrecoverable harm.

In the edge infrastructure, the scenario described above may get even more complex if the intermediary edge infrastructure is outsourced to sub-CSPs. The sub-CSP and the CSP both may have their own bundle of hardware, software, firmware and other tools, and they all collectively should be considered by the customer organization. Besides, if the infrastructure is situated at the customer's premises, or if the infrastructure includes a BYOD provision as part of its architecture, considerations must include these too.

### 4.5 TRUST

Understanding the concept of trust in computing is important for organization adopting CC/CbC as the reliance on trust in a distributed computing environment may become a security problem. First, it is important for the organization to identify the right CSP; the choice of a CSP is a critical success factor (CSF) in CC/CbC deployment and has a significant impact on the implementation of the cloud approach. Second, as mentioned earlier, a CSP may have its own sub-CSPs. Therefore, adopting CC/CbC may mean involving external entities in the organization's business operations. As a consequence, organizations using CC/CbC may put themselves in a position where they have given third (external) parties a high level of access to their core business processes, to people (employees, customers) and to the organization's digital assets. Both intra- and inter-organizational trust are important for achieving secure computing. In this section, we explore the role of trust as a CSF for organization using CC/CbC.

### 4.5.1 Intra-organizational Trust

Intra-organizational trust is associated with privacy and security concerns for both cloud- and non-CbC. One sensitive element within an organization is its people. A trust-based approach within an organizational computing practice may open doors to cyber incidents instigated through social engineering or by malicious insiders. From the perspective of access to information, the different functional units in an organization should be treated as external entities to each other. Since such considerations are normally within the scope of the organization's information security policy, we limit our discussion only to mentioning that operationally speaking, there is not much conceptual difference between inter-organizational and intra-organizational trust in computing.

### 4.5.2 Inter-organizational Trust

CSPs are external entities to whom customer organizations hand over their digital assets to. Thus, inter-organizational trust is a core defining factor for the protection of privacy and security in the cloud. Since edge computing is a variant of CC, the principles of inter-organizational trust apply to edge computing as well. In fact, if the edge infrastructure is provided by sub-CSPs, even more external parties are involved in the provision of cloud services and the trust relationships between the entities (or lack of trust thereof) affect the security and privacy of the customer organization's data.

As already discussed, the digital assets of the customer organization reside in an infrastructure owned and managed by CSPs (i.e., external parties). Through SLA provisioning as well as through the binding rules and regulations of the legislative and regulatory environment, a CSP may be legally prohibited to carry out unintended operations on a customer's digital assets. However, the organization still needs to consider how to monitor their CSP's activity. Assumptions and trust that a CSP will abide by the terms and conditions of the SLA may not be realistic and may contribute to the creation of security loophole(s). Rather, there needs to be a mechanism where a customer can monitor a CSPs activity in relation to the customer's digital assets. A question for organizations to ask is 'can our CSP carry out unauthorized activities on our digital assists, and do we have the capability to learn about any malicious activities by our CSP?'

An audit trail will help to discover activity footprints left in cyberspace. However, if the CSP is also the owner of the audit trail, the problem remains. One of the approaches to eliminate the enforced reliance on CSPs is to decentralize the audit trail itself. This can be achieved by applying identity and access management (IAM) processes that ensure that the customer's CSP has no controlling power over the management of the audit trails. In CC/CbC, IAM processes can be quite complex due to the distributed nature of the computing environment which makes the effective application and management of the security-related aspects for CC/CbC also complex. While decentralized computing involving multiple parties may help reduce or eliminate the organization's dependency on its CSP, the means and tools used to maintain the integrity of a large and complex and distributed system may become more complex than the system itself.

It is appreciable that CSPs apparently have started providing better safeguards for the digital assets of their customers. However, customers still need to acquire an understanding of the implications of relying on a rogue CSP. Trust by default may easily lead to privacy and security breaches. It needs to be underlined that in terms of privacy and security, trust-based computing in a CC/CbC environment may be a dangerous approach.

The issues with trust-based computing have led to considering zero-trust computing models. According to Mehraj and Banday (2020), a zero-trust strategy may improve the security aspects of CC. In summary, any level of trust in a CC/CbC implementation may lead to detrimental consequences for the cloud users as trust-based computing model is highly likely to be compromised at some point.

## 4.6 GEOGRAPHIC LOCATION

A CSP's infrastructure may have a global span and spread across different geographical location. The geographic dispersion of CC/CbC is illustrated in Figure 4.3. The business operating office of a CSP may be in one country but their cloud infrastructure or data centers may reside in different countries and even continents. At the same time, the CSP's customers may very well come from yet another country/continent; in particular, a customer may come from

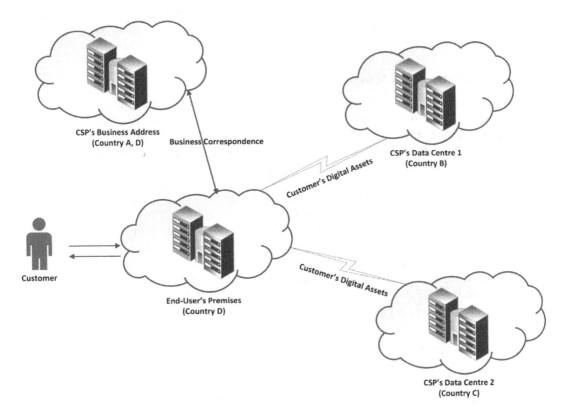

*Figure 4.3* The geographic dispersion of CC/CbC.

a country where their CSPs have no infrastructure. In other words, the customer organization may become involved in a business relationship with an entity residing in a country that may not be the same as the customer's, while storing and processing of the customer's digital assets may be taking place in other different countries.

The geographic dispersion, as illustrated in Figure 4.3, plays a crucial role with regard to the privacy and security of the organization's digital assets. In this section, we explore how the architectural dispersion may affect digital asset protection. We explore regulatory and jurisdictional as well as compliance and governance aspects and consider their impact on the privacy and security of geographically dispersed computing architectures.

### 4.6.1 Regulations and Jurisdictions

A customer from one country may sign a contract with a CSP from another country. In such a case, the established regulations and the requirement of the respective jurisdictions will need to be followed. However, when the customer and the CSP reside in different countries, it is not uncommon to find differences (sometimes substantial) in the respective laws and other regulations. This raises the question about which country's regulations and jurisdictions should apply to the contract between the customer and the CSP, and in what contexts. Therefore, considering local government regulations is a specific legal aspect of CC/CbC deployment. Without a proper understanding of the concrete legal requirements and their implications for the geographically dispersed cloud environment, a customer organization may find themselves not only in breach of security and privacy but also creating legal problems for its stakeholders.

Additionally, a CSP's infrastructure may be distributed across several countries where it stores or processes its customers' digital assets. The customer organization must have a clear understanding about the applicable laws concerning digital assets in relation to using the CSPs infrastructure as well as in relation to the management of security breaches.

### 4.6.2 Compliance and Governance

The meaning of compliance and governance, and the related standards, conditions and applicable regulations may differ from one country to another. Therefore, the requirements for being compliant may differ from one country to another. For a cloud customer, it is important to fully understand the compliance standards of the different geographic locations where their data may be kept by the CSP. Cloud customers also need to carry out a feasibility study on delegating the control over the organization's digital assets to different parties in different countries, should the organization decide to let their CSP store digital assets in an infrastructure situated at a different geographic location.

As an intermediary infrastructure used by the CSP, the edge infrastructure is 'closer' to the customer compared to the main CSP infrastructure. How close is close enough? This is not defined well for edge computing; for example, an edge infrastructure in a neighboring (different) country could be considered as a 'closer' infrastructure for a particular customer, given the location of the CSPs main cloud infrastructure. Thus, the geographic dispersion of CC/CbC architecture may be a challenge for edge computing as well.

### 4.7 CONCLUSIONS

The biggest problem with cybersecurity breaches is that, unlike a dent on the body of a vehicle, a cyber incident (or an attack) as well as the reasons for the incident does not become visible right at the moment it happens. The incident or attack may go unnoticed for a long time or forever; this is by far the most alarming aspect of a cybersecurity breach. Where information theft is the main motivation behind an attack, the attacker may try to steal the information without leaving any footprint. As digital assets can be replicated (i.e., by creating copies) unlimited times, and without distorting the original, stealing digital assets only requires copying the information without moving the original assets to a different location. In other words, a diamond necklace may not be stolen without this getting noticed at some point, but digital assets can very much be stolen without the theft being ever noticed!

In some cases, the unauthorized disclosure of information may be so devastating that finding the guilty parties may not provide a remedy. For example, if the data and information that relate to a scholarly research project are stolen, the damage to the owner is irreparable. Moving to CC/CbC does not minimize the risk of sensitive data being stolen. Despite of all the amazing benefits CC/CbC has to offer, for some organizations a resounding 'no' may be the answer to the question to adopt or not a CC/CbC approach. While CC/CbC may bring apparent benefits to organizations from an operational effectiveness and efficiency perspective, these benefits need to be considered along with the negative impacts on the privacy and security of the organization's digital assets.

## REFERENCES

M. Ahmed and N. I. Sarkar, 2020. Privacy in Cloud-based Computing. In G. Cornetta, A. Touhafi, & G. Muntean (Eds.), *Social, Legal, and Ethical Implications of IoT, Cloud, and Edge Computing Technologies*. IGI Global, USA.

M. Al Yami and D. Schaefer, 2019. "Fog computing as a complementary approach to cloud computing." In *2019 International Conference on Computer and Information Sciences (ICCIS)*, USA, 1–5, IEEE.

S. Almasi and G. Pratx, 2019. Cloud computing for big data. *Big Data in Radiation Oncology*, 61–78, CRC Press.

U. D. Ani, H. He and A. Tiwari, 2019. "Human factor security: Evaluating the cybersecurity capacity of the industrial workforce." *Journal of Systems and Information Technology*, 21(1), 2–35.

R. Arora and A. Parashar, 2013. "Secure user data in cloud computing using encryption algorithms." *International Journal of Engineering Research and Applications*, 3(4), 1922–1926.

W. C. Basto, A. P. Villalobos, C. A. U. de la Cruz, J. de la Hoz Hernández and O. B. P. Lezama, 2019. "Hybrid cloud computing architecture based on open source technology." *Dependability in Sensor, Cloud, and Big Data Systems and Applications: 5th International Conference*, 1123, 191, Guangzhou, China.

K. S. Bo, 2018. "Cloud computing for business." *International Journal of Advances in Scientific Research and Engineering*, 4(7), 156–160.

M. De Donno, K. Tange and N. Dragoni, 2019. "Foundations and evolution of modern computing paradigms: Cloud, IoT, edge, and fog." *IEEE Access*, 7, 150936–150948.

T. Dillon, C. Wu and E. Chang, 2010. "Cloud computing: issues and challenges." *24th IEEE International Conference on Advanced Information Networking and Applications*, 27–33, IEEE.

I. Ghafir, J. Saleem, M. Hammoudeh, H. Faour, S. Prenosil, S. Jaf and T. Baker, 2018. "Security threats to critical infrastructure: The human factor." *The Journal of Supercomputing*, 74(10), 4986–5002.

M. Gusev and S. Dustdar, 2018. "Going back to the roots—the evolution of edge computing, an IoT perspective." *IEEE Internet Computing*, 22(2), 5–15

P. Hopkin, 2018. *Fundamentals of Risk Management: Understanding, Evaluating and Implementing Effective Risk Management*. Kogan Page Publishers, UK.

J. S. Hurwitz and D. Kirsch, 2020. *Cloud Computing for Dummies*. John Wiley & Sons, USA.

I. R. Khan and M. Alam, 2017. "Cloud computing: Issues and future direction." *Global Sci-Tech*, 9(1), 37–44.

S. Khan, S. Parkinson and Y. Qin, 2017. "Fog computing security: A review of current applications and security solutions." *Journal of Cloud Computing*, 6, 1–22.

V. Kumar, A. A. Laghari, S. Karim, M. Shakir and A. A. Brohi, 2019. "Comparison of fog computing & cloud computing." *International Journal of Mathematical Sciences and Computing (IJMSC)*, 5(1), 31–41.

S. Mehraj and M. T. Banday, 2020. "Establishing a zero trust strategy in cloud computing environment." In *2020 International Conference on Computer Communication and Informatics (ICCCI)*, 1–6, IEEE.

A. Narang and D. Gupta, 2018. "A review on different security issues and challenges in cloud computing." In *2018 International Conference on Computing, Power and Communication Technologies (GUCON)*, 121–125, IEEE.

L. J. Nieuwenhuis, M. L. Ehrenhard and L. Prause, 2018. "The shift to cloud computing: The impact of disruptive technology on the enterprise software business ecosystem." *Technological Forecasting and Social Change*, 129, 308–313.

G. Platsis, 2019. "The human factor: Cyber security's greatest challenge." In *Cyber Law, Privacy, and Security: Concepts, Methodologies, Tools, and Applications*, 1–19, IGI Global, USA.

V. K. Prasad, M.D. Bhavsar and S. Tanwar, 2019. "Influence of monitoring: Fog and edge computing." *Scalable Computing: Practice and Experience*, 20(2), 365–376.

B. B. Rad, T. Diaby and M.E. Rana, 2017. "Cloud computing adoption: a short review of issues and challenges." *International Conference on E-commerce, E-Business and E-Government*, 51–55.

O. Santos, 2019. *Developing Cybersecurity Programs and Policies*. Pearson Education Inc. ISBN-13: 978-0-7897-5940-5.

K. Sha, T. A. Yang, W. Wei and S. Davani, 2020. "A survey of edge computing-based designs for IoT security." *Digital Communications and Networks*, 6(2), 195–202.

W. Shi, J. Cao, Q. Zhang, Y. Li and L Xu, 2016. "Edge computing: Vision and challenges." *IEEE Internet of Things Journal*, 3(5), 637–646.

P. J. Shih, 2018. "From the cloud to the edge: The technical characteristics and application scenarios of fog computing." *International Journal of Automation and Smart Technology*, 8(2), 61–64.

A. Singh and K. Chatterjee, 2017. "Cloud security issues and challenges: A survey." *Journal of Network and Computer Applications*, 79, 88–115.

B.E. Strom, A. Applebaum, D. P. Miller, K. C. Nickels, A. G. Pennington and C. B. Thomas, 2018. "Mitre ATT&CK: Design and philosophy." Technical report.

B. Varghese, N. Wang, S. Barbhuiya, P. Kilpatrick, and D. S. Nikolopoulos, 2016. "Challenges and opportunities in edge computing." In *2016 IEEE International Conference on Smart Cloud (SmartCloud)*, 20–26, IEEE.

D. Velzen, M. de Jong and S. Jansen, 2019. *Business Continuity Risks Through the Use of Software-As-A-Service: A Descriptive Survey*. Utrecht University, Netherlands. Available at: https://saas-continuiteit.nl/wp-content/uploads/2019/11/vanVelzen-5493994-OZPSaaSContinuity-CompleteV2.pdf

S. Wang, X. Zhang, Y. Zhang, L. Wang, J. Yang and W. Wang, 2017. "A survey on mobile edge networks: Convergence of computing, caching and communications." *IEEE Access*, 5, 6757–6779.

Chapter 5

# An Overview of Cognitive Internet of Things
## Cloud and Fog Computing

*Fariha Eusufzai, Tahmidul Haq, Sumit Chowdhury,*
*Shohani Sahren, and Saifur Rahman Sabuj*

BRAC University, Bangladesh
Hanbat National University, South Korea

## CONTENTS

## 5.1 INTRODUCTION

Wireless networking is one of the most dynamic fields of modern technology. Signals such as speech, images and multimedia are transmitted through a wireless medium. Additionally, cellular networks have many benefits, including versatility, as coverage is being accessed, an increase in ability to extend availability, lower ownership costs and many more. The new advances in the Internet of Things (IoT) have attracted worldwide focus to an extensive range of 'things' in our real environment, including education and business, to extend Internet access. The number of IoT devices is projected to expand in a broad range with the transition of IoT theory into practice. This makes it challenging to give adequate spectrum bands to specific devices. Careful research on the history of spectrum use has indicated the low use of the available spectrum. This motivates the spectral reuse principle. This permits secondary networks to access the authorized or shared radio spectrum to primary networks, while the spectrum is momentarily unavailable [1]. Cognitive Radio (CR) is the primary technique of motivating spectrum reuse. CR allows the signal to choose the shortest path to complete the transmission by connecting both the signals with the licensed and unlicensed device. The best possible transmission bands must be chosen automatically by intelligent radio Internet services. The secondary purchasers must sense, track and identify frequency ranges that are not dominated by the principal network within their operational field. CR, combined with random access techniques, can help reduce network congestion [2]. A CR system will customize its transmitting parameters to allow effective use of the available ever-changing spectrum in a self-serving manner. Spectrum detection performs a significant role in recognizing unused channels throughout the CR and IoT networks [3]. A CR system will adjust the propagation specifications to make the most of the continually altering spectrum resources (carrier wavelength, distance, transmitting capacity, etc.) [2].

With the combination of CR and IoT devices, Cognitive IoT (CIoT) devices provide a broad spectrum range. This ensures that all the available spectrums are used effectively. The network enhances more with the combination of CIoT and Cloud. Improved performance, stability, privacy and reliability are the motivations for combined Cloud-IoT. CIoT can be connected to millions of devices, and hence it generates a considerable amount of semi-structured or unstructured data [4]. Cloud-IoT is the cheapest and most effective method to handle or store this vast amount of data. After the data is stored in the Cloud-IoT, the data can be protected by applying security measures, and only then authorized devices can access the same data from anywhere. Cloud-IoT also provides scope for new data integrations and the sharing of the data with authorized third-party devices. CIoT alone has limited data processing capacities, whereas Cloud-IoT allows unlimited virtual data processing and also provides on-demand usage of data. CIoT requires IP enabled telephony devices to communicate through specific hardware. The communication costs for such systems are expensive. Cloud-IoT allows a method to connect and track any data from anywhere and thus making this communication cheap. As people communicate with one another, various data is produced, and Cloud-IoT provides features that allow this data to be easily accessible and usable, whenever necessary, at a meager cost [5].

To solve bandwidth shortage, geographically distributed, ultra-low latency and sensitive to privacy, a computing model that is closer to connected devices is necessary. Industry and academia have suggested that Fog Computing [6] can solve the problems mentioned earlier and extinguish the need for a computer model, which is relatively close to network devices. Fog Computing fills the void among Cloud and CIoT devices by allowing close contact to CIoT devices for computing, storing, networking and data processing of the entire network. As a consequence, computation, data storage, routing, decision-making and network security not only exist within the Cloud but also happens in the CIoT-to-Cloud path. This is because data travels through the Cloud. Fog Computing is a much more typical approach of computing, mostly because of its widespread nature and versatility. Another model close to Fog Computing is Edge Computing. As its tremendous performance capabilities in delivering real-time data processing, low running costs, fast scalability, reducing latency and enhanced network Edge Computing have created a suitable position in the digital world. Edge Computing will dramatically change different fields such as health maintenance, education, transport infrastructure, e-commerce and public networks with its tremendous processing capabilities. The program running on Edge Computing must execute locally until it connects to the Cloud. It maintains a dispersed architecture with data computation at the edge of boundary network nodes to make an independent resolution. As a result, it would reduce concerns about network congestion as well as security problems. Besides, using Edge computing, other wireless networking systems, such as mobile ad hoc network, ad hoc vehicle networks, can quickly make decisions by eliminating the delay in life-saving incidents [7].

In this chapter, we have proposed three separate applications that would enable the users to transfer their data without any significant problem. Several CIoT devices will be using one Fog node. Thus, they can quickly access and pass data to their nearest Fog server. There can be issues depending on network flow and bandwidth when there are more essential users. To address this issue, we suggested Reconfigurable Intelligent Surface (RIS) operation. By using this, the data will practically move through the closest and fastest path. This will use any pathway, and it does not depend on the authorization of the channel. Besides, it would remove the data-loss issue. We also include cloud computing in this chapter. Therefore, it will do all the complicated computing and offer powerful storing capabilities. This chapter's significant contributions are outlined as follows:

1. We have implemented fog computing to address the limited battery power issue of CIoT devices connected in cellular networking that would be nearest to the user's end and process data rapidly while supplying us with a real-time response. This is also the easiest way to protect details because it is directly linked to the user.
2. To prevent data latency issues that can arise when a single Fog node is being used more than the expected user. When the Cloud network is overloaded with data, we have implemented RIS. Any unused route near the consumer would be used for the data transfer by reflecting from one RIS to another.
3. Fog may be the best choice to avoid the problem of downtime, as we have used multiple Fog nodes for better propagation of the details. Furthermore, even if a single Fog node crashes, the whole network system and data will not be collapsed.
4. We have implemented Cloud infrastructure specifically to do all the dynamic computations that are not feasible with multiple Fog nodes. This is because the processing capacity is better than Fog nodes. It has infinite storage space, where it can store both incoming and outgoing data in this two-way contact model.

The continuation of the chapter is ordered, as described. The background of Cloud, Fog and Edge Computing, including merits and demerits, is demonstrated in Section 5.2. Section 5.3 explains the literature review and motivation of Fog, Edge and Cloud Computing. In Section 5.4, we have illustrated our system model. This section also includes all the mathematical expressions and analysis between Fog-Cloud and Fog-Fog. Section 5.5 provides the evaluation of performance or simulated results of the implemented network infrastructure with appropriate measurements. Finally, we have concluded in Section 5.6 of this chapter.

## 5.2 BACKGROUND OF FOG, CLOUD AND EDGE COMPUTING

Cloud computing is a form of processing where the information is stored on different servers and accessed from any device online. Besides, with the assistance of fog and edge computing, it has been possible to improve operating performance by allowing end-users to view smaller, more detailed data instead of storing information through a centralized, Cloud-based database, along with data that they would never need to access. We will briefly discuss the background information of fog computing, cloud computing and edge computing in the following sections: 5.2.1, 5.2.2 and 5.2.3.

### 5.2.1 Fog Computing

Fog computing is aimed at providing the IoT with robust recognition. [4]. The Fog is a collaborative framework for recording and processing data from consumers and the Cloud distribution centers [8]. Fog computing is based on a design that completely incorporates terminal devices computation functions and local processing advantages [9]. A fog processing paradigm refers to a virtual environment, in which data storage is carried out and managed by the individual [10]. Fog computation eliminates the distance between the Cloud and IoT devices by allowing network nodes to be measured, processed, interconnected and data controlled in IoT devices' proximity. Fog Computing is characterized as 'a device horizontal infrastructure that deploys user proximity to computation, storage, management and connectivity via a continuous Cloud-to-thing system'. The 'horizontal' framework in Fog Ccomputation enables the distributions of computational functions across various mechanisms and businesses and promotes soiled implementations through the vertical platform [4].

#### 5.2.1.1 Benefits of Fog Computing

1. It consumes less power.
2. Fog Computing enables real-time computation, which facilitates data analysis as quickly as our local area network [9].
3. It improves the utilization of network resources [10].

#### 5.2.1.2 Disadvantages of Fog Computing

1. Huge amount of Fog nodes are required.
2. Increased power usage in Fog nodes often rises in IoT terminals.
3. When communicating with nodes at wider distances, nodes need a lot of energy [10].

### 5.2.2 Cloud Computing

On-demand wireless network services, Cloud infrastructure, supports data processing without specific, active control by the consumer. To offer Software-Defined Networking (SDN), Network Virtualization (NFV), Mobile Edge Computing (MEC) and Cloud access network (C-RANs) for potential 5G services, telecommunications providers are expected to provide their Cloud processing and maintenance capabilities, combined with their heterogeneous data and transmission platforms [11]. By exploiting developments in network technology Cloud infrastructure provides a practical approach. Not only the model for Cloud storage focuses on data centers that are equipped to manage massive data stores but also its operation. Cloud avails groundwork, program and software as a service (IaaS, PaaS, SaaS). Infrastructure as a service (IaaS) enables Cloud users to connect IT framework for executing, memory and networking allocation [12]. Such data centers are also interconnected with one another in a way that it gives a unique terminal advantage through optical networks, providing data center networks with low-latency connectivity between data centers [13].

#### 5.2.2.1 Benefits of Cloud Computing

1. It has extensive storage capabilities.
2. It has far more processing power and does all the complex computations.

3. It is suitable for long-term analysis.
4. It helps to save sustainable capital costs by avoiding the use of physical hardware investment.
5. If the Internet is accessible, it has the benefit of operating from all over the global community.

### 5.2.2.2 Disadvantages of Cloud Computing

1. Huge device loads on one Cloud server contribute to delays in loading and queuing [14].
2. Cloud management is complicated because of the complexity of intelligent arrangements when it comes to utilizing the service.
3. Safety is a vital issue since the Cloud is freely accessible globally.
4. Needs continuous Internet connection for a better service.

## 5.2.3 Edge Computing

We live in an era dominated by advanced technology in cloud computing, and billions of people use personal Cloud storage to store their data using the Internet. Due to the increasing number of users, excess delay and bandwidth utilization have become an issue nowadays. To leverage 5G wireless technology and enable a real-time response, lower latency and easier maintenance, a concept called 'Edge Computing' came as an extension to the Cloud. Edge Computing serves as an intermediate layer between the Cloud and the end devices, enabling the storing, interpretation and transmission of the information at the edge of a networking system. The Edge layer in the middle of end-users and the Cloud is executed for various aspects regarding the devices that operate as the intermediate Edge nodes, the transmission protocols and system utilized by the Edge layer and the assistance that the Edge layer provides. The Architecture of the edge layer can be categorized into three categories: MEC, Fog Computing (FC), and Cloudlet Computing [15]. However, Edge Computing can be implemented to cellular and wireless communications scenarios as a revolutionary Edge technology, incorporating software and hardware systems placed at the edge of the network in the proximity of end-users. The key hypothesis of Edge Computing is to bring convenience, such as operating and bandwidth to the network edge. The storage capacity is brought adjacent to IoT devices to diminish data congestion and retaliation delay and to promote space-intensive IoT applications [16]. The data initiated by the end devices will be operated at the edge nodes, and just a specific segment of the information will be transmitted to the Cloud for further computation. Thus, the backbone network and the communication load can be minimized.

1. QoS and Latency: While edge devices are efficient, many of them lack adequate capacity to meet the delay-sensitive necessities. Cloud Computing offers resource-enhanced technology with enormous processing ability and storage power. However, most IoT devices are susceptible to delays. In contrast to Cloud models, all these devices are usable via Wide Area Network (WAN), which causes latency. Thus, typical Cloud cannot address issues, such as accessibility and necessities in real-time. The applications that require more operating potential and storage resources that cannot be developed competently utilizing Cloud services can be numerous network hops apart from where the end-user is located. To achieve high QoS at the boundary of the network, operating

resources are necessary. For instance, in autonomous vehicles, the information obtained from the camera needs to be processed promptly to satisfy the QoS requirement in real-time. Due to insufficient Internet bandwidth and WAN delay, user experience is hampered by the consolidated Cloud servers. If the databases are installed adjacent to the end network, the general latency can be minimized. The advantage of servers closest to the consumers is the high availability of the local area network (LAN) as well as a relatively small quantity of demands.

2. Reduction of Core Network Traffic: Due to IoT, the number of devices can produce an immense volume of raw information to be analyzed and preserved. According to [16], 15 petabytes of traffic is initiated every month. Allowing to send entire traffic to the Cloud network will cause cloud servers overload due to the shortage of storage capacity in the Cloud servers. To minimize the bandwidth usage and decrease congestion on the core network, the data must be processed at the edge servers. In this way, billions of end-users can be managed at edge servers to solve the data traffic and latency issue. Thus, the Edge Computing approach can play a significant part in reducing traffic on the whole networking system.

3. Scalability: It is interpreted that, in the future, a considerable amount of IoT devices will give rise to a severe scalability challenge. As a result, sending vast amounts of data to the Cloud servers will end in data blockage. Therefore, in this case, Cloud Computing will not work efficiently anymore. In this context, Edge server virtualization will offer an ability to facilitate scalability. The congestion in the Cloud servers will be solved when this data will be processed at the Edge servers since a relatively small number of data will be sent to the Cloud servers.

In the coming years, endless sensors, computing systems and Internet-based mobile apps will quickly dominate the digital industry. A stable Edge Computing system should be introduced to satisfy the enormous demands, which can handle both processing and communication efficiently, making it an integrated system.

### 5.2.3.1 Benefits of Edge Computing

1. Edge computing occurs near the devices where the sensors are linked. As a result of the shorter distance from the end devices, the data is processed quickly and gives us a real-time response [15].
2. Edge Computing is more secured as data is processed locally on the device users are using [6].
3. It does not require an Internet connection as the data is stored in the Local Area Network (LAN).
4. The quality of service in Edge Computing is higher than the Cloud since the linked devices do not have to wait for the service.
5. According to the companies, they can reduce their cost by reducing the bandwidth needed.

### 5.2.3.2 Disadvantages of Edge Computing

1. Edge Computing collects and processes only a subset of data instead of taking the full information from the Cloud. As a result, some necessary information or data can be lost.
2. For Edge Computing, more local hardware is needed (Table 5.1).

*Table 5.1* Difference among Edge Computing, Fog Computing and Cloud Computing.

| Characteristics | Edge computing | Fog computing | Cloud computing |
| --- | --- | --- | --- |
| 1. **Location** | The edge is located near or directly on the end devices. | Data is processed within the Fog nodes, which covers the LAN network. | Cloud is located far away from the source of information. |
| 2. **Processing power** | It has less processing power since it is performed near the source of information. | It has more processing power than the edge. | It has far more processing power and also does all the complex computations. |
| 3. **Storage capability** | It has a lesser capability. | It has more storage capacity. | More than Edge and Fog. |
| 4. **Internet access** | It does not require any Internet access. | It also does not need any Internet. | Requires an Internet connection. |
| 5. **Security** | Since it is the closest one to the user, so it is the most secure. | Less secure than the Edge. | Less secured as the data is stored in one place. |
| 6. **Purpose** | Edge is more suitable for quick analysis. | Fog is also fit for short-term interpretation. | It is befitting for the long-term, in-depth analysis. |
| 7. **Downtime** | Less possibility of collapsing the whole system. | Data is distributed among nodes. As a result, if something goes wrong, then the whole system does not collapse. | Everything is stored in one place. As a result, if something goes wrong, then it takes down the whole system. |

## 5.3 LITERATURE REVIEW OF EXISTING WORKS

Reviewing the literature is an important aspect that provides a useful framework for information advancement, which initiates discovering areas where there is a need for development. In Cloud Computing, Fog Computing and Edge Computing, many professionals have proposed different mechanisms and models to establish their thoughts, motivating us to research more on this topic. In Sections 5.3.1, 5.3.2 and 5.3.3, we will provide a literature review of the work performed in Fog Computing, Cloud Computing and Edge Computing.

## 5.3.1 Review of Fog Computing

In this model, Fog Computing is used to process data continuously while transferring with a real-time response. In this way, details can be protected as it is linked up straight to the user. Although Fog Computing reserves many advantages of Cloud Computing, data security is a critical challenge. However, T. H. Dang [13] proposed three models for data protection and performance issues to demonstrate the feasibility and the productivity of the structure. Therefore, an all-inclusive assessment of industrial IoT operating procedures to meet the threat of security issues in Fog Computing was provided by R. Basir et al. [10]. Also, J. Li et al. [17] proposed a Fog Computing-Assisted Trustworthy Forwarding (FCTF) scheme where the authors were the first ones to investigate an organized method to point out the threats, attacks in Fog Computing and then establish some possible solutions which could solve the security issues of IoT.

A single Fog node may affect the whole network system by collapsing the data. For setting up a stable propagation, multiple Fog nodes are more preferable. Cross-domain technology enables data sharing among different networks and levels to make the overall network model steady. Based on cross-domain IoT function, the authors of [16] and [17] proposed a Fog-based multi-level service framework and a solution for auto-driving, respectively, which is related to a Cloud/Fog-Computing structure and the IoT AI service. Furthermore, Fog service overlay activates services allocation at the edges of the network, and for seamless service provisioning and ordered Fog network was established.

Fog networking infrastructure leads on to strengthen the configuration, structure, and administration over network mainframe to build a well-coordinated safe computing proto-type to guide the future of IoT operations. Similarly, M. R. Anawar et al. [18] emphasized that Fog Computing became a comfortable platform because of some suggested research work's critical properties. Hence, systems like healthcare, smart cities, linked automobiles and smart grid Fog applications greatly influence the next generation of IoT systems. Similarly, by using the perception of Fog Computing, the authors of [19] focused on health monitoring, [20] on authentic time-oriented Heart Attack Mobile Detection Service, [21] on remote nodes applied in the smart home and [22] on SDN infrastructure in the smart industry. In addition to this, a music perception system based on machine learning methods to interconnect music and spontaneously write scores was introduced by L. Lu [23].

The proposed system model is established upon multiple Fog nodes, where selecting an ideal path to complete the mission of transferring data on time is a real challenge. Hence, N. Mostafa [24] developed a Fog resource distribution algorithm that allows programmed Fog selection and allotment for IoT structure. This result is diminished in the comprehensive end to end latency of the model. Additionally, K. Ma et al. [9] proposed a Fog Computing model based on IoT, including numerous-layer called IoT-FCM. This uses a genetic formula computation for resource distribution between the terminal and Fog layers and a multi-sink model of the Least Interference Beaconing Protocol (LIBP) to amplify the error permissiveness. Thus, it reduces the power usage of a terminal layer.

Ensuring low-cost management and energy efficiency while framing a system model is a crucial aspect. To reduce communication costs and energy consumption in 5G services, different authors have experimented with different applications. Similarly, C. Mouradian et al. [25] used the non-linear route point mobility prototype for Fog nodes to evaluate the desired timespan and function implementation cost. They then modeled an Integer Linear Programming (ILP) expression, which reduced the timespan and price's accumulated weighted operation. F. Jalali et al. [26] presented strategies and surveys for energy-efficient IoT applications. On the other hand, the recent survey [27] focuses on a Fog-based model that utilizes local computation, memory, connection, monitor and policymaking and thus overcomes the cost issue in 5G deployment. Again, L. Velasco et al. [28] reviewed a safe, supremely circulated and excessive-dense Fog Computing architecture provided at the top edge of a wireless network for a Telecommunication Carrier to deliver several integrated, budget-friendly and new 5G services. Similarly, R. Shahzadi et al. [29] highlighted challenges like resource allocation, users' privacy, the non-availability of programming models, and testing software and support for heterogeneous networks. Furthermore, M. S. Elbamby et al. [30] researched the complication of task administration and dynamic edge caching in Fog networks with intermission and authenticity constraints.

Along with the energy consumption strategy, the data transmission rate of Fog nodes was being experimented. As a result, E. Balevi [31] determined the ideal nodes which must be improved to Fog nodes with subsidiary computing proficiency caused by increase in the standard data rate and reduction in the channeling obstruction. I. Yildirim, [32] worked on the possible profit of using RISs for inner–outer configuration and different frequency bands (from 2 GHz to 100 GHz). First, a common propagation framework with a particular RIS was examined. The development of the overall amount of reflecting equipment on the most assumed allocation of the transmitted signal-to-noise ratio and delusion act was observed.

## 5.3.2 Review of Cloud Computing

Cloud networking is closely associated with Fog computing. The multiple Fog nodes are not sufficient enough to stable the network system of the given model. Thus, Cloud is also attached in this system model with the Fog nodes to provide the highest performance within the shortest time. The authors [12] highlighted the challenges and issues of Cloud Computing adoption perspective. Furthermore, they focused on interoperability issues, including IaaS, PaaS, SaaS, for further research and development. F. Bonomi et al. [14] presented emerging applications' requirements to make the Fog a suitable framework for several demanding IoT applications. The author also aimed at the relation between the Fog and the Cloud while identifying Cloud Computing's disadvantages. Once again, S. Prabavathy [33] introduced a central Cloud intelligence framework for detecting a fast-moving Attack for the IoT feature spread to local Fog Nodes, allowing for an upgradable mobility and interoperability distributed intrusion monitoring process. The system demonstrates to be proficient in terms of feedback and identifying reliability. Separating for MCC and FC, the application's principle was experimentally evaluated and discussed by C. Fiandrino et al. [34].

Fog is the expansion of Cloud Computing that includes multiple Edge nodes instantly attached to physical equipment. Therefore, N. Moustafa [8] proposed a systemic interaction between IoT, Fog and Cloud for successfully executing big data analytics and computer security structure with safety issues, possible solution and further investigation instruction in the architecture. The authors of paper [11, 35] proposed the TelcoFog architecture as an excessive-dense Fog Computing structure which can be assigned at the highest edge of a wireless system to deliver multiple merged, cost-efficient and new 5G applications. The paper aimed to build up the place of the cell phone network and cloud markets.

Like Fog, Cloud Computing infrastructure also needs to be concerned about the cost, timeliness and power usage for a more accurate system model. Afterward, M. A. Rahman et al. [36] proposed a Fog-Cloud hybrid architecture to compose a massive social network by supporting a massive ad hoc crowd and circulated IoT nodes over a smart city surrounding. The authors presented a transmission structure between device users and Fog nodes, Fog nodes, and the Cloud and a durability and power consumption model, including significant data architecture. Sequentially, A. Mebrek et al. [37] proposed an effective system pattern in which the energy utilization and the delay were taken in observation. The authors also stated three different energy-proficient methods to reduce the total price of IoT Service implementation in a Fog-Cloud system. Apart from this, S. Sthapit et al. [38] introduced a sensor network using an Open Jackson network model, which was prepared as a network of chains in need of load stabilizing when Cloud and Fog are missing.

## 5.3.3 Review of Edge Computing

Although the combination of Fog and Cloud structure can expand the ability of data transmission, yet the excessive use of the same Fog node and massive loads on the Cloud network can slow down the entire network model. Thus, Edge Computing is introduced to the model for supporting the weak point of Fog and Cloud. Recently [15, 39] highlighted the straightforward concept of Edge Computing by including the basic ideas and new capabilities of Edge Computing along with the reasons behind emerging and future research works. N. Abbas et al. [40] aimed to present the definition of MEC, its usage benefits, system models and usage areas together with highlighted related research and future directions. Again, F. A.

Salaht et al. [41] presented a survey on research performed on Service Placement Problem (SPP) in the Fog/Edge Computing. A classification of suggestions was given and detected issues and difficulties were examined, like the variety of user outlook and IoT devices feature complexity and deployment problem.

Furthermore, to meet the latency requirements, G. Premsankar has experimented with Edge Computing [42]. As a paradigmatic sample of mobile gaming, it was viewed as a resource-intensive 3-D application as they measured the response delay of various implementation scenarios. As a consequence, they found Edge Computing a requirement of virtual and augmented reality applications. F. N. Nwebonyi et al. [43] explained how mobile Edge-Cloud, a less favored Edge Computing prototype, could be used at a lower cost to attain similar or lower latency. The authors also proposed a lightweight safety and fairness mechanism for e-Health protocols based on mobile Edge-Clouds and other prototypes. Similarly, T. Muhammed et al. [44] proposed an omnipresent healthcare platform, UbeHealth, by utilizing its three significant elements: four Edge Computing layers, deep learning, big data high-geared computing and IoT.

After implementing the latency requirements, Edge Computing needs to focus on the issue of longevity, reducing overload and quick response while sharing data with Fog nodes or Clouds for an unbreakable super-fast network. X. Sun et al. [45] proposed a novel IoT model approach toward mobile Edge Computing, Edge IoT, to manage data streams at the mobile edge. Following this, T. Nguyen et al. [46] presented a transferred and reviewed content-centered networking (CCN) protocol and forum for the deployment/discovery of MEC services. According to a tri-tiered hierarchical MEC network topology, they configured a gateway in each region to reduce overhead computing at the centralized controller. Md. A. Rahman et al. [47] proposed a blockchain-based framework to promote security and Spatio-temporal smart contract services for sustainable IoT sharing in mega smart cities. R. Ullah et al. [16] integrated NDN with ECC to ensure fast response time to information. Their system was based on architecture from N-Tier, and consisted of three main tiers.

In terms of storage, processing power and security, the three terms Fog, Edge and Cloud Computing can be differentiated. Consequently, A. Yousefpour et al. [6] provided concepts on Fog Computing and difference among other computing prototypes, such as Cloudlets and MEC Besides, H. E. Sayed et al. [7] studied the system's different network characteristics to determine that EC structures performed better than Cloud Computing structures. Moreover, K. Dolui [15] discussed and compared in depth the Fog Computing, Cloudlet and MEC, which are three different applications of Edge Computing. The authors also defined a set of guidelines to select one of these most acceptable applications based on the situation and present a decision chart to select the optimum application.

Motivated by the above discussion of the existing research literature, there is a gap in studies that directly compares these three terms CIoT, RIS, Fog and Cloud within the same framework. We have analyzed these terms through our contribution to this chapter.

## 5.4 NETWORK ARCHITECTURE

Here, we consider the concept of IoT devices as multiple users connecting to the Fog nodes, which is then connected to the RIS. Finally, the network is based on the connection of the Cloud Computing network. We can divide the connection in three ways so that there is less power consumption, low latency and high scalability (Figure 5.1).

Firstly, from the diagram, we see that the CIoT devices (devices-1-9) will be connected to each of its corresponding Fog nodes (Fn-1-3). The data will be passed from the devices through one Fog node to another by their respecting paths. As Fog nodes can be used instead

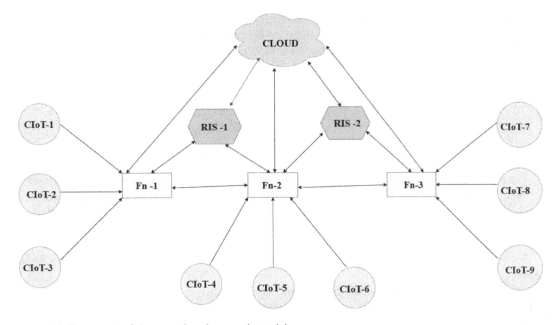

*Figure 5.1* Illustration of the considered network model.

of BaseBand Units (BBU), all user information will be stored at the nodes. In this way, a limited number of users will be able to access their closest Fog node. Thus, storage computation will be less time-consuming due to the reduction of physical distance between the Fog nodes.

Two cases are considered based on the system model: (i) Computation between Fog and Cloud and (ii) Computation between Fog and Fog.

## 5.4.1 Computation Between Fog and Cloud

Suppose the packet (a particular number of bits create a single packet) size is K-bits. The packet is partly analyzed in the Fog node, e.g., the packet's $Q$ bits are analyzed also the remaining, i.e., $K–Q$ Cloud bits are interconnected. Thus, the transmission delay is defined as

$$\tau_{tD}^{FC} = \frac{K}{R_{fog}} + \frac{K-Q}{R_{cloud}} \tag{5.1}$$

Here, the data rates at the Fog node and Cloud rate are $R_{fog}$, and $R_{cloud}$ can be expressed as

$$R_{fog} = B\log_2\left(1 + SNIR_{fog}\right) \tag{5.2}$$

$$R_{cloud} = B\log_2\left(1 + SNIR_{cloud}\right) \tag{5.3}$$

Here, $B$ represents bandwidth. Also, $SINR_{fog}$ and $SINR_{cloud}$ both represent the signal-to-interference ratio (SINR) at the Cloud and Fog node, respectively. The SINR for the $n^{th}$ device at the Fog node, we get

$$SINR_{fog}\left(n\right) = \frac{P_{cn}h_n d_n^{-\alpha}}{\sigma^2 + I_{fog1}} \tag{5.4}$$

Here, $n = 1, 2, 3, \ldots\ldots N$, $N$ is the total number of CIoT devices. $P_c$ denotes the transmission power of the CIoT device, $h$ represents the channel coefficient, $d$ is the distance between the CIoT device and the Fog node, $\alpha$ is the path-loss exponent, $\sigma^2$ is the noise variance and $I_{fog}$ is the interference from other CIoT devices at the Fog node. The SINR of the $m^{th}$ Fog node at the Cloud can be written as

$$SINR_{cloud}(m) = \frac{P_{fm}\left[h_{fcm}d_{fcm}^{-\alpha} + \left(d_{frm}^{-\alpha} + d_{rcm}^{-\alpha}\right)\sum_{i=1}^{Z} h_{fr}^i h_{rc}^i e^{j\varphi_i}\right]}{\sigma^2 + I_{cloud}} \tag{5.5}$$

Here, $m = 1, 2, 3, \ldots\ldots M$. $M$ is the total number of Fog devices. $P_f$ denotes the transmission power of Fog devices. $h_{fc}$, $h_{fr}$ and $h_{rc}$ represent the channel coefficient of Fog-Cloud, Fog-RIS and RIS-Cloud, respectively. $d_{fc}$, $d_{fr}$ and $d_{rc}$ are the distances between Fog to Cloud, Fog to RIS and RIS to Cloud, respectively, and $I_{cloud}$ is the interference strength from the other Fog nodes at the Cloud.

Secondly, the diagram depicts direct connections between Fog nodes (Fn-1-3) and Cloud. Also, there are indirect connections between Fog nodes (Fn-1-3) to RIS and RIS to Cloud. So, the data can be transferred to the Cloud using the direct path between Fog nodes and Cloud, or it can also be passed to Cloud through RIS from Fog nodes. Since it is a two-way communication system, the transmitted and received data will be stored in Cloud Computing [31].

Substituting the Equations (5.4) and (5.5) into Equations (5.2) and (5.3), we get,

$$R_{fog} = B\log_2\left(1 + \frac{P_{cn}h_n d_n^{-\alpha}}{\sigma^2 + I_{fog1}}\right) \tag{5.6}$$

$$R_{cloud} = B\log_2\left(1 + \frac{P_{fm}\left[h_{fcm}d_{fcm}^{-\alpha} + \left(d_{frm}^{-\alpha} + d_{rcm}^{-\alpha}\right)\sum_{i=1}^{Z} h_{fr}^i h_{rc}^i e^{j\varphi_i}\right]}{\sigma^2 + I_{cloud}}\right) \tag{5.7}$$

Finally, plugging the Equations (5.6) and (5.7) into Equation (5.1), we find,

$$\tau_{trans} = \frac{K}{B\log_2\left(1 + \frac{P_{cn}h_n d_n^{-\alpha}}{\sigma^2 + I_{fog1}}\right)} + \frac{K - Q}{B\log_2\left(1 + \frac{P_{fm}\left[h_{fcm}d_{fcm}^{-\alpha} + \left(d_{frm}^{-\alpha} + d_{rcm}^{-\alpha}\right)\sum_{i=1}^{Q} h_{fr}^i h_{rc}^i e^{j\varphi_i}\right]}{\sigma^2 + I_{cloud}}\right)} \tag{5.8}$$

## 5.4.2 Computation Between Fog and Fog

Suppose the packet size is K-bits, and the packet is partly analyzed in the Fog node, e.g., the packet's Q bits are analyzed, and the remaining, i.e., $K–Q$ Cloud bits are interconnected. Thus, the transmission delay is defined as

$$\tau_{tD}^{FF} = \frac{K}{R_{fog}} + \frac{K-Q}{R_{fog-fog}} \tag{5.9}$$

Hence, the diagram demonstrates that the Fog nodes (Fn-1-3) are specifically linked. Moreover, this is a two-way communication network where the data can be sent and received simultaneously in the nodes. Even here, the Fog nodes accumulate and store the information as per the owner [48, 49]. Thus, the data is quite simple to access.

$$R_{fog-fog} = B\log_2\left(1 + \frac{P_{fm}\left[h_{ffm}d_{ffm}^{-\alpha} + \left(d_{frm}^{-\alpha} + d_{rfm}^{-\alpha}\right)\sum_{i=1}^{Z}h_{fr}^{i}h_{rf}^{i}e^{j\varphi_i}\right]}{\sigma^2 + I_{fog2}}\right) \tag{5.10}$$

Finally, plugging the Equations (5.6) and (5.10) into Equation (5.9), we find,

$$\tau_{tD}^{FF} = \frac{K}{B\log_2\left(1 + \frac{P_{cn}h_n d_n^{-\alpha}}{\sigma^2 + I_{fog1}}\right)} + \frac{K-Q}{B\log_2\left(1 + \frac{P_{fm}\left[h_{ffm}d_{ffm}^{-\alpha} + \left(d_{frm}^{-\alpha} + d_{rfm}^{-\alpha}\right)\sum_{i=1}^{Z}h_{fr}^{i}h_{rf}^{i}e^{j\varphi_i}\right]}{\sigma^2 + I_{fog2}}\right)} \tag{5.11}$$

## 5.5 NUMERICAL RESULTS

In this section, we have described the numerical results of our proposed model. We have investigated two cases as 1) Computation between Fog and Cloud; 2) Computation between Fog and Fog.

Figure 5.2 shows the position of all the objects in the system model, including the CIoT devices, which are approximately 40–60 meters away from the three Fog nodes. The Fog nodes are about 260–350 meters apart from one another. Each Fog node can store and

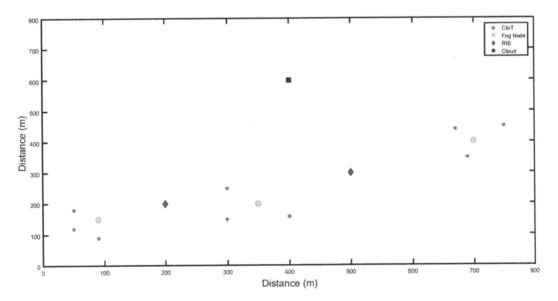

*Figure 5.2* The position of CIoT, Fog, RIS and Cloud.

process all data from the three nearby CIoT devices. A RIS was positioned between two Fog nodes at a distance of around 110–200 meters away from them. Additionally, a central Cloud is placed at around 200–450 meters from the three Fog nodes, which can store and process all the data from the system's nine CIoT devices. According to Figure 5.1, we assume the simulation parameters: $B = 15$ kHz, $\alpha = 4$ and $\sigma^2 = -174$ dBm. All channels are assumed to be Rayleigh fading.

In Figure 5.3, comparisons of data rate between three paths: CIoT-Fog, Fog-Fog and Fog-Cloud are shown where the transmission power lies along the $x$-axis, and the data rate lies along the $y$-axis. The figure shows a rise in the data rate with the increase in transmission power. Moreover, CIoT-Fog displays a maximum data rate of 2037 bps when the transmission power is 30 dBm. On the other hand, at the same transmission power, Fog-Fog shows a data rate of 12.93 bps, and the Fog-Cloud path shows 1003 bps, respectively. Therefore, from the above analytics, we can say that the CIoT-Fog path indicates better performance for next-generation wireless networks as it is possible to get a higher data rate.

Figure 5.4 shows the improvement found in the CIoT-Fog-Cloud path after the transmission power of –93 dBm. The variations in propagation delay and transmission power between both CIoT-Fog-Cloud and CIoT-Fog-Fog paths are seen in the figures, which indicate an exponential declination of the parameters used to compare. The CIoT-Fog-Cloud path displays a minimum transmission delay of around 0.07439 seconds when its transmission power is –35 dBm while the lowest transmission delay for the CIoT-Fog-Fog path is 3.893 seconds when its transmission power is –68 dBm. By contrast, the CIoT-Fog-Cloud path has a more significant transmission delay than the other system. As an example, the CIoT-Fog-Cloud path has a transmission delay of $1.998 \times 10^4$ seconds at –130 dBm transmission energy. In contrast, the CIoT-Fog-Fog path has a transmission delay of 1108 seconds at the same transmission power.

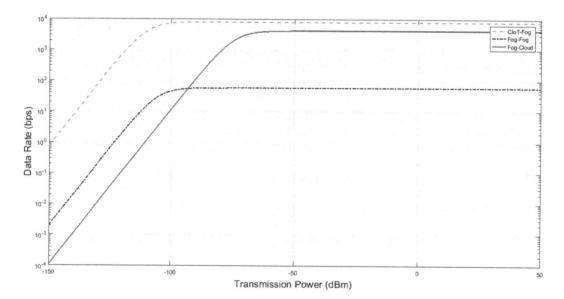

*Figure 5.3* Data rate comparison between CIoT-Fog, Fog-Fog and Fog-Cloud.

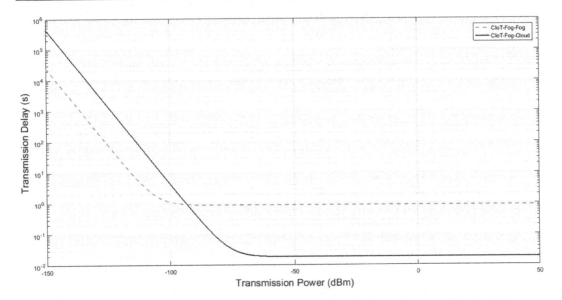

*Figure 5.4* Transmission delay comparison between CIoT-Fog-Cloud and CIoT-Fog-Fog.

## 5.6 CONCLUSION

The IoT devices increase technological innovation and support various sectors, including production, electricity, infrastructure, smart cities, schooling, banking, healthcare and government. In this chapter, a structure was suggested to explain the relationships between CIoT, Cloud, RIS and Fog layers for wireless networks' successful operation. Key features of this chapter involve Fog, Cloud and RIS. Here, the three layers were discussed not only to transfer information with lower scalability and lower energy usage but also to store and measure data very quickly. Fog networking is one of the most successful approaches for managing the big data delivered by the CIoT, which is always crucial in terms of protection and resources. Using RIS may be one of the simplest and easiest ways to transmit the data in terms of data flow. The Cloud framework has been used to manage all the complicated computing processes and advanced analytics to store and transfer data within a few seconds. Throughout this chapter, we presented a model for maintaining transmitting data with low bandwidth.

Finally, we demonstrated that our results have a wider reach than the specific application can provide. Decisively, the above model may be extended to future developments for the detection of Friend or Foe (FoF) research using physical-layer network coding to identify secondary users [50], random CR network quality in Rayleigh-lognormal environment [51], energy harvesting [52] and CR network energy efficiency analysis [53].

## REFERENCES

1. X. Zhang et al., "Distributed Compressive Sensing Augmented Wideband Spectrum Sharing for Cognitive IoT," *IEEE Internet of Things Journal*, vol. 5, no. 4, pp. 3234–3245, August 2018.
2. Y. Liang, Y. Zeng, E. C. Y. Peh and A. T. Hoang, "Sensing-Throughput Tradeoff for Cognitive Radio Networks," *IEEE Transactions on Wireless Communications*, vol. 7, no. 4, pp. 1326–1337, April 2008.

3. T. Li, J. Yuan and M. Torlak, "Network Throughput Optimization for Random Access Narrowband Cognitive Radio Internet of Things (NB-CR-IoT)," *IEEE Internet of Things Journal*, vol. 5, no. 3, pp. 1436–1448, June 2018.

4. H. F. Atlam, A. Alenezi, A. Alharthi, R. J. Walters and G. B. Wills, "Integration of Cloud Computing with Internet of Things: Challenges and Open Issues," in *Proceedings of IEEE International Conference on Internet of Things (iThings) and IEEE Green Computing and Communications (GreenCom) and IEEE Cyber, Physical and Social Computing (CPSCom) and IEEE Smart Data (SmartData)*, pp. 670–675, Exeter, 2017.

5. A. Botta, W. Dedonato, V. Persico, "On the Integration of Cloud Computing and Internet of Things," in *Proceedings of 2014 International Conference on Future Internet of Things and Cloud*, December 2014.

6. A. Yousefpour, C. Fung, T. Nguyen, F. Jalali, A. Niakanlahiji, J. Kong and J. P. Jue, "All One Needs to Know about Fog Computing and Related Edge Computing Paradigms: A Complete Survey," *Journal of Systems Architecture*, Vol. 98, pp. 289–330, September 2019.

7. H. E. Sayed et al., "Edge of Things: The Big Picture on the Integration of Edge, IoT and the Cloud in a Distributed Computing Environment," *IEEE Access*, vol. 6, pp. 1706–1717, 2018.

8. N. Moustafa, "A Systemic IoT-Fog-Cloud Architecture for Big-Data Analytics and Cyber Security Systems: A Review of Fog Computing," [online] https://arxiv.org/abs/1906.01055

9. K. Ma, A. Bagula, C. Nyirenda, and O. Ajayi, "An IoT-Based Fog Computing Model," *Sensors*, vol. 19, pp. 1–17, 2019.

10. R. Basir, S. Qaisar, M. Ali, M. Aldwairi, M. I. Ashraf, A. Mahmood, and M. Gidlund, "Fog Computing Enabling Industrial Internet of Things: State-of-the-Art and Research Challenges," *Sensors*, vol. 19, pp. 1–38, 2019.

11. R. Vilalta et al., "TelcoFog: A Unified Flexible Fog and Cloud Computing Architecture for 5G Networks," *IEEE Communications Magazine*, vol. 55, no. 8, pp. 36–43, August 2017.

12. T. Dillon, C. Wu and E. Chang, "Cloud Computing: Issues and Challenges," in *Proceedings of 24th IEEE International Conference on Advanced Information Networking and Applications, AINA 2010*, pp. 27–33, 2010.

13. T. D. Dang and D. Hoang, "A Data Protection Model for Fog Computing," in *Proceedings of 2nd International Conference on Fog and Mobile Edge Computing, FMEC 2017*, pp. 32–38, 2017.

14. F. Bonomi, R. Milito, J. Zhu, and S. Addepalli, "Fog Computing and Its Role in the Internet of Things," in *Proceedings of the 1st ACM Mobile Cloud Computing Workshop, MCC 2012*, pp. 13–15, Finland, 2012.

15. K. Dolui & S. K. Datta, "Comparison of Edge Computing Implementations: Fog Computing, Cloudlet and Mobile Edge Computing," in *Proceedings of Global Internet of Things Summit (GIoTS)*, 2017.

16. R. Ullah, M. A. U. Rehman and B. Kim, "Design and Implementation of an Open Source Framework and Prototype for Named Data Networking-Based Edge Cloud Computing System," *IEEE Access*, vol. 7, pp. 57741–57759, 2019.

17. J. Li, X. Li, J. Yuan, R. Zhang and B. Fang, "Fog Computing-Assisted Trustworthy Forwarding Scheme in Mobile Internet of Things," *IEEE Internet of Things Journal*, vol. 6, no. 2, pp. 2778–2796, April 2019.

18. M. R. Anawar, S. Wang, M. Azam Zia, A. K. Jadoon, U. Akram, and S. Raza, "Fog Computing: An Overview of Big IoT Data Analytics," *Wireless Communications and Mobile Computing*, vol. 2018, pp. 1–22, 2018.

19. P. Verma and S. K. Sood, "Fog Assisted-IoT Enabled Patient Health Monitoring in Smart Homes," *IEEE Internet of Things Journal*, vol. 5, no. 3, pp. 1789–1796, June 2018.

20. S. Ali and M. Ghazal, "Real-time Heart Attack Mobile Detection Service (RHAMDS): An IoT Use Case for Software Defined Networks," in *Proceedings of 2017 IEEE 30th Canadian Conference on Electrical and Computer Engineering (CCECE)*, pp. 1–6, Windsor, ON, Canada, 2017.

21. A. Kanyilmaz and A. Cetin, "Fog Based Architecture Design for IoT With Private Nodes: A Smart Home Application," in *Proceedings of 2019 7th International Istanbul Smart Grids and Cities Congress and Fair (ICSG)*, pp. 194–198, Istanbul, Turkey, 2019.

22. J. Wang and D. Li, "Adaptive Computing Optimization in Software-Defined Network-Based Industrial Internet of Things with Fog Computing." *Sensors*, vol. 18, 8 2509, Basel, Switzerland, 1 August 2018.

23. L. Lu, L. Xu, B. Xu, G. Li and H. Cai, "Fog Computing Approach for Music Cognition System Based on Machine Learning Algorithm," *IEEE Transactions on Computational Social Systems*, vol. 5, no. 4, pp. 1142–1151, December 2018.

24. N. Mostafa, I. A. Ridhawi and M. Aloqaily, "Fog Resource Selection Using Historical Executions," in *Proceedings of 2018 Third International Conference on Fog and Mobile Edge Computing (FMEC)*, pp. 272–276, Barcelona, 2018.

25. C. Mouradian, S. Kianpisheh, M. Abu-Lebdeh, F. Ebrahimnezhad, N. T. Jahromi and R. H. Glitho, "Application Component Placement in NFV-Based Hybrid Cloud/Fog Systems with Mobile Fog Nodes," *IEEE Journal on Selected Areas in Communications*, vol. 37, no. 5, pp. 1130–1143, May 2019.

26. F. Jalali, S. Khodadustan, C. Gray, K. Hinton and F. Suits, "Greening IoT with Fog: A Survey," *2017 IEEE International Conference on Edge Computing (EDGE)*, pp. 25–31, Honolulu, HI, 2017.

27. N. Khumalo, O. Oyerinde and L. Mfupe, "Fog Computing Architecture for 5G-Compliant IoT Applications in Underserved Communities," in *Proceedings of 2019 IEEE 2nd Wireless Africa Conference (WAC)*, pp. 1–5, Pretoria, South Africa, 2019.

28. L. Velasco and M. Ruiz, "Flexible Fog Computing and Telecom Architecture for 5G Networks," in *Proceedings of 2018 20th International Conference on Transparent Optical Networks (ICTON)*, pp. 1–4, Bucharest, 2018.

29. R. Shahzadi et al., "Three tier Fog Networks: Enabling IoT/5G for Latency Sensitive Applications," *China Communications*, vol. 16, no. 3, pp. 1–11, March 2019.

30. M. S. Elbamby, M. Bennis and W. Saad, "Proactive Edge Computing in Latency-Constrained Fog Networks," in *Proceedings of 2017 European Conference on Networks and Communications (EuCNC)*, pp. 1–6, Oulu, 2017.

31. E. Balevi and R. D. Gitlin, "Optimizing the Number of Fog Nodes for Cloud-Fog-Thing Networks," *IEEE Access*, vol. 6, pp. 11173–11183, 2018.

32. I. Yildirim, A. Uyrus, E. Basar and I. Akyildiz, "Propagation Modeling and Analysis of Reconfigurable Intelligent Surfaces for Indoor and Outdoor Applications in 6G Wireless Systems," 2019. [online] https://arxiv.org/abs/1912.07350

33. S. Prabavathy, K. Sundarakantham and S. M. Shalinie, "Design of Cognitive Fog Computing for Intrusion Detection in Internet of Things," *Journal of Communications and Networks*, vol. 20, no. 3, pp. 291–298, June 2018.

34. C. Fiandrino, N. Allio, D. Kliazovich, P. Giaccone and P. Bouvry, "Profiling Performance of Application Partitioning for Wearable Devices in Mobile Cloud and Fog Computing," *IEEE Access*, vol. 7, pp. 12156–12166, 2019.

35. P. Bellavista, L. Foschini and D. Scotece, "Converging Mobile Edge Computing, Fog Computing, and IoT Quality Requirements," in *Proceedings of 2017 IEEE 5th International Conference on Future Internet of Things and Cloud (FiCloud)*, pp. 313–320, Prague, 2017.

36. M. A. Rahman, M. S. Hossain, E. Hassanain, and G. Muhammad, "Semantic Multimedia Fog Computing and IoT Environment: Sustainability Perspective," *IEEE Communication Magazine*, vol. 56, no. 5, pp. 80–87, May 2018.

37. A. Mebrek, L. Merghem-Boulahia and M. Esseghir, "Energy-Efficient Solution Using Stochastic Approach for IoT-Fog-Cloud Computing," in *Proceedings of 2019 International Conference on Wireless and Mobile Computing, Networking and Communications (WiMob)*, pp. 1–6, Barcelona, Spain, 2019.

38. S. Sthapit, J. Thompson, N. M. Robertson and J. R. Hopgood, "Computational Load Balancing on the Edge in Absence of Cloud and Fog," *IEEE Transactions on Mobile Computing*, vol. 18, no. 7, pp. 1499–1512, 1 July 2019.

39. K. Peng, V. C. M. Leung, X. Xu, L. Zheng, J. Wang and Q. Huang, "A Survey on Mobile Edge Computing: Focusing on Service Adoption and Provision," *Wireless Communications and Mobile Computing*, Hindawi Limited, 2018.

40. N. Abbas, Y. Zhang, A. Taherkordi, and T. Skeie, "Mobile Edge Computing: A Survey," *IEEE Internet Things Journal*, vol. 5, no. 1, pp. 450–465, February 2018.

41. F. A. Salaht, F. Desprez, A. Lebre, "*An Overview of Service Placement Problem in Fog and Edge Computing*," pp.1–43, France, 2019.

42. G. Premsankar, M. Di Francesco, and T. Taleb, "Edge Computing for the Internet of Things: A Case Study," *IEEE Internet of Things Journal*, vol. 5, no. 2, pp. 1275–1284, 2018.

43. F. N. Nwebonyi, R. Martins and M. E. Correia, "Security and Fairness in IoT Based e-Health System: A Case Study of Mobile Edge-Clouds," in *Proceedings of 2019 International Conference on Wireless and Mobile Computing, Networking and Communications (WiMob)*, pp. 318–323, Barcelona, Spain, 2019.

44. T. Muhammed, R. Mehmood, A. Albeshri and I. Katib, "UbeHealth: A Personalized Ubiquitous Cloud and Edge-Enabled Networked Healthcare System for Smart Cities," *IEEE Access*, vol. 6, pp. 32258–32285, 2018.

45. X. Sun and N. Ansari, "EdgeIoT: Mobile Edge Computing for the Internet of Things," *IEEE Communications Magazine*, vol. 54, no. 12, pp. 22–29, December 2016.

46. T. Nguyen, E. Huh and M. Jo, "Decentralized and Revised Content-Centric Networking-Based Service Deployment and Discovery Platform in Mobile Edge Computing for IoT Devices," *IEEE Internet of Things Journal*, vol. 6, no. 3, pp. 4162–4175, June 2019.

47. M. A. Rahman, M. M. Rashid, M. S. Hossain, E. Hassanain, M. F. Alhamid and M. Guizani, "Blockchain and IoT-Based Cognitive Edge Framework for Sharing Economy Services in a Smart City," *IEEE Access*, vol. 7, pp. 18611–18621, 2019.

48. E. Björnson, O. Özdogan, and E. G. Larsson, "Intelligent Reflecting Surface vs. Decode-and-Forward: How Large Surfaces are Needed to Beat Relaying?" *IEEE Wireless Communications Letters*, vol. 9, no. 2, pp. 1–1, February 2020.

49. E. Basar, "Reconfigurable Intelligent Surface-Based Index Modulation: A New Beyond MIMO Paradigm for 6G," *IEEE Trans. Commun.*, vol. 68, no. 5, pp. 3187–3196, May 2020.

50. S. R. Sabuj, M. Hamamura and S. Kuwamura, "Detection of Intelligent Malicious User in Cognitive Radio Network by Using Friend or Foe (FoF) Detection Technique," in *Proceedings of 2015 International Telecommunication Networks and Applications Conference (ITNAC)*, pp. 155–160, Sydney, NSW, 2015.

51. S. R. Sabuj and M. Hamamura, "Random Cognitive Radio Network Performance in Rayleigh-Lognormal Environment," in *Proceedings of 2017 14th IEEE Annual Consumer Communications & Networking Conference (CCNC)*, pp. 992–997, Las Vegas, NV, 2017.

52. S. R. Sabuj and M. Hamamura, "Two-slope Path-loss Design of Energy Harvesting in Random Cognitive Radio Networks," *Computer Networks*, vol. 142, pp. 128–141, 2018.

53. S. R. Sabuj and M. Hamamura, "Energy Efficiency Analysis of Cognitive Radio Network Using Stochastic Geometry," in *Proceedings of 2015 IEEE Conference on Standards for Communications and Networking (CSCN)*, pp. 245–251, Tokyo, 2015.

54. N. Chen, Y. Yang, J. Li and T. Zhang, "A Fog-Based Service Enablement Architecture for Cross-Domain IoT Applications," in *Proceedings of 2017 IEEE Fog World Congress (FWC)*, pp. 1–6, Santa Clara, CA, USA, 2017.

55. H. Lu, Q. Liu, D. Tian, Y. Li, H. Kim and S. Serikawa, "The Cognitive Internet of Vehicles for Autonomous Driving," *IEEE Network*, vol. 33, no. 3, pp. 65–73, June 2019.

# Chapter 6

# Privacy of Edge Computing and IoT

*David G. Glance and Rachel Cardell-Oliver*

The University of Western Australia Crawley, Australia

## CONTENTS

## 6.1 INTRODUCTION

Individuals are adapting rapidly to the proliferation of IoT (Internet of Things) they interact with on a pervasive and continuous basis. Sensors are carried around in smartphones and other wearables, smart devices in the home are used to monitor, entertain, inform and carry out commands. Individuals will also interact with IoT in cars, on public transport and more generally in smart cities. Although all of the devices that individuals interact with serve distinct and specific purposes, they are all potentially capable of collecting personally identifiable information. Although the collection of this information in a personally identifiable form may be justifiable in order for the IoT device to fulfill its primary role, the danger to the privacy of the individual is that the data is subsequently used or sold for purposes that the individual was not aware of and also possibly had no means of consenting to before interacting with the devices that collected it.

IoT devices collect data about human activity and the environment. This sensor data can be used in combination with other sensor data where it may reveal unintended personal information. An example of this is a motion sensor in a smoke alarm that on its own can only report on the presence of movement in a space, but that can with other sensors, together with machine learning applied to the data they collect, calculate a profile of the Activities of Daily Living (ADL) of a person who occupies that space. The ability to use a group of IoT sensors to measure ADL could be important for allowing an elderly person to continue to live at home and be monitored for falls or other changes in their activities. ADL could also be used to measure and predict rates of deterioration in an illness and conversely state and rates of recovery. But all of this goes far beyond the imagined functionality of the individual sensors that the user puts in their personal space and beyond what they might have agreed to in terms of the individual privacy agreements that accompanied the specific sensors and the systems they used to collect and store data.

IoT data gathered from individuals is particularly valuable when combined into datasets for large populations. Population datasets can be used to train machine learning algorithms which can then be used for prediction or classification. Before it is shared, a user's IoT data is typically de-identified. That means all personal identifying information is removed from the shared data points. However, de-identification alone is not sufficient to protect privacy. Montjoye et al. (2013) demonstrated that in a mobility dataset with millions of users 95% of users could be uniquely identified using only four spatio-temporal points. In population data scenarios the use of an individual's data can be far removed from its original collection purpose. Protecting an individual's privacy in this de-coupled, population setting is a challenging problem.

Privacy is the ability for individuals or a group to protect their data from unauthorized use by third parties. Privacy in an IoT system is the system's ability to protect users' privacy. Edge devices connect a private sensor network, such as the sensors in a smart home, to an external network. Edge devices are information gateways that have sufficient resources to manage privacy policy and implementation. Edge computing refers to the algorithms and frameworks, including privacy protection, that run on edge devices. The devices are typically owned by the user and so can act as guardian for the user before their data is published to the wider world. Using edge devices to manage privacy is also efficient for performance because it distributes the processing load and limits data transmission. This chapter explores how edge computing can protect users' privacy and allow them to benefit from the functionality that IoT can deliver, at the same time as providing data to drive population applications using machine learning that could potentially benefit the wider community.

The complexity of privacy and security with IoT devices arises from the fact that IoT operate as an ecosystem of hardware, software, communications and networks. Personal data is collected by IoT device and can be transported over networks and stored and processed in multiple locations. One can conceptualize this as *sense spaces* that the IoT ecosystem creates through the IoT and their sensory realm. At the borders of these spaces there will be one or more edge devices that interface the IoT on the inside of the space to other edge devices or cloud services on the outside. For wearables the sense space is usually a person with the edge device being the person's smartphone. In the home, IoT would normally communicate with edge devices such as smart hubs, smart speakers or smart screens.

Edge devices define the boundary of a private space comprising the IoT sensors, the network they communicate over and the physical domain that is being sensed. All data collected by the sensors pass through the edge devices. At that point decisions can be made about what data is stored or shared, who can subsequently access it and under what conditions it is accessed. Edge devices have storage, processing power and potentially means of interacting with users either directly through physical interfaces such as screens or indirectly mediated through an application on a computer or smartphone. The potential for increasing user control of privacy through the edge device is far greater than if this is done through the IoT devices themselves or where raw data that has already been transferred to a remote location under an organization's control.

This chapter examines how edge computing can be used to protect users' privacy in IoT sense spaces. Section 6.2 provides an overview of the IoT ecosystem. Section 6.3 describes state-of-the-art technologies for privacy on edge devices with examples from Google Home and Apple HomeKit. Section 6.4 outlines four main technologies for privacy protection: authorization, de-identification, data obfuscation and encrypted query processing. A case study on contact tracing mobile phone apps shows how these technologies can be combined to achieve a high level of privacy. Section 6.5 summarizes existing standards, policy and regulation for privacy and edge IoT and Section 6.6 concludes the chapter.

## 6.2 IoT ECOSYSTEM

The OECD (OECD, 2015) defined the Internet of Things as:

> "An ecosystem in which applications and services are driven by data collected from devices that sense and interface with the physical world"

The structure of this IoT ecosystem can be split into four layers according to the functions carried out by those layers:

1. **Sensing/Acting**
   At a basic level, IoT digitalize the physical, analog, world through sensors and can potentially act on the physical world through actuators. They have limited local physical memory and storage.
2. **Communication/networking**
   IoT communicate with other devices through Machine-to-Machine communication (M2M). This includes edge devices that allow for communication outside of the local network that the IoT operate on. IoT may also be directly Internet accessible, as in the case of Internet-based cameras or with other application services that may be cloud-based.
3. **Data storage/computation**
   Data generated by IoT devices is communicated and stored through the use of databases and other middleware either on an **edge** device (a network device that controls data flow and has immediate or direct connection to the Internet or an external network), a mobile device or computer under an individual's local control, or through **cloud computing** where the data of many devices belonging to many users may be stored.
4. **Data aggregation and analytics/processing**
   This layer allows for the analysis of the data and the processing that can take actions based on that data. It also potentially provides user access to the digital representation of the world that is being managed by the IoT devices. This layer may be located at the **edge of a network,** a mobile device or computer, or scaled up through **cloud computing** to utilize big data techniques for analysis of the IoT data (Figure 6.1).

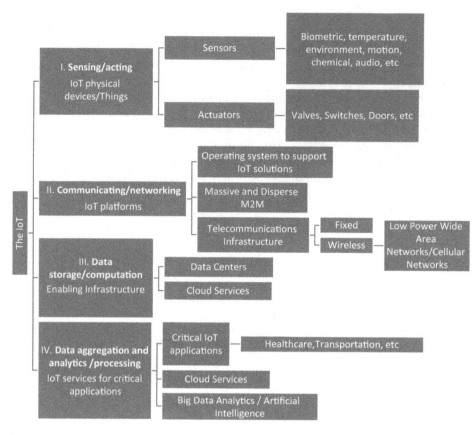

*Figure 6.1* IoT Ecosystem.

## 6.3 PRIVACY SPACES

From a privacy perspective, it is the data that IoT collects and the context under which this data is collected that defines its impact on an individual's privacy. Measuring movement of an individual in a home for example carries an expectation of privacy that is, by definition, largely absent when taken in the context of public spaces. It is useful to consider the field over which IoT operate as a 'Privacy Space' that we define as the space that a collection of IoT operate in to collect data through the range of their sensors. The boundary of the space is defined by one or more edge devices that are responsible for collecting data from these particular sensors. Edge devices operating on the boundary of a privacy space are also responsible for the security of the devices inside that space (Figure 6.2).

A Privacy Space also has other attributes that characterize the level of sensitivity of the data within it. This sensitivity corresponds to the notion of sensitive data defined by privacy regulations of a range of countries and includes the following:

- Health information
- Sexual preferences or practices
- Biometrics
- Personality
- Drug addictions
- Age

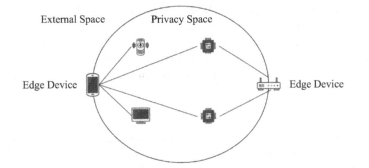

Figure 6.2 A Privacy Space is defined as a collection of IoT and an edge device at the border.

- Anything done or said within the Privacy Space
- Movement: where you go and when
- Interactions: whom you meet or come into contact with

Much of this data can be directly monitored or inferred from other data being collected in a Privacy Space.

Another characteristic of the data within a Privacy Space is the degree of control the individuals within the Privacy Space have over the data. If all the data stays within the Privacy Space and only leaves with the explicit understanding and consent of the Privacy Space owner. Once data has left a Privacy Space to the cloud that is controlled by a third party, the original owner of that data loses control and oversight of how the data will be used subsequently.

Other individuals who are not the owner of the Privacy Space may also be part of that Space. This is an important consideration because they may not even be aware that data about them is being collected. Their interests are implicitly delegated to the Privacy Space owner. Some of the participants in a Privacy Space may be minors and the owner their guardian or parent – but in other cases, it may be co-habiting individuals who have not agreed to delegate these rights (McKenna et al., 2012).

Multiple Privacy Spaces relating to an individual may collectively interoperate or be discrete. We may consider a Privacy Space consisting of IoT in a bedroom and a separate Privacy Space in the living room of a house. Separately they provide different information about the individuals living in those spaces. Indeed, the software and systems in both spaces may be created by different manufacturers and interact with different edge devices. Together however, the data from both living spaces provide a different perspective on the individual that could not be inferred from either of the Privacy Spaces individually.

## 6.4 THE TECHNOLOGY OF PRIVACY SPACES

IoT use a variety of protocols to communicate with edge devices including ZigBee, MQTT, CoAPP, AMQP, Thread, Z-Wave and Bluetooth Low Energy (BLE). In general, IoT, especially at the consumer level, implement a particular protocol to communicate with a hub device that can, in turn, connect to the Internet and to software that interacts with the device owner. Examples of distinct IoT systems include the Philips Hue[1], Google Home[2] and Apple HomeKit[3]. Each of these systems implements different communication technologies and protocols but they also differ in their approach to the Privacy Space they implement. As an illustration of this, we will consider the technical architectures of Apple's HomeKit and Google

Home that take different approaches to their treatment of data from a Privacy Space. In the case of Apple's HomeKit, the architecture uses an edge device to collect and store data from a Privacy Space without transmitting this data externally unless it is under the direct instruction of the owner after they have consented. Google Home processes all data collected within a Privacy Space in the cloud with little to no local storage and processing on an edge device.

### 6.4.1 Apple HomeKit

Apple's HomeKit provides a specification and framework for interfacing applications on an Apple device with an IoT. Commercial devices are required to certify with Apple according to a 'Made for iPhone' (MFi) certification. MFi used to require IoT devices to incorporate a security chip called a MFi chip, but this changed with iOS 11 to allow software-based authentication and encryption.

Once the device has been registered to HomeKit, it can be accessed only through the application on an Apple smart device (iPhone, iPad). Data can be synchronizedby the manufacturers' apps and potentially stored outside of the Privacy Space, but only with the consent of the user. Apple HomeKit does not allow background data collection and transportation. The app has to be run explicitly by the user. Some vendors of IoT devices have adopted this principle and highlight the fact that their IoT devices do not transmit data to the cloud and it all remains on the phone[4] (Figure 6.3).

Apple has also introduced HomeKit Routers which act to allow users control over how HomeKit IoT devices communicate. In particular, a "Restrict to Home" setting will restrict traffic from the devices to a home hub and not be allowed to leave that local network. This places some of the burden of controlling the access these devices have to the user and may have unintended side-effects such as not being able to update the device's firmware.

Another feature that Apple is introducing to implement further privacy through HomeKit is HomeKit Secure Video. This carries out processing of the video locally before video is encrypted and stored on iCloud, Apple's cloud backup system. Apple uses end-to-end encryption for Home data using keys that are generated by the user and so not available to Apple itself.

The principle behind Apple's strategy for HomeKit is to keep data within the Privacy Space and to give users control over what data can leave, and when it does, to ensure it is with the knowledge of the user and is encrypted before transportation.

Contrasting this approach taken by Apple is that taken by Google, which we will turn to next.

### 6.4.2 Google Home

Google operates an IoT architecture that has similarities to Apple's HomeKit. Google provides hub devices such as the Nest Hub Max and Nest Hub that have screens and the smart speaker-based hubs called Google Home.

Google takes a different approach to Apple's HomeKit when integrating IoT devices with their services, specifically the Google Assistant. Connecting a device so that it can communicate with Google Assistant to respond to commands requires a Cloud Service that can link accounts using OAuth (Figure 6.4)

This architecture is an example of loose coupling. Privacy of data on the IoT device is left up to the company providing the device, but there is no concept of keeping data confined to the Privacy Space.

Google abstracts devices for the purposes of interactions with Google Assistant. Each device has a device type that stipulates what class the device is such as a light or fan. Each

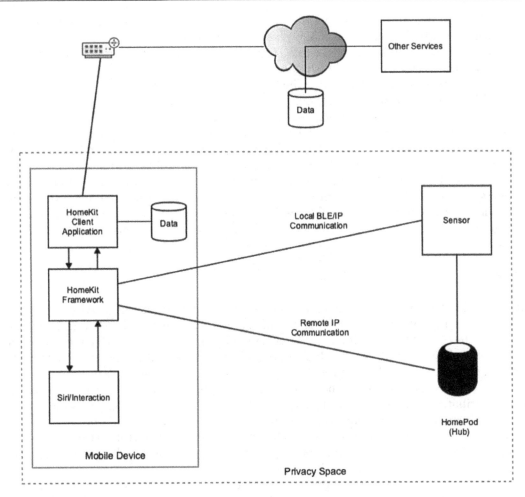

*Figure 6.3* Architecture of Apple HomeKit.

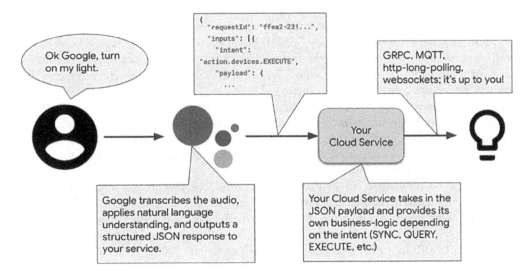

*Figure 6.4* Integration of an IoT device with Google Assistant.

device also has device traits which are the capabilities of the device. A light, for example, can be turned on or off, whereas a fan can have its speed altered.

Information about devices is stored in a Home Graph which adds contextual information such as the device's location within a home.

Google is updating the process by which commercial vendors of IoT devices can integrate with Google Nest products. This involves agreeing to Google's Device Access Terms of Service and submitting to a security assessment, among other things[5].

This does not alter the fundamental architecture which largely circumvents the use of an edge device to maintain the Privacy Space. Even if not all of the data is shared with Google, the architecture is such that data from the Privacy Space would be available in its entirety on a real-time basis with the cloud service of the provider. This is a good example of how Google's architectural choices determine what other companies are obliged to do to interoperate with a particular ecosystem. Whereas Apple's HomeKit enforces the Privacy Space to a large degree, Google encourages vendors to utilize cloud-based solutions.

## 6.5 PRIVACY SPACE DATA FLOWS

As can be seen from the two architectures detailed above, data from sensors within a Privacy Space are initially collected and potentially aggregated at the individual user level by an edge device. In the case of Google Home, the data simply flows directly out to different cloud services provided by the vendors of the IoT sensors. That data may individually be controlled by the user, but as soon as it has left the Privacy Space, the level of control that a user has over this data diminishes as soon as it has left the user's physical domain. Other users who may have contributed data, knowingly or otherwise, would have even less control as they would need to rely on the Privacy Space controller to ensure data privacy on their behalf.

This is not to say that privacy is not possible in this type of architecture. There are a range of technological techniques that could be applied to preserve privacy of the user who the data originated from which we will shortly discuss.

The control of data to preserve privacy needs to be balanced by the competing requirements of that data. There is the use of the data to train machine learning algorithms that could use the data from large numbers of users to personalize useful functionality for the individual users including managing their health and well-being. Much of the benefit of data from IoT sensors in a Privacy Space will only arise when combined with other data from within and also between other Privacy Spaces. For this to occur, there would need to be an overall interoperability provided by the framework that the IoT devices operate within. This is the case with Apple HomeKit, for example, but this relies on a proprietary system that is ultimately under the control of one company, Apple.

Another requirement might be the interchange of information between Privacy Spaces. An example of this would be data that is collected from sensors on a person's body being used in combination with data from a Privacy Space that is that person's home. In this situation, different edge devices could communicate with each other, exchanging information that allowed for software to use to direct some action.

An example of how different Privacy Spaces could collaborate through the sharing of data is in the measurement and tracking of human Activity of Daily Living (ADL). In the past an ADL assessment would have been performed by human observation or questioning with the aim of establishing a baseline from which any subsequent differences can be compared (Eakin, 1989). In an IoT-enabled household, aggregated data from IoT can be used to recognize activities automatically by comparing the values against machine learning models (Wan et al., 2017) (Figure 6.5).

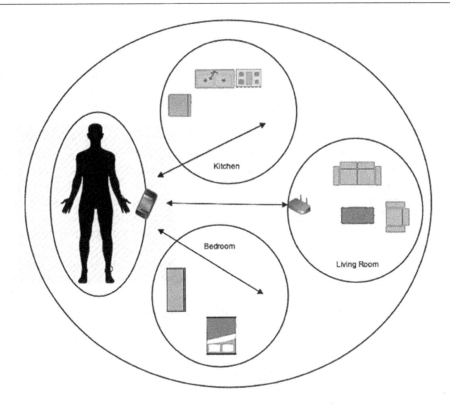

*Figure 6.5* Collaborating Privacy Spaces to calculate and monitor activities of daily living.

## 6.6 REMOTE ACCESS

A system such as the one outlined to measure ADL would not need to share this data outside of the overall Privacy Space. However, there are reasons why a person might be asked to share some, or all of the data, with third parties. The first might be for remote monitoring purposes by a doctor, health worker, family member or security firm that is able to respond in an emergency. Another reason for sharing might be to contribute the data for the purpose of health research or ongoing refinement and training of the machine learning models that the system is itself using.

Returning to Apple HomeKit, remote access to data from HomeKit devices is done through the mediation of iCloud, Apple's cloud services working with the HomeKit Home Hub device such as the Apple TV, HomePod or iPad. Data and settings are shared via iCloud. Communication is still performed over encrypted sessions and authenticated using a user's iCloud account. Remote access in this way has the same guarantees as local access that it has to be done explicitly under the user's control.

## 6.7 PERSONAL DATA STORE

If data from IoT in Privacy Spaces is preserved by edge devices, this data could be stored collectively within a Personal Data Store that itself resides on an edge device. Access to this data store could be controlled, dictating who the data is shared with and how that data is shared. We have already mentioned HomeKit above that controls data collected and distributed to other applications. Two data stores that manage different data from HomeKit as personal data stores are Apple's Home application and Health. Both of these stores control consenting process by which data is shared with other users. The issue with this approach however is that the personal data stores are of a proprietary format, still very much under the control of Apple. Backup of this data is end-to-end encrypted using device data and the device passcode, and so the security of this data relies on keeping the 6-digit passcode secret. Of course, if at any time, another application has been allowed access to the raw Home or Health data, then the data in the personal data store is no longer solely under the control of the owner.

A different type of Personal Data Store is illustrated by the openPDS project (Montjoye et al., 2014). Although this personal data store is aimed at a user's general app usage metadata, it illustrates an approach where underlying raw data is not provided to third parties but instead allows queries to be executed on the dataset to return a specific answer. This type of approach will be discussed in detail below, but at present, it suffices to illustrate a mechanism by which data can be stored on an edge device and the control of its underlying data maintained as the owner.

In practice, it is likely that there will be multiple Personal Data Stores that relate to specific Privacy Spaces and potentially deal with different classes of data. Three that have been outlined above are Home, Health and Internet Metadata, but one could imagine other stores relating to the Privacy Space in a car or GPS data relating to movement through public spaces.

## 6.8 PRIVACY-PRESERVING TECHNIQUES

As mentioned above, there are many potential benefits of being able to share data between Privacy Spaces and with third parties like researchers and health organizations. The owner of the data may simply also decide that the data has economic value and share it on a commercial or exchange-for-use basis. In order for this to be possible, guarantees need to be made to the owner that (Ziegeldorf et al., 2014):

- They are made aware of the privacy risks imposed by IoT and the software and services that make use of data provided by IoT.
- They will be provided with potential individual control over the collection and processing of personal information and data from IoT.
- They are made aware of, and are able to control, subsequent use and dissemination of personal information by the organizations deploying IoT and any other organization outside the subject's personal sphere of control.

While personal data stores on an edge device maintain control of data for the owner of that data, there need to be mechanisms by which data can be shared with specific authorized parties, ideally in a way that preserves privacy even once the data has left the Privacy Space.

Before data can be shared, there needs to be a mechanism by which the owner of the data is given notice about the request for personal information stating what the information will be used for, by whom, for how long and what the owner can do once the data has been shared. This notice obliges the owner to give informed consent, but the entire process has been frequently criticized for its many shortcomings (Lipman, 2016). With IoT, the obvious issue has been the fact that there is no way for IoT devices to provide proper notice given the absence of screens or in fact, a mechanism to interact with the device. Edge devices can provide a better way of providing notice and obtaining consent before data is even collected in the first place by providing a screen and a better mechanism for informing the data owner.

A full discussion about the complexity of notice and consent with IoT is beyond the scope of this chapter and we are going to focus on general technical approaches to preserving privacy on the assumption that informed consent has been obtained after appropriate notice.

Methods for protecting the privacy of data, especially in the context of data stored on an edge device, fall into two main approaches: anonymization of the data before sharing and controlling queries on the data on the device in such a way that they are privacy preserving and do not reveal personal, identifying information. We will look at these two approaches in turn.

## 6.8.1 Anonymization

Anonymization aims to anonymize personal data by removing any personally identifying information before that data is shared. There are many methods for anonymizing data. For example, a user's name and address can be replaced by a randomly assigned customer identification variable. However, this approach alone is not sufficient to protect privacy because individuals can potentially be re-identified using quasi-identifier variables: identifiers that are not unique but through their combination can be sufficiently correlated to enable re-identification of an individual. The risk of this type of attack is sometimes referred to as 'Prosecutor Risk' (El Emam & Dankar, 2008) since it involves the de-identification of a specific individual through pre-existing knowledge. A second risk or re-identification of anonymized data is referred to as 'Journalist Risk' and also through the use of other datasets that provide side channels to enable re-identification of a random group of people.

Three different approaches to anonymization of data are $k$-anonymity, unicity and epsilon-differential privacy. Each tries to balance the trade-off between privacy through anonymity and being able to use the data for analysis and research.

## 6.8.2 k-Anonymization

A popular way of anonymizing a dataset is to use k-anonymity (Loukides & Shao, 2007) that aims to provide anonymity while preserving utility of the data.

A dataset with data about individuals has $k$-anonymity if an attacker cannot distinguish any individual from at least $k-1$ other individuals present in a dataset. $k$-anonymity can be achieved by suppression, generalization or global recoding (El Emam & Dankar, 2008). Suppression involves removing individuals with distinctive features from the dataset that can also be achieved by generalization, i.e., by reducing the dimensionality of the raw data though various forms of aggregation. For example, reporting hourly or daily demand in a smart metering application uniquely identifies fewer individuals than 1- to 15-minute readings. Finally, global recoding involves replacing sensitive identifiers with ranges or other codes. An age of 27, for example, could be replaced by the interval 20–29.

AnonySense is an architecture based on collaborative, opportunistic sensing by mobile devices (Cornelius et al., 2008). Participating users can be asked to complete submitted sensing tasks when the opportunity arises. AnonySense uses an anonymity-protecting protocol to distribute sensing tasks and retrieve user reports. The protocol provides secure task assignment and data report collection. The system aims to provide k-anonymity by blurring, or obfuscating, location data at the edge before the data is sent anonymously to a server.

Obfuscating sensor data obscures the original data by hiding some information or adding noise in order to enhance privacy. The same sensor time series can be represented in different ways and this property can be used to make trade-offs between the utility of the data for external analysis and privacy for the user who owns the sensor data. But obfuscation may also impact utility. Sharing the original series maximizes utility for further analysis but likely also compromises users' privacy.

In the case of AnonySense, locations are obfuscated using a *tessellation* approach. This works by mapping the location of an individual to a *tile* that is a region that k users normally visit during a typical time interval. This ensures that any given individual cannot be identified uniquely among a group of k other users.

### 6.8.3  Unicity

Unicity is a metric designed for mobility data to quantify the re-identifiability of a dataset (Montjoye et al., 2013). It determines uniqueness for a set of location traces given $I_p$ a specific set of $p$ spatio-temporal points. The tester finds the set of users whose trajectories match $p$ points in $I_p$. If the size of this set is 1 then the point set $I_p$ uniquely identifies an individual. Unicity is the proportion of such unique traces for $p$ randomly chosen points, i.e., the ratio of uniquely identified individuals to all individuals. The closer E is to 1 the lower the privacy of the dataset since a high proportion of individuals are uniquely identified. If the dataset has E = 0 then no users are uniquely identified. For a mobile phone dataset for 1.4 million people, it was shown that using sets of only $p$ = 4 spatio-temporal points was sufficient to uniquely characterize 95% of users (Montjoye et al., 2013).

### 6.8.4  Differential Privacy

Differential privacy is a system for publicly sharing information about a dataset by describing the patterns of groups of individuals within the dataset while withholding information about individuals in the dataset (Dwork, 2011). Suppose the raw data has been processed by some function K. For example, an origin–destination matrix is a summary of a mobility dataset where $c_{ij}$ is the number of times a trip is made from any origin $i$ to $j$. The resulting data is differentially private if by looking only at the output you cannot tell whether any individual's data was in the dataset or not. That guarantee must hold for any dataset. Intuitively, it captures the increased risk to an individual's privacy that is incurred by participating in a database. The idea is that if there is a very small probability of distinguishing between the published output from a dataset when one individual is or is not included, then that dataset protects privacy.

Formally (Dwork, 2006), a randomized algorithm K gives $\epsilon$-differential privacy if for all datasets D and $D^t$ differing on at most one row (one individual), and all $S \subseteq range(K)$,

$$\Pr\big[K(D) \in S\big] \leq \exp(\epsilon) \times \Pr\big[K(D') \in S\big]$$

$\epsilon$ is typically a value such as 0.01, 0.1.

A concrete mechanism for achieving $\epsilon$-differential privacy is to add appropriate random noise to the answer of a query function $f$ on a database X. Suppose the answer is $a = f(X)$ then for an appropriately chosen noise parameter, Each output $a$ is perturbed by adding a random value drawn from a Laplace distribution $L(0, p)$.

Differential privacy is increasingly used as a technique to anonymize data that is collected by mobile phone. Apple has adopted a *local model* of differential privacy where the data collected on a phone is randomized before being shared (Apple, 2017). The central model of differential privacy always leaves open the possibility that the raw data is used instead of the anonymized data.

## 6.8.5 Privacy-Preserving Data Queries

Controlling access to information in a database as a security or privacy measure is well known in the field of information security. Privacy can be preserved in a database by only allowing summarization methods to execute against the data that aims to represent the salient features of the data while preserving its information content (Ahmed, 2019). Summarization methods include statistical summaries of the data such as the mean, standard deviation, moving averages, clusters, table summaries or rules. The exact level of summarization that is provided will depend on what the data needs to be used for. In the example of a smart water or electricity meter time series (McKenna et al., 2012), the sub-second to minute temporal data can be used to identify the use of specific appliances by their demand signature. The electricity demands for a fridge, kettle or washing machine each having a unique signature which is visible at a fine temporal grain but obscured if the data is aggregated to 15 minutes, hourly or more.

On the other hand, hourly data for water or electricity can show occupancy whether a house is occupied or not, and potentially by how many people. Daily or quarterly data exposes only the mean electricity or water demand of a household.

In the spatial domain, data can be aggregated by a single power point, a wiring circuit or the whole house. This spatial aggregation does not protect privacy on its own, because devices are often used one at a time, and so with fine temporal granularity it is still possible to identify specific devices. However, when combined with temporal aggregation, spatial aggregation does enhance privacy. Another type of aggregation coarsens the units used for reporting values. For example, if water use is reported to the nearest Liter or less, then it is straightforward to distinguish between activities by the rate of water use. However, by reporting to the nearest 10 L or 1000 L users' privacy about their activities is enhanced.

As mentioned previously, *openPDS* is a personalized framework that allows users to manage the collection and storage of their data and sharing their data with third parties via *SafeAnswers* (Montjoye et al., 2014) Instead of trying to anonymize individuals' metadata, users store their metadata in a personal data store. SafeAnswers allows services to ask questions of an individual's data store (Montjoye et al., 2014). This system uses the data obfuscation approach: a user protects their privacy by reducing the dimensionality of the data before it is released.

How does the user know the required level of data aggregation to protect their privacy? Suitable functions can be decided by rules learned from previous datasets. For example, the 4 spatial-temporal location points rule could be used to decide the appropriate release granularity of personal mobility data (Montjoye et al., 2013). Similarly, rules learned from linked datasets can guide the level of dimension reduction required for protection. The user of SafeAnswers can also monitor possible querying attacks on their data store using anomaly detection methods to check for suspicious behavior such as high rates of querying. The main advantage of the openPDS approach is that the users own their data and maintain control of it. However, it makes the assumption that the user is able to determine 'safe' dimension reduction methods. There can be no guarantee that the user will not be identifiable in a population dataset.

## 6.9 CASE STUDY: CONTACT TRACKING MOBILE APPLICATIONS

Each of the privacy-preserving techniques described above can be used alone or in combination to further enhance privacy. In this section, we illustrate the benefits of the combined approach by considering the privacy implications of two different approaches to contact tracking applications that have been taken during the Covid-19 pandemic: Singapore's TraceTogether initiative (TraceTogether, 2020) and the Apple and Google Privacy-Preserving Contact Tracing initiative (PPCTI) (Apple, 2020). This is a good example of how data from Privacy Spaces can be exchanged with the consent of the respective owners while preserving anonymity. The essential difference between the two approaches is whether a third party has visibility of personal information about the individuals involved. In the TraceTogether approach, each participant registers with the central service and is provided with cryptographic tokens to exchange with other contacts. In the case of the Apple and Google approach, keys are generated on the mobile device and central authorities have no visibility of who the contacts of an infected individual are. The details of these protocols will become clear as they are described.

TraceTogether is a mobile-phone-based application designed to improve the traditional manual process of tracing the contacts of someone who has been diagnosed with Covid-19. Users download the TraceTogether app and in doing so consent to sharing their contact data with a trusted central server: The Ministry of Health of the Government of Singapore. The app downloads TempIds from the central server (Bay et al., 2020). These TempIds are unique encrypted tokens that have a set expiry time of 15 minutes that can be exchanged with other app users via BLE to indicate a contact encounter.

By using time-varying tokens the app aims to provide *anonymization* with respect to the information provided to other individuals. However, the BLE messages also contain details of the mobile device models that are involved, and this alone may be sufficient to identify specific individuals.

In the case of a positive diagnosis of Covid-19 infection by an individual, they are asked to consent to the upload of their contact information that is stored on the device. This is then used to identify potential contacts over the previous 21 days by a health authority who can then use the decrypted TempIds provided to identify and contact individuals concerned.

The Apple and Google PPCTI takes a different approach with the tokens that are generated coming from the phones themselves and do not involve a centralized server to allocate them. Likewise, there is no requirement to register with a service when using the app. In the case of a positive diagnosis, an individual can agree to upload Diagnosis Keys with a central server. These keys do not provide any information about individual contacts. The keys can then be released to be downloaded by all users running the app which then checks if these keys are in their individual lists of contacts. If so, they can then elect to notify the health authorities or self-isolate. Keys are only released on validation that the individual providing them was diagnosed with a positive test.

The two approaches taken by these contact tracing applications are good illustrations of the trade-offs made when balancing individual privacy using a decentralized system with the benefits to the health authorities and society generally of allowing for a centralized management of the system. In the case of the PPCTI, the health authority has no visibility into the extent of possible contacts and would still need to rely entirely on conventional contact tracing mechanisms. In the case of TraceTogether, the data collected from the app may provide support to these conventional means of contact tracing in identifying contacts that the Covid-19 positive individual may have forgotten, or didn't know, that they encountered.

Researchers have suggested ways in which the protocols of the TraceTogether app could be modified to increase privacy without compromising their utility for tracking contacts. One approach is to replace the proactive role of the central server in contacting people by allowing users to poll the central server sending a list of their contacts for confirmation of whether or not they have been in touch with an infected person (Cho et al., 2020). This solution is still susceptible to linkage attacks, where a user can time their queries in order to identify an infected person, especially where the number of contacts has been low. The polling approach can be improved by mixing, in which infected users divide their tokens and send them to many different servers. These servers combine the tokens from multiple infected users and send those to the central server. Other versions of this idea split the roles of the authority parties in such a way as to preserve the privacy of people's interactions (Bell et al., 2020). The mixing approach protects against linkage attacks by *obfuscating* the identity of contact reporters.

## 6.10 CONCLUSIONS

Edge devices are capable of protecting privacy of data collected from sensors that exist within a set of Privacy Spaces relating to an individual. That data can be subsequently shared in both its raw form that may include personal information or in a privacy-preserving manner. In contrast, where data from IoT devices is preserved on the cloud, the privacy of that data rests solely in the hands of the company providing that service.

There are disadvantages to the use of edge devices to preserve privacy. To begin with, a great onus is placed on the Privacy Space owner to manage the data under their control. This data may be that of other individuals who have spent time there or in fact share the space on an ongoing basis. One disadvantage is that processing of data for the purposes of monitoring is limited by the requirements that all uses of data be under the control of the user and usually when applications are running in the foreground.

The case study of contact tracing illustrates other trade-offs between privacy-preserving sharing of data between Privacy Spaces as exemplified by the Apple/Google contact tracing framework and the centralized approach taken by the Singapore Government with the TraceTogether application. The technical decisions taken in these approaches are based on wider social considerations with regard to public health and safety versus preserving privacy at all costs. The fact that there are technical solutions to preserving privacy in this manner does not necessarily mean that those solutions are acceptable to the societies that they operate in.

## NOTES

1. Philips Hue https://www2.meethue.com
2. Google Home https://store.google.com/product/google_home
3. Apple HomeKit https://www.apple.com/au/ios/home
4. https://www.evehome.com/en/privacy
5. https://developers.nest.com/guides/tos

## REFERENCES

Ahmed, M. (2019). Data summarization: A survey. *Knowledge and Information Systems*, 58(2):249–273.

Apple. (2017). Learning with privacy at scale. Accessed from https://machinelearning.apple.com/docs/learning-with-privacy-at-scale/appledifferentialprivacysystem.pdf on May 8th 2020.

Apple. (2020). Privacy-preserving contact tracing. Accessed from https://www.apple.com/covid19/contacttracing/ on May 11th 2020.

Bay, J., Kek, J., Tan, A., Hau, C.S., Yongquan, L., Tan, J., Quy, T.A. (2020). BlueTrace: A privacy-preserving protocol for community-driven contact tracing across borders. Accessed from https://bluetrace.io/static/bluetrace_whitepaper-938063656596c104632def383eb33b3c.pdf on May 11th 2020.

Bell, J., Butler, D., Hicks, C., and Crowcroft, J. (2020). TraceSecure: Towards privacy preserving contact tracing.

Cho, H., Ippolito, D., and Yu, Y. W. (2020). Contact tracing mobile apps for COVID-19: Privacy considerations and related trade-offs.

Cornelius, C., Kapadia, A., Kotz, D., Peebles, D., Shin, M., and Triandopoulos, N. (2008). AnonySense: Privacy-aware people-centric sensing. In *Proceeding ACM 6th International Conference on Mobile Systems, Applications and Services (Mobisys)*, pages 211–224.

Dwork, C. (2006). Differential privacy. In *Lecture Notes in Computer Sci- ence (including subseries Lecture Notes in Artificial Intelligence and Lecture Notes in Bioinformatics)*, 4052 LNCS, pages 1–12.

Dwork, C. (2011). A firm foundation for private data analysis. *Commu- nications of the ACM*, 54(1):86–95.

Eakin, P. (1989). Assessment of activities of daily living: A critical review. *British Journal of Occupational Therapy*, 52(1):11–15.

El Emam, K., Dankar, F.D. (2008). Protecting privacy using k-anonymity. *Journal of the American Medical Informatics Association*, 2008(15):627–637. doi: 10.1197/jamia.M2716

Lipman, R. (2016). Online privacy and the invisible market for our data (January 18, 2016). 120 Penn State Law Review 777. Accessed at SSRN: https://ssrn.com/abstract=2717581

Loukides, G., & Shao, J. (2007, March). Capturing data usefulness and privacy protection in k-anonymisation. In *Proceedings of the 2007 ACM Symposium on Applied Computing*, pp. 370–374.

McKenna, E., Richardson, I., and Thomson, M. (2012). Smart meter data: Balancing consumer privacy concerns with legitimate applications. *Energy Policy*, 41:807–814.

Montjoye, Y.-a. D., Hidalgo, C. A., Verleysen, M., and Blondel, V. D. (2013). Unique in the crowd: The privacy bounds of human mobility. *Scientific Reports*, 3(1376):1–5.

Montjoye, Y.-a. D., Shmueli, E., Wang, S. S., and Pentland, A. S. (2014). OpenPDS: Protecting the privacy of metadata through SafeAnswers. *PloS one*, 9(7):e98790.

OECD. (2015). Digital security risk management for economic and social prosperity. doi: 10.1787/9789264245471-en

Shafagh, H. (2018). *Retaining Data Ownership in the Internet of Things*. Phd, ETH Zurich.

Shafagh, H., Hithnawi, A., Droescher, A., Duquennoy, S., and Hu, W. (2015). Talos: Encrypted query processing for the internet of things. In *Proceedings of the 13th ACM Conference on Embedded Networked Sensor Systems - SenSys '15*, pages 197–210, New York, NY, USA. ACM Press.

TraceTogether. 2020 Accessed from https://bluetrace.io on May 11th 2020.

Wan, J., Gu, X., Chen, L., Wang, J. (2017). Internet of things for ambient assisted living: Challenges and future opportunities. In *International Conference on Cyber-Enabled Distributed Computing and Knowledge Discovery*. IEEE.

Ziegeldorf, J. H., Morchon, O. G. and Wehrle, K. (2014). Privacy in the Internet of Things: Threats and challenges. *Security and Communication Networks*, 7: 2728–2742. doi:10.1002/sec.795.

# Section II

Chapter 7

# Reducing the Attack Surface of Edge Computing IoT Networks via Hybrid Routing Using Dedicated Nodes

*James Jin Kang, Leslie F. Sikos, and Wencheng Yang*
Edith Cowan University, Perth, Australia

## CONTENTS

## 7.1 INTRODUCTION

As edge computing increases in prevalence and more enterprises deploy use cases to share topologies, processes and technologies, challenges arise in the areas of equipment and device management, security and data management and architecture [1]. This chapter focuses on how edge computing deployment can be secured when the deployment location is beyond their control or management capacity. In heterogeneous network environments, such as IoT networks across various autonomous systems from a source node to a destination node, one viable solution is to avoid suspicious networks while maintaining the highest possible security level, such as by focusing on defending against MITM attacks.

The popularity of Internet of Things (IoT) devices has led to them gradually replacing or integrating embedded sensors with Internet connectivity capabilities. IoT devices are being increasingly used for applications such as smart environments (smart homes, smart grids), and edge computing have now become closer to the devices that generate and collect data using an inference algorithm for efficient data processing [2]. The development and mainstream deployment of 5G networks will provide more rapid transmission speeds and wider bandwidth capacities which would enable the necessary conditions for widespread uptake and usage of IoT sensor devices within our daily activities and environments. One example of an IoT-integrated private network is the use of a Low-Power Wide Area Network (LPWAN) to manage large geographical areas, such as in agriculture or in bushfire disaster monitoring applications [3]. Another example of a private network which consists largely of IoT devices is Wireless Body Area Networks (WBAN), which use personal IoT-enabled devices such as wearable sensors that collect and handle sensitive personal data [4].

These aforementioned private networks are typically connected to the public network and can access the Internet, which may have a functional relationship with the private network such as in mediating the transfer of data for storage to a cloud server or for accessing outsourced services. The Internet is vastly more complex in its network composition, and it is almost a certainty that packets traveling from a source would pass through various sub-networks, both trusted and untrusted, in its journey to the destination. There is little assurance given to users or IoT devices regarding the security of these sub-networks, and little control is afforded outside of the private network [5]. In light of this situation, it is therefore of great importance to be able to determine the possibility of an attack, for example whether adversaries may be observing traffic leaving the private network and transiting through other networks.

There are a few useful packet analysis tools to inspect content of the packet to identify suspicious traffic [6]. *Tcpdump*[1] is very simple but useful to examine individual packets and sequence of communication flows. Firewalls are widely used to screen for bad packets (every packet, unless they have been endorsed by a trusted certificate authority (CA), which will classify packets based on the layer 2 and layer 3 headers, such as the credit score rating system against a predefined database. Application-aware firewalls, also called next-generation firewalls, operate at a high level to identify applications, which send packets to pass through firewalls. Web application firewalls can block specific sites or types of Internet traffic by inspecting web traffic. While traditional port matching has been widely used to identify packets with layer 4, deep packet inspection (DPI) inspects headers and payload unencrypted to identify the originating network applications. It ensures data to be in a correct format, and in the case of malicious codes, actions to block, re-route and log events. Port mirroring, also called Span Port, is a common way to acquire packets. Deep flow inspection (DFI) is 'a packet filtering technique that analyzes statistical characteristics like packet lengths, ratio of large packets and small payload standard deviation, and connection behavior of flows, to determine the actions to be applied to application flow or session packets' [7].

Machine learning constitutes algorithms such as Bayesian classification, support vector machines and C4.5 [8] is used to identify traffic based on traffic and packet characteristics for decision-making. They enable the full automation of DPI by detecting against registered or predefined rules as well as traffic patterns, which can be hard to detect by individual packet inspections.

This chapter focuses primarily on the detection of man-in-the-middle (MITM) attacks, particularly when the attacks are actively in progress and when there is a risk that messages are being tampered with or manipulated during transmission. Eavesdropping is not considered to be an active attack within this context, due to the fact that there is no modification to the data. During message manipulation, there is a substantial delay in transmission and communication time that can be observed, and the solution being proposed utilizes these observations. While there have been multiple routing protocols, e.g. [9], which focus on improving packet travel time and overall network capacity, none have been designed with the ability to detect anomalies in packet exchange time durations for the purpose of attack detection.

The routing protocol outlined in this chapter is integrated with an anomaly detection mechanism that determines the likelihood of data manipulation by a potential MITM attacker and classifies traffic accordingly The protocol provides for a consistent transmission time with little variability, enabling a predefined time threshold to be set with which time delays can be measured. This then allows for the assumption that unexpected delays and/or differences between source and destination travel times could represent a possible MITM attack. Additionally, a trusted third party (TTP) is used in the solution in order to account for the differences in performance from multiple networks. The use of this protocol at a network level enables this anomaly detection mechanism and time measurement to be enabled without requiring IoT sensors and devices to implement this on a device level.

This chapter is based on a previously published study [10] and extends it with additional insights. An enhanced hybrid routing method is used, which combines a defined static route with dynamic routes between a source and the destination [10] and uses probability analysis to understand the effect of a dedicated node on routing efficiency. Having dedicated devices with increased battery and computational capacity would offer three main benefits: 1) to be able to define secure pathways within the network and avoiding routing through suspicious or untrusted nodes/networks, 2) help stabilize travel time (by reducing fluctuations) within a trusted time server (TTS) that would result in more accurate time estimations and 3) allow for packets to be inspected through security checks. TTS servers across heterogeneous servers are synchronized with the use of a centralized server which also uses a software-defined wide area network (SD-WAN). This will improve IoT network security by enabling real-time detection of intruders.

The structure of this chapter is organized as follows: Section 7.2 provides an overview of related and relevant literature in the area; Section 7.3 presents an overview of the high-level solution design; Section 7.4 explains the test methodology and the simulation environment; a case study of the proposed method is presented in Section 7.5 and Section 7.6 ends with the conclusion.

## 7.2 RELATED WORKS

Dynamic routing protocols are widely used to improve packet routing efficiency through the Internet; however, it does not necessarily result in the best throughput [11]. Many attempts have been made to find the best routing option for wireless sensor networks, focusing on protocols with data transmission that is reliable [12], secure, trustworthy [13], cluster-based [14] and have prolonged and stable routings [15]. Messages are often relayed in order to maximize energy efficiency given the limitations of battery and computational power of sensors within wireless sensor networks. Luo et al. [16] proposed an algorithm to improve network performance, hence minimizing power consumption during data relay with low residual energy. Shen et al. achieved an improvement in performance of packet delivery with the use of a normalized routing overhead [12]. A comparison and analysis between three different forms of routing protocols were made, which included reactive, proactive and geographic types. The characteristics that were compared were latency, resource usage, overhead and effectiveness. They found that sufficient reliability and message transmission validity could be achieved using a location-aware routing protocol.

Wang et al. [9] focused on routing efficiency in order to improve overall network capacity as well as data packet travel time by combining both static and dynamic routing. Larger degree nodes were used to achieve this by generating an optimal parameter value, which combines local static and dynamic information and proposes a similar strategy. However, the methodology was not based on this and instead an additional address field was introduced to contain the transit, source and destination addresses within the header field. Section 7.3 expands on this aspect in greater detail.

Improvements have been made in sensor networks that focus on routing protocols; however, the literature has not addressed solutions that establish route paths which generate consistent transmission times with minimal time variance. Time variance is important to infer and determine the likelihood of an active MITM attack as time is required for adversaries to establish a session after breaching into a network.

The implementation of a software-defined network (SDN) on already existing switches as a form of hybrid network offers a feasible and cost-effective alternative than replacing an entire network to SDN. A spanning tree protocol could be used to implement this in order to have a global view of older legacy switches and the hybrid network through the use of a learning bridge protocol. This would overcome the need of having to change older, legacy switches [17].

Traffic engineering (TE) within IP networking and routing has been used extensively to maximize efficiency of network resources. Both intra-domain as well as inter-domain traffic have been extensively studied, with several protocols such as Open Shortest Path First (OPSF) and Intermediate System-Intermediate System (IS-IS). These protocols work to provide optimal TE by splitting traffic evenly across the shortest paths, using link weights by link state routing with hop-by-hop forwarding [18–20]. Segment Routing TE has been proposed to simplify route enforcement and provides a framework that allows the integration of the SDN paradigm and to overcome the issue of traditional per-flow routing which would require direction interaction from other nodes in the traffic pathway and the SDN controller [21]. The Segment Routing proposed by the Internet Engineering Task Force (IETF) splits the routing path into different segments to improve network utilization. This also allows for finer control over routing paths to route traffic through middle boxes [22].

The SDN separates the control and forwarding data layers, the TE is able to improve network resources and design reasonable routing mechanisms for more effective network utilization. SDN can benefit from TE with a centralized control that can monitor and analyze network traffic in real-time and apply rules rapidly and in an efficient manner to meet quality of service (QoS) requirements [23]. Wei et al. [24] proposed an energy aware TE with the use of hybrid SDN and IP backbone networks. This uses a quick heuristic algorithm for multi-path routing and splitting traffic flow by the SDN controller. TE usually relies on a network configuration with static link weights to split traffic between the shortest paths through the equal-cost multi-path (ECMP). An optimal link weight configuration can be achieved by a TE with ECMP, therefore achieving optimal traffic distribution without the need to change forwarding mechanisms or the routing protocols [25–27].

Maintaining and guaranteeing a high level of network optimization and QoS is a challenge for larger scale networks. One way to overcome this challenge is to use the Resource Description Framework (RDF)[2] that captures contextual information for network path estimation, as well as data inferring at the node via automated reasoning prior to transmitting on to the next hop [28, 29]. Multiprotocol Label Switching (MPLS) is a popular protocol that is used by Internet Service Providers and can be combined with SDN network frameworks. MPLS TE is proposed as a dynamic, smart and efficient model for bandwidth management and allocation to manage QoS, SDN and legacy network equipment [30].

To summarize our literature findings, there has been little focus on current routing protocols to establish route paths with consistent transmission times and variation; thus, these protocols are not suitable for effectively detecting anomalies in data transmission times. Several works relating to SDN TE and popular protocols, e.g. MPLS, have been conducted; however, they have not used the approach of a dedicated node for traffic pass-through for specific purposes such as avoiding untrusted or suspicious networks and ASes.

## 7.3 THE SOLUTION

The proposed solution consists for four core functions.

### 7.3.1 Inference System of Trusted Time Server

Once a service is registered with a CA for sender A, and the TTS is triggered with session details (these could include timestamps and source/destination addresses), an inference algorithm is activated to check a threshold value. This threshold value is determined by the inferencing system at the TTS, which works by identifying anomalies in comparison to previous route information already determined between a sender and receiver. An existing CA can be used, which will notify a TTS to gain access to that service. An overview of the server and access flow design is described in more detail in [31].

It is necessary to have an appointed TTS that has reliable network access to the Internet when being used in private networks such as LPWANs that cover a large geographical area and consist of many wireless sensors/devices. Many sensors may only have a simple function, such as collecting data and transferring to a cluster head device which could be equipped with greater battery and computational capacities.

### 7.3.2 Security Features

Sensor nodes in an LPWAN (e.g. Sigfox, NB-IoT, LoRa and DASH7 [32]) are typically battery-powered and these power constraints pose a challenge when implementing security measures for them. Such nodes are designed with simple functions in mind such as data gathering and data transfer to a nearby node as according to the routing protocol. Therefore, there are often minimal or simple security/cryptography methods suitable for wireless networks. A gateway device can have much greater capabilities, such as a range of up to 50 kilometers which contrasts to more simplified and limited sensor devices. It is more effective to therefore implement full or complex security features at the gateway as well as dedicated cluster head nodes. IoT networks are at risk of attacks such as replay, jamming and wormhole attacks. Therefore, the aforementioned gateways and/or cluster head nodes which have access to the Internet are required to have strong security features within large IoT networks [33].

Authentication of IoT devices is critical to IoT security and can help prevent unauthorized access to IoT networks. For a long time, using passwords or passphrases used to be the only way to authenticate users in computing systems, but times have changed. Over the past decade, biometrics has evolved rapidly, spreading to almost every part of our daily lives, offering a viable alternative to secure and reliable user authentication. With the proliferation of powerful IoT devices, the winning combination of IoT devices and biometrics in the consumer market has made biometric authentication widely accepted. Gateways and cluster head nodes have relatively robust battery life and computing power and, as such, can be equipped with biometric authentication systems, thereby benefiting from the security and convenience this attractive authentication technology brings [34].

### 7.3.3 Synchronization with a Trusted Time Server

A CA can act as a TTP and can register a service request and subsequently allocate a TTS (for user A) for a user who may connect to a server in an LPWAN. Other TTSs can be available for the recipient (user B) once the session is established across heterogeneous AS networks. In this case, it is necessary to synchronize data with accurate timestamps and existing network timing protocols (NTP) can be used for this synchronization and security. A security mechanism has been recommended by IETF for network time synchronization protocols that are lightweight with minimal burden onto the network infrastructure [35, 36].

Figure 7.1 outlines the procedures in triggering CA and TTS, and Figure 7.2 outlines the establishing process of the call session across heterogeneous networks with dedicated nodes.

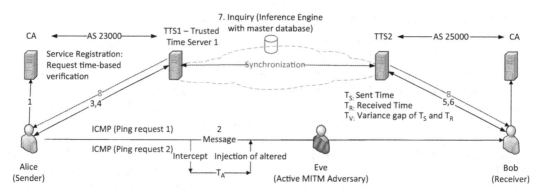

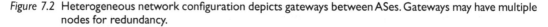

*Figure 7.1* Information flow of MITM attack detection scenario. TTS1 in Autonomous System (AS) 23000 are synchronized with servers in AS 25000 via a centralized server in the cloud.

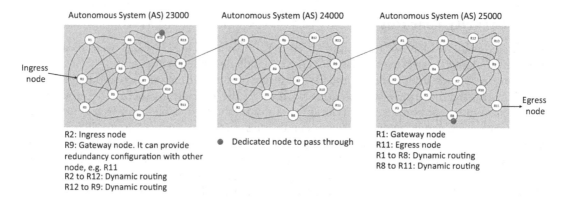

*Figure 7.2* Heterogeneous network configuration depicts gateways between ASes. Gateways may have multiple nodes for redundancy.

### 7.3.4 Transit Addresses

The transit, source and destination addresses for dedicated nodes are carried on an additional field at layer 3 header fields for IP routing. This would need to be accommodated for and is not considered within the scope of this chapter as it would require real-life discussion and protocol agreement by standards bodies such as International Telecommunication Union Telecommunication (ITU-T) Standardization Sector.

## 7.4 TEST METHODOLOGY AND ENVIRONMENT

The accuracy of the inference system can be measured by comparing the difference in the variance gap of the minimum/maximum travel times in this anomaly detection system prior to and after applying the inference algorithm. Hybrid routing can suggest the effect of additional functions such as security features implemented onto a dedicated node, and the means of bypassing untrusted or suspicious networks.

Experimental testing of simulated data and analyzing their results can support the feasibility of this solution. The detailed testing environment, network topology, procedures and results are discussed to compare the performance both with and without implementing the proposed solution for the TTS inference system and the hybrid routing scheme.

### 7.4.1 TTS Server and Data Collection for Inference

The process of registration and information flow for the TTS to collect data and respond with the inference results with a measure of likelihood (in the form of standard deviation) is as follows (see Figure 7.1):

*Step 1:*     Registration is requested and approved by a TTP such as a CA.

*Step 2:*     When Alice sends a message to Bob, a ping request can be sent to B before and/ or after the message to record the travel time to be sent to the TTS with details of the message (e.g. message ID, timestamp source and destination address).

*Steps 3–4:* The TTS records the data and sends an acknowledgment to A. The server records the timestamp and responds to A with acknowledgment.

*Steps 5–6:* When the message is received by recipient B, detailed information of the message is sent to the TTS, which also sends an acknowledgment back to B.

*Step 7:*     Having the received data, the TTS executes inferencing algorithms to check the anomaly against a predefined threshold table with the variance gap.

*Step 8:*     In the case of a possible attack, the TTS sends the result to trigger the alarm to relevant parties, such as the sender's host or network operator and security service provider.

Figure 7.3 depicts the information flow of the TTS inferencing system and procedure of data collection. A is a source node and B is a destination node. CA is a trusted authority combined with a TTS providing inference engine with alarm notification functionality using machine learning algorithms designed to detect anomaly.

### 7.4.2 Heterogeneous Network Environment

Two scenarios are considered for simulation. These are situations for normal routing (case 1) and hybrid routing (case 2).

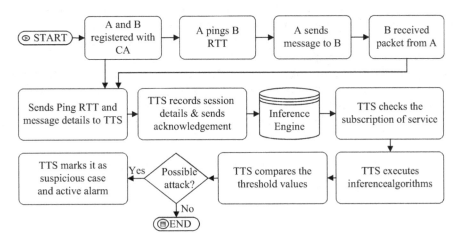

*Figure 7.3* Workflow of determining possible attacks based on inferred network knowledge.

***Simulation Case 1:***

Within a normal routing configuration, 100 attempts are given with unique link costs for each attempt in order to determine the best route decided by the routing protocol. The best route is determined from the routing protocols based on the route table built by route update for each routing protocol such as RIP, OSPF, BGP and so on. A static route may be configured and used by a network operator of each autonomous system (AS); however, the basic assumption is that there should not be any extra configuration other than the dedicated nodes to pass through. The outcome of the simulation will be the mean travel time with minimum and maximum values. Smaller variance of the min/max values is considered better for inferencing at the TTS.

***Simulation Case 2:***

A few nodes are allocated as dedicated fixed nodes which have all routes passing through them during each attempt and with results shown in Table 7.1.. For example, LS protocol depicts a shorter travel time but a larger variance of travel time than DV protocol. Several assumptions have been made when considering these simulation experiments:

1. The AS consists of two routing methods which are distance vector (DV) and link state (LS). These methods are simulated as separate cases.
2. The link cost among nodes has been allocated randomly for LS with a single natural integer, e.g. 1–9.
3. The link is randomly allocated among the nodes for DV.
4. The cost is considered to be the transmission time to travel between nodes. This has been simplified for the purpose of simulation.
5. Various ASes are connected in series to represent a WAN and thus the simulations are represented with multiple ASes connected in series.
6. The network can be an IP-based WAN or other ad hoc networks, e.g. LPWAN.

### 7.4.3 Graph-based Representation

To make explicit statements based on implicit knowledge automatically via automated reasoning, the inference engine requires heterogeneous network data to be stored in a uniform machine-interpretable language and serialization format. Having Semantic Web standards used for reasoning, the rich semantics of the corresponding network entities must be captured in the dataset as a prerequisite.

Network connections and routing scenarios in communication networks can be efficiently represented as directed, and usually acyclic, graphs [37]. Graph-based representations can hold information on not only how network devices are interconnected but also how information flows around a network [38]. This includes autonomous systems, network devices, and

*Table 7.1* Measurement of travel time (ping request and results).

| Ping results | DV (ms) | LS (ms) |
| --- | --- | --- |
| Minimum | 400 | 150 |
| Maximum | 800 | 700 |
| Mean time | 600 | 450 |
| Variance | 400 | 550 |

depending on the network, selected properties of routing messages (such as OSPF link state advertisements and BGP update messages).

A graph-based data model such as RDF can be used to describe network concepts and their properties with machine-interpretable definitions for data aggregation and data fusion and to facilitate automated reasoning over network knowledge. This relies on formalisms that utilize not only graph theory but also set theory and description logics, most of which are decidable fragments of first-order logic. To ensure decidability so that reasoner's inferencing over the corresponding datasets will be guaranteed not to run in an infinite loop, the computational properties of the description logic underlying the knowledge organization system used for capturing the semantics of a communication network must be considered. To increase the expressivity of such formalisms, mathematical constructors of special-purpose description logics, such as spatial and temporal description logics, may also be used, although doing so might break decidability. Another way of increasing expressivity is to use *SWRL*[3] rules that contain an antecedent/body and a consequent/head, both of which can be an atom (an expression having a predicate symbol representing concepts, properties and individuals; and arguments for individuals, data values or variables) or a positive/unnegated conjunction of atoms.

The nodes of graphs representing network knowledge can also have metadata, such as provenance data, associated data source depending on the mechanisms (e.g. named graphs, GraphSource) and the graph database (e.g. Neo4j, AllegroGraph) used [39, 40]. The choice depends heavily on the underlying data model, which determines the range of options to semantically enrich the typed links represented by the edges between graph nodes, and the tuple type of the representation. Storing metadata with network data is important so that statements about the origin of data can be captured, and statements can be made about a network knowledge statement or a set of such statements.

While not all routing paths are equally likely, the probability of getting to a node can be iteratively calculated by the sum of the probabilities of getting to any of its predecessors multiplied by the probability of following the edges from those predecessors to the node in question. The values calculated this way can be used for aggregating and/or fusing routing data via automated reasoning, logging network data for incident response and network forensics, as well as for the visualization of network paths.

## 7.5 CASE STUDY

To see the proposed method in action for setting nodes to be dedicated nodes the network traffic must go through, take the network segment shown in Figure 7.4 as an example.

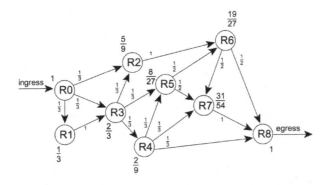

*Figure 7.4* Probability values for the traffic passing through a particular node.

By default, the probability of the traffic passing through the nodes can be calculated as follows:

$$P(R0) = 1$$

$$P(R1) = P(R0)\frac{1}{3} = 1\frac{1}{3} = \frac{1}{3}$$

$$P(R2) = P(R0)\frac{1}{3} + P(R3)\frac{1}{3} = 1\frac{1}{3} + \frac{2}{3}\frac{1}{3} = \frac{1}{3} + \frac{2}{9} = \frac{3}{9} + \frac{2}{9} = \frac{5}{9}$$

$$P(R3) = P(R0)\frac{1}{3} + P(R1)1 = 1\frac{1}{3} + \frac{1}{3}1 = \frac{1}{3} + \frac{1}{3} = \frac{2}{3}$$

$$P(R4) = P(R3)\frac{1}{3} = \frac{2}{3}\frac{1}{3} = \frac{2}{9}$$

$$P(R5) = P(R3)\frac{1}{3} + P(R4)\frac{1}{3} = \frac{2}{3}\frac{1}{3} + \frac{2}{9}\frac{1}{3} = \frac{2}{9} + \frac{2}{27} = \frac{6}{27} + \frac{2}{27} = \frac{8}{27}$$

$$P(R6) = P(R2)1 + P(R5)\frac{1}{2} = \frac{5}{9}1 + \frac{8}{27}\frac{1}{2} = \frac{5}{9} + \frac{8}{54} = \frac{30}{54} = \frac{38}{54} = \frac{19}{27}$$

$$P(R7) = P(R4)\frac{1}{3} + P(R5)\frac{1}{2} + P(R6)\frac{1}{2} = \frac{2}{9}\frac{1}{3} + \frac{8}{27}\frac{1}{2} + \frac{19}{27}\frac{1}{2} = \frac{2}{27} + \frac{8}{54} + \frac{19}{54} = \frac{4+8+19}{54} = \frac{31}{54}$$

$$P(R8) = P(R4)\frac{1}{3} + P(R6)\frac{1}{2} + P(R7) = \frac{2}{9}\frac{1}{3} + \frac{31}{54}1 + \frac{19}{27}\frac{1}{2} = \frac{2}{27} + \frac{31}{54} + \frac{19}{54} = \frac{4+31+19}{54} = \frac{54}{54} = 1$$

Without our approach of setting a dedicated node, the probability that the traffic goes through node R4 when not taking the path selection of advanced routing algorithms into account is 1/3 P(R3), i.e., 2/9.[4] By setting R4 to be a dedicated node the traffic has to go through, this probability would be 1 (by definition). Inherently, this also means that some of the path segments originally leading to node R4 would definitely be bypassed, i.e., the segment formed by nodes R2, R5 and R6 (regardless of the routing algorithms used for dynamic routing), thereby achieving the goal of bypassing a non-desired network segment altogether, whether that may be a set of bad nodes, an entire autonomous system or a country (see Figure 7.5).

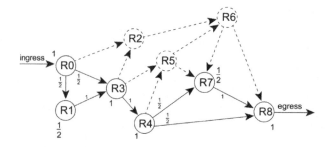

*Figure 7.5* Changed probability values for the traffic passing through a particular node when setting R4 to be a dedicated node.

*Table 7.2* Traffic forced through a dedicated node restricts the potential sets of nodes for traffic routes.

| Node | Default case | With R4 dedicated |
|---|---|---|
| R0 | 1.00 (ingress) | 1.00 (ingress) |
| R1 | 0.33 | 0.50 |
| R2 | 0.55 | 0.00 (bypassed) |
| R3 | 0.66 | 1.00 (forced path) |
| R4 | 0.22 | 1.00 (dedicated) |
| R5 | 0.29 | 0.00 (bypassed) |
| R6 | 0.70 | 0.00 (bypassed) |
| R7 | 0.57 | 0.50 |
| R8 | 1.00 [egress] | 1.00 [egress] |

Note that using R4 as a dedicated node the traffic must go through would also slightly change the probability of the traffic passing through node R7. Table 7.2 summarizes the probability value changes of the case study.

By setting R4 to be a dedicated node the traffic has to go through, its probability is increased to 1. Because in this network segment the only edge coming to R4 is the one from R3, the probability of that edge also changes to 1. This is only possible if the probability of going through R3 is 1 as well, in other words, this part of the traffic path is enforced. Considering the two incoming edges from R0 and R1, one from each node, this means that if the traffic goes through R1, that path segment is definitely used. All in all, the traffic bypasses R2, R5 and R6. This leaves the following paths from which the routing algorithm can choose (while also considering the edge costs):

- R0→R1→R3→R4→R7→R8
- R0→R3→R4→R7→R8
- R0→R1→R3→R4→R8
- R0→R3→R4→R8

To facilitate automation, first the paths are represented using Semantic Web standards. To demonstrate this, describe the last path in *RDF/Turtle:*[5]

```
@prefix : <http://www.example.org/routingdataset#> .
@prefix net: <http://purl.org/ontology/network/> .
@prefix prov: <http://www.w3.org/ns/prov#> .
@prefix xsd: <http://www.w3.org/2001/XMLSchema#> .

:PATH2 a net:Path .

:DedicatedR4 a prov:Activity ; prov:startedAtTime "2020-10-06T11:2
6:00+08:00"^^xsd:dateTime .

:PATH2 {
        :R0 net:nextHop :R3 .
        :R3 net:nextHop :R4 .
        :R4 net:nextHop :R8 .
        :SEGMENTR3R4 :hasLikelihood "1" .
}
```

```
:PROV {
        :PATH2 prov:wasGeneratedBy :DedicatedR4  .
}
```

By using a named graph for a path, not only the hops and the likelihood of going through particular nodes can be captured, but also additional metadata, such as provenance (using another named graph), in the above case, the time when the R4 node has been set as a dedicated node.

Next, a SELECT query can be executed in *SPARQL*[6] to calculate the number of hops between the ingress (R0) and egress (R8) node for the above paths as follows:

```
select ?R0 ?R8 (count(?hops) as ?length) {
    ?R0 (<>|!<>)* ?hops .
    ?hops (<>|!<>)+ ?R8 .
}
group by ?R0 ?R8
```

Finally, automated reasoning can be performed, such as to infer new network knowledge using *RDFS/OWL/D/pD* entailment regimes[7][8][9] [41], compare the path lengths using *SWRL built-ins*[10] or validate paths against constraints using *SHACL*.[11] Paths of large RDF graphs can be processed efficiently using the MapReduce-based *RDFPath* [42].


## 7.6 CONCLUSION

This chapter has presented a novel scheme for reducing the attack surface and to facilitate detection of possible MITM attacks within IoT networks. An algorithm has been proposed as part of this scheme, which appoints dedicated nodes whereby routing is enforced through among IoT devices, which allows for the detection of anomalies in the TTS. Multiple scenarios for routing have been described and suitable metrics that can be used for performance evaluation of the model have been outlined.

In order to validate this solution in heterogeneous networks, dedicated nodes must be set up across different networks with the addition of transit addresses being communicated to dedicated nodes. This requires modification of existing header fields in layers 2 and 3 of the TCP/IP suite in IP networks. In addition, existing protocols in private networks (e.g. LPWAN or mHealth networks) would require modification to implement changes needed for this solution. One of the challenges of implementation is the need to find a spare field that could be used; this requires addressing in future research. This process may also require relevant organizations and parties to discuss an agreement with international standardization bodies.

Moreover, further study is required to determine the optimal way to designate dedicated nodes while considering the network traverse history of packets. As IoT devices in PWAN are powered by batteries, it is difficult to implement full-scale security measures. Therefore, it is important to consider lightweight security, which is optimized to be adequate and has efficient computational and battery power consumption. The more complicated algorithms are implemented, the more power is required. Thus efficient and lightweight algorithms which will not overload devices are essential to overcome the dilemma. To satisfy this requirement, dedicated nodes in this hybrid routing solution may be embedded with more hardware capacity for computational and battery power as they serve a purpose for cluster head.

## NOTES

1. https://www.tcpdump.org
2. https://www.w3.org/RDF/
3. https://www.w3.org/Submission/SWRL/
4. Because dynamic routing employs advanced routing algorithms, in real-world applications this value would typically be lower, with some of the less favorable potential paths ignored.
5. https://www.w3.org/TR/turtle/
6. https://www.w3.org/TR/sparql11-overview/
7. https://www.w3.org/TR/2004/REC-rdf-mt-20040210/#RDFSRules
8. https://www.w3.org/TR/owl2-profiles/#Reasoning_in_OWL_2_RL_and_RDF_Graphs_using_Rules
9. https://www.w3.org/TR/2004/REC-rdf-mt-20040210/#D_entailment
10. http://www.daml.org/2004/04/swrl/builtins.html
11. https://www.w3.org/TR/shacl/

## REFERENCES

1. Bittman, T., Exploring the Edge: 12 Frontiers of Edge Computing Gartner.
2. Kang, J.J., Larkin, H., and Luan, T.H., 2016. Enhancement of sensor data transmission by inference and efficient data processing. In *Applications and Techniques in Information Security*, L. Batten and G. Li Eds. Springer Singapore, 81–92. doi: 10.1007/978-981-10-2741-3_7.
3. Kang, J. and Adibi, S., 2017. Bushfire disaster monitoring system using low power wide area networks (LPWAN). *MDPI Technologies 5*, 65 (2017/10/08/). doi: 10.3390/technologies5040065.
4. Kang, J. and Adibi, S., 2015. A Review of Security Protocols in mHealth Wireless Body Area Networks (WBAN). In *Future Network Systems and Security*, R. Doss, S. Piramuthu and W. Zhou Eds. Springer International Publishing, 61–83. doi: 10.1007/978-3-319-19210-9_5.
5. Yang, W., Johnstone, M.N., Sikos, L.F., and Wang, S., 2020. Security and forensics in the internet of things: Research advances and challenges. In *2020 Workshop on Emerging Technologies for Security in IoT (ETSecIoT)*, 12–17. doi: 10.1109/ETSecIoT50046.2020.00007.
6. Sikos, L.F., 2020. Packet analysis for network forensics: A comprehensive survey. *Forensic Science International: Digital Investigation 32*, 200892, (2020/03/01/). doi: 10.1016/j.fsidi.2019.200892.
7. Mohamed, B. and Christian, J., 2015. *Handbook of Research on Redesigning the Future of Internet Architectures, IGI Global*, Hershey, PA, USA, IGI Global is the Publisher, 1–621. doi:10.4018/978-1-4666-8371-6.
8. Krasser, S., Tang, Y., Gould, J., Alperovitch, D., and Judge, P., 2007. Identifying image spam based on header and file properties using C4. 5 decision trees and support vector machine learning. In *2007 IEEE SMC Information Assurance and Security Workshop IEEE*, 255–261.
9. Wang, W.-X., Yin, C.-Y., Yan, G., and Wang, B.-H., 2006. Integrating local static and dynamic information for routing traffic. *Physical Review E 74*(1), 016101.
10. Kang, J.J., Fahd, K., Venkatraman, S., Trujillo-Rasua, R., and Haskell-Dowland, P., 2019. Hybrid routing for Man-in-the-Middle (MITM) attack detection in IoT networks. In *2019 29th International Telecommunication Networks and Applications Conference (ITNAC)*, 1–6. doi: 10.1109/ITNAC46935.2019.9077977.
11. Jain, K., Padhye, J., Padmanabhan, V.N., and Qiu, L., 2005. Impact of interference on multi-hop wireless network performance. *Wireless networks 11*(4), 471–487.
12. Shen, J., Tan, H.-W., Wang, J., Wang, J.-W., and Lee, S.-Y., 2015. A novel routing protocol providing good transmission reliability in underwater sensor networks. *Journal of Internet Technology 16*(1), 171–178.
13. Liu, Y., Dong, M., Ota, K., and Liu, A., 2016. ActiveTrust: Secure and trustable routing in wireless sensor networks. *IEEE Transactions on Information Forensics and Security 11*(9), 2013–2027.
14. Singh, S.P. and Sharma, S., 2015. A survey on cluster based routing protocols in wireless sensor networks. *Procedia Computer Science 45*, 687–695.

15. Naranjo, P.G.V., Shojafar, M., Mostafaei, H., Pooranian, Z., and Baccarelli, E., 2017. P-SEP: A prolong stable election routing algorithm for energy-limited heterogeneous fog-supported wireless sensor networks. *The Journal of Supercomputing* 73(2), 733–755.

16. Luo, J., Hu, J., Wu, D., and Li, R., 2015. Opportunistic routing algorithm for relay node selection in wireless sensor networks. *IEEE Transactions on Industrial Informatics* 11(1), 112–121. doi:10.1109/TII.2014.2374071.

17. Lin, C., Wang, K., and Deng, G., 2017. A QoS-aware routing in SDN hybrid networks. *Procedia Computer Science 110*, 242–249, (2017/01/01/). doi: 10.1016/j.procs.2017.06.091.

18. Fortz, B., Rexford, J., and Thorup, M., 2002. Traffic engineering with traditional IP routing protocols. *IEEE Communications Magazine 40*(10), 118–124. doi: 10.1109/MCOM.2002.1039866.

19. Lagoa, C.M., Che, H., and Movsichoff, B.A., 2004. Adaptive control algorithms for decentralized optimal traffic engineering in the internet. *IEEE/ACM Transactions on Networking* 12(3), 415–428.

20. Xu, D., Chiang, M., and Rexford, J., 2011. Link-state routing with hop-by-hop forwarding can achieve optimal traffic engineering. *IEEE/ACM Transactions on Networking* 19(6), 1717–1730. doi: 10.1109/TNET.2011.2134866.

21. Davoli, L., Veltri, L., Ventre, P.L., Siracusano, G., and Salsano, S., 2015. Traffic engineering with segment routing: SDN-based architectural design and open source implementation. In *2015 Fourth European Workshop on Software Defined Networks*, 111–112. doi: 10.1109/EWSDN.2015.73.

22. Bhatia, R., Hao, F., Kodialam, M., and Lakshman, T.V., 2015. Optimized network traffic engineering using segment routing. In *2015 IEEE Conference on Computer Communications (INFOCOM)*, 657–665. doi: 10.1109/INFOCOM.2015.7218434.

23. Shu, Z., Wan, J., Lin, J., Wang, S., Li, D., Rho, S., and Yang, C., 2016. Traffic engineering in software-defined networking: Measurement and management. *IEEE Access 4*, 3246–3256. doi: 10.1109/ACCESS.2016.2582748.

24. Wei, Y., Zhang, X., Xie, L., and Leng, S., 2016. Energy-aware traffic engineering in hybrid SDN/IP backbone networks. *Journal of Communications and Networks* 18(4), 559–566. doi: 10.1109/JCN.2016.000079.

25. Chiesa, M., Kindler, G., and Schapira, M., 2017. Traffic engineering with equal-cost-multipath: An algorithmic perspective. *IEEE/ACM Trans. Netw.* 25(2), 779–792. doi: 10.1109/tnet.2016.2614247.

26. Sridharan, A., Guerin, R., and Diot, C., 2005. Achieving near-optimal traffic engineering solutions for current OSPF/IS-IS networks. *IEEE/ACM Transactions on Networking* 13(2), 234–247. doi: 10.1109/TNET.2005.845549.

27. Xu, K., Shen, M., Liu, H., Liu, J., Li, F., and Li, T., 2016. Achieving optimal traffic engineering using a generalized routing framework. *IEEE Transactions on Parallel and Distributed Systems* 27(1), 51–65. doi: 10.1109/TPDS.2015.2392760.

28. Kang, J.J.W., 2017. *An inference system framework for personal sensor devices in mobile health and internet of things networks*. Deakin University.

29. Philp, D., Chan, N., and Sikos, L.F., 2020. Decision support for network path estimation via automated reasoning. In *Intelligent Decision Technologies 2019*, Switzerland, Springer, 335–344.

30. Bahnasse, A., Louhab, F.E., Ait Oulahyane, H., Talea, M., and Bakali, A., 2018. Novel SDN architecture for smart MPLS Traffic Engineering-DiffServ Aware management. *Future Generation Computer Systems 87*, 115–126, (2018/10/01/). doi: 10.1016/j.future.2018.04.066.

31. Kang, J.J., Fahd, K., and Venkatraman, S., 2018. Trusted time-based verification model for automatic man-in-the-middle attack detection in cybersecurity. *Cryptography* 2(4), 38.

32. Chacko, S. and Job, M.D., 2018. Security mechanisms and vulnerabilities in LPWAN. *IOP Conference Series: Materials Science and Engineering 396*, 012027, (2018/08/29). doi: 10.1088/1757-899x/396/1/012027.

33. Mekki, K., Bajic, E., Chaxel, F., and Meyer, F., 2019. A comparative study of LPWAN technologies for large-scale IoT deployment. *ICT Express 5*(1), 1–7, (2019/03/01/). doi:10.1016/j.icte.2017.12.005.

34. Yang, W., Wang, S., Hu, J., Ibrahim, A., Zheng, G., Macedo, M.J., Johnstone, M.N., and Valli, C., 2019. A cancelable iris-and steganography-based user authentication system for the Internet of Things. *Sensors* 19(13), 2985.

35. IETF, 2017. Network Time Security for the Network Time Protocol NTP Worling Group.
36. O'Donoghue, K., 2017. A new security mechanism for the network time protocol. *IETF Journal: Internet Security* (31 October).
37. Sikos, L.F. and Philp, D., 2020. Provenance-aware knowledge representation: A survey of data models and contextualized knowledge graphs. *Data Science and Engineering*(2020/05/08). doi: 10.1007/s41019-020-00118-0.
38. Sikos, L.F., Philp, D., Howard, C., Voigt, S., Stumptner, M., and Mayer, W., 2019. Knowledge Representation of Network Semantics for Reasoning-Powered Cyber-Situational Awareness. In *AI in Cybersecurity*, L.F. Sikos Ed. Cham, Springer International Publishing, 19–45. doi: 10.1007/978-3-319-98842-9_2.
39. Sikos, L.F., 2015. *Mastering Structured Data on the Semantic Web: From HTML5 Microdata to Linked Open Data*. California USA, Apress.
40. Sikos, L.F., Stumptner, M., Mayer, W., Howard, C., Voigt, S., and Philp, D., 2018. Representing network knowledge using provenance-aware formalisms for cyber-situational awareness. *Procedia Computer Science 126*, 29–38, (2018/01/01/). doi: 10.1016/j.procs.2018.07.206.
41. Ter Horst, H.J., 2005. Completeness, decidability and complexity of entailment for RDF Schema and a semantic extension involving the OWL vocabulary. *Journal of Web Semantics 3*(2), 79–115, (2005/10/01/). doi: doi:10.1016/j.websem.2005.06.001.
42. Przyjaciel-Zablocki, M., Schätzle, A., Hornung, T., and Lausen, G., 2012. RDFPath: Path Query Processing on Large RDF Graphs with MapReduce. In *The Semantic Web: ESWC 2011 Workshops*, R. García-Castro, D. Fensel and G. Antoniou Eds. Berlin Heidelberg, Berlin, Heidelberg, Springer, 50–64.

Chapter **8**

# Early Identification of Mental Health Disorder Employing Machine Learning-based Secure Edge Analytics

## A Real-time Monitoring System

*Naveen Kumar Oburi, Tahrat Tazrin, Akshai Ramesh, Prem Sagar, and Sadman Sakib*

Lakehead University, Canada

*Mostafa M. Fouda*

Idaho State University, USA

*Zubair Md Fadlullah*

Lakehead University, Canada
Thunder Bay Regional Health Research Institute (TBRHRI), Canada

## CONTENTS

## 8.1  INTRODUCTION

Across the globe, anxiety and depression are emerging as high-impact mental health challenges across all age, gender, ethnicities. Both anxiety and depression have been linked with a significantly adverse effect on social and economic progress. The individuals suffering from these conditions are likely to eventually suffer from physical disorders including cardiovascular diseases, diabetes and so forth [1–2]. Depression has become an unavoidable piece of life and a few techniques have been proposed to combat it. For instance, a changed and solid eating routine, working out, relaxing, keeping a pet, stopping smoking, tuning to music, a progressive perspective of life and laughing help diminish such problems. Let us consider the situation that we are all going through at present, i.e., the COVID-19 status quo. The country is on the verge of a complete lockdown, and people are scared to get out of their homes. It is a global pandemic, and we face this together. But every one of us would have personally felt very helpless and wondered when this would come to an end and when we would get back to our normal lives. If this feeling of loneliness or sadness prolongs, then one can be considered depressed. That longevity would determine if the severity is high or low.

There is additionally developing proof that individuals are keen on accessing mental health services by means of the web and mobile applications [3]. Recent reports suggest that depression and anxiety represent the best weight of illness among all psychological wellness issues and are expected to end up being the second-most elevated health problem among all medical issues in 2020. In 2017, it was found that around 792 million people were suffering from such conditions [4]. In the current day and age when technology is growing at an unimaginable rate and the role that social media has in our lives, even a small tweet or a post about something that is very sensitive can end up being disastrous. People are very open about what they want to share and convey nowadays. Importantly, the notion of speaking out what they feel is very critical and strong irrespective of the topic. Such small repercussions can build up to something extremely alarming in the future that can affect the person mentally and physically and jeopardize their health data privacy.

Depression is a major concern among people of all ages in various parts of Canada, especially in the Northern Ontario region [5–6]. Hence, it is of utmost significance to develop a predictive model for the automated detection of anxiety and depression given specific security and/or privacy concerns. To address this issue, our proposed AI-based model will employ real-time facial expression analysis at the edge device using a pre-trained model to determine the mental status of a subject and generate customized alerts or messages based on the depression level detected by the system to inform the subject and the care providers. Since the automated analysis will take place locally at the edge device, the privacy concern will be largely mitigated in contrast with the traditional cloud-based solutions.

People with such problems lead an inspired and constructive life while being treated for their mental disorder. It can be assumed that almost everyone can be associated with at least a relative, acquaintance or friend, who in turn experienced a mental disorder a priori and can share his/her experience in an emotionally relevant context. The need to assess oneself is also very vital. When you feel low at times, there is nothing wrong to question yourself, for example, 'Do you have worries or anger?' and 'Are you considering irresponsible things which could jeopardize safety of yourself and/or others?' Most importantly, we once again stress that early detection is crucial for prompt intervention. What makes us think we can treat such problems without a measure? Do you think we can treat diabetes without measuring the blood sugar level? No, right? That is why it is essential to assess the user based on certain rating scales. Those scales would broadly be based on the user symptoms, their side effects, day-to-day activities and the quality of life. By doing this, we would have a comprehensive understanding of the people who are being treated for depression and anxiety. Similarly, the user's privacy is not compromised when they provide such information.

Utilization of secured mobile-based applications can be considered as a promising answer for expanding access to mental healthcare. Applications can be utilized to obtain data about psychological wellness upkeep, provide guided or self-improvement systems and offer continuous and efficient communications with healthcare experts. Presently, less is thought about the monetarily accessible applications that are touted to address anxiety signs and depression. When applications are promptly accessible for the general population that may be enticed to get to them instead of mental healthcare, it is imperative to examine their subject matter, mediation approaches, methods and the manner in which they are helping to solve this challenge. It is extremely crucial to know the problems that people confront. There are people who never leave their comfort zone and avoid mingling with anyone. They might think that it is their own problem and they alone should fight through this. So, unless they come out and share it with someone whom they feel comfortable with, it is difficult to comprehend what they are suffering from. We also notice many people trying to beat this with a positive attitude by understanding themselves and learning about the problems and the reasons that brought them to the current situation.

The conventional approach of implementing such mobile applications, to address the crucial challenges of mental health, involves collecting data in the edge devices and sending the data to cloud for further analysis. While transferring the data over the Internet, the data might be vulnerable to various security issues such as data breaches, DoS attacks, malicious attacks and so forth. Hence, the user might not feel comfortable to rely on such services even if it brings benefit to them. With these issues in mind, the primary aim of this chapter is to develop a reliable and secured architecture that would help to recognize the distress level that a user is experiencing and automatically generate different levels of alerts based on the conditions. The application will collect various types of data from the user such as numeric data through a set of questionnaire and also image data collected through the camera sensor. After performing a set of analysis in the collected data, our model will predict the emotion of the user and take actions accordingly. To ensure a secured mobile application, this model employs the concepts of federated learning where the AI model training is performed on the edge devices. The trained models are then transferred to cloud where a global training is performed. Therefore, this method secures data collected from the application by avoiding transmission of the collected data over the Internet.

## 8.2 TRADITIONAL METHODS IMPLEMENTED IN EDGE COMPUTING

Edge computing is created because of the exponential development of IoT [7] gadgets, which are associated with the web for either receiving data from the cloud or conveying information back to the cloud. Furthermore, numerous IoT gadgets produce gigantic measures of information over the span of their activities. The fast development of web-associated gadgets, i.e., the IoT, gives rise to new applications which need real-time monitoring and analytics as well as continuous computational power. This is recently driving various edge-computing frameworks. Fast-growing innovations, for example, Fifth Generation (5G) networks, are taking into account edge frameworks to accelerate the creation or support of constant applications including real-time streaming and processing of multimedia contents, recommendation systems, autonomous cars, robotics, AI, medical analytics and so forth. [8–9]. In any case, issues emerge when the quantity of gadgets transmitting information simultaneously develops. The data is transmitted from thousands of gadgets rather than just one single camcorder transmitting live video stream. This does not mean that this will exclusively ascertain quality because of inactivity, the expenses for data transfer can be enormous.

In customary IoT models as depicted in Figure 8.1, all gathered sensor information is moved to a common repository where it is put together, and the information is prepared considering all things. This functions only if the information is gathered and cumulatively analyzed. Be that as it may, imagine a scenario in which it's not important to have the information to get the ideal outcomes. One interesting point with edge processing is that since information isn't stored for a long time, it's not helpful for big data analytics since it gets deleted eventually. All things considered, edge computing is appropriate for IoT organizations where both limited and batch processing can be utilized [10]. A totally substantial IoT configuration might be one where the sensors possibly associate with the cloud when they have something critical to report. This structure gives the chance to lessen IoT organizing costs by utilizing technologies, for example, cell-based innovations that adapt a lower-cost, pay-per-kilobit charging strategy instead of an always-on connection. It's critical to note that, in any case, even edge-based AI and Machine Learning (ML) applications frequently require productive access to essential resources so as to work viably [11]. Right now, the connection between edge and cloud is exceptionally correlative.

By considering that AI is practically fundamental to evaluate the big data involving medical records and medical data streams which need to be secured and kept private, researchers have been intrigued to incorporate Edge Computing and AI, which offers a boost to secure Edge Intelligence. The concept of Edge Intelligence is the basic blend of Edge Computing and

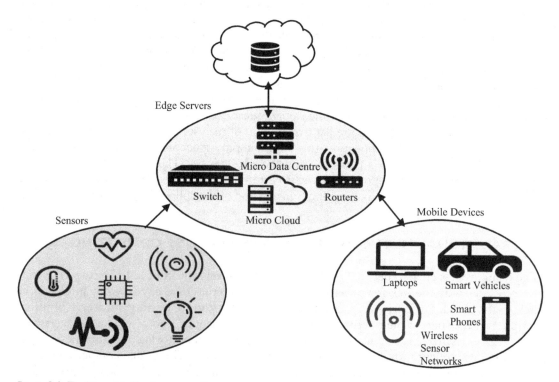

*Figure 8.1* Traditional IoT edge computing.

AI that is receiving much research attention, covering a plethora of ideas and innovations, interlaced together in a complex manner. In addition, to ensure data security in these smart models, federated learning has been implemented as an effective method while having lower latency and less power consumption on the edge [12]. Thus, it is employed in various applications ranging from medical domain [13] to recommendation system [14] in order to make them more reliable and efficient for the users. It is also discussed to be very efficient for training IoT models such as wearable devices, autonomous vehicles or smart homes in real-time while maintaining privacy [15].

## 8.3 SECURE ANALYTICS OF SMART HEALTHCARE AT THE EDGE

The advancement of smart healthcare has facilitated an improved management of medical resources by introducing efficient IoT systems that will consume less resources while being more efficient. The resources in healthcare industries can be categorized into consumable and non-consumable resources. Consumable resources are the resources that become worthless with time, for example, clinical guides and instruments. On the other hand, non-consumable resources are those that don't terminate after some time. Among the non-consumable resources are doctors, medical caretakers, enrolled attendants and all those associated with the procedure of healthcare. Having the right personnel in this setup is very important and making the maximum use of it in an efficient manner would be the perfect path toward an excellent healthcare system.

The success of a secure healthcare system requires a robust and reliable approach to constantly ingest, process and analyze the large streams of medical information to make informed decisions and possible intervention decisions close to the data source. In case of cloud and edge computing, planning and creating an efficient smart healthcare system is currently possible since it has been established that the cloud paradigm is supposedly more capable in contrast with the more traditional, stand-alone servers [16]. Usually, patient-privacy is still managed or protected by the cloud computing vendors and suppliers. Essentially, both cloud and edge computing, when put together in a balanced approach, may act as facilitators toward developing a truly smart and privacy-preserving healthcare ecosystem.

The significance of conveying IoT of portable hubs into healthcare is practiced so as to improve the framework and, in this manner, it advances the system and improves execution measures. Healthcare is an essential part of our life and the surge of people requiring healthcare increases every passing day, hence increasing the significance of integrating smart healthcare with our life. With the exponential increase in population and chronic diseases with time, it has become difficult for healthcare sectors to cope up. Thus, cloud computing was used to address these problems of data and resource usage as traditional methods were not effective.

Computerized healthcare frameworks that influence EHRs (Electronic Health Records) and use technologies, for example, IoT and big data are relied upon to flawlessly interface patients and suppliers across different healthcare systems. These frameworks are being progressively associated with the Internet to different sorts of clinical wearable devices that are being worn for monitoring real-time health [17]. But a lot of problems should be tended to before smart healthcare can create a steady and adaptable system. Unapproved access to IoT gadgets could make a genuine hazard to the patient's well-being just as to their private data. Connected devices including cell phones obtain, calculate, process and move the clinical data to the cloud. The gadget layer is defenseless against tag cloning, spoofing, RF jamming and cloud polling. Denial of Service (DoS) attack can influence medicinal services and harm the patient's well-being.

In a healthcare system, the duplication of assets may not generally be conceivable since a portion of the devices is embedded. The quick recognition of potential security issues is always challenging due to the number and multifaceted nature of fast-growing software and hardware technologies. This issue is deteriorating as an expanding number of gadgets are being associated with the Internet. Moreover, we have additionally observed a flood in the expansion of wearable gadgets in recent times. Secrecy and security are significant worries for doctors too. Patients may not have any desire to share their clinical records as a result of the sensitive nature of the health data. Protection concerns increment when the patient's data is shared among a few applications. The systems which transmit information are frequently heterogeneous and are as often as possible controlled by third parties. As a result, the security and privacy of the data become even more difficult.

The IoT medical sensors and devices are among the most important edge computing use cases since they have the potential to entirely revolutionize the healthcare ecosystem by substantially improving the patient and caregiver experiences. They can help mental health patients to assess their own situations on a daily basis given that the edge device security is considered while designing the relevant mobile application, allow them to schedule appointments and share their current situation in a secure manner with the appropriate healthcaregivers and so forth.

## 8.4 RELATED WORK: OVERVIEW OF MOBILE APPLICATIONS FOR MENTAL HEALTH

In this section, we briefly list a number of related mobile applications for mental health that are available on the mobile marketplaces and describe the security/privacy challenge associated with them at the end of the section.

### 8.4.1 Anxiety Reliever

The anxiety reliever application tracks symptoms of anxiety and provides relaxation exercises accordingly. The application has a free limited version, and to access the full app, it needs to be purchased.

### 8.4.2 Anxiety Coach

Anxiety Coach is a counseling application that uses Cognitive Behavioral Therapy (CBT) strategies to focus on fears and worries. It identifies a person's fear by making a list and comes up with solutions to overcome them. It also has the options to self-test severity, track anxiety and view their own progress.

### 8.4.3 Breath2Relax

The Breath2Relax, established by the National Center for Telehealth and Technology, is a phone application that helps to deal with stress and provides lessors for breathing techniques. The skills taught using the application can be applied to the people having anxiety disorders, Post-Traumatic Stress Disorder (PTSD) and other stress. The users can modify it according to their comfort and it has other resources like video demo, charts and reading materials to keep track of personal progress. One of the great advantages of this application is that it can be customized according to the user for their ease of use. There are other attractive features such as video demonstration, personal improvement tracker, reading materials, etc. This app can assist the people who have recently started treatment of mental health, and breathing techniques are involved in the treatment.

### 8.4.4 Happify

The goal of Happify application is to spread positivity through activities supported by positive psychology and mindfulness research. The state of the user is determined through a set of questions and they are suggested various activities to cope with worry, chronic pain, increase fitness and building relationships. The reasoning behind the suggested activities is also provided for their reading.

### 8.4.5 Head Space

Head Space application provides meditation guidelines to decrease stress and anxiety and improve attentiveness and awareness. It is good for people who want to set a regular meditation routine. Various skills such as cognitive diffusion and meditation and tasks like breathing workouts, stress-release tips, meditation practice and attentiveness can be learned from the app. This application is used among people with anxiety and depressive disorders, Obsessive Compulsive Disorder (OCD) and PTSD. This application has a fascinating user-interface which describes basic concepts, and it also gives instructions about meditations in a user-friendly manner, builds an online forum, supplies podcasts, normalizes mind-wandering and illustrates main points with videos. However, it cannot be used as an alternative for treatment for people having considerable mental health issues such as anxiety or depression.

### 8.4.6 Mindshift

Mindshift is an application that helps people from all walks of life to acquire awareness and gather elementary skills to control any syndromes related to anxiety, including generalized anxiety disorder, particular fears/phobias, social anxiety, anxiety attacks, etc. Also it manages other kinds of anxiety, worries and perfectionism. Users can apply the learned skills in order to deal with difficult situations by organized way of thinking. It provides a range of coping strategies for anxiety in various formats. Users can mark their recommended activities as favorite. However, people who want to keep track of symptoms and advancement or who get overwhelmed by various options will not get much help from the app.

### 8.4.7 MoodKit

This application helps individuals with their depression, issues regarding rage control, anxiety disorders, etc. Various abilities can be learned like monitoring oneself, building healthy thought patterns and engaging in nourishing activities. It provides information about CBT so that people can work on by themselves or with a therapist.

### 8.4.8 Panic Relief

This application aims to help individuals with panic disorder by providing simple and analytical tools to overcome panic attacks easily. There is a trial version that only gives permission to access the progressive muscle relaxation section, but the paid upgrade gives full access to other skills such as square breathing, progressive muscle relaxation and diaphragmatic breathing.

### 8.4.9 PTSD Coach

PTSD Coach is an app that is provided by the National Center for PTSD to help oneself. The purpose of this app is to help people who are suffering from mild to moderate versions of PTSD and provides information about the disorder for people to learn. However, people who suffer from serious PTSD issues, or who need further clinical assistance, or those who are unable to make safe decisions must refrain from using this app. Hence, it provides education, assesses PTSD, offers tips to manage common PTSD symptoms and has search option for additional treatment resources.

The aforementioned mobile applications, however, do not consider the privacy concern of the collected health data from individual patients. The data are typically shared with the remote server. Even if the data are encrypted during transmission, they are revealed at the cloud server during analytics. The data can be either sold to third-party companies, which is in violation with the medical data privacy of various countries or be reconstructed using a plethora of state-of-the-art techniques. So in this chapter, we aim to address this issue and present our adopted methodology for automated assessment of anxiety and depression levels in the edge with privacy-preservation capability.

## 8.5 METHODOLOGIES FOR AUTOMATED REAL-TIME MOOD DETECTION FOR ASSESSING ANXIETY AND DEPRESSION LEVELS IN THE EDGE WITH PRIVACY-PRESERVATION CAPABILITY

Initially, the mobile application requires collecting data from the users via two methods – a set of questionnaires and image data collected by the camera. In this section, we have demonstrated the series of pre-processing steps required to handle the image data in order to feed it to the machine learning algorithm. We have also applied machine learning algorithm in a questionnaire dataset to show the efficacy of our proposed system in terms of performance. Furthermore, we have implemented federated learning which can be used to provide the users more security by conducting the analysis precisely at edge. The elaborated methodology is presented in the sections below.

### 8.5.1 Data Preparation and Pre-processing

In this method, we take data from users' mobile by providing an interface to take pictures using their mobile camera for mood detection. This process involves the following steps:

- Tracking
- Optic flow Establishment in Facial Areas

#### Face-tracking

The face-tracking part was built based on an upgraded ratio template algorithm version. It uses a spatial face model and then matches the ratios of mean luminance using that. In our system, the biological proportions of the face mode were also considered with the algorithm. Figure 8.2 determines the functioning of the ratio template algorithm for detecting facial expressions.

The face tracker detects facial structures taking various light settings into consideration except for when light is shone from below to the subject. Activities such as yaw, roll and

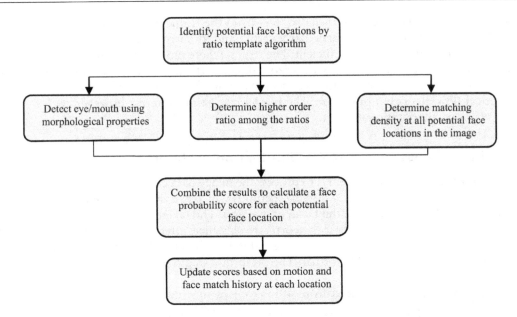

*Figure 8.2* Face-tracking method flowchart using the ratio template algorithm.

head tilting can be detected by the system. At indoor, it can detect various illumination characteristics with great speed that makes it more efficient. The ratio template algorithm offers more focused facial filter search by providing a rough spatial map by using the spatial face template. The rough map provides information of various features of the face prior to finding the relative motion which acts a very important component in facial expression detection.

### 8.5.1.1 *Identifying Optic Flow in Facial Regions*

The optical flow algorithm is used to find the motion of the face after the face is traced in the scene by the face tracker. Motion information is used to determine expressions because the expressions are dynamic events and also the different textures of people's face can be ignored using motion. Therefore, the motion pattern of people's expression is similar regardless of the person showing it. Face detection using motion has been a booming field and it is able to even determine gender of a person. In order to determine the facial optical flow, we have employed Multi-Channel Gradient Model (MCGM) in the system.

MCGM is built from the human cortical motion pathway system and it runs in multiple dimensions while regarding for the dense velocity field of the whole image. Various temporal and spatial differential filters are applied to the image in addition to their appropriate ratios to recover speed and direction of the model. MCGM has been proven to act similarly as human cortical motion pathway as the number of motion-based optical illusions can be correctly predicted by the model [18]. There are various reasons as to why MCGM is implemented in order to retrieve motion information like it does not vary with variation in scene luminance as it calculates speed using ratio of differentials. Therefore, the contrast normalization problem caused by template matching or Fourier energy methods of retrieving optical flow can be eliminated. Another reason is Matrox Genesis DSP boards were used to implement a real-time MCGM model using a machine which provides an accurate measure of optical flow even though the real-time version was optimized for hardware. A speed of 18fps is attained on the target image using the referred board, hence, making it suitable for determining expression real-time.

The tracker detects a location (usually face) from the frame and uses a motion computation of local area and uses that particular location and its surroundings instead of the whole face in order to make the system efficient. The region where motion of the face is computed is bordered in order to let the face move horizontally or vertically during expression, otherwise the rigid movements may cause the face to move outside the bordered region and intrude the optical flow algorithm operation. The border size can be altered, however, with a slight expense in the computational speed.

## 8.5.2 Pre-processing and Noise Elimination of the Image Data

One of the objectives of this system is to process the image data collected from the application by removing the noises using the following methods which can then be passed to the machine learning algorithm to determine the facial expression. The facial expression (non-expression or the six basic emotions) needs to be correctly classified after the facial motion has been determined. In order to train the model, the dataset needed to be pre-processed so that the sequences were in an acceptable format. The pre-processing steps are described below:

- The frame rate was reduced from 40fps to 4fps in order to match with the speed of completed systems.
- The face sizes on the pictures were decreased so that the face tracker can detect it and emotion detection system (roughly 45 pixels) can easily employ it. The images were all condensed to the same size so that the only change in position of the faces are due to different poses adopted by people or normal human differences.
- The start frame of every individual sequence was labeled at the beginning of facial expression
- Motion pattern examples for the six basic emotions were then produced from these sequences. In the proposed system, data were automatically generated in order to train the model after the construction of pre-processed sequences. As stated above, the face tracker collected facial positions and generated a mapping of the positions of face feature approximately. Then the facial motions were determined from this spatial map using the MCGM. Subsequently, the facial motions were used in the training phase of the classifiers without any additional requirement for labeling of the locations of features on the face manually. In order to represent each facial expression, four successive motion frames produced using MCGM were considered. These four frames denote beginning phase of the facial motion on one second (i.e. from normal expression to indicative expression). The data were condensed and modified before using them in the classification which the expression recognition system employed by taking the average of data regarding motion and calculating ratios of the mean motion.
- Averaging of the Motion – The motion data produced by MCGM can be compressed in a precise structure by taking the average of specific predefined regions of the face instead of using the raw optical flow output to train the classifier. Thus, the classification task can be simplified with this data condensation process as the information is reduced.
- Ratios of averaged motion – Ratios of motion are calculated to measure relativity of various facial parts so that the effects due to rigid head translation can be removed. A drastic change that can be observed is the optical flow output of MCGM when someone gives an expression while moving their head as a whole. Therefore, in such cases, relative motions are used so that the system does not vary with global head translations.

A non-expression training and testing set was also used to train the classifier in addition to the active expression examples. It was done to make the system more realistic because this will ensure that all the emotions are classified properly if the input image does not belong to one of the six basic emotions. The non-expression collection has a length of 4800 frames and contains ten different people recorded indoor using normal illumination in a computer without any specific constraints.

## 8.5.3 Questionnaire Data Description

Another objective of our developed system was the questionnaire part that was used to collect data from the users. In order to show the efficacy of our machine learning model, we have employed a similar mental health dataset containing answers of questionnaires to determine resilience of a person. The dataset is collected from Data Dryad. The dataset consisted of various information from medical students regarding their mental health from 22 Brazilian health institutions. Various standard scales were used to measure the attributes such as Dundee Ready Educational Environment Measure (DREEM), Wagnild and Young's resilience scale, the World Health Organization Quality of Life (WHOQOL) measure, the State-Trait Anxiety Inventory (STAI) and the Beck Depression Inventory (BDI). Some other personal features of each student like their gender, age, school status and school location were also available. There were a total of 22 features with around 1350 instances. To measure the overall resilience, the Wagnild and Yong's resilience scale was employed. Here, the resilience was measured based on five criteria which are – perseverance, existential aloneness, meaning, self-reliance and equanimity. The students' quality of life was recorded both in terms of their medical aspect as well as the overall aspect. For measuring the overall quality of life, a set of questionnaires certified by world health organization quality of life (WHOQOL-BREF) was employed and an additional global self-evaluation was also performed. In WHOQOL-BREF, 26 items were clustered in four fields: environment, psychological, social relationships and physical health that ranged from 0 to 100. The higher the scores are, the better is their quality of life. Another set of features are the educational environment in terms of five domains – learning, teachers, social self-perception, academic self-perception and atmosphere which was measured by Dundee Ready Educational Environment questionnaire. BDI was used to get an approximation of depression and STAI were used to get a measure of state anxiety and trait anxiety of the students. The values of resilience score ranges from 0 to 100; therefore, we converted the scores to resilience level having two values – high and low. People having values higher than 75 were considered to have high resilience and any value below that was considered as low resilience.

## 8.5.4 Proposed Architecture

The adopted architecture has two major elements: 1) a phone application and 2) a real-time system to deliver advice from a server. The proposed architecture for the whole application is represented in Figure 8.3. It is seen that the mobile application has four parts which are primary engine, request handler, local database and communicator. Initially the request handler receives a request which is then dispatched toward the core. The core then uses components like Solution Provider, Processor and Questionnaire Analyzer to determine the thought process of a real psychologist. The request is verified in the processor and is either processed or forwarded to the next component. The questionnaire analyzer assesses the user's condition and generates a questionnaire and provides solution according to the answer. According to the information provided by the other components, the solution provider provides the appropriate solutions. The information of each individual user is stored in the database.

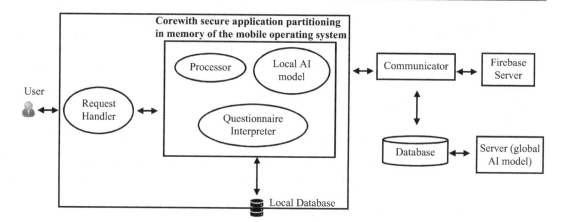

*Figure 8.3* Architecture of the considered system for secure anxiety and depression data collection, transmission and analysis at the edge.

The users' whereabouts are collected from Facebook using communicator and through Google Map nearby doctors are suggested. The communicator also gives authorization to server to update questions and receive data of the application for statistical purposes, research centers and doctors. Doctors will use this to collect patient's information and research centers will use it to collect system statistics. All statistics will be completely anonymized and will only be accessible if authorized by the user.

## 8.5.5  Data Analysis Using AI Techniques

Various machine learning algorithms can be employed to determine the facial expression of a person. We have employed a questionnaire dataset, which was discussed in earlier section, to determine the performance of the model for the collected questionnaire data. To achieve this, we have utilized various algorithms such as Random Forest (RF), K Nearest Neighbors (KNN), Support Vector Machine (SVM), AdaBoost and Gradient Boosting (GB). The algorithms are discussed in detail in the following part of this section.

**RF** is an ensemble learning method for classification, regression. Multiple decision trees are formed at the time of training and a bootstrap sample technique is used for outputting the class that is the mode of the classes of the individual trees for classification purposes. A set of decision trees is constructed from a randomly selected subset of the training set. Then it aggregates the majorities from all the decision trees to decide the final class of the test instance. Choosing the number of decision trees that should be regarded to make a voting decision is also very important. If the number of trees is very small, the algorithm will not use enough data to build a proper model; on the other hand, if the number of trees is very high, same features will be used several times increasing the correlation between trees. Therefore, in RF, the number of trees can be considered as a hyper-parameter for the model.

**KNN** is a lazy learning method that was used to classify this problem. It is considered to perform optimally as it only considers the k nearest points around it instead of computing for the whole dataset. Based on the k neighbors, the algorithm determines class label by taking the most frequent value among the neighbors. The neighbors are determined by calculating distance of all the points from test data points. The k data points having minimum distance from the points are considered as k neighbors. In order to calculate distance, various distance measures can be used. In our case, we used Euclidean distance to calculate the distance between instances. In KNN, K is a hyper-parameter that can be altered to find the optimal value of K.

**SVM** is a classification method where a decision boundary is constructed using various kernels in the high-dimensional data. Since higher dimensions are also considered while developing a hyperplane, SVM is said to separate the class values even more accurately than other algorithms. Therefore, a kernel value must be defined in order to perform classification with this algorithm. However, in some cases, the data cannot be perfectly separated if an optimal boundary is built. In that case, a penalty factor (C) can be introduced that is a trade-off between an optimal boundary and more accurate classification.

**AdaBoost** or Adaptive Boosting is an ensemble learning method that assigns weight values to observations, where more weight is given to the critical instances which are challenging to classify and less weight to the instances that are comparatively easier to classify. Therefore, the model concentrates on finding deeper interpretation based on the weak trees. Multiple weak models are constructed based on their weights and the final class label is determined based on the majority votes of the weak learners.

**GB** algorithm also has similar properties as AdaBoost. However, instead of finding out weak learners based on their weight, this algorithm employs the gradient of the loss function to find the weak learners. This algorithm trains multiple models in a sequential and additive manner.

## 8.5.6 Privacy Preservation of the Model

In such applications, it is very crucial to preserve privacy of collected data, particularly when the data are used for building a model centrally. This is also applicable for the proposed application in this chapter. We tackle this issue by using an emerging concept called federated learning in our model that can be achieved through federated learning as stated below.

### 8.5.6.1 Federated Learning

Federated learning enables training the algorithm across multiple decentralized edge devices or servers holding the local data samples. The integration of federated learning with our model is discussed in the next part. In Figure 8.4, it is seen that information can be shared without sharing the actual data and can be implemented efficiently. Here, $M_n$ is the mobile device of user n, $L_n$ is the load of user n and $W_n$ is the weight of user n. Federated learning allows devices situated on the edge to participate in the training of the machine learning models. The trained model on each edge device participating in the federation is then sent to the centralized server instead of the raw data. The collected models are re-trained with all the local models collected from various decentralized edge devices to make a more robust global model. Hence, the data that we have (user data) does not get out of the device (e.g., mobile, laptop or an IoT device). By this method, we can limit data sharing and preserve data security while contributing toward building a more precise model.

We have demonstrated the federated learning model in a particular number of mobile devices. To evaluate the performance of the model, we have implemented two deep learning algorithms which are – Artificial Neural Network (ANN) and Convolutional Neural Network (CNN). To construct the federated learning model, at first the global model was trained. Subsequently, using this model, the local models were trained. The local models were aggregated and the global model was then updated accordingly. The updated model was then again transferred to the local devices.

ANNconsists of one or more layers of neurons. The three major components of this model are input layer, hidden layers and output layer. Each input in the hidden layer is assigned

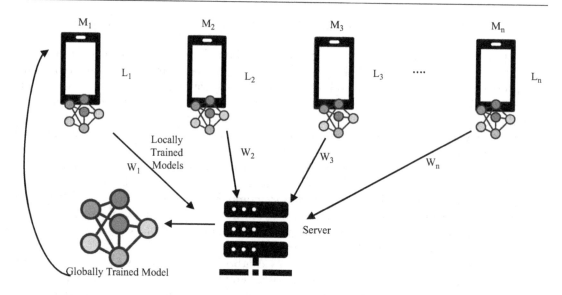

*Figure 8.4* Federated learning in our model.

a weight which is determined by various forward and back propagation techniques in the previous layer. The model is trained upon these weights which denotes the importance of the input. Then the data is passed to output layer where the class label is determined. There are two types of ANN – shallow and deep ANN. The shallow ANN consists of one hidden layer, whereas deep ANN consists of multiple hidden layers.

CNN is a more robust algorithm that employs additional convolutional and max pooling layers along with the hidden layers to train the model. It can interpret the data in a more profound level by constructing relevant features of its own using the convolutional filters. Just like ANN, CNN can also be categorized into two forms – shallow and deep CNN. The shallow CNN consists of one convolutional layer, whereas deep CNN consists of multiple convolutional layers.

## 8.5.7 Model Deployment on Edge Devices

To deploy this model into smart edge devices, the application should be released in either any globally connected apps provider (e.g., Google Play) and deploy the generated APK using the following steps:

- First, create a developer account and then set up a merchant account.
- Then create an application with default language and choose the title of the application.
- As for the next process, finish preparing the store listing and give the product details.
- Next, add the user graphics and add screenshots and icons that showcase the app's features.
- Google offers multiple ways to upload and release your APK. Before you upload the file, however, you need to create an app release, and then release the app.
- Offer an appropriate content rating.
- Set up pricing and distribution.
- Roll out the release to publish the app.

## 8.6 EXPERIMENTAL RESULTS

### 8.6.1 SqlLite Analysis

In this analysis, we present the scores of both anxiety and depression using a scoring procedure and demonstrate a simple, easy-to-understand visualization of the severity levels on a daily basis in the course of a week. The severity level of anxiety and depression collected from the mobile application questionnaire part is represented in Figure 8.5 and Figure 8.6.

### 8.6.2 Machine Learning Algorithm Analysis

In the questionnaire data, we applied several machine learning algorithms. For the ensemble learning models such as RF, AdaBoost and GB algorithm, the number of trees was considered to be 100. For KNN, the number of neighbors was considered to be 3. For SVM, the value of penalty factor was 1 and the kernel was radial basis function. The accuracy, precision and F1-score of the algorithms in the dataset is illustrated in Figure 8.7. It can be seen from the figure that RF and SVM is performing comparatively well with an accuracy and precision of 80% and 79%, respectively. Other algorithms such as KNN and AdaBoost's performance was relatively lower compared to the other algorithms.

### 8.6.3 Federated Learning Analysis

The performance of federated learning models implemented with the deep learning algorithms for 20 mobile devices are reported in Figure 8.8. For deep ANN and CNN algorithms, both the number of hidden layers and convolutional layers were considered to be 4. 'Adam'was

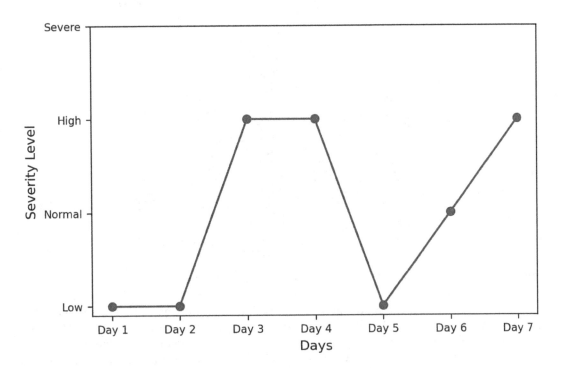

*Figure 8.5* Analysis of anxiety using test quiz scores using the developed mobile app for a user.

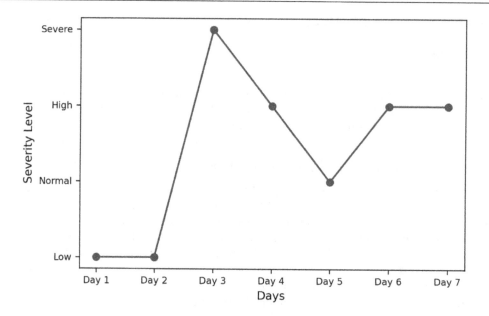

*Figure 8.6* Analysis of depression using test quiz scores using the developed mobile app for a user.

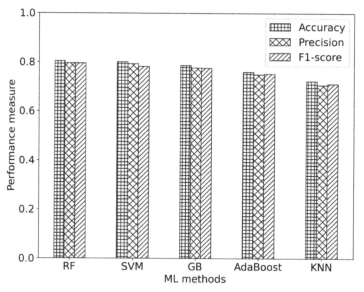

*Figure 8.7* Performance comparison of various machine learning algorithms.

used as the optimizer of the model and the activation function was ELU. The results reveal that deep ANN performed the best with an accuracy, precision and F1-score of 94% which is much higher than the other algorithms. Shallow ANN performed with the second best among the other algorithms; however, CNN models did not perform up to the mark for this particular case. Since deep ANN performed the best, a confusion matrix was also plotted to obtain a deeper interpretation of the results which is represented in Figure 8.9. It can be seen that majority of the instances of both high and low resilience classes were predicted correctly.

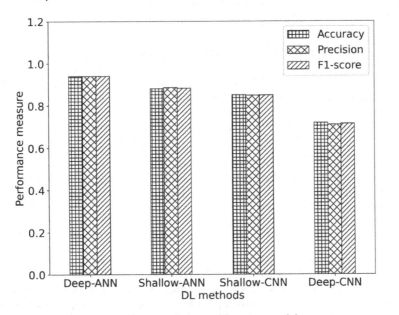

*Figure 8.8* Performance comparison of various federated learning models..

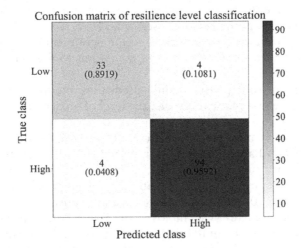

*Figure 8.9* Confusion matrix of deep-ANN model.

The overall performance evaluation of the machine learning models and federated learning models showed that federated learning models perform much more precisely while providing greater security for the architecture. Therefore, such models can be a better selection to be employed in the application to make it more reliable for the users.

## 8.6.4 Comparative Analysis

A comparative analysis was performed with previous studies that employed mental health data as is presented in Table 8.1. It is seen that our federated learning model performs superiorly

*Table 8.1* Comparative analysis of the proposed model with earlier studies.

| Study Type | Model | Performance (Accuracy %) |
| --- | --- | --- |
| Resilience detection (Proposed approach) | Federated learning employing deep ANN | 94 |
| Stress detection [19] | J48 decision tree classifier | 78 |
| Manic and depressed state detection [20] | Naïve Bayes classifier | 76 |
| Anxiety detection [21] | Markov chain | 73 |
| Short-term depression prediction [22] | Random forest | 70 |

compared to other studies who have conducted similar analysis using mental health data. Thus, this confirms the efficiency of the model in terms of performance comparison.

## 8.7 CONCLUSION

Early Identification of Mental Health Disorder is a secure interactive mobile application designed to recognize the symptoms of depression and anxiety. Although several applications are available online to detect various health problems, they are of limited use. They are more time consuming and not developed for multipurpose. Therefore, our system addresses the issue and offers new features that are not currently available in addition to providing a diagnosis. Our aim is to make the user find the best solutions for the illness while keeping their data secured. Our analysis of the existing users who have recovered from the same health problems makes us provide the best solutions to the new users in a quicker way. Different questionnaires will be given to users with same symptoms to figure out the effectiveness of each of the questionnaire.

Our model consists of four phases mainly prediction, monitoring, analysis and stress-relieving methods. In the first phase to predict the level of anxiety and depression, we used a quiz approach.

The questionnaire set is based on real-time issues in an individual's life. The questionnaire includes symptoms of apparent sadness, reported sadness, inner tension, reduced sleep, reduced appetite, lack of concentration, lassitude, inability to feel, pessimistic thoughts, suicidal thoughts, etc. The questionnaire set is an array of questions. Each time a user takes the test, they can answer 10 questions on anxiety and depression. In order to increase the effectiveness of the questionnaire, we employed the Fisher-Yates Algorithm. The main idea for employing this method is to shuffle the questionnaire set. We further classified levels of severity from mild to severe. The Montgomery-Asberg Depression Rating Scale (MADRS-S) has been used to evaluate the severity of depression, while Hamilton Anxiety Rating Scale to rate the severity of anxiety.

In the monitoring phase, the data or the scores generated from both the test modules depression and anxiety are stored in the history module. This module consists of subclasses of History_Anxiety and History_Depression. History_Anxiety displays the score of the anxiety test module and the History_Depression shows the score of the depression test module.

In the next phase, the analysis is done on the generated user data using firebase analytics and machine learning approach. The firebase analysis helps in monitoring the number of users of the application, activities the users are using, the location of the users, the stability of the app, daily retention, etc. This analysis helps us to understand the growth in usage of the application and the development needed in the application to render efficient services to the users. The machine learning algorithms are required to analyze the collected data. In this chapter, we have demonstrated the efficacy of our algorithm in a similar questionnaire dataset where algorithms such as RF, KNN, SVM, GB and AdaBoost were implemented. We have also implemented a federated learning model using ANN and CNN. Among all the analysis, deep-ANN performed the best with a highest accuracy of 94% in the federated learning model. This indicates that the federated learning model can perform much more accurately offering a more secured analysis platform.

Our secured Depression and Anxiety mobile application will help those who are unsure if they are in a condition that needs treatment. The evaluation after the screening gives more certainty about the mental health of the user. Moreover, a notification will be sent to the guardian when the user meets a certain level of anxiety and depression. The application generates an automated clinical report for the user. The clinical report helps the user to have a clear idea of his/her levels of depression and anxiety. Over a period, by day-to-day analysis, we generate the graph which shows the levels of depression and anxiety. The user is further allowed to refer to some stress-relieving methods like music or games which are present by default in the application. The users with less severity level can spend time on stress-relieving methods while the high severity levels are processed to the guardian for the treatment. This application can be made reliable to the users by integrating the concepts of federated learning, which will help construct a more accurate model while not sharing user data over Internet. Hence, data can be collected and stored securely within the local device.

## REFERENCES

1. P. Winkler, J. Horáček, A. Weissová, M. Šustr, and M. Brunovský, "Physical comorbidities in depression co-occurring with anxiety: A cross sectional study in the Czech primary care system," *Int. J. Environ. Res. Public Health*, 2015, doi: 10.3390/ijerph121215015.
2. H.-J. Kang et al., "Comorbidity of depression with physical disorders: Research and clinical implications," *Chonnam Med. J.*, 2015, doi: 10.4068/cmj.2015.51.1.8.
3. P. Chandrashekar, "Do mental health mobile apps work: Evidence and recommendations for designing high-efficacy mental health mobile apps," *mHealth*, 2018, doi: 10.21037/mhealth.2018.03.02.
4. H. Ritchie and M. Roser, "Mental health," Apr. 2018. [Online] Available: https://ourworldindata.org/mental-health.
5. Canadian Mental health Association, "Rural and northern community issues in mental health," 2009. [Online] Available: https://ontario.cmha.ca/documents/rural-and-northern-community-issues-in-mental-health/.
6. Doetsch, Karl H. and Garry Lindberg. "Canadarm," *The Canadian Encyclopedia*, 04 Mar. 2015, Historica Canada. Available: https://www.thecanadianencyclopedia.ca/en/article/canadarm. Accessed 12 April 2021.
7. Z. M. Fadlullah, M. M. Fouda, N. Kato, A. Takeuchi, N. Iwasaki, and Y. Nozaki, "Toward intelligent machine-to-machine communications in smart grid," *IEEE Commun. Mag.*, vol. 49, no. 4, pp. 60–65, 2011.
8. T. X. Tran, A. Hajisami, P. Pandey, and D. Pompili, "Collaborative mobile edge computing in 5G networks: New paradigms, scenarios and challenges," *IEEE Commun. Mag.*, 2017, doi: 10.1109/MCOM.2017.1600863.
9. J. Zhang and K. B. Letaief, "Mobile edge intelligence and computing for the internet of vehicles," *Proceedings of the IEEE*. 2020, doi: 10.1109/JPROC.2019.2947490.
10. P. C. Pijush Kanti Dutta Pramanik, Saurabh Pal, Aditya Brahmachari, "Processing IoT data: From cloud to fog—it's time to be down to earth," in *Applications of Security, Mobile, Analytic, and Cloud (SMAC) Technologies for Effective Information Processing and Management*, IGI Global, 2018.

11. Z. Zhou, X. Chen, E. Li, L. Zeng, K. Luo, and J. Zhang, "Edge intelligence: Paving the last mile of artificial intelligence with edge computing," *Proc. IEEE*, 2019, doi: 10.1109/JPROC.2019.2918951.

12. B. McMahan and D. Ramage, "Federated learning: Collaborative machine learning without centralized training data," *Post*, 2017, doi: 10.1080/00173130902749999.

13. S. Silva, B. A. Gutman, E. Romero, P. M. Thompson, A. Altmann, and M. Lorenzi, "Federated learning in distributed medical databases: Meta-analysis of large-scale subcortical brain data," In *2019 IEEE 16th international symposium on biomedical imaging (ISBI 2019)*(pp. 270–274). IEEE. 2019, doi: 10.1109/ISBI.2019.8759317.

14. M. Ammad-ud-din et al., "Federated collaborative filtering for privacy-preserving personalized recommendation system," 2019, [Online]. Available: http://arxiv.org/abs/1901.09888.

15. T. Li, A. K. Sahu, A. Talwalkar, and V. Smith, "Federated learning: Challenges, methods, and future directions," *IEEE Signal Process. Mag.*, 2020, doi: 10.1109/MSP.2020.2975749.

16. B. Kumawat, S. Chaudhary, and S. Gaur, "A study of cloud technologies-research issues, challenges, engineering, platforms and applications: A survey," *International Journal of Multimedia, Image Processing and Pattern Recognition*, vol. 1, no. 1, pp. 1–10, 2018, [ISSN: 2581-625X (online)].

17. A. Pantelopoulos and N. G. Bourbakis, "A survey on wearable sensor-based systems for health monitoring and prognosis," *IEEE Trans. Syst. Man, Cybern. Part C: Apps Rev.*. 2010, doi: 10.1109/TSMCC.2009.2032660.

18. K. Anderson and P. W. McOwan, "A real-time automated system for the recognition of human facial expressions," *IEEE Trans. Syst. Man, Cybern. Part B Cybern.*, 2006, doi: 10.1109/TSMCB.2005.854502.

19. D. Carneiro, J. C. Castillo, P. Novais, A. Fernández-Caballero, and J. Neves, "Multimodal behavioral analysis for non-invasive stress detection," *Expert Syst. Appl.*, 2012, doi: 10.1016/j.eswa.2012.05.065.

20. A. Grünerbl et al., "Smartphone-based recognition of states and state changes in bipolar disorder patients," *IEEE J. Biomed. Heal. Informatics*, 2015, doi: 10.1109/JBHI.2014.2343154.

21. D. Miranda, J. Favela, and B. Arnrich, "Detecting anxiety states when caring for people with dementia," *Methods Inf. Med.*, 2017, doi: 10.3414/ME15-02-0012.

22. A. G. Reece and C. M. Danforth, "Instagram photos reveal predictive markers of depression," *EPJ Data Sci.*, 2017, doi: 10.1140/epjds/s13688-017-0110-z.

Chapter 9

# Harnessing Artificial Intelligence for Secure ECG Analytics at the Edge for Cardiac Arrhythmia Classification

*Sadman Sakib*
Lakehead University, Canada

*Mostafa M. Fouda*
Idaho State University, USA

*Zubair Md Fadlullah*
Lakehead University, Canada
Thunder Bay Regional Health Research Institute (TBRHRI), Canada

## CONTENTS

## 9.1 INTRODUCTION

Due to the rapid advancement in Artificial Intelligence (AI) and Internet of Things (IoT) technologies, automated health monitoring of subjects with chronic diseases such as cardiovascular diseases (CVDs) is emerging to be a striking necessity to introduce intelligence into the healthcare system. However, traditional health analytics and monitoring systems mostly employ cloud computing, which can raise an obvious privacy concern for the subjects and care providers [1]. Therefore, to integrate intelligence into the healthcare system and make the analytics process more robust and secure, we choose electrocardiogram (ECG) analysis for arrhythmia detection. The proposed AI-aided heartbeat classification system, if deployed at the edge devices, can identify irregular heartbeats with high accuracy and can be deployed at the edge device for localized intelligence without the obligation to transfer health data to a remote server decision-making.

As a proof of concept of the localized analytics of health data, we choose cardiac arrhythmia since it is one of the major causes of CVDs. CVDs are the leading reason for death globally, and more people die yearly from CVDs than from any other cause, according to the world health organization (WHO) [2]. These CVDs arise due to the long-term result of cardiac arrhythmia, which may not seem life-threatening initially but can result in heart failure in the long run if not detected timely. Arrhythmia causes the heart not to pump blood adequately. Patients suffering from arrhythmia ordinarily feel signs of quicker or slower heart pulsations. Some other symptoms encompass fainting, dizziness, weakness and pain in the chest. However, various patients with arrhythmia do not perceive every indication. Hence, automatic arrhythmia detection is vital to avoid any extreme adverse CVD conditions. Continuous observation of the ECG signals over hours is very critical for detecting various CVDs. The conventional method of long-time ECG monitoring is known to be invasive, time-consuming and extremely expensive, where the daily activity of the subject becomes confined during the ECG data retrieval phase. Lately, due to the massive advancement in Machine Learning (ML), Deep Learning (DL) techniques for efficient data analysis and the wearable IoT devices and wireless technologies, the ECG signal can be transmitted using wireless transmission techniques and analyzed automatically. Figure 9.1 manifests the traditional cloud-based health monitoring system and our focused secure AI-aided edge analytics for smarter IoT with embedded intelligence. It is usually analyzed at the remote cloud to get insights into the health status of a subject. However, in this way, the private sensitive health data gets shared with the cloud server, which can raise a potential privacy concern. Moreover, this paradigm of ECG analytics results in bandwidth consumption, delay in transmitting the enormous data and privacy concerns.

Although the traditional cloud-based architecture has aforementioned potential pitfalls, the adaptation of localized intelligence at the edge devices is still lacking focus in the literature. To diminish the communication delay, extensive network bandwidth, and preserve user-data privacy, we should consider the localized analysis of the health data. Thus, a more automated and effective analytics technique should be designed and integrated with the edge devices. Therefore, in this chapter, as the primary step of integrating intelligence with edge devices, we focus on developing the efficient multi-class heartbeat (HB) classification system and we considered several ML techniques to pave the way to relocate the ECG monitoring system for arrhythmia detection from the centralized cloud paradigm to edge IoT to enhance

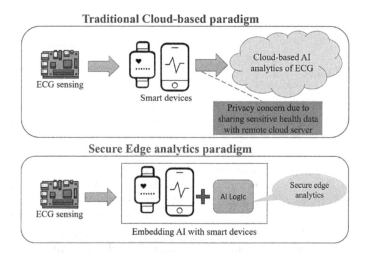

*Figure 9.1* Traditional cloud-based ECG monitoring architecture vs secure edge analytics paradigm.

the privacy of the subject's health data. We employ state-of-the-art AI and data analytics techniques to efficiently develop the ML models and assess the models' effectiveness in multiple experimental setups. Among the ML models, we have explored the random forest (RF), Decision Tree (DT), K Nearest Neighbor (KNN), Quadratic Discriminant Analysis (QDA) and Linear Discriminative Analysis (LDA) classifiers to compare the models' performance employing a clinically graded ECG dataset [3–5]. The RF model outperformed the other two ML models with exceptional classification accuracy (95.74% and 99.45%), which indicates the model's eligibility for deploying at the programmable smart edge devices for secure ECG monitoring.

## 9.2 LITERATURE REVIEW

An efficient arrhythmia classification is a vital task for secure ECG monitoring, which comprises detecting irregular heartbeats from the ECG signal. Arrhythmia subjects usually experience symptoms of faster or slower heartbeats compared to a regular rhythm [6]. Due to the availability of IoT devices that can facilitate health data transmission, researchers have been working on ECG analysis for detecting these diverse abnormal heart conditions. It is indispensable to identify CVDs timely, and hence, constant measurement of ECG for an extended time is imperative. However, the traditional method of long-time ECG monitoring is invasive and costly, and it limits the daily activity of the subjects. To surmount this issue and introduce automation in the ECG monitoring system, cloud-based ECG analytics has been employed where the ECG signal is customarily broadcasted adopting wireless transmission methods such as Bluetooth, Zigbee or Wi-Fi [7, 8]. Therefore, most of these conventional automatic ECG monitoring systems analyze the data at the cloud servers to carry out the system models and then send feedback to the user or care providers. Authors in [9] proposed cloud-based analytics where the ECG signals are gathered employing a wearable monitoring node and transmitted straight to the IoT cloud using Wi-Fi. An IoT-based patient monitoring system is introduced where data is then processed utilizing a Raspberry Pi, temperature sensor, heart rate sensor and accelerometer sensor and then after the analysis phase decision regarding the heart condition is delivered to the IoT cloud for cloud-based analytics [10].

Arrhythmia is often attached to other kinds of heart disease, which means subjects may require treatment to prevent further severe issues. Hence, recently automatic heartbeat classification is getting widespread attention to automate the process with enhanced efficiency and security. The most common medical test for arrhythmia is the ECG. Due to the ECG signal's noise and the heartbeat signal's non-stationary nature, it is difficult for cardiologists to deal with manual arrhythmia detection. Arrhythmia can be discovered when the heartbeat's electrical activity is unusual and can result in a faster or slower heartbeat than normal conditions. Arrhythmia can happen at random times as ECG is a non-stationary signal. The ECG data volume is enormous, and the manual process can be delayed and time-consuming [11]. Hence, the automatic classification needs to implement with the IoT sensors to embed the intelligence or the analytics phase of the detection of arrhythmia efficiently and securely. A few notable examples of ECG analysis are performed by employing time-domain analysis [12], neural networks [13], wavelet analysis [14], wavelet analysis combined with radial basis function neural networks (RBFNN) [15] and non-linear delay differential equations [16].

In the cloud-based ECG arrhythmia monitoring systems, numerous techniques are utilized, for example, feature extraction and classification techniques such as ML and Deep Learning (DL). The authors in [17] have proposed a Support Vector Machine (SVM)-based classification model for arrhythmia detection with high accuracy. The authors in [18] use a deep learning-based CNN model to classify heartbeats with high correctness. Another method employed a Deep Neural Network (DNN) architecture [19] to classify the ECG signal as natural or unusual, checked with ground-truth, and demonstrated exceptional performance. Furthermore, AdaBoost and Gradient Boosting algorithms were implemented by the authors in [20] to classify ECG using single-lead ECG. In another research, an accurate arrhythmia classification method for ECG is proposed based on extreme weighted gradient boosting (XGBoost) using a broad range of feature sets [21]. Although most researchers have focused on cloud-based ECG analytics, the concept of localized intelligence for ultra-edge IoT-based efficient arrhythmia classification technique is proposed in [1].

## 9.3 DATASET PREPARATION

To develop the arrhythmia classification model, we have employed the MIT-BIH arrhythmia database [22] taken from Physionet, which comprises records of several traditional and life-threatening cases of arrhythmia and normal samples sinus rhythm. Since 1980, this dataset has been utilized for fundamental research on cardiac diseases and ECG. The database contains 48 examples of 30 mins excerpts of two-lead (lead A and B) ECG recordings acquired from 47 subjects at a sampling rate of 360 Hz. At least two cardiologists annotate each beat. Most of the dataset recordings consist of either lead II, V2, V4, or V5. The recordings can be divided into two sets:

i. 23 subjects (100 series) are determined at random from a group of over 4000 Holter recordings
ii. 25 subjects (200 series) were chosen to incorporate samples of unusual but essential cases of arrhythmia.

The datasets comprise a text header file, a binary file, and a binary annotation file with .txt, .dat, and .atr extensions, respectively.

i. Header file (.hea): These files comprise a brief text file that defines the contents of the signals, such as the name of the signal file, number of examples, signal format, type of signal, and so forth.
ii. Binary file (.dat): The binary files include digitized representations of the ECG signals.
iii. Annotation files (.atr): The annotation files contain compilations of heartbeat labels that represent the nature of ECG signals at a stipulated time in the record.

Annotations can be used in this dataset to generate five different beat categories in accordance with the Association for the Advancement of Medical Instrumentation (AAMI) EC57 standard [23]. Table 9.1 illustrates a summary of mappings between beat annotations in each category.

The labeled ventricular beats are from 15 different heartbeat types in the MIT-BIH arrhythmia dataset, as shown in Table 9.1. Also, there exists considerable variation in the number of examples of the heartbeat types presented in Table 9.2. Here, the most prominent class is Normal (N), with over 75,000 samples, whereas the minority class with the least number of samples is the Fusion beat (F). Among the five classes in the dataset, for the multi-class heartbeat detection task, we have employed the three prominent classes with a high number of samples (i.e., N, S, and V) in the experiment. Even after considering the majority classes with a higher number of heartbeats, there is a significant class imbalance within the three categories, and we adopted up-sampling the instances from the classes with lower samples compared to the majority class.

*Table 9.1* Mapping the MIT-BIH Arrhythmia dataset heartbeats to the AAMI heartbeat classes.

| Heartbeat Super Class | Heartbeat Annotation |
|---|---|
| N (Normal) | N (Normal) |
| | L (Left bundle branch block beat) |
| | R (Right bundle branch block beat) |
| | e (Atrial escape beat) |
| | j (Nodal (junctional) escape beat) |
| S (Supraventricular ectopic beat) | A (Atrial premature beat) |
| | a (Aberrated atrial premature beat) |
| | J (Nodal (junctional) premature beat) |
| | S (Supraventricular premature beat) |
| V (Ventricular ectopic beat) | V (Premature ventricular contraction) |
| | E (Ventricular escape beat) |
| F (Fusion beat) | F (Fusion of ventricular and normal beats) |
| | Q (Unclassifiable beat) |
| Q (Unknown beat) | / (Paced beat) |
| | f (Fusion of paced and normal beat) |

*Table 9.2* Frequency of heartbeats of each class of the dataset.

| Heartbeat Super Class | Number of Samples |
|---|---|
| N (Normal beat) | 90,083 |
| S (Supraventricular ectopic beat) | 2,779 |
| V (Ventricular ectopic beat) | 7,009 |
| F (Fusion beat) | 15 |
| Q (Unknown beat) | 803 |

## 9.4 METHODOLOGY

This section illustrates the proposed ML-based heartbeat classification methods and the potentiality of deploying at the edge node for secure ECG analytics. AI logic can be integrated with edge sensors for a long time, efficient ECG monitoring of a subject [1] [24]. Hence, in this work, we aim to develop a practical ECG filtering, feature extraction method, which can pave the way to a secure classification method by deploying at the edge node. The deployment and integration of the efficient AI-aided models at the edge devices will enhance the privacy and security of the sensitive ECG trace as the data will not be required to be transferred to any remote server for analysis. The results produced by the edge analytics can then be transmitted to the care-providers for cardiac activity monitoring. In order to implement the AI-aided system at the edge sensors for faster and secure analysis, the classification of heartbeat is a crucial segment. Consequently, our primary goal is to design such an AI-aided model that can be deployed at the edge node for secure ECG monitoring with high precision.

The proposed AI-aided system requires four distinct phases for efficient ECG analytics:

   i. ECG signal pre-processing
  ii. Heartbeat segmentation

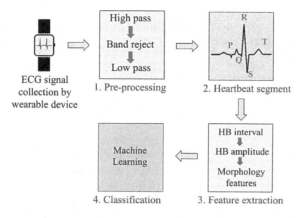

ECG signal
collection by
wearable device

*Figure 9.2* Steps of ECG heartbeat classification.

   iii. Feature extraction
   iv. Learning or Classification

As presented in Figure 9.2, the ECG heartbeat classification task mainly comprises four steps. The first step is the pre-processing phase, which involves eliminating the ECG's undesired interference and noises. The segmentation technique creates parts into simple data for additional analysis. A unique set of significant features extracted for further investigation of the ECG is produced in the feature extraction phase. Lastly, the classification phase includes the detection and learning of the type of heartbeat based on ECG features. The techniques utilized during the pre-processing step directly influence the results, and hence, it should be cautiously accumulated. The classification of heartbeat mainly consists of the combination of an efficient feature extraction technique followed by ML or deep learning algorithms. The following subsections explain the methodology employed in each of the four steps of the analysis.

## 9.4.1 ECG Pre-processing Phase

There are several kinds of noise associated with the raw ECG signal. Among these include the noise due to muscle contraction, power-line interference, baseline wander. Hence, pre-processing is essential for efficient recognition of ECG signals. Several approaches have been taken for the pre-processing step of ECG signals. To decrease the impacts of artifacts of ECG before handling the information. In perspective on this, we utilized a course of three filters:

- A high-pass Butterworth filter with cut-off frequency 1 Hz is used to eliminate DC component and baseline wander
- A band-reject Butterworth filter is utilized to reduce the 60 Hz AC interference
- A low-pass Butterworth filter is applied to high-frequency noise with cut-off frequency 25 Hz

Butterworth filter produces frequency response as flat as possible in the passband. In Figures 9.3 and 9.3, a portion of raw ECG from record 100 of the MIT-BIH arrhythmia dataset is exhibited that contains noise and pre-processed clean ECG, respectively. As the figures illustrate that the exploited three-phased noise-filtering can eliminate different segments of unwanted noise from the ECG signal and produce a clean ECG trace for further analysis.

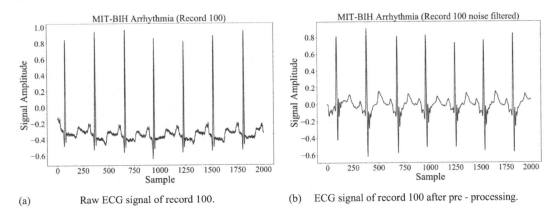

(a)           Raw ECG signal of record 100.

(b)    ECG signal of record 100 after pre - processing.

*Figure 9.3* Effect of the noise filtering of the raw ECG signal.

## 9.4.2 Heartbeat Segmentation Phase

In the heartbeat segmentation phase, we have taken the fiducial points provided with the MIT-BIH datasets. These provided fiducial focuses are at the moment of the significant nearby outrageous of a QRS complex of the ECG signal. The fiducial focuses were obtained on beat-by beat premise. All heart pulsates are isolated into fifteen beat types in the datasets. However, as indicated by AAMI, all the heart thumps, which are accessible in the database, were arranged into five groups as per their physiological source. In our analysis, we have taken the three classes of beats to be specific normal (N), supraventricular (S), and ventricular (V).

Therefore, we have utilized the database's annotations associated with heartbeat segmentation, such as identifying the R peak in the QRS complex, which is distinguished and labeled earlier. Employing the R peak location, we have also segmented the location of the other peaks (i.e., Q, S, T, etc.). Figure 9.4 illustrates the heartbeat segmentation phase's QRS complex detection. The figure exhibits the result of Q, R, and S peak detection of the record 100 from the dataset. The R peaks' locations are already annotated in the dataset; hence, we utilized that information to determine the exact positions of the Q and S peaks from each ECG cycle. We employed the peak location from each cycle to identify the unique features in the feature extraction phase.

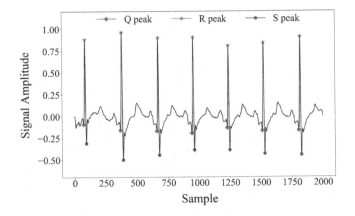

*Figure 9.4* Detection of QRS peaks from the ECG sample (record 100 from the dataset).

### 9.4.3 Feature Extraction Phase

The feature extraction stage is an essential phase for the success in the secure heartbeat classification of the arrhythmia using the ECG signal. Any information obtained from the heartbeat used to distinguish its type can be acknowledged as a feature. Figure 9.5 manifests different segments and peaks of an ideal ECG cycle and illustrates the typical locations of the four significant peaks in an ECG cycle, namely, P, Q, R, S, and T peaks. The Q, R, and S wave peaks comprise the QRS complex, which is a vital distinguishing portion of an ECG cycle. We utilize the position of these peaks to find discriminative features of the regular and irregular ECG signals.

In this study, the features have been categorized into four different groups:

i.   RR intervals features
ii.  Heartbeat intervals features
iii. Heartbeats waves' amplitude features
iv.  Morphology features

The most distinguishing feature is determined from the heartbeat interval, also recognized as the RR interval, which is the interval between the R peak of a heartbeat to another different heartbeat, which could be its previous or follower heartbeat. We determined the pre-RR and post-RR intervals by calculating the R peak range with respect to the predecessor and successor cycle's R peak's location. Features related to RR interval have a high aptitude to distinguish the kinds of pulses, and the RR interval features play a vital role in efficient ECG analysis. Features linked with heartbeat intervals are determined after heartbeat segmentation. The QRS duration is the time interval between the QRS onset and the QRS offset. The T-wave duration is established as the time interval between the QRS offset and the T-wave offset. The full set of unique features employed in this study is presented in Table 9.3. The features are utilized for both ECG leads, namely, lead A and lead B. Therefore, combining lead A and B, we get our full feature set consisting of 34 features, 17 for each lead A and B. Features related to heartbeat amplitude can be divided into five categories, one per P, Q, R, S, and T wave where each of these contains the corresponding amplitude values. For the morphology features, five samples were taken in the QRS complex (between onset and offset point of the QRS complex).

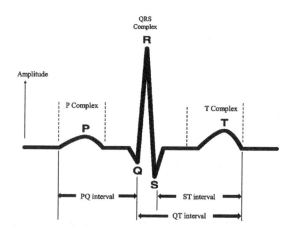

*Figure 9.5* Different components of one ideal ECG cycle.

Table 9.3 The unique set of extracted features from the ECG signal.

| Feature Group | Lead A and B |
| --- | --- |
| RR Intervals | Average RR |
| | Pre-RR |
| | Post-RR |
| Heartbeat Intervals features | PQ Interval |
| | QT Interval |
| | ST Interval |
| | QRS Duration |
| Heart beats amplitude features | P peak |
| | T peak |
| | R peak |
| | S peak |
| | Q peak |
| Morphology features | QRS morph feature 1 |
| | QRS morph feature 2 |
| | QRS morph feature 3 |
| | QRS morph feature 4 |
| | QRS morph feature 5 |

In our study, after extracting the features from the ECG trace, we have used the standard scaling technique to scale the features in a specific range. The standardization technique scales the features by excluding the mean and adjusting to unit variance. Standardization considers that the observations fit a Gaussian distribution with a proper mean and standard deviation. This scaling technique also serves to normalize the data within a selective range, which also benefits in speeding up the computations. The standard score of sample feature $x$ can be calculated from the Equation (9.1),

$$\bar{X} = (x - \mu)/\sigma \tag{9.1}$$

Here, $\mu$ = the mean of the feature $x$ and $\sigma$ = standard deviation

## 9.4.4 Learning/Classification Phase

We utilize the RF-based ML technique to deploy the AI-aided model to the edge devices for secure analysis of ECG. After defining a set of features from the heartbeats from the feature extraction phase, models can be trained with these features using AI algorithms from ML and data mining specialties for arrhythmia heartbeat classification. Some of the commonly used AI approaches for this purpose are SVM, Artificial Neural Networks (ANN) and Linear Discriminant Analysis (LDA), etc. In this research, we have applied the RF algorithm and compared the results with traditional ML models, namely the DT, KNN, QDA and LDA.

The RF is an ensemble learning method for classification, regression. Multiple decision trees are formed at the time of training. The fundamental concept behind the RF method is to combine many decision trees into a particular model. Separately, predictions made by decision trees may not be accurate, but the predictions will be more efficient when combined from multiple decision trees. A bootstrap sample technique is adopted for outputting the class that is the mode of the classes of the individual trees for classification purposes. In RF, a large number of nearly uncorrelated trees function as a combination. A set of decision trees from a randomly selected subset of the training set. Then it aggregates the majorities from all the decision trees to decide the final class of the test instance. In the RF, the measure of the split's quality can be calculated using Gini impurity or entropy. In the adopted RF architecture, we exploited the Gini index for splitting. The RF performance is linked to the correlation among trees and the strength of each individual tree. If there is a higher correlation among the trees, the error will decrease, whereas the strength of each tree will increase the forest's performance. We considered $\sqrt{M}$ (M = number of features) several features when looking for the best split. In the adopted RF architecture, we have selected $N_t$ number of decision trees, and the optimal value of $N_t$ is selected based on the hyper-parameter tuning of the number of trees. One other essential property of the RF is that they are beneficial when trying to determine feature importance as essential features tend to be at the top of each tree. Therefore, the importance score of each of the extracted ECG features has been determined after applying the RF classifier. The RF classifier's feature importance can facilitate the model to use a lower number of features and still obtain excellent classification efficiency. The adopted RF model with optimal hyper-parameters will be integrated with programmable smart-edge devices to increase the security of the ECG trace of a subject.

## 9.5 EXPERIMENTAL SETUPS, RESULTS AND DISCUSSION

In this section, we exhibit the results of the systematic experiments we conducted for the proposed RF model and compared it with other traditional ML methods. We evaluate the proposed ML-based method's efficiency across different experimental setups. The systematic analyses were carried in different phases which are noted as follows:

- Experimental setup 1: The full dataset is divided into two parts, one for training and another part for testing. The training part consists of 22 records, whereas the testing part also consists of 22 files. We also perform hyper-parameter tuning to find the optimal parameters for the ML methods.
- Experimental setup 2: The full dataset is employed in this scheme. To evaluate the models, we conducted stratified cross-validation [25]. We also considered the class imbalance in the dataset by applying up-sampling of the minority class.

The experiments were conducted on a workstation with Intel Core i7, 3.00GHz CPU, 16 GB RAM, powered by Nvidia RTX 2060 GPU. For implementing the ML algorithms and other data analytics methods, we intended to utilize python programming language. We employed the Scikit-learn library for adopting the ML models, the matplotlib library for visualizing the results and ECG signals. To analyze the locations of different peaks from ECG, we employed a library named waveform-database (WFDB) [26] package for reading, writing and processing WFDB signals and annotations.

### 9.5.1 Performance Indicators

To evaluate the classification performance of the adopted ML models, we utilized the sequence of three measurement indicators, accuracy, weighted precision and weighted F1 score. The accuracy of a test is its ability to differentiate the three cases correctly. Considering, $C$ = Number of classes in the considered ECG classification, $N_j$ = Number of samples in the $j^{th}$ class and $|N|$ = the total number of samples in all the class, the accuracy can be denoted using the Equation. (9.2):

$$\text{Accuracy} = \frac{\sum_{j=1}^{C} TP_j}{|N|} \tag{9.2}$$

Here, $TP_j$, $FP_j$ stands for true positive and false positive classification for the $j^{th}$ class, respectively. The weighted precision can be represented as Equation (9.3). It addresses how well defined the model is out of those predicted to be in $j^{th}$ class, how many of them are genuinely in $j^{th}$ class and the amount is multiplied by the weight of the $j^{th}$ class. The precision of the $j^{th}$ class can be expressed as the Equation (9.3):

$$\text{Precision} = \sum_{j=1}^{C} \left( \frac{N_j}{|N|} * \frac{TP_j}{TP_j + FP_j} \right) \tag{9.3}$$

As the third performance indicator, we employed the weighted F1 score, which is essentially the weighted average of precision and recall. The weighted F1 score can be achieved as Equation (9.4). Here, $P_j$ and $R_j$ are the precision and recall of $j^{th}$ class, respectively. $P_j$ can be expressed as $TP_j/(TP_j + FP_j)$ and $R_j$ can be denoted as $TP_j/(TP_j + FN_j)$. $TP_j$ indicates the number of cases correctly identified to be in the $j^{th}$ class; $FP_j$ depicts the number of cases incorrectly identified to be in the $j^{th}$ class and $FN_j$ indicates the number of cases wrongly identified as a class other than the $j^{th}$ class.

$$\text{F1 Score} = \sum_{j=1}^{C} \left( \frac{N_j}{|N|} * \frac{2(P_j * R_j)}{P_j + R_j} \right) \tag{9.4}$$

## 9.5.2 Results for Experimental Setup 1

In the experimental setup 1, we firstly performed hyper-parameter tuning for KNN and RF to find the optimal value of K and the number of trees, respectively, which produces the best performance. We considered N (Normal), S (Supraventricular ectopic beat) and V (Ventricular ectopic beat) heartbeats for our classification purpose. The distribution of these beats in the training and testing set for the experimental setup 1 is manifested in Table 9.4.

Figure 9.6 exhibits the results after performing hyper-parameter tuning for KNN and RF employing experimental setup 1. We used a grid search with three-fold cross-validation for this purpose. For the training purpose of the hyper-parameter tuning phase, we utilized 50% of the training data from Table 9.4. This portion of training data was preserved and separated only for training purposes in both experimental setups. According to the hyper-parameter tuning results, the best accuracy (96.9%) of KNN was recorded when the value of K was 3. For RF, the best accuracy (97.5%) was recorded when the number of trees was 101.

Table 9.4 Heartbeat distribution in train and test set for the experimental setup 1.

| Heartbeat super class | Train set | Test set |
|---|---|---|
| N (Normal) | 45,845 | 44,238 |
| S (Supraventricular ectopic beat) | 943 | 1,836 |
| V (Ventricular ectopic beat) | 3,788 | 3,221 |

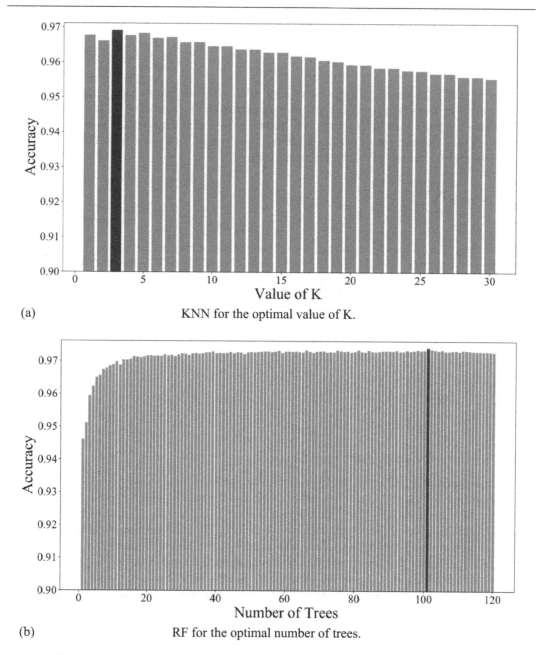

(a)          KNN for the optimal value of K.

(b)          RF for the optimal number of trees.

*Figure 9.6* Hyper-parameter tuning results for K Nearest Neighbor (KNN) and random forest (RF).

After selecting the optimal configuration for the ML models, we conducted the training of the models utilizing the training and testing data portion of experimental setup 1, illustrated in Table 9.4. In our experiments, we have employed singular value decomposition (SVD) as the solver for LDA. In terms of the KNN model, we have used Minkowski distance as the distance measurement technique. The experimental results are exhibited in Figure 9.7. The results show that the RF model outperformed the other four ML methods (DT, KNN, QDA and LDA). For further experiments, we have selected the best performing three ML methods (RF, KNN and LDA). The accuracy, precision and F1 score of the RF model were 95.74%,

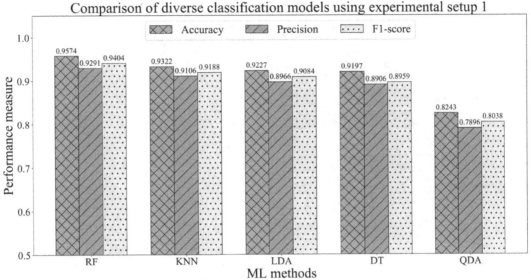

*Figure 9.7* Performance comparison of the classification models employing the experimental setup 1.

0.9291 and 0.9404. Hence, the RF model's efficiency in all three performance matrices proves its efficiency for deploying at the edge node for secure ECG analytics.

As the RF method produced the best classification efficiency, we investigate the model's performance by using the crucial features from the whole feature list. To find out more useful features in distinguishing irregular heartbeats from the ECG signal, we have utilized RF feature importance scores and used the experimental setup 1 for this purpose. In Figure 9.8, all the feature's importance is plotted in descending order from left to right direction. Analyzing feature importance, we can perform feature selection to reduce the feature set's dimension and use more essential features to train the classifiers [27]. In this manner, we can eliminate less significant features from the feature set to make the classifier more efficient in integrating with the edge devices. As in many cases, the edge devices are often limited in terms of resources; therefore, finding out the optimal set of features is vital to designing a model that can perform efficiently even with a lower number of features.

Figure 9.8 demonstrates that the features related to RR intervals are more significant for RF to identify patterns in heartbeats. The first and second features in the ranking of feature importance are the pre-RR feature for lead A and lead B. These results confirm the significance of the R peak and the features related to RR intervals. Out of the top 10 features, six features are from the RR interval group. According to the feature importance score, the morphology features are the least important features as none of the top 10 features are from that feature group.

The top three ML models acquired from the previous results are compared when the reduced features (top 10 features) are utilized with the full set of features (34 features). Table 9.5 represents the results of the performance of RF when the reduced feature set is employed. The RF model outperformed the other two methods in terms of classification efficiency. The results illustrate that the RF model is robust enough to classify irregular heartbeats with 93.95% accuracy, 0.9101 precision and 0.9118 F1 score. The performance for the reduced feature set is slightly lower than that of when the full feature set is employed. However, the decrease in performance is not that massive considering that the dataset has become almost half in terms of the number of features. The encouraging classification performance proves

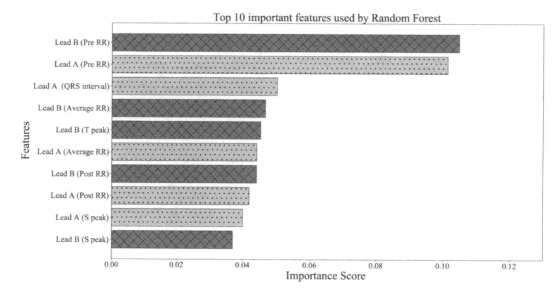

*Figure 9.8* Top 10 features from the random forest in terms of feature importance.

*Table 9.5* Performance comparison of the top performing three ML methods employing the full feature set and the reduced feature set after selecting top 10 features based on feature importance of experimental setup 1.

| Method | Full feature set | | | Reduced feature set with top 10 features | | |
|---|---|---|---|---|---|---|
| | Accuracy | Precision | F1 score | Accuracy | Precision | F1 score |
| RF | **95.74%** | 0.9291 | 0.9404 | **93.95%** | 0.9101 | 0.9118 |
| KNN | 93.22% | 0.9106 | 0.9188 | 91.27% | 0.9014 | 0.9095 |
| LDA | 92.27% | 0.8966 | 0.9084 | 91.99% | 0.8846 | 0.8904 |

that using only the top significant features; the RF model can be integrated with the edge devices. The RF model's robust performance, even with the reduced feature set, proves that in terms of integrating with computational resource-constrained edge devices, the model can identify discriminative features from the ECG signal even with fewer features, facilitating the edge devices to generate faster decisions with enhanced security due to localized analytics.

### 9.5.3 Results for Experimental Setup 2

For the classification of experimental setup 2, we have considered the full MIT-BIH dataset without any pre-defined training and testing data. We have used ten-fold stratified cross-validation for all three methods. Stratified k-fold cross-validator splits data into train and test sets by maintaining the ratio of representations for each class. Before the training phase of k-fold cross-validation, 20% of the whole dataset was split into the testing ECG data. The remaining 80% of the ECG trace was employed for the training purpose.

In this experimental setup, we also applied the up-sampling technique for the minority classes to deal with the class imbalance. After filtering out the noise from the ECG signal, we applied Synthetic Minority Over-sampling Technique (SMOTE) in terms of experimental setup 2 to balance the four classes. SMOTE is a technique for increasing the number of

Table 9.6 Performance Comparison of the machine learning models before and after employing Synthetic Minority Over-sampling Technique (SMOTE) for experimental setup 2 using stratified 10-fold cross-validation.

| Method | Without applying SMOTE | | | After applying SMOTE | | |
|---|---|---|---|---|---|---|
| | Accuracy | Precision | F1 score | Accuracy | Precision | F1 score |
| RF | **99.17%** | 0.9916 | 0.9916 | **99.45%** | 0.9945 | 0.9945 |
| KNN | 99.31% | 0.9931 | 0.993 | 98.86% | 0.9896 | 0.9889 |
| LDA | 95.55% | 0.9524 | 0.9531 | 90.84% | 0.9443 | 0.9252 |

cases in the dataset in a balanced procedure [28]. This technique works by generating new examples from existing minority cases that are supplied as input. However, SMOTE does not increase or reduce the number of samples in the majority class. SMOTE receives representatives of the feature space and produces discrete cases that blend features of the target case with features of its neighbors for the minority class.

Table 9.6 manifests that the efficiency of the RF model raises after balancing the classes by adopting SMOTE. The classification accuracy of the RF model increases from 99.17% to 99.45% due to applying the SMOTE to balance out the classes. However, SMOTE did not have a positive influence on the performance of KNN and LDA as the accuracy reduced slightly for both the methods. The encouraging experimental outcomes prove that the RF model can be a viable solution for efficient and secure ECG analytics tool if integrated with the edge devices. Therefore, as the AI-based module, we can deploy this pre-trained RF model into the programmable edge devices for secure, faster and efficient analysis of the subjects' sensitive health data with enhanced privacy due to localized inference by the ML models.

## 9.6 CONCLUSION

The proliferation of wearable sensors and IoT devices generate a large stream of health data, and it is essential to keep safe from any unwanted third-party access. The pitfalls of traditional cloud-based solutions for health data analytics can cause severe concerns for the subjects and the care providers as well, and if the private health data gets compromised, it can cause a dire circumstance for both. Hence, with the developing processing power of IoT devices and smart devices, traditional analytics can be driven away from the cloud to the edge, and it can assist in overcoming significant privacy concerns as well as overall communication delay and bandwidth consumption. Hence, this chapter aims to employ AI and data analytics techniques to classify heartbeats by analyzing the ECG signal, which can be integrated with edge devices for efficient and secure heartbeat classification. This regular and irregular heartbeat classification can pave the path to overcome privacy issues of the traditional cloud-based health analytics and moving toward local intelligence. Different ML and data analytics techniques are employed to decide the most suitable model for this ECG analysis at the edge. The proposed method depicts an automatic multi-class heartbeat classification system according to the guidance of ANSI/AAMI EC57:1998 standard so that it can be integrated with sensors to produce sensors with embedded intelligence. A clinically graded dataset from PhysioNet is utilized to evaluate the proposed method, and multiple experimental setups are arranged to ensure the generalization ability of the proposed RF-based model. The selected AI-aided technique is optimized by choosing the best hyper-parameters by tuning different sets of values for the parameters. Finally, the trained model can be integrated with the edge devices to achieve localized embedded intelligence. In the proposed architecture for secure ECG analysis, a selected use-case from the health domain, the edge devices will take part in the analytics, and this way, the private and sensitive data will persist within their local device for faster and enhanced privacy.

## REFERENCES

1. S. Sakib, M. M. Fouda, Z. M. Fadlullah, and N. Nasser, "Migrating intelligence from cloud to ultra-edge smart IoT sensor based on deep learning: An arrhythmia monitoring use-case," in *2020 International Wireless Communications and Mobile Computing (IWCMC)*, Limassol, Cyprus, Jun. 2020, pp. 595–600, doi: 10.1109/IWCMC48107.2020.9148134.

2. "Cardiovascular diseases (CVDs)," 2017. [Online]. Available: https://www.who.int/news-room/fact-sheets/detail/cardiovascular-diseases-(cvds). [Accessed: 14-Jun-2020].

3. A. J. Prakash and S. Ari "AAMI standard cardiac arrhythmia detection with random forest using mixed features," *2019 IEEE 16th India Counc. Int. Conf. INDICON 2019 - Symp. Proc.* pp. 24–27 2019 doi: 10.1109/INDICON47234.2019.9030317.

4. M. Emu and S. Sakib, "Species identification using DNA barcode sequences through supervised learning methods," in *2nd International Conference on Electrical, Computer and Communication Engineering, ECCE 2019*, 2019, pp. 7–9, doi: 10.1109/ECACE.2019.8679166.

5. L. Yang, X. Liu, F. Nie, and Y. Liu, "Robust and efficient linear discriminant analysis with L2,1-Norm for feature selection," *IEEE Access*, vol. 8, pp. 44100–44110, 2020, doi: 10.1109/ACCESS.2020.2978287.

6. S. Sahoo, M. Dash, S. Behera, and S. Sabut, "Machine learning approach to detect cardiac arrhythmias in ecg signals: A survey," *Innovation and Research in BioMedical engineering (IRBM)*, vol. 41, pp. 185–194, 2020, doi: 10.1016/j.irbm.2019.12.001.

7. T. Shaown, I. Hasan, M. M. R. Mim, and M. S. Hossain, "IoT-based portable ECG monitoring system for smart healthcare," in *1st International Conference on Advances in Science, Engineering and Robotics Technology (ICASERT)*, Dhaka, Bangladesh, May 2019, doi: 10.1109/ICASERT.2019.8934622.

8. M. Bansal and B. Gandhi, "IoT big data in smart healthcare (ECG monitoring)," in *2019 International Conference on Machine Learning, Big Data, Cloud and Parallel Computing (COMITCon)*, Faridabad, India, Feb. 2019, pp. 390–396, doi: 10.1109/COMITCon.2019.8862197.

9. A. Rahman, T. Rahman, N. H. Ghani, S. Hossain, and J. Uddin, "IoT Based patient monitoring system using ECG sensor," in *1st International Conference on Robotics, Electrical and Signal Processing Techniques (ICREST)*, Dhaka, Bangladesh, Jan. 2019, pp. 378–382, doi: 10.1109/ICREST.2019.8644065.

10. A. Kamble and S. Bhutad, "IOT based patient health monitoring system with nested cloud security," in *4th International Conference on Computing Communication and Automation (ICCCA)*, Greater Noida, India, Dec. 2018, pp. 1–5, doi: 10.1109/CCAA.2018.8777691.

11. E. Izci, M. A. Özdemir, R. Sadighzadeh, and A. Akan, "Arrhythmia detection on ECG signals by using empirical mode decomposition," in *2018 Medical Technologies National Congress (TIPTEKNO)*, Magusa, Nov. 2018, pp. 1–4, doi: 10.1109/TIPTEKNO.2018.8597094.

12. Y. R. Tsai, Z. Y. Chang, and C. W. Huang, "Time-domain multi-level R-peak detection algorithm for ECG signal processing*," in *2019 IEEE Eurasia Conference on Biomedical Engineering, Healthcare and Sustainability (ECBIOS)*, Okinawa, Japan, 2019, pp. 35–38, doi: 10.1109/ECBIOS.2019.8807887.

13. M. Kachuee, S. Fazeli, and M. Sarrafzadeh, "ECG heartbeat classification: A deep transferable representation," in *2018 IEEE International Conference on Healthcare Informatics (ICHI)*, New York, NY, Jun. 2018, pp. 443–444, doi: 10.1109/ICHI.2018.00092.

14. K. Giri, S. Saraswat, A. K. Yadav, and S. Singh, "Classification of supraventricular arrhythmias using wavelet decomposition," in *9th International Conference on Cloud Computing,*

*Data Science & Engineering (Confluence)*, Noida, India, Jan. 2019, pp. 387-391, doi: 10.1109/CONFLUENCE.2019.8776624.

15. S. Raj and K. C. Ray, "Sparse representation of ECG signals for automated recognition of cardiac arrhythmias," *Expert Systems with Applications*, vol. 105, pp. 49–64, 2018, doi: 10.1016/j.eswa.2018.03.038.

16. C. Lainscsek and T. J. Sejnowski, "Electrocardiogram classification using delay differential equations," *Chaos*, vol. 23, no. 2, pp. 1–9, Jun. 2013, doi: 10.1063/1.4811544.

17. V. Mondéjar-Guerra, J. Novo, J. Rouco, M. G. Penedo, and M. Ortega, "Heartbeat classification fusing temporal and morphological information of ECGs via ensemble of classifiers," *Biomedical Signal Processing and Control*, vol. 47, pp. 41–48, 2019, doi: 10.1016/j.bspc.2018.08.007.

18. A. Rajkumar, M. Ganesan, and R. Lavanya, "Arrhythmia classification on ECG using Deep Learning," in *5th International Conference on Advanced Computing & Communication Systems (ICACCS)*, Coimbatore, India, Mar. 2019, pp. 365–369, doi: 10.1109/ICACCS.2019.8728362.

19. R. Nanjundegowda and V. A. Meshram, "Arrhythmia detection based on Hybrid features of T-wave in Electrocardiogram," *International Journal of Intelligent Engineering and Systems*, vol. 11, no. 1, pp. 153–162, 2018, doi: 10.22266/ijies2018.0228.16.

20. J. Bogatinovski, D. Kocev, and A. Rashkovska, "Feature extraction for heartbeat classification in single-lead ECG," in *42nd International Convention on Information and Communication Technology, Electronics and Microelectronics (MIPRO)*, Opatija, Croatia, 2019, pp. 320–325, doi: 10.23919/MIPRO.2019.8757135.

21. H. Shi, H. Wang, Y. Huang, L. Zhao, C. Qin, and C. Liu, "A hierarchical method based on weighted extreme gradient boosting in ECG heartbeat classification," *Computer Methods and Programs in Biomedicine*, vol. 171, pp. 1–10, 2019, doi: 10.1016/j.cmpb.2019.02.005.

22. G. B. Moody and R. G. Mark, "The impact of the MIT-BIH arrhythmia database," *IEEE Engineering in Medicine and Biology Magazine*, vol. 20, no. 3, pp. 45–50, May 2001, doi: 10.1109/51.932724.

23. American National Standards Institute, "Testing and reporting performance results of cardiac rhythm and ST segment measurement algorithms ANSI/AAMI EC57," *Association for the Advancement of Medical Instrumentation*, 2012.

24. A. Mohsen, M. Al-Mahdawi, M. M. Fouda, M. Oogane, Y. Ando, and Z. M. Fadlullah, "AI aided noise processing of spintronic based IoT sensor for magnetocardiography application," in *IEEE International Conference on Communications (ICC)*, Dublin, Ireland, Jun. 2020, pp. 1-6, doi: 10.1109/ICC40277.2020.9148617.

25. X. Zeng and T. R. Martinez, "Distribution-balanced stratified cross-validation for accuracy estimation," *Journal of Experimental & Theoretical Artificial Intelligence*, vol. 12, no. 1, pp. 1–12, 2000, doi: 10.1080/095281300146272.

26. "wfdb PyPI," [Online]. Available: https://pypi.org/project/wfdb/. [Accessed: 14-Jun-2020].

27. J. Rogers and S. Gunn "Identifying feature relevance using a random forest," in *SubspaceLatent Structure and Feature Selection. SLSFS 2005. Lecture Notes in Computer Science* C. Saunders, M. Grobelnik, S. Gunn J. Shawe-Taylor Ed. vol 3940. Springer, Berlin Heidelberg. doi: 10.1007/11752790_12.

28. T. Pan, J. Zhao, W. Wu, and J. Yang, "Learning imbalanced datasets based on SMOTE and Gaussian distribution," *Information Sciences.*, vol. 512, pp. 1214–1233, Feb. 2020, doi: 10.1016/j.ins.2019.10.048.

## Chapter 10

# On Securing Electronic Healthcare Records Using Hyperledger Fabric Across the Network Edge

*Sarthak Kothari, Tahrat Tazrin, Dhruvi Desai,*
*and Anam Parveen*
Lakehead University, Canada

*Mostafa M. Fouda*
Idaho State University, USA

*Zubair Md Fadlullah*
Lakehead University, Canada
Thunder Bay Regional Health Research Institute (TBRHRI), Canada

## CONTENTS

## 10.1  INTRODUCTION

Recently, healthcare systems have been identified as a critical infrastructure, often targeted by malicious adversaries. Healthcare data interception due to improper handling of the patient-data may result in not only financial losses for both the care-giving entities (hospitals, clinics, physicians, nurses, insurance companies) and victims but also identity theft, damage of reputation and other social issues. While healthcare systems are currently supported by an assortment of technologies to improve the patient-experience within the entire healthcare ecosystem, numerous operational challenges still exist [1]. In particular, the challenge related to unified management of Electronic Health Records (EHRs) requires researchers to design a scalable technique to enable multiple physicians to have access to the complete health history of a given patient, at the same time, maintaining privacy of the health data. This challenge has become even more daunting recently because the patients are nowadays able to collect their own physiological and mental health data using Internet of Things (IoT) sensors and wearables, use pain-management applications and so forth, which need to be collected from their edge devices (e.g., user-smartphones), and converted and stored as EHRs. The proliferation of patients' edge devices generating a large stream of medical data from IoT-based, remote monitoring means that it is important to secure their data across the healthcare ecosystem so that they are not exposed to third parties. In order to have a secure access control of the health data, our aim in this chapter is to put the patient in control of their respective health data, by empowering them to share which relevant physicians and other caregivers they are willing to share their data with in a unified format. The use of blockchain in various domains, including healthcare, has recently garnered much attention from government, academicians and industry [2]. Due to its ability to support such unified medical records, data security, privacy improvement and insurance decisions/transactions, the blockchain technology may be regarded as an effective solution for the aforementioned healthcare technology challenges. Apart from several function of blockchain in financial domains, it also has usage in the non-financial domains such as reputation systems [3], public services [4], protection and IoT [5, 6]. However, blockchain also faces some technological difficulties, some of them being consistency, safety and scalability [7].

Blockchain is an advanced technology which has modified the ways to store, transact and record the data. The concepts partially match to that of a conventional database; however, the only difference is that the intermediary can be avoided here. The issues of interoperability in data safety are largely studied in recent years. The critical issue is to figure out a way to enable public access to confidential health data, anonymity, safeguarding the protection of personal data and preventing abuse of data. Blockchain technology and smart contracts offer a creative and exciting way for EHRs to hold a reference. With the help of the proposed concept, patients, healthcare providers and hospitals can have better control over their data, which are collected by other organizations. In brief, blockchain has the potential to boost the safety and interoperability of EHR solutions. This chapter discusses how to use blockchain and smart contracts to develop EHR. We address some non-technical aspects that make data on health valuable first. Next, we are proposing an architecture that could boost the existing EHR structures. The key goal is to ensure safe access to patient data without permission, restricting access by third parties, and only permitting access to the patient and doctor and the medical centers.

E-Health is a value-developing technology that can access medical data remotely as well as share patient data in real-time that are collected from various sensors. This had stated that the use of EHRs had grown largely from 9% in 2008 to a peak of 96% by 2015 [8]. An EHR is typically the automated patient health data collection which has different attributes such as text documents, video, image data, etc. The main purpose of EHR systems is to store and manipulate patient data in order to monitor the health of a patient over time. For cross-EHR sharing, the question of legal interoperability arises because there are legal requirements many healthcare systems and providers have to utilize EHRs, which prohibits any medical data sharing. The absence of structured management of data and sharing contributes to a fragmentation rather than unity of personal medical data [9]. This kind of technology is important nowadays because it encourages patients to engage in activities concerning their healthcare and restore intermediaries about their health records [10]. The concepts of blockchain provide exciting prospects for technical progress to tackle these healthcare problems [11].

In short, it is decentralized, authenticated and a database that keeps a series of transactions in the form of blocks where a consensus-driven mechanism is implemented with the help of the ledger to achieve consensus between various individuals who might not be trusted. This will require any individual in the medical system, such as provider, patient, insurance company, pharmacist, to apply the required credentials and identities to get control on the blockchain. Every participant will have permission to access the ledger and other digitally collected data with the authorization of candidate or if they are sanctioned. [5]. The failure to access healthcare data is a persistent issue specially while collecting it efficiently in the provision of healthcare worldwide. The EHRs placed in position presume that one patient only visits one doctor at a clinic. Also, patients are not limited to only one doctor or clinic. In a study it was seen that on average a U.S. patient can have approximately 19 different health records, and in 2010, a study reported that patients see18.7 different doctors in their lifetime [7]. Patients are not limited to a single zone protected by EHR. People move for jobs, for recreation and they relocate for a long period of time. Individuals are also willing to protect their health by using data created by wearable gadgets.

In this chapter, we first discuss the contribution of the state-of-the-art blockchain technology and smart contracts in various practical situations of healthcare industries which is regarding data access, interoperability and management. The concept of implementing an extensive information architecture is proposed in order to maintain EHRs based on hyperledger fabric model. The hyperledger fabric model is a distributed ledger that consists of assets, chaincode, ledger features, channels, security and membership services and consensus. Setting distributed ledger of the blockchain node (assigned patient to doctor) can be used for setting up central network of the edge computing; this could be visualized as the vectorized decentralized edge computing. The act of ensuring that the patients have access to their data can be referred to as data privacy, and data accessibility ensures that the access of information is unconstrained. Data accessibility by the user always raises a concern of privacy, which should be taken into account specially in the field of healthcare [12]. The issues regarding data health interoperability are being studied more than ever [13]. One of the crucial challenges is to enable open access to sensitive health data while maintaining personal data privacy and avoiding data misuses while maintaining anonymity. Blockchain can contribute significantly in order to manage data of such patients. It is a set of distributed ledger architectures that is heavily applied for various cryptocurrency applications starting from Ethereum to bitcoin. These permission-less blockchains can affect the financial services industry by being disruptive [14]. Permissioned chains can be prone to demands of resource storage [3]. Therefore, our main contribution, in this chapter, is to use the concepts of an integrated blockchain-based architecture to address the issues related to accesibility and data privacy in healthcare. The limitation that is addressed through this chapter is – the use of permissioned blockchain integrated with off-chain storage of data which is accessed with the help of a mobile application or browser. The framework is implemented by employing an example use of healthcare data which are patient centered.

The proposed architecture consists of three parts which are the access control module based on blockchain, off-chain data storage and a role-centered web interface. The resource containing all kinds of data such as test results, diagnostic images and other paperwork of the patient are made secured through encryption which are then stored on a cloud repository in order to maximize the performance of the model and also make it economically reasonable. These methods can associate the on-chain and off-chain data without having to pay any additional computational or storage-related expense in the user edge devices, which is common aspect in blockchain architectures [15]. The smart contracts facilitate doctors and patients to provide access to their respective users with their edge device flexibly and securely. The web interfaces can then be used by the doctors and patients to carry out multiple activities such as writing a prescription, allowing the read-only access to other doctors over the patient who require the medical attention from specialists, revoke rights from doctors once the patient has acquired the treatment, patients can track their medical records from any place, check current prescription, book appointments for recommended test, etc. more easily. In order to keep track of EHRs, blockchain technology and smart contracts are employed as an effectual solution [16]. Therefore, the concerns regarding privacy and interoperability of the data can be addressed through the concepts of blockchain and smart contracts to improve EHR systems which arepropositioned in this chapter.

## 10.2 EXISTING DECENTRALIZED SECURITY METHODS: CAN BLOCKCHAIN BE USED AT THE EDGE?

Blockchain technology is at the core of digital cryptocurrency and its applications are being considered for various application domains. The topic of how blockchain could be leveraged at the edge is garnering much research attention. The crucial growth of blockchain has fascinated a wide range of people starting from technology giants to manufacturers. The change from a centralized model to the decentralized model has made blockchain a foundational technology. Because of the features like decentralization, security, automation, immutability and transparency, all the agreed mental obligations and rights and ownership of assets can be recorded on the blockchain. However, there is an essential and critical disadvantage of a blockchain, i.e., lack of ability to scale. This drawback of scalability restricts to see the success of applications. Nevertheless, with the development of computing technology, a multitude of applications are devised. Due to this, mobile cloud and fog computing are introduced like an addition to the cloud edge computing. The edge computing facilitates execution of programs at the edge of the network. Moreover, edge computing also provides a superior solution to data storage, low latency maintenance, computation power and application services. Therefore, integrating the concepts of edge computing with blockchain has facilitated the construction of exceptional systems by providing better storage of distributed nodes, reliable access of the network, better computation and so forth. Therefore, the systems are better in terms of security, data integrity and computation validation. However, the fusion consumes a lot of storage and computational resources, which affects the computation of mining and storage of the blockchain in resource-constrained devices. Additionally, the computation and storage on the blockchain are facilitated by off-chain computation and storage in edge nodes. The concepts of blockchain with edge computing are very popular; however, there are some problems that need to be addressed. Many approaches will be used at different levels for scalability refinement. Although by adding new autonomic mechanisms, the complexity of management reduces these additional results to security problems that still need to be studied. Furthermore, from different views and with stability and flexibility, the blockchain and edge computing-based functionalities need to be incorporated deeply. Also, the relationship between edge computing and blockchain needs to be promoted by AI and Big Data [15].

## 10.2.1 Current EHR System in Canada

It is seen that the healthcare industry has done many developments in their respective territory, and the development graph of healthcare is still growing. The expansion in the popularity of the medical field enables health professionals and service providers to enhance their specializations. Daily life habits like less workout, junk food diet, and less sleep, etc. result in chronic diseases [17]. Apart from primary and secondary prevention, there is a need to pay heed to early diagnostics. Having an incorporated electronic well-being record makes it workable for the specialist co-ops to put together their activities concerning what is as of now known about the client's well-being history. In any care delivery setting, EHR is known as a longitudinal electronic record of patient health information, which includes the medical history of the patient, radiology reports, problems, medications. Personal health records (PHR) which are also called Electronic Personal health record is a complimentary record which has been created as a need for people to take an interest in their health. With the help of electronic health tools and information data set, PHR manages health-related data, assists the management of chronic. As far as EHRs are concerned, the primary key point is secured documents, which include current as well as past medical records. These health records include information from labs, different hospitals, clinics, etc. Executing electronic well-being records in Canada is a Canadian skillet activity that requires the cooperation of partners, including the government, Canada Health Infoway Inc. and the commonplace and regional governments, just as different associations engaged with the conveyance of medicinal services. Each inspected purview has, in any event, one center electronic well-being/health record (EHR) framework setup, and a few territories have nearly wrapped up their EHR frameworks. Given the noteworthy difficulties of this venture and the considerable potential advantages of EHRs, partners need to report on progress made and benefits accomplished to lawmaking bodies and Canadians. The Auditor General of Canada and the auditor generals of Alberta, Nova Scotia, Ontario, Prince Edward, British Columbia and Saskatchewan conducted execution reviews of the implementation of EHR in their jurisdictions [18, 19]. For EHR studies, the common objective has been created by different representatives of a committee. The main focus and concentration are being given to organizations like ministries of health who are answerable and liable for implementing EHR. Ensuring the compatibility of EHR is a primary task before implementing it. EHR, with excellent compatibility, result in better accessibility of medical information to healthcare professionals. At the administration level, Infoway was practicing due respect in managing assets from the national government to achieve its goals and objective in implementing EHR in Canada [18]. Infoway, as a fundamental and essential speculator, backs up each venture that relies on task potential. Moreover, based on project potential, Infoway accepts and approves each project to satisfy the needs of the project. Nevertheless, Infoway has done many works in support of implementing EHR across Canada:

1. Infoway has employed approval process to figure out the EHR requirements and inspect them.

2. Infoway funds the projects through a gated funding model. This gated funding model operates by binding repayment to the accomplishment of project milestone.
3. Infoway also settles legal agreements for each project in order to verify the projects.

However, when it comes to testing the system to check whether the projects have satisfied the requirements, Infoway does not involve the conformance testing results of the EHR system. Also, Infoway does not provide a guaranteed compatibility to EHR across Canada. It is surely compatible in cases where the standards have variances in the conformance. It is found that most of the people in Canada prefer to get healthcare from their native province but not all provinces have assurance about the compatibility of their EHR systems [18]. The compatibility of EHR systems has still not been properly established. To have a decent EHR system, it is important to have effective systems with better performance monitoring and reduced risks. However, it is found that there are different ways of handling project management. It depends and varies from province to province as follows:

1. In Ontario, projects expenditures with insufficient supervision, insufficient deliverable was reported [18].
2. In Saskatchewan, according to recognized project management, by ignoring the timelines and overall cost projects were managed [18].
3. In Prince Edward Island, cost for monitoring the projects was always a problem [18].
4. In Alberta, according to accepted project technique, EHR projects were handled. But monitoring of total cost for EHR systems still needs to be addressed [18].

## 10.2.2 Challenges with the Traditional EHR Systems

While there is no doubt that the EHR system is progressing day by day across Canada, there are still some issues regarding challenges listed below in implementing EHR system that needs to be addressed.

1. Achieving the goal: In March 2009, it was found that EHR healthcare professionals were available to only 17% of Canadians [18]. The main goal is to have 100% EHR of Canadians available to healthcare professionals which was stated to be very difficult by Infoway.
2. System upgradation: Compatibility funds are essential to construct the complete EHR, but it is often tough to determine how these funds will be provided and when.
3. Realizing benefits: From research conducted by Infoway it is found that $6 billion will be saved each year once they are deployed. However, jurisdictions are failing to realize the various advantages.
4. Patient healthcare solutions: The advancement of healthcare industries have enabled patients to access their own records. But the new EHR systems are not compatible with the old systems and therefore, there is a need for more solutions [18].
5. Sharing personal health information: EHR should be available across the country since many people move from one place to another place in search of jobs or living, sharing the personal medical data from one province to another is important. There are different laws for collection of medical data in different provinces. Thus, the laws also should be compatible between jurisdictions for an easier transfer of data between provinces.
6. Initiation of funding: At long last, questions stay about how the activity will be financed. The absolute expense to build the EHR system is also a crucial part to consider [18].

## 10.2.3 Security Measures for Health Records

As the technologies are advancing in every field, the risk of data loss and cybercrime is also increasing which results in destructive ramifications. Data security should be given the highest priority in all domains including healthcare industries. Data security is important in healthcare domain because losing healthcare data of a patient brings the question of life and death. As cybercrime in healthcare is a serious issue, the department of health and human services (HHS) in the USA has launched centers of cybersecurity and communication integration center. The main goal of these centers is to familiarize consumers and healthcare organizations about the risks of using mobile technology in the industry. There are many ways through which data can flow in and out of healthcare systems. EHR is considered to be one of the foremost information hubs from which the data can be lost. Since cloud-based EHRs effectively manage the exchange of data for the providers, the data is also at risk there. Although the sharing of data is helpful for the healthcare industries, there is a risk of data integrity being disrupted. The best way to eliminate threats to data integrity can be addressed by the four security measures that can provide security to the patient's data:

1. Compliance to HIPAA and HITECH as a standard: Health Insurance Portability and Accountability Act (HIPAA) and Health Information Technology for Economic and Clinical Health Act (HITECH) provide best information security baseline standard and administrative guidelines for information security. For example, a bank-level (SSL) encryption algorithm is employed to check for secure transmission.
2. Critical clues provided by an audit trail: The main objective of audit trail is to track user actions to eliminate loss of information of hacking from the system. This tracking answers what, when, where and who, i.e.,
    - What was the data that was retrieved?
    - When was the data retrieved?
    - Where was the data retrieved?
    - And who retrieved the data?
3. State-of-the-art data centers: The state-of-the-art data centers maintain real-time surveillance, bank-level security and so forth. These data centers stop private information from being hacked, and also it shields from physical threats. For example, web apt saves the data in the IO data center which provides a qualified advantage for securing the data.
4. Accessibility to expertise on real-time: It is very crucial to have specialized staff in online security measures. The staff should be able to solve any data security related problems and other issues including security threat as protecting data means protecting people from these threats [20].

## 10.3 CURRENT CHALLENGES FACED BY THE HEALTHCARE WORKERS IN COVID-19 PANDEMIC

In the current state of rise in number of people impacted by Coronavirus Disease 2019 (COVID-19) in every corner across the world, clinical trials for the development of life-saving drugs have seen enormous growth [21]. Since its first detection in China, Coronavirus Disease 2019 (COVID-19) has now spread to over 210 countries/territories, with reports of local transmission happening across the world. According to World Health Organization (as of 10th April 2020), there have been a total of 15,21,252 confirmed cases and 92,798 deaths due to COVID-19 worldwide [22] and the number is still increasing. Recently, the FDA released guidance for industries, investigators and institutional review boards to consider for ongoing trials, incorporate policies and procedures, and solutions for trials that are impacted by COVID-19 in this pandemic [21].

### 10.3.1 Importance and Role of Medical Records During Pandemic

Medical records are an important part of the management of a patient. It is crucial for the doctor to responsibly record the patients' health data who are under their care. The record keeping of health data can be considered a significant part of the system. This document can be used as both private and impersonal document which will address any patient management issues and help with scientific evaluations. The private documents are considered to be very confidential, and hence it cannot be accessed by anyone else without the patients' consent, except for some cases. On the other hand, impersonal document can be accessed without patient's permission and it can be used for multiple purposes, one of them being research. It is very important to maintain confidentiality of a patient and therefore hospitals must maintain privacy of patient's private medical data. If confidentiality is breached, the patient has the right to file complaints claiming the negligence of the doctor or hospital authorities [23].

### 10.3.2 Challenges Faced by Doctors

In recent scenario, coronavirus is spreading to other countries by means of traveling. Most of the cases found positive in the first wave of the coronavirus were the people traveling to or contacting the locals in Wuhan, China. Locals and internationals who reported the initial symptoms and did not have access to their medical records had to follow the standard procedure in clinics which includes getting the blood report, EMR, ECG, stool and urine reports, etc. as the symptoms start to grow. These reports take time, and, in the meantime, patient is given antibiotics and anti-allergen supplements by the doctor to make sure the patient's condition doesn't worsen further which can have a reverse impact on the patient like allergic reaction or so forth. In absence of medical records of the patient chances of such mishaps are high. Another possible error could be misinterpretation of the symptoms shown by the patients, for example, if a patient has respiratory issues and has common fever and cough but the patient hides this information and with absence of medical records doctors might suspect it to be another coronavirus positive case and start with the medications.

Such accidents could be avoided by making the medical records electronic. If all the medical records were made electronic following same standards across the world it would have been easier to share, update, maintain and preserve the medical records. With easy access to medical records of each patient, doctors would be able to identify it much quickly whether the patient is showing positive symptoms for coronavirus disease or it is one of the other health irregularities causing it. Doctors would also be able to learn about the patient's dietary restrictions, past and current medications and all the other medical history of the patient since the first logged entry.

### 10.3.3 Understanding the Proposed Architecture Using COVID-19 Example

We look forward to three main roles/participants in proposed consensus mechanisms which are committer, endorsers and consenters. In the current state of Pandemic, the doctors update the number of positive cases, new cases, total deaths to their respective Country Health Organizations. These organizations update their statistics to World Health Organization, and

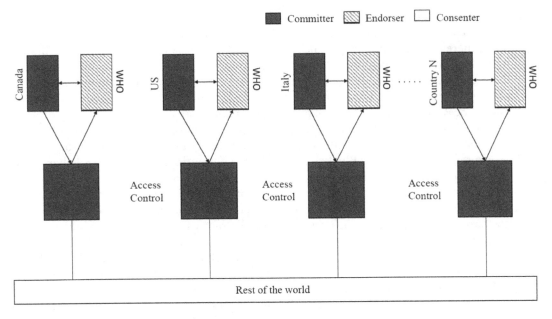

*Figure 10.1* Proposed consensus mechanism.

they update it on their website which is then acknowledged by the rest of the world. In this scenario, the country passing the stats becomes the committer, WHO becomes the endorser and rest of the World becomes the consenters as shown in Figure 10.1.

## 10.4 SCALABLE SECURE MANAGEMENT AND ACCESS CONTROL OF ELECTRONIC HEALTH RECORDS AT THE EDGE

The primary concern of blockchain refers to the capacity to allow the number of different participants in a distributed shared ledger to document the system. The crux of blockchain is having better privacy and security with the need for enhancement in scalability. Among the various advantages of edge computing like achieving better scalability, better network performance, computing in distributed edge and storage, edge computing mainly focuses on management and service support along with the need for efficient control. Therefore, the main aim of coupling blockchain with edge computing is to take storage, computation and network into consideration while satisfying the requirements of the applications.

### 10.4.1 The Importance of Integrating Blockchain and Edge Computing?

1. Security of Edge Computing: In edge computing, there are high chances of losing the data packets or even storing the data incorrectly which might hamper integrity of data. This is due to data being stored across different storage locations. Also, as edge computing provides heavy storage overhead, ensuring the reliability of data has become a challenge in edge computing. In addition to this, uploading computational tasks to edge computation nodes while maintaining privacy and security is also another challenge for edge computing. Thus, these security problems need to be addressed while taking the problem of excessive encryption overheads into consideration.

2. Technical Challenges and Limitations of Blockchain: There are many advantages of blockchain like immutability, security that makes blockchain appealing, but at the same time, there are many challenges that obstruct its wide usage. There are various limitations like low scalability, high latency, low throughput that blocks the efficacy of the blockchain-based solution. In blockchain, with the increase in transactions, the issue of storage capacity arises. For example, public blockchains like Ethereum and bitcoin can only process 8–20 records each second that is smaller than common payment processor. However, if the block size is increased for a greater throughput, it results in centralization risk and cost of security increasing and thus it is not considered as an option.

3. Advantages of Integrating Blockchain and Edge Computing: Coupling blockchain with edge computing is advantageous as it increases the automation resource usage, security and privacy. The edge nodes can be employed to implement distributed control in blockchain technology. Moreover, with the help of mining process blockchain assures the accuracy, validity and consistency of data. Privacy of edge computing is being challenged as data is stored among multiple parties. Since there is no role of the third party to access and control data in the blockchain, privacy preservation with blockchain is comparatively easier. Resource is exchanged among edge nodes with dynamic coordination. But with the help of blockchain, the resources in edge computing is enabled, as by running a specified resource algorithm to run a demanded service of smart contracts of blockchain the on-demand resources can be used [15].

## 10.4.2 Challenges

When it comes to using blockchain with edge computing despite of having so many advantages there are still some challenges that need to be addressed:

1. Scalability Enhancements
2. Security and Privacy
3. Self-Organization
4. Function Integration
5. Resource Management

## 10.5 OVERVIEW OF BLOCKCHAIN AND HYPER LEDGER METHODOLOGIES

Our platform is a blockchain framework based on Hyperledger that addresses the previously discussed issues by constructing an architecture that will allow the software to be scalable and extensible. This model has three key device components which are an access control module based on blockchain, an off-chain data storage and a web user interface that is dissented for patient and doctor. In order to construct an efficient model, the different kinds of data that are collected such as laboratory test results, diagnostic images, care plans, prescriptions, etc. are encoded and saved in the cloud server and a hash value of the data is kept in the model. Smart contracts help the patient to control access permits flexibly and safely to each of their data assets. The web interface lets patients, physicians, quickly access the application. Today this technology is the foundation of most recent cryptocurrencies in circulation. A publicly distributed ledger is the key feature of this system, where the ledger is not owned by any individual, and a duplicate of the ledger is stored in all the nodes of the network. In the following sections, a further discussion of the methodologies has been provided.

### 10.5.1 Blockchain

Blockchain was originally created as the underlying technology in 2008 that enabled transactions of cryptocurrencies like bitcoin between peers. After recovering from the economic crisis of 2008, bitcoin being a new cryptocurrency was expected to address the double expenditure dilemma by blockchain usage. Stuart Haber and W. Scott Stornetta initially suggested the concept of cryptographic timestamps to store digital data in a block network [24]. In 1991, it was nevertheless initially introduced by creator(s) being named Satoshi Nakamoto, to create a bitcoin transaction blockchain in 2009. The transactions take place in this decentralized network which is peer-to-peer (P2P) instead of relying or requiring confirmation from third parties. The Economist article, published in 2015, announced blockchain technology as a trusted system by referring it as the 'trust machine' which is expected to change the operating style of the world economies. Blockchain provides a simple and sophisticated system despite of looking complex in various cases. Blockchain is a robust database or distributed digital ledger which allows direct P2P transactions of financial assets such as bonds and stocks, money, intellectual property, art, contracts, music, data and votes in some cases. Blockchain achieved this trust through a systematic consensus, collaboration and cryptography network rather than by banks, governments or intermediaries of third parties. The data blocks are stored securely and will be continuously updated with every new transaction. All parties involved in the transaction are provided a list through a distributed computer network. The concept of blockchain includes chronological blocks of transactions acting as distributed database where all the blocks are assigned individual hash values of newly verified transactions as well as the entire blockchain and are connected to the adjacent blocks based on the block's hash value. For validating transactions, various algorithms are used by blockchain utilizing consensuses. A block can only be erased or removed when the copies on the distributed nodes are out of synch with them. Thus, three main characteristics are attained which are immutability, longevity and reliability characteristics. Figure 10.1 represents a generic application focused on blockchain. Participants in the blockchain system are not reviewed before transaction, and without involving any third parties, the transactions can be carried out. It is a licensing setting in which participants can stay unknown. Such resources have progressed the rise of blockchain technology to build cryptocurrencies along with transacting them. It has been the dominant cryptocurrency since the introduction of bitcoin. Its success has highlighted weaknesses in feature. The calculation cycles necessary to employ the proof of work consensus require heavy computation, often exceeding the expense of a transaction of bitcoin.

A timely upgrade of a blockchain of this size requires substantial computational and storage capacity, underlining existing nodes. The chain has developed to the size of around 160 GB [25], while still continuing to expand. Bitcoin's block size is actually 1MB which is not likely to rise in the immediate years. The use cases that can be included in the architecture are also limited in this system along with the complexity of the carried out transactions. Ethereum is a newer blockchain platform that has no fixed block size in MB. For every individual transaction, the overall cost is limited. Businesses can, theoretically, ensure efficient and economical operation of an Ethereum-based chain. Ethereum has introduced features called smart contracts which allow virtually unlimited complexity of the transaction rules. Smart contracts [6] automatically try to validate conditions and implement the actions in the blockchain by building programmable triggers. By the time of launch of the blockchain the structure of each form of smart contract is decided. Participants possess individual values for each contract duration which allows flexibility as well as complexity of transactions. The above adds to the list of drawbacks of permission-less blockchains by being an obstacle to their usage in a wide variety of cases of business usage.

### 10.5.2 Electronic Health Records (EHRs)

EHRs are digital data of patient's records such as their history and knowledge of medication that are traditionally kept on paper. The database can be accessed by certain healthcare providers and doctors for efficient treatment purposes as it allows long-term tracking of patient data. With the use of EHR, a large amount of paperwork can be avoided by removing a large amount of patient data from paper-based tracking.

### 10.5.3 Smart Contract

Smart contracts are electronic executable programs. A high-level computer programming language is needed to write these contracts to apply arbitrary business logic or pre-determined parameters to cause value transfer. A blockchain transaction has a specified target smart contract method, a payload that includes input values for the feature call and is always signed by the submitter. A transaction can be sent to any node in the blockchain network that transmits the transaction to the entire network. At some point the transaction is performed by any single node using the smart contract. With a successful execution of transaction, the internal state of the blockchain may change. However, the state is not affected when the input is detected to be invalid by the smart contract and the transaction will be rejected as failed. A majority of blockchain nodes run with this independently where each node maintains its own state database by conducting its own transactions using the chaincode.

### 10.5.4 Access Control in Medical Domain

The perfect way to address the health and medical data resource problems outlined in the introduction is through a blockchain which is based on hyperledger. A permitted smart contract in a blockchain gives the stakeholders (i.e., doctors and patients) full authority, enables immutability and cryptography, provides security and privacy and also permits identified participants to carry out trusted transactions. A basic digital transfer can be attained by used interface of data by drag and drop. Hyperledger blockchains have the disadvantage of storing large block sizes in addition to the cost of their computation. The digital asset's size, and therefore the network size, would model performance problems that are going to deteriorate experience of the users and increase operating expenses in many companies [3]. Our implementation strategy is constructed to address such issues

### 10.5.5 Hyperledger

Hyperledger is a project that is a distributed ledger having open source, which is approved by the Linux Foundation. It consists of various subprojects like: Fabric, Sawtooth, Indy, Burrow, Iroha, etc. In this chapter, we have concentrated on the hyperledger fabric project only. Hyperledger fabric provides an open source platform which is enterprise-grade developed by the IBM and Linux Foundations. Like Ethereum and bitcoin, there is no blockchain in it, where limited network participants can access the network, and no one can join it. The utilized approach to validate the transactions and generate blocks at hyperledger fabric is PBFT (Practical Byzantine Fault Tolerance) [26]. The transactions are handled using chaincode in hyperledger fabric, which is a software code that allows writing and configuration of the application to communicate with the network. An insulation mechanism known as the channel is used to assess the privacy of the participant's network transactions. The channel only shares data with the nodes which are channel members and have the transaction and the data. The hyperledger fabric's official documentation defined transaction as an instant request or invoke transaction which is submitted by the peer to order and validate. A chaincode is generated from the instilled request in each path, when the invoked transactions perform operations such as read/write on the ledger. The key elements of hyperledger fabric Architecture are ordering nodes, peer nodes and client applications [27]. The task of responsible certificate authorities is to create identities of the component. The transactions are received and ordered by the ordering nodes from various requests inside a block [6].

### 10.5.6 Composer Tools

Hyperledger technologies are very popular for designing and decentralizing blockchain applications. The most widely used tools are especially the hyperledger fabric and Hyperledger Composer. Hyperledger Composer is a stable, open tool set and framework for designing blockchain applications. Hyperledger Composer follows the existing hyperledger fabric blockchain architecture and runtime, which uses pluggable blockchain consensus protocols to ensure that the transactions are being authenticated by authorized business network participants with respect to the policy. Everyday applications can use business network data and provide end-users with simple and controlled access points. Hyperledger Composer is a series of collaboration resources used by business owners and developers that render hyperledger fabric and Decentralized Applications (also known as smart contracts) easy to write chaincode. Proof-of-Concept can be quickly build using Composer and adopt chaincode in the blockchain within a short time. Composer Hyperledger consists of the following toolkits:

- Modeling language called CTO: a domain modeling language that defines the requirements of the principle, business model and business network.
- Playground: It is used for rapid business network configuration, deployment and testing.
- Command-line interface (CLI) tools: The client command-line interface is used to integrate business networks with hyperledger fabric Composer-CLI as the most effective tool for business networking. Some other effective tools are REST servers, Hyperledger Composer Generator, Yeoman and Playground. Composer CLI offers many useful tools for the developers. The Composer REST server is used to build a REST interface to a blockchain-deployed business network.

### 10.5.7 Playground

The Hyperledger Composer Playground offers a user interface for configuring business network, deployment and testing. Playground has a wide range of advanced features that allow users to control the business network security, invite business networking participants and connect to multiple business blockchain networks.

### 10.5.8 Off-chain Storage

Off-chain storage is used to store the medical and health data assets securely to preserve the efficiency and economic viability of an application, and the block's data item which is dedicated to the chain is considered as the hash of the data asset's URI. The transactions of data asset are authorized with a sign of the data owner with a private key (patient or caregiver). An extra layer of data asset security is added when the size of an individual block can be reduced by employing URI hash.

### 10.5.9 User Experience From Patient's Side

Playground is a software framework used to access the application functionality. The general idea is to always keep the patient at the center of a treatment circle. Patients have the liberty to choose the people to be included in their circle of treatment and what knowledge is exchanged with each of them. For the patients who require a reliable assistance, the domain is further expanded to involve a secondary opinion like a caregiver / another doctor who can work on behalf of the patient. The web platform connects using the well-known RESTful API to the network. Hyperledger Composer can call external APIs utilizing smart contracts or transaction processor function. We have built a stable, reliable and accessible component for introducing modularity and unified extensibility by connecting users to the blockchain. This portion is partly developed with Secure Hypertext Transfer Protocol (HTTPS). The users can then keep tract of their digital assets by running the application in any device that supports HTTPS requests.

## 10.6 HYPER LEDGER-BASED PROPOSED ARCHITECTURE FOR PROTECTING ELECTRONIC HEALTH RECORDS

As discussed above, our system is a permissioned blockchain where nodes are organized in committer, endorser and consenter.

- The committers' ordered and validated transactions are appended to their respective ledger once it is returned by the consenter.
- Endorsers run the transactions related to the network and also prevent the occurrence of non-deterministic and unstable transactions.
- Consenters provide the validation of the transaction and update the distributed ledger with the latest transaction details that took place between the Committers and Endorsers.

### 10.6.1 Proposed Architecture of the Blockchain System

The novel technology blockchain is gaining popularity in every field, especially in healthcare industries since it has many benefits. Figure 10.2 represents the conceptual architecture where all the medical data (prescriptions, read access and IoT data) is stored in the medical blockchain. This medical data is an independent medical lake that is not only limited to hospital usage but also for disease prevention and research, and it is referred as the stored-off blockchain.

More specifically, the medical blockchain network is made up of trusted authenticating peers, and for the network every single peer holds copies of the ledger to keep the distributed ledger secure. The database is a part of the ledger which stores the unchangeable record of the transaction, blocks sequence record, and a data lake in order to hold different kinds of health data. The role of blockchain is to basically act as a logbook and document any alterations related to data lake. The data lake is the database having an off-chain state that carries, for example, latest digital patient data and the current data collection values. Medical IoT devices are capable of continuously collecting and transmitting data which can be used in data analyzing and eventually create a range of resources starting from response to critical care to preventive care.

A rapid transmission and processing of data enables healthcare providers to treat their patients more efficiently. For example, the user group includes people in various positions:

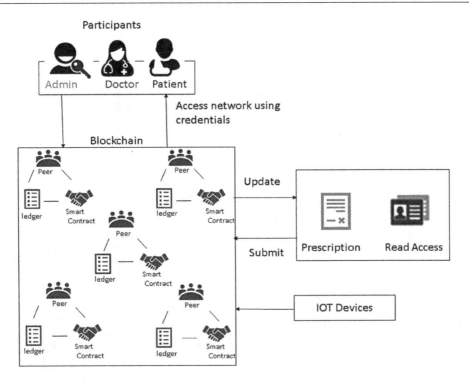

*Figure 10.2* Overview of Proposed Architecture.

the administrator who is capable of handling all the resources inside the hospital, the doctor who is able to review all patient details and give a prescription for the medication, the pharmacists who instruct and advise about the right usage and consequences of the medications and products that are prescribed. The patients can therefore access their medical data through the peer networks containing their health records. In addition, the patient can set up permission to allow access to any physician of their medical information who is in the same network. That can be achieved by defining the smart contract's policies of access control which is distributed across complete network of blockchain to make sure that the patient's data has privacy and protection. All end-user interactions in a blockchain require a digital signature so that the device is secured.

Figure 10.3 describes the key components and offers a good overview of the medical blockchain framework being proposed. Both the technical framework and user interface system have been depicted in the architecture where both the smart contract and distributed ledger are presented as services in the applications. The users (doctor, patient, admin, nurse, etc.) may send offers for transactions via the application toward the network of blockchain to obtain booking, EHR, payment and many other services. A transaction refers to the course of producing, modifying, transferring or deleting EHR data that exist between the peers that are connected.

For facilitating transactions that are confidential and private, we split the complete network into various private networks to make it subnetwork which requires interactions between multiple departments that are listed. When the agencies wish to store health data privately so that it is not accessible by other agencies, they are permitted to initiate their subnetworks, which include the required units that need access to data. It is of particular significance for the use of businesses, because some participants might be rivals who do not want any deal, it is made available to everyone, for instance, an exclusive rate given to specific people. The

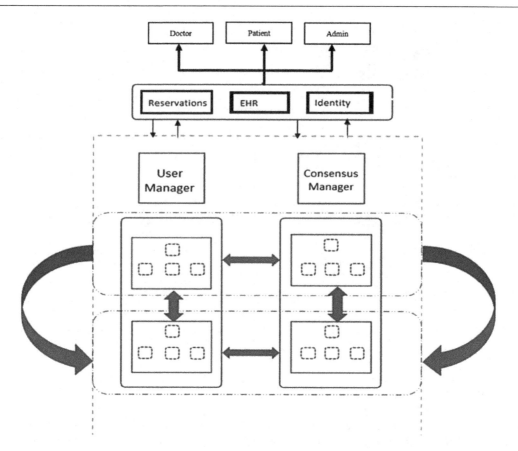

*Figure 10.3* Integrity management of proposed medical blockchain platform for EHR.

proposed platform stands out from other blockchain systems because it is constructed on a permissioned network. Instead of using an open program which is permission-less and will permit unknown participants to enter the network, participants of the built network are added via a user manager that is trusted. Their role is to make every cryptographic process abstract and offer multiple resources for the certification. More specifically, these services include user registration, rules governing such identities and authentication and protected communications among the components or user of the blockchain.

The design of the proposed framework in the architecture enables the accommodation of complex business use case requirements, where the order of transactions in the pluggable consensus can be switched to and fro, the operation of smart contracts takes place inside a container environment and it supports various identity management protocols and finally multiple storage technologies can be used to store the ledger data. Departments attach to sub-network through an interface that is provided by the consensus manager in addition to the order of transactions, and they also decide how it should be integrated with the final block. The medical blockchains have different peers in each of their departments which include storage of data and smart contract to support the transaction pitch or write a block of transaction in the ledger. The distributed ledger is responsible for recording the clear and fixed past that refers to all events which occurred in the network. Services such as hashing and digital signatures that are part of consensus protocol and cryptographic primitives are used to make the process more secure by ensuring the precision of the ledger.

## 10.6.2 Data Flow Diagrams

### 10.6.2.1 Doctors

Doctor/Physicians need to login to the application using their valid individual credentials. On login, they can see multiple options under their profile. Doctors can update their personal information under the profile tab. Doctors can view the list of other doctors available, the medical records of the assigned patients, grant/revoke the read-only access rights to/from the other doctors, transactions list over the blockchain and the list of patients assigned to them (Figure 10.4).

Figure 10.5 shows the Data Flow Diagram for GRANT/REVOKE the READ-ONLY Access Rights to/from Other Doctors.

### 10.6.2.2 Patient

Patient needs to login to the application under the profile tab; they can view their own medical records, name of the assigned doctor, current and past prescriptions and transactions list over the blockchain as shown in Figure 10.6.

### 10.6.2.3 Transaction Flow

Figure 10.7 shows the transaction control flow from point of login to transaction posted over the blockchain.

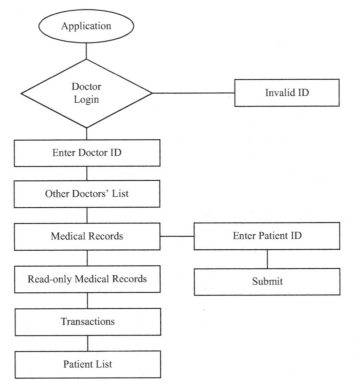

Figure 10.4 Data Flow Diagram for Doctor.

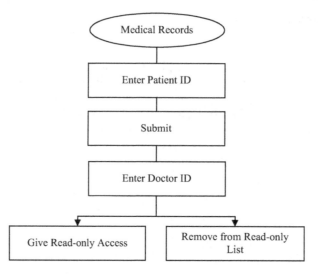

*Figure 10.5* Data Flow Diagram for Sharing Medical Records.

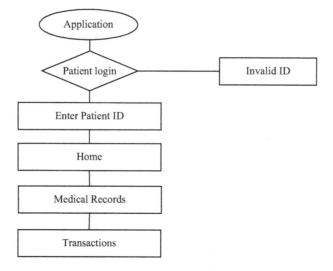

*Figure 10.6* Data Flow Diagram for Patient.

## 10.7 PERFORMANCE EVALUATION

### 10.7.1 Performance of the Proposed Model

We have used Quad core Skylake Processor: Intel® Core™ i5-6300U Processor (3M Cache, up to 3.00 GHz) along with 8 GB DDR3 RAM as the basic hardware to implement our project on the local system.

Figure 10.8 depicts the time taken to create number of patients and doctors. Since there are more parameters to be passed in creating the records for doctors, it is taking slightly higher time for creating the record as compared to the patients. Here, number of participants created are visible by the numbers used over the line graph and vertical columns/bar represent the time taken by doctors and patients. The performance was quite steady in the controlled environment and it was able to perform with great stability and provide better results.

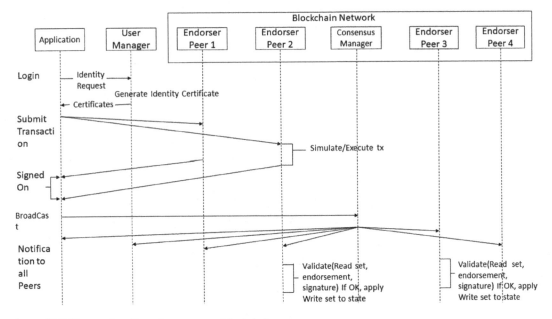

Figure 10.7 Transaction flow diagram over blockchain.

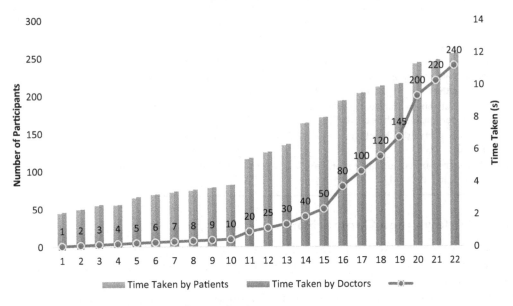

Figure 10.8 Time taken to create records in application.

Figure 10.9 depicts the time taken to grant the read-only access over the medical records of a patient to one doctor or multiple doctors. Our reading shows that it took around 1second per transaction to complete when a single doctor was given read-only access rights over a patient. Similarly, when a batch of 240 doctors was granted read-only access over the medical records of a patient by the assigned doctor, it took about 6 seconds for the transaction to complete. According to these results, we can predict that one Cuda Core 600 MHz GDDR3 BUS type GPU computing module could be sufficient for a single hospital setup handling multiple transactions per second.

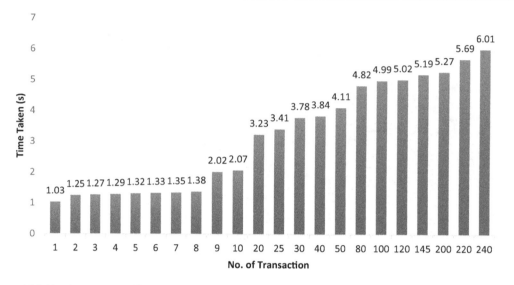

*Figure 10.9* Read access over Electronic Health Records.

*Table 10.1* Comparative analysis between various blockchain-based studies.

| Blockchain-based studies | Smart contract | Resource storage | Accessibility scheme | Website/Mobile application |
|---|---|---|---|---|
| Our approach | Yes | Off-chain | Permissioned | Yes |
| MediBchain: A Blockchain Based Privacy Preserving Platform for Healthcare Data [28] | Yes | Blockchain | Permissioned | No |
| OmniPHR: A distributed architecture model to integrate personal health records [29] | No | Blockchain | Permissioned | Yes |
| Managing IoT devices using blockchain platform [30] | Yes | Blockchain | Permission-less | No |
| Toward blockchain-based auditable storage and sharing of IoT data [31] | No | Off-chain | Permission-less | No |

## 10.7.2 Performance Comparison

A comparative analysis was performed in Table 10.1 to compare our model with some of the existing relevant studies. It was found that our system provides a combination of features that is efficient and secured for the users. The study in [29] comes close to our model in terms of accessibility, smart contract employment and provides a developed application; however, due to resource management technique of the model, it did not surpass the performance of our model.

## 10.8 CONCLUSIONS AND FUTURE CAVEATS

It can be concluded that many accessories are benefited for incorporating the concepts of blockchain technology in healthcare industries by enabling data sharing and tracking with required privacy and transparency for the users. This chapter proposes a unique way of designing and implementing a decentralized system to deal with EHRs with the help of blockchain technologies. The purpose of the system is to offer an essential secured and clear platform to aid the stakeholders such as patients, doctors and hospitals. Specific performance indexes are used to conduct experiments, showing a reasonable resource usage while maximizing efficiency. Also, a comparative analysis was performed which showed the efficacy of our proposed model compared to previous studies in terms of various characteristics. While the evolution of blockchain technologies in the field of healthcare is still evolving, the aim of this study is to propose a viable approach to construct an application integrating healthcare applications and healthcare, benefiting stakeholders and revolutionizing innovations throughout the healthcare industry.

Furthermore, we could replicate 60% of the setup activities and installation over Cloud platform using Ubuntu as OS and Google Cloud as the service provider. We would be working further in this direction to find an alternative for the REST server for composer tools to launch the application over the cloud environment instead of local computers, which could be a leading research area in itself as the IT giants are working in this area. In addition, the proposed work can be extended based on the developed framework to several other business settings. Some of the challenges of this work largely depend on scale of the blockchain network and the requirements of a device. Some of the future research directions are to address the problem of extending the size of network to a larger scale and incorporating the propositioned architecture in cloud.

## REFERENCES

1. K. M. Cresswell and A. Sheikh, "Health information technology in hospitals: current issues and future trends," *Futur. Hosp. J.*, 2015, doi: 10.7861/futurehosp.15.015.
2. S. A. Bragadeesh and A. Umamakeswari, "Role of blockchain in the Internet-of-Things (IoT)," *Int. J. Eng. Technol.*, 2018, doi: 10.14419/ijet.v7i2.24.12011.
3. S. Rouhani, L. Butterworth, A. D. Simmons, D. G. Humphery, and R. Deters, "MediChainTM: A secure decentralized medical data asset management system," In *2018 IEEE International Conference on Internet of Things (iThings) and IEEE Green Computing and Communications (GreenCom) and IEEE Cyber, Physical and Social Computing (CPSCom) and IEEE Smart Data (SmartData)* (pp. 1533–1538). IEEE, 2018, doi: 10.1109/Cybermatics_2018.2018.00258.
4. R. Sharma, "Blockchain in Healthcare: 2017s successes," *Fr. Canada Chamb. Commer. Ontario*, pp. 2017–2019, 2018, [Online]. Available: https://www.coindesk.com/blockchain-healthcare-2017s-successes/.
5. L. Hang, E. Choi, and D. H. Kim, "A novel EMR integrity management based on a medical blockchain platform in hospital," *Electron.*, 2019, doi: 10.3390/electronics8040467.
6. Q. Nasir, I. A. Qasse, M. Abu Talib, and A. B. Nassif, "Performance analysis of hyperledger fabric platforms," *Secur. Commun. Networks*, 2018, doi: 10.1155/2018/3976093.
7. R. J. Krawiec et al., "Survey: Patients see 18.7 different doctors on average," In *Proc. NIST Workshop Blockchain Healthcare*, 2010. [Online], Available: https://www.prnewswire.com/news-releases/survey-patients-see-187-different-doctors-on-average-92171874.html.
8. Charles, D., M. Gabriel, and T. Searcy. "Adoption of electronic health record systems among U.S. non-federal acute care hospitals: 2008-2014," 2015. ONC Data Brief, no.23. Office of the National Coordinator for Health Information Technology: Washington DC.
9. K. D. Mandl, P. Szolovits, and I. S. Kohane, "Public standards and patients' control: How to keep electronic medical records accessible but private," *Br. Med. J.*, 322, 283, 2001.
10. N. Rifi, E. Rachkidi, N. Agoulmine, and N. C. Taher, "Towards using blockchain technology for eHealth data access management," In *2017 fourth international conference on advances in biomedical engineering (ICABME)* (pp. 1–4). IEEE, 2017, doi: 10.1109/ICABME.2017.8167555.
11. S. Al-Megren et al., "Blockchain use cases in digital sectors: A review of the literature," In *2018 IEEE International Conference on Internet of Things (iThings) and IEEE Green*

*Computing and Communications (GreenCom) and IEEE Cyber, Physical and Social Computing (CPSCom) and IEEE Smart Data (SmartData)* (pp. 1417–1424). IEEE, 2018, doi: 10.1109/Cybermatics_2018.2018.00242.

12. J. Lane and C. Schur, "Balancing access to health data and privacy: A review of the issues and approaches for the future," *Health Serv. Res.* 2010, doi: 10.1111/j.1475-6773.2010.01141.x.

13. M. Reisman, "EHRs: The challenge of making electronic data usable and interoperable," *Pharm. Ther.*, 42, 572, 2017.

14. Y. Guo and C. Liang, "Blockchain application and outlook in the banking industry," *Financ. Innovation.* 2016, doi: 10.1186/s40854-016-0034-9.

15. R. Yang, F. R. Yu, P. Si, Z. Yang, and Y. Zhang, "Integrated blockchain and edge computing systems: A survey, some research issues and challenges," *IEEE Commun Surv Tutor.* 2019, doi: 10.1109/COMST.2019.2894727.

16. A. da Conceição, F. Silva, V. Rocha, A. Locoro, and J. Barguil, "Eletronic health records using blockchain Technology," 2018.

17. F. W. Booth, C. K. Roberts, and M. J. Laye, "Lack of exercise is a major cause of chronic diseases," *Compr. Physiol.*, 2012, doi: 10.1002/cphy.c110025.

18. "2010 April report of the auditor general of Canada," 2010. [Online]. Available: https://www.oag-bvg.gc.ca/internet/English/parl_oag_201004_07_e_33720.html.

19. A. Boonstra, A. Versluis, and J. F. J. Vos, "Implementing electronic health records in hospitals: A systematic literature review," *BMC Health Serv Res.* 2014, doi: 10.1186/1472-6963-14-370.

20. H. Jannenga, "4 Crucial data security measures every EMR must have in place," Available: https://www.beckershospitalreview.com/healthcare-information-technology/4-crucial-data-security-measures-every-emr-must-have-in-place.html (accessed Aug. 10, 2017).

21. D. Cohn-Emery, "Challenges for clinical trials and treating patients with cancer in light of the coronavirus," Available: https://www.targetedonc.com/view/challenges-for-clinical-trials-and-treating-patients-with-cancer-in-light-of-the-coronavirus (accessed Mar. 20, 2020).

22. WHO, "Coronavirus disease 2019 (COVID-19) Situation Report –81," 2020. [Online]. Available: https://www.who.int/docs/default-source/coronaviruse/situation-reports/20200410-sitrep-81-covid-19.pdf?sfvrsn=ca96eb84_2.

23. J. Thomas, "Medical records and issues in negligence," 2009, doi: 10.4103/0970-1591.56208.

24. S. Haber and W. S. Stornetta, "How to time-stamp a digital document," *J. Cryptol.*, 1991, doi: 10.1007/BF00196791.

25. "How to build an electronic medical record secured by blockchain?" Available: https://www.devteam.space/blog/how-to-build-an-electronic-medical-record-secured-by-blockchain/.

26. M. Castro and B. Liskov, "Practical byzantine fault tolerance," *Proc. Symp. Oper. Syst. Des. Implement.*, 1999, doi: 10.1145/571637.571640.

27. C. Cachin, "Architecture of the hyperledger blockchain fabric," *Leibniz Int. Proc. Informatics, LIPIcs,* 2017, doi: 10.4230/LIPIcs.OPODIS.2016.24.

28. A. Al Omar, M. S. Rahman, A. Basu, and S. Kiyomoto, "MediBchain: A blockchain based privacy preserving platform for healthcare data," In *International conference on security, privacy and anonymity in computation, communication and storage* (pp. 534–543). Springer, Cham, 2017, doi: 10.1007/978-3-319-72395-2_49.

29. A. Roehrs, C. A. da Costa, and R. da Rosa Righi, "OmniPHR: A distributed architecture model to integrate personal health records," *J. Biomed. Inform.*, 2017, doi: 10.1016/j.jbi.2017.05.012.

30. S. Huh, S. Cho, and S. Kim, "Managing IoT devices using blockchain platform," 2017, doi: 10.23919/ICACT.2017.7890132.

31. H. Shafagh, L. Burkhalter, A. Hithnawi, and S. Duquennoy, "Towards blockchain-based auditable storage and sharing of IoT data," 2017, doi: 10.1145/3140649.3140656.

# Chapter 11

# AI-Aided Secured ECG Live Edge Monitoring System with a Practical Use-Case

*Amit Kumar, Tahrat Tazrin, Arti Sharma, Shivani Chaskar, and Sadman Sakib*
Lakehead University, Canada

*Mostafa M. Fouda*
Idaho State University, USA

*Zubair Md Fadlullah*
Lakehead University, Canada
Thunder Bay Regional Health Research Institute (TBRHRI), Canada

## CONTENTS

## 11.1 INTRODUCTION

### 11.1.1 Background

The evolution of the Internet of Things (IoT) has propelled various areas of research including real-time user monitoring to smart vehicles. IoT technology has been established as a convenient alternative to traditional approaches for developing various wearables, monitoring systems, early diagnosis systems, etc. to make healthcare systems more efficient [1]. Various techniques are being developed recently that has made communication between doctors and patients more convenient, efficient and reliable. However, there are still some problems that need to be addressed to make smart health a state-of-the-art technology. Hospital managements can be made more responsible and liable by sharing patient's condition and updates with healthcare providers and relatives. In cases where patient's condition is critical, their health should be continuously monitored so that accidents can be avoided. However, in most cases this can be achieved with the help of large medical equipment to measure health data. Over the last few years, ECG monitoring systems have become very popular for monitoring heart activities of various kinds and therefore there was a need to improve the communication quality, i.e., ECG signal's reception and transmission for remote operation [2, 3]. Nevertheless, there exists a plethora of challenges such as packet loss in remote transmission, security [4], sensor noise, wearability [5] and so forth. With the increased inclination of people toward relying on technology, it is important to address the problems of health industries and come up with solutions such as smart health monitoring system that will enable effective communication between network devices. The smart health technologies are therefore expected to provide viable solutions to help the doctors and patients by monitoring, tracking and recording the patient's medical data conveniently at the edge [6, 7]. In this vein, we have developed an ECG monitoring system to detect supraventricular arrhythmia which will collect patient's information and send the data securely to the healthcare providers and attendants of patients on their edge devices by monitoring them through the Internet remotely. To achieve this, the health data of patients can be collected through e-Health sensor platform in edge devices such as Raspberry Pi. Raspberry Pi provides the entire environment in a smaller platform for a cheaper cost and enables communication via several input/output pins. All the collected data will be stored and processed on the device, hence facilitating the local intelligence at the edge devices ensuring the privacy of each user. This system can be installed in the hospitals as well as at homes because of its simplicity and accessibility. Moreover, implementing such a system will make the healthcare monitoring more efficient by reducing cost and space requirement. In addition to classifying arrhythmia, we have also proposed the concepts of bio-authentication, where the machine learning algorithms will also differentiate between heartbeats of different people in order to use this model as a mode of authentication. Therefore, the ECG data collection process will be consistent as the system will only collect information of the authorized user and third parties will not be able to get hold of the data without authorization. This kind of authentication system does not currently exist in the developed health monitoring systems and therefore, we have proposed the novel approach of authenticating such systems with the help of machine learning (ML) algorithms.

In our considered system, a user's heart rate is measured through Electrocardiogram (ECG) which is regarded as a vital biomedical signal. The ECG sensor value is an analog signal. MCP3008 analog to digital converter (ADC) can be utilized to digitize ECG signals and then displayed in real-time using the Raspberry Pi microcontroller. A single ECG trace consists of different segments, i.e., the QRS complex, the ST segment and the PR segment. The QRS complex can be leveraged to identify major heart abnormalities. To understand and do the prediction of the abnormalities four machine learning classification algorithms are used including the decision tree, Random Forest, Artificial Neural Network (ANN) and Convolutional Neural Network (CNN). These algorithms are applied and validated on the MIT-BIH Supraventricular database available in the PhysioNet data repository [8].

## 11.1.2 Problem Statement

The IoT allows the connection of various objects with people through Internet for collecting and processing various kinds of data through sensors and analyzing them to figure out a particular trait for time monitoring, tracking and management of data [9]. Medicinal service is a basic piece of life and it is essential for every human being. The rapid increase in population and illness is placing a significant role in healthcare system. With the advancement of smart health all around, it is essential to develop more efficient and precise continuous health monitoring systems. This can be easily achieved in the current era because of the accessibility of mobile technologies, which makes the control of these technologies easier than ever. However, with the development of these technologies, the question of security also arises as user's personal system can be accessed by any other people and hence there is a risk of their private profile being exposed. Therefore, in most cases many people are not comfortable using these kinds of technologies. Thus, there is a growing need to address the privacy concerns with the developments of such techniques. In case of constructing an ECG monitoring system, it is important to ensure, the data is collected from the authorized user in order to maintain the integrity of the system and preserve privacy of user data. This can be considered as a significant challenge because the existing system has no method of distinguishing between authorized and unauthorized users, and therefore data is more vulnerable to third parties.

In addition, heart diseases such as arrhythmia can be considered as very fatal and therefore needs immediate medical attention. However, as the number of doctors in a particular city or area is limited, compared to the total number of people, there are times when highly qualified and efficient physicians need to travel from one part of the country to other parts in order to treat patients with such serious conditions. There are also patients with emergency cases who are unable to go to the doctors because of their severity and hence, are unable to get proper treatment due to transportability. In order to avoid such crucial cases, a health monitoring system can be utilized to continuously monitor patient's heart condition remotely and warn the users about any probable heart abnormalities that might trigger an arrhythmia. In order to achieve this, the concepts of IoT can be combined with Raspberry Pi which will provide an effective secured solution for monitoring the heart conditions of patients [10, 11].

## 11.1.3 Objective and Scope

The aim is to execute an Artificial Intelligence (AI) aided secured live checking framework of ECG on edge to detect signs of arrhythmia utilizing Raspberry Pi device during emergency circumstances particularly when a patient is separated from everyone else at home or while the patient is travelling. The system needs to be constructed is such a way so that it is lightweight, economical and efficient so that maximum number of users are benefited by the model and can rely on them. In critical events, e.g., if an individual has an abrupt heart stroke, an alert will be produced to notify the responsible people like the doctors, nurses and patient's attendants in order to take crucial precautions to assist the patients. This technology can be used by a doctor to study a patient's condition even if they are not present at the scene and still suggest medications to the patient. The primary goal, therefore, is to decrease the workload of healthcare providers and provide the patients with less complicated secured medical services. To ensure reliability of the system, the bio-authentication part of the system is introduced for authorized access of the user. Applications can be made more secure by using unique ECG signals of the person to authenticate the user so that their private data can be secured. This will encourage more people to use the secured systems and keep their data private.

## 11.2 RELATED WORK

In the medical domain, monitoring is the observation of a disease, condition or one/several medical parameters over time. In hospitals, patients' ECG must be monitored constantly, which is usually done by doctors or paramedical staff. They observe ECG of patients continuously and maintain a record of it. This process is quiet slow and bit expensive [12] for which there is a great need of developing advanced monitoring system to monitor ECG continuously.

Rahman et al. [13] discussed about a smart patient monitoring system which will display the health information of patients automatically using multiple sensors as shown in Figure 11.1. The collected information is stored in IoT cloud after it is being processed through Raspberry Pi. The system extracts the primary data as ECG by using ECG sensor (single lead heart rate monitor (AD8232)) and secondary data as temperature by using temperature sensor (DS18B20) and by continuous monitoring the patient's health conditions can be tracked by doctors, nurses and relatives remotely. Based on the criticality of the condition, a warning is conveyed to the user, and the doctors/nurses/relatives can start a video call. This helps in constant remote caregiving facilities for monitoring condition of patients, where the

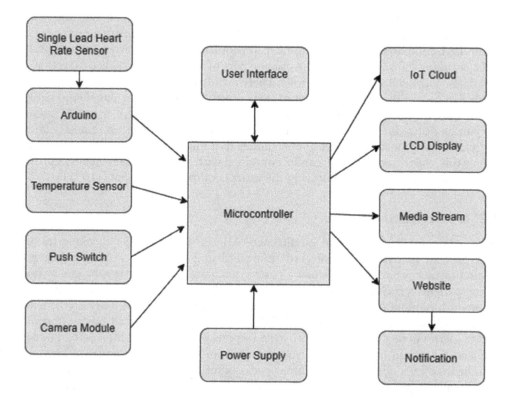

Figure 11.1 Elements of the considered ECG monitoring system. Note that the microcontroller is at the centerpiece which provides the resources for local signal processing and/or ECG analytics.

physicians received the text notification if there are any changes in the patient's condition. The system contains a push switch that can be pressed by the patient during emergencies like when they get uncomfortable. This will send an SMS notification and make a video call to the people who are responsible for attending like doctors/relatives in order to enable access to the patient's condition through multimedia such as video. Additionally, there is also an option of live stream to monitor condition of the patient through the website. This can be attained using the camera module of Raspberry Pi positioned near the patient.

Budida et al. [14] suggested an idea of smart healthcare system utilizing the concepts of IoT as shown in Figure 11.2. Patients' data are collected using various IoT sensors and are transferred to the microcontroller ATMEL 89s52, which stores the data in the MySQL database server. The MySQL database server is employed to control the collected information and provide accessibility, and it can then be viewed using available android application by patients. If any abnormality is detected in the collected data, the patient is warned through a notification and a message is dispatched to their respective caregiver. The abnormality in the trend in data is detected by employing various decision-making algorithms. People can then have access to the database in order to check their medical records. Hence, this system can provide a better health monitoring framework. Thus, the system in [14] can be exploited to detect the condition of the patient and hence provide a rapid and effective mechanism. The attributes of the patient required for patient monitoring are collected using different sensors. Then, the collected data are analyzed and stored, and the results are presented on the server to be accessed by doctors and patients. The data is also available on mobile applications and webpage to be viewed by doctors and patients in addition to booking appointments, emergency button, patient's review, alert, single and family registration and so forth.

Riaz et al. [15] proposed an IoT-based system to capture various vital signs such as ECG signals, blood pressure, body temperature and heart rate of patients. Their proposed system also utilizes a Wireless Sensor Network (WSN) with IoT to build a continuous monitoring system. The data are transferred through wireless medium, for instance Internet cloud computing and Zigbee, so that doctors can view the data. The proposed system can be implemented in areas lacking proper healthcare facilities where it is difficult to get reasonable healthcare. Using wireless transmission to acquire data, the work showed that such a

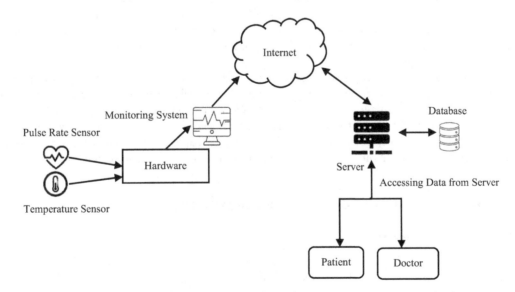

*Figure 11.2* A smart health monitoring system at the edge leveraging IoT.

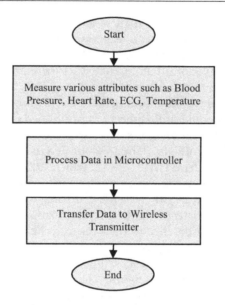

*Figure 11.3* Process of patient data collection.

continuous monitoring system can be built to monitor and report patient's condition over Internet. The data collected from the sensor are processed and analyzed in the microcontroller and then sent to doctors and patients' receiver-end node through wireless module of Zigbee. The data then are dispatched to the mobile application as well as the caregiver's web repository. The flowchart of the whole process is represented in Figures. 11.3 and 11.4.

Bhoyar et al. [16] indicated the progress in multiparameter health tracking system using Arduino to detect illness. A disease identifying algorithm was formulated to identify certain illnesses such as Hyperthermia, Dysautonomia and so on, using various parameters, e.g., metabolic conditions, weight, oxygen level, temperature, heartbeat pulse, stress level and blood pressure. Their introduced system acts as a monitoring and early detection system utilizing the Arduino environment. The collected sensor data are sent to a gateway over Bluetooth. Thus, this research focused on the WSN; different sensor devices are present in a wireless network that are used to collect users' data in order to monitor their health conditions by taking into consideration two aspects, namely sensor deployment (Figure 11.5) and disease detection algorithm.

The common shortcoming of the aforementioned related work is their lack of consideration for developing a portable secured edge device capable of locally processing and analyzing the data for localized decision-making. We consider this to be the contribution in this chapter by showing how to employ distinct technologies to build a simple yet accurate enough ECG monitoring device that can be leveraged for patient-monitoring applications and further leveraged for bio-signal authentication in specific use-case scenarios.

## 11.3 PROPOSED AI-BASED SYSTEM ARCHITECTURE

### 11.3.1 Block Diagram

The main motivation of the model includes monitoring the patient's health conditions periodically and developing a secured and cost-efficient remote patient monitoring edge-based ECG system using sensors that predict results using machine learning algorithm which decides

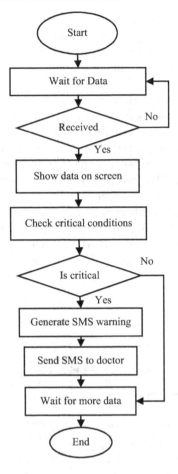

Figure 11.4 Process of analyzing patient data.

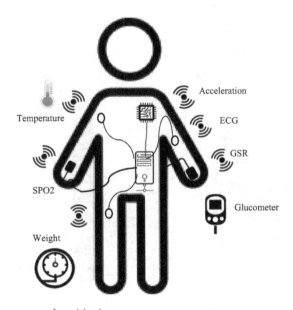

Figure 11.5 Sensor deployment and positioning.

the patient's abnormalities. Our proposed system will be using sensors that detects health problem with high accuracy by using some AI technology that tracks patients' health on edge devices. The patient dataset obtained is preprocessed before any algorithms or analysis is performed. The dataset used for training the system is MIT-BIH Supraventricular dataset and the test data is the live data which is obtained from the Raspberry Pi module. The training dataset is classified and trained with multiple machine learning algorithms as mentioned earlier, and the best algorithm based on the performance accuracy is selected to process the test data. The pre-trained data model is loaded on the SoC, and the result and evaluation are displayed on the screen. The entire proposed procedure is summarized in Figure 11.6 below.

To connect the heart rate sensor to SoC, we need to have an idea about the GPIO pin diagram of SoC as shown in Figure 11.7, which helps us in identifying which pins are to be used to connect the device and the sensor together.

Figure 11.8 shows how the connection is to be made between the sensor and the board, and we can also see how analog to digital converter acts as an intermediate device between the sensor and the board. Here, the pins of ADC, such as voltage supply and ground, are connected to the respective supply and ground pins in raspberry pi. Other pins such as clock, input and output are connected to the GPIO pins of the Raspberry Pi module.

Figure 11.6 Block diagram of proposed system.

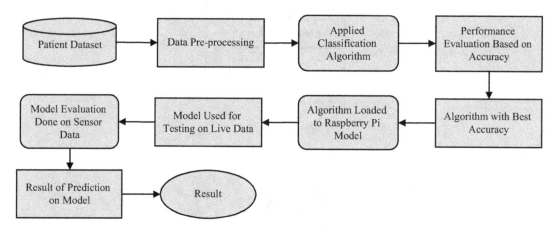

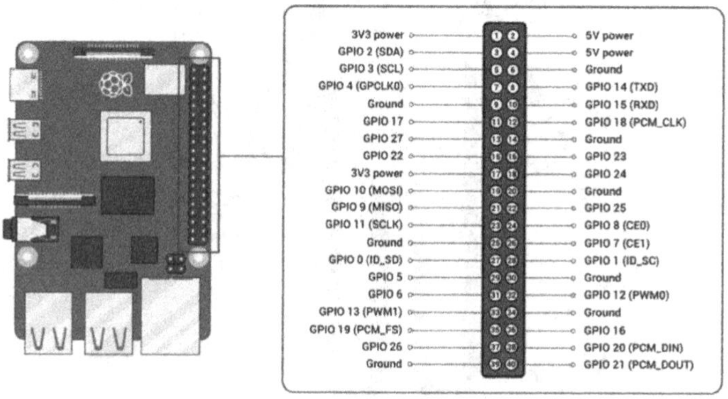

Figure 11.7 GPIO layout Raspberry Pi [17].

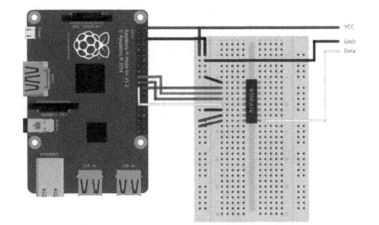

*Figure 11.8* Circuit diagram [18].

## 11.3.2 Data Collection and Pre-Processing Steps

MIT-BIH Supraventricular dataset from PhysioNet is used for the evaluation of the adopted early warning system involving ECG-based arrhythmia classification. Altogether, the data was divided in two cycles which includes futures of ECG such as PQRST wave as depicted in Figure 11.9. The main feature is the QRS complex which identifies heart abnormalities. The dataset contains 184428 total records and 33 total attributes. It is divided into five main target classes which are – Normal (N), Supraventricular ectopic (SVEB), Ventricular ectopic (VEB), Fusion (F) and unknown (Q) beats.

Figure 11.10 depicts a representation of the raw ECG signals collected from the heart rate sensors which are later preprocessed to use as test set for the system. This preprocessing step of the signals consists of the following steps: data cleaning, matching, combining and removing noise and irrelevant data. Initially, the collected raw ECG signals were cleaned using three filters which were Band reject, High pass and Low pass filter. The purpose of these filters is to eliminate various noises from the raw signals and clean the data. The cleaned data is then passed to the heartbeat segmentation phase where various peaks of the heartbeat such as Q peak, S peak, R peak and so forth are identified to further extract features from the peaks. Finally, to extract meaningful features from the peak, the distance between the peaks is calculated. The distance between the peaks gives us an idea about the situation of the peak, which can help us assume various crucial features of the ECG signal. Therefore, various features regarding the heartbeat amplitude, heartbeat interval, morphological features and so forth are comprehended in this way. These extracted features are considered as the final feature set for feeding to the machine learning algorithms.

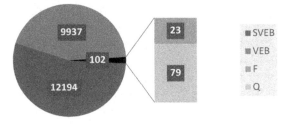

*Figure 11.9* Abnormal heartbeat distribution.

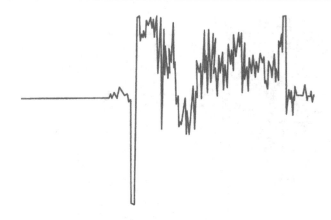

*Figure 11.10* Raw ECG output of the monitoring system.

## 11.3.3 Detecting Heart Abnormalities Using AI-Aided Techniques

All the preprocessed data obtained from the previous step is then processed on a high-end computing device and the results in terms of accuracy rate are determined. Therefore, the pre-trained model having the best performance is then loaded on the Raspberry Pi.

The following steps are the intermediate steps for training the dataset and saving it into a pickle file.

Figure 11.11 demonstrates a chunk of the dataset that was extracted from the ECG signals. Here, the columns such as 0_pre_RR, 1_qrs_morph2, 1_qrs_morph3 etc. are the features of the dataset and the type column is our class label to detect supraventricular arrhythmia. The dataset was scaled using standard scaling method before passing it to the machine learning algorithms. The scaling was performed to normalize the range of the features

The problem was converted to a binary classification case where the Normal and SVEB classes in the dataset were converted as Type 0 and 1. The total number of records in the two classes are 162240 and 12480, respectively.

During the evaluation, a 'pkl' file is created for all the models. This file is used to load the trained ML model on to Raspberry Pi. The pkl file of the model having best performance is copied to Raspberry Pi for displaying the results on the device. The pkl file has a pre-trained model, and this model can be later used for testing the live data which will be obtained from the ECG sensor connected to the raspberry pi device. Once the file is downloaded it is ready

| record | type | 0_pre-RR | ... | 1_qrs_morph2 | 1_qrs_morph3 | 1_qrs_morph4 |
|---|---|---|---|---|---|---|
| 800 | N | 168.0 | ... | 0.003311 | 0.077157 | 0.060548 |
| 800 | N | 167.0 | ... | -0.011806 | -0.011806 | -0.011806 |
| 800 | N | 169.0 | ... | -0.009710 | -0.009710 | -0.009710 |
| 800 | N | 170.0 | ... | 0.011955 | 0.039944 | 0.066575 |
| 800 | N | 166.0 | ... | -0.029659 | -0.005076 | -0.005076 |
| ... | ... | ... | ... | ... | ... | ... |
| 894 | N | 102.0 | ... | -0.366454 | -0.489696 | -0.489696 |
| 894 | N | 96.0 | ... | -0.489704 | -0.710598 | -0.710598 |
| 894 | N | 79.0 | ... | -0.225756 | -0.505484 | -0.505484 |
| 894 | N | 96.0 | ... | -0.326364 | -0.326364 | -0.423273 |
| 894 | SVEB | 59.0 | ... | -0.887602 | -0.887602 | -0.887602 |

*Figure 11.11* Preprocessed data obtained from raw ECG signal.

to be run on the raspberry pi device provided all the requirements mentioned in 3.1 are already satisfied. The program can be executed by writing a simple python program and it displays the current health status of the person.

## 11.4 CONSIDERED SMART ECG MONITORING SYSTEM

In this section, we present the hardware (sensing) and AI-logic components of our considered smart ECG monitoring system.

### 11.4.1 Edge Hardware Components

The centerpiece of the hardware setup for the considered smart ECG monitoring system is a microcontroller. Among various off-the-shelf microcontroller devices, Raspberry Pi 3 Model B+ is considered due to its cost-efficiency and performance for deploying pre-trained AI model for ECG classification with reasonable accuracy. The microcontroller and other hardware devices needed to construct the ECG monitoring system are described next.

#### 11.4.1.1 System-on-a-Chip (SoC) Model

After rigorous study of different microprocessors which are readily available in the market, the Raspberry Pi 3 Model B+ is selected as the SOC model for constructing our considered smart ECG monitoring system. Figure 11.12 illustrates an image of the raspberry pi 3B+ model. This hardware model is based on an ARM Cortex-A53 1.4GHz processor operating on the Raspbian Operating System, a dual-band 2.4GHz and 5GHz Wireless Local Area Network (WLAN) interface, Bluetooth 4.2/BLE, and Ethernet with 300Mbps. A 700mA power supply is used for the operation of the SoC and the IoT peripherals.

#### 11.4.1.2 IoT Sensor for Heart Rate Data Acquisition

An off-the-shelf optical pulse sensor is used to measure the heart rate of the user as shown is Figure 11.13. This has the capability of collecting reliable pulse readings from the fingertip or earlobe of the user by using the state-of-the-art on-sensor noise-cancellation and signal amplification circuits. The sensor does not require soldering to a system board since

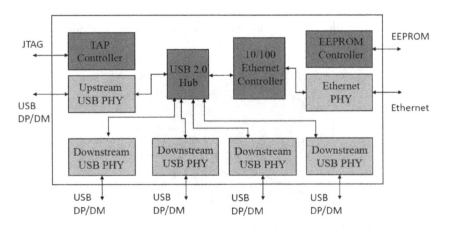

*Figure 11.12* Raspberry Pi 3B+ [17].

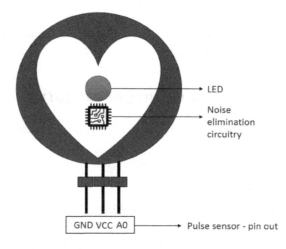

*Figure 11.13* Pulse Heart Rate Sensor [19].

it consists of a three-pin cable that is terminated with standard male headers. Furthermore, the sensor consists of a luminous Light Emitting Diode (LED) and a light detector that allow light to pass through the finger and detected, respectively. As the heart pumps a pulse of blood through the blood vessels, the finger turns opaque to such an extent that a less amount of light reaches the detector. Furthermore, the light signal captured at the detector varies with each heart pulse that is translated into an electrical pulse and amplified so that a +5 V logic level output signal is generated. The LED blinks on the generation of each output signal that corresponds to each heartbeat. This analog output is connected to the microcontroller for converting the electronic signal to number of heart beats per minute.

### 11.4.1.3 Microprocessor and Analog to Digital Converter

Arduino microprocessor is selected to connect the analog pulse sensor to the SoC with the support of a cost-efficient, eight-channel and 10-bit analog to digital converter (MCP3008) which is illustrated in Figure 11.14. This converter uses serial interface employing successive approximation algorithm to sample the signal at 75 ksps and 200 ksps with the operating voltages of 2.7 and 5 V, respectively.

The above-mentioned set of hardware was integrated to develop our desired secured ECG monitoring system for collecting ECG signals. Figure 11.15 shows a demonstration of our developed system. Here, the ECG signal data are collected using the pulse heart rate sensor,

*Figure 11.14* Analog to digital converter (MCP3008) [20].

*Figure 11.15* Diagram illustrating the developed system.

which with the help of MCP3008 is converted to digital data. The digital data can then be accessed through the raspberry pi SoC.

## 11.4.2 AI-Logic Component

For the AI-logic component at the SoC to construct the heartbeat monitoring and corresponding arrhythmiaclassification system from ECG signals, an open-source graphical library and integrated development environment, referred to as 'Processing', is exploited. This offers a powerful visualization framework for incorporating the AI-logic component to the considered SoC to simplify the compilation and execution steps of a pre-trained AI logic. The reason behind choosing this framework is its ability to seamlessly connect with MCP3008 analog to digital converter that was challenging with other available frameworks.

For the AI-logic component of the system, the following requirements with latest versions of python with TensorFlow and Keras were downloaded and installed on the SoC. Sklearn, Numpy and Scipy libraries were required for executing the pre-trained AI model on the edge device (i.e., the SoC).

On the other hand, for training the AI-logic model, a more powerful centralized computing environment was used. Four machine/deep learning classification algorithms were taken into consideration for building a model using supervised training based on public repository data of ECG signals and underlying diseases. Classification is a process to identify a model which describes and differentiates data classes or concepts for the purpose of employing the model to predict the class of objects whose class label is unknown. The four classification algorithms used in this work are decision tree, Random Forest, ANN and CNN. These algorithms are used for performing a comparative study and obtaining the best accuracy which can be further used for predicting supraventricular arrhythmia locally at the considered edge device. An overview of these algorithms is presented in the remainder of this section.

### 11.4.2.1 Decision Tree

First, we select the decision tree to be trained at a central computing environment with sufficient computational power based on publicly available ECG data. The reason behind investigating the decision tree algorithm is its popularity and practicality to deploy on edge nodes for fast inference for sensed bio-signal without much complexity. Decision tree is trained in a supervised manner to predict a class by employing decision rules on nodes generated from previous data. The instances are classified in the root nodes of a decision tree. By employing various features, the root nodes are able to classify the instances with different features. At the root nodes, there may be more than two branches. Finally, in the leaf nodes, the classification result is reported. The decision tree construction is performed step by step by using the highest information gain value among all the attributes.

### 11.4.2.2 Random Forest

The next model that we consider for facilitating the edge intelligence is Random Forest, which is also a supervised learning algorithm. In essence, Random Forest offers a classification method based on numerous decisions trees to significantly improve the prediction accuracy in contrast with a single decision tree model. In the literature, Random Forest is referred to as an ensemble learning method whereby a multitude of decision trees are formulated during the training time and the output class is obtained as the mode of the classes or mean prediction of the individual trees. The Random Forest model employs bagging and feature randomness while constructing each individual tree. This attempts to build an uncorrelated forest of trees, prediction accuracy of which is significantly improved in a systematic manner.

### 11.4.2.3 ANN

While decision tree and Random Forest models work with small-scale preprocessed ECG data, more sophisticated techniques may be required with large ECG datasets where preprocessing and manual feature extraction may not be trivial. Therefore, we also consider the ANN structure consisting of neurons deployed over three layers which are input, output and hidden layer. The ANN model is trained by varying their weights using forward and backward propagation techniques. The data of the input layer are propagated to the hidden layer neuron units where each input is assigned a weight based upon the importance of the input. The output layer neuron units represent the predicted class (e.g., whether the user is exhibiting normal or abnormal heartbeats and so forth).

### 11.4.2.4 CNN

Deep neural networks with more than one hidden layer are becoming more prominent for solving various computational-intensive tasks in today's literature of biomedical engineering. CNN is an advanced variant of deep neural networks that has a plethora of application in image and speech recognition. The one-dimensional CNN model may be useful in processing complex time-series of heartbeat signals to accurately identify associated cardiac conditions. While the adoption of convolutional layers consisting of local filters, max-pooling and weight sharing makes the CNN model much more robust and powerful over the simple ANN, its training and inference tradeoff for predicting heart disease needs to be carefully considered.

## 11.5 BIO-AUTHENTICATION APPLICATION OF THE CONSIDERED ECG MONITORING SYSTEM FOR SPECIFIC USE-CASES

By implementing this IoT-based system in a single chip of logic, improved and economical health services can be provided for the users. The system can authenticate users based on their bio-signals such as ECG signals and make the procedure safe and secure. Since user can access the system on the edge, the entire process of heart monitoring becomes easily accessible. Thus, it is able to offer improved and reliable services related to healthcare in situations where the patient is far away from the doctor. Thus, this allows doctors to acquire data of the patients from far away and prescribe medicine accordingly more quickly and efficiently. It also enables patients and doctors across a country to connect for superior treatments by tracking and recording patient data in real-time. The proposed system can save hospital bill, valuable time and in some cases might avoid long queues in the hospitals. The proposed design provides a cost-efficient, lightweight alternative to the current technologies present in the medical centers which are less efficient and more expensive.

Next, the propositioned system can have a multitude of applications. Several continuous user monitoring applications such as car insurance monitoring apps observe user data to study the user's vehicle-driving behavior and conditions to decide when claims are made to the companies. These apps usually monitor the car speed, road conditions and weather conditions using various features of the user mobile phone. However, to activate and use the application, there is only one-time authentication, and it does not guarantee whether the registered user or any other unauthenticated person is driving the car. We introduce an ECG-based continuous biometric authentication scheme for all such applications where continuous user monitoring is required. We aim to identify the change from authenticated users to the unauthorized user for user monitoring apps. The proposed AI-aided model will analyze and find patterns or trends in the user's heart activity by analyzing the ECG wave of each individual. The ECG data will be collected from the user and will be processed locally on edge devices adopting AI-aided techniques to also monitor if the person's health condition is normal or not.

In order to demonstrate our bio-authentication system, we have constructed a machine learning model that will be able to differentiate authorized user from unauthorized user. For implementing it using ECG signals, we have utilized the same dataset containing the extracted features that were used for classifying supraventricular arrhythmia. The classification was carried out on only the normal cases of the dataset to show the efficacy of our proposed concept. In this case, we have classified the users, i.e., the record column as our goal is to authenticate the user. Therefore, we have considered two classes: authorized and unauthorized. We have run the experiment five times, where at each run, only one of the records (i.e., person) will be considered authorized and the rest of the users will be unauthorized. The ECG recordings of both authorized and unauthorized were shuffled and considered in both train and test set. We have applied Random Forest algorithm to classify the records because initially Random Forest performed better for supraventricular arrhythmiaclassification.

## 11.6 PERFORMANCE EVALUATION

Evaluation on performance of a classification algorithm is usually done on its accuracy. The estimations of an instance to that instance's genuine value to the level of familiarity is known as accuracy. The dataset was split into train and test set with the ratio of 70 and 30, respectively. The models were validated using stratified five-fold cross-validation.

### 11.6.1 Supraventricular Arrhythmia Classification

This research used four machine learning models; decision tree, Random Forest, CNN and ANN to predict the chances of heart failure in a patient from the MIT-BIH Supraventricular dataset. The comparative study is performed on the results (Accuracy) of all the ML models as shown in Figure Figure 11.16. In Figure Figure 11.16 it is seen that the model with the best performance is Random Forest with 97.38% accuracy. Thus, the Random Forest model is used as the prediction model for integrating with raspberry pi.

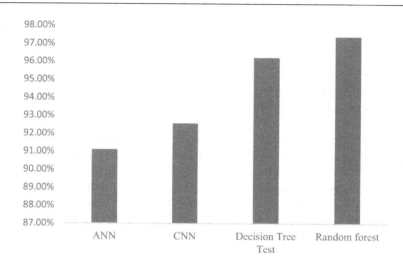

*Figure 11.16* Algorithm accuracy chart.

*Table 11.1* Comparative study of our model with existing methods.

| Problem | Classification model | Performance |
| --- | --- | --- |
| Our model for classifying supraventricular arrhythmia | Random Forest | 97.38% |
| Arrhythmiaclassification using ECG signals [21] | Convolutional Neural Network | 93.31% |
| Classification of arrhythmia in selected feature set [22] | K Nearest Neighbor | 92.8% |
| ECG-based arrhythmia classification [23] | Deep belief networks | 96.94% |

The performance also depends on the sensor manufacturer as the capacity of accurate sensing varies from sensor to sensor and also depends on the manufacturer. The system requires high electronic circuit's knowledge to reduce the noise from the sensor and get accurate results. The experimental results for the patient's health status is 100% accurate for normal patients according to the live data which was tested against the training data using the machine learning algorithms.

The result achieved while classifying supraventricular arrhythmia data was compared with the performance of previous studies where similar analysis is performed. Table 11.1 shows a comparative analysis of our model with three studies, using the MIT-BIH Supraventricular dataset, in terms of their performance.

## 11.6.2 Authorized User Classification for Bio-Authentication System

The performance was evaluated based on Accuracy, Precision, Recall, F1 Score and their respective confusion matrix. For Random Forest algorithm, the number of trees was considered to be 150. As mentioned earlier, the experimentation was repeated for five users. The performance evaluation on the proposed bio-authentication system is illustrated in Table 11.2. Here, record represents the authorized user. It can be seen from the table that Random Forest is performing remarkably while classifying users based on their ECG signal features. The accuracy, precision, recall and F1-score are giving near-perfect values denoting that the ECG signals of each person is distinct from the other person and hence can be thoroughly identified.

*Table 11.2* Performance evaluation on the proposed bio-authentication system.

| Record | Accuracy | Precision | Recall | F1-score |
|--------|----------|-----------|--------|----------|
| 800 | 0.999918 | 0.999918 | 0.999918 | 0.999918 |
| 801 | 0.999938 | 0.999938 | 0.999938 | 0.999938 |
| 802 | 0.990094 | 0.995021 | 0.990094 | 0.991723 |
| 803 | 0.992396 | 0.995277 | 0.992396 | 0.993286 |
| 804 | 0.998993 | 0.999038 | 0.998993 | 0.999005 |

The confusion matrix of the results was also plotted for the five experiments. The results are stated in Figure 11.17. It can be seen that the results of false positives and false negatives are almost insignificant and most of the instances are classified accurately.

Thus, we can conclude that implementing the bio-authentication system using Random Forest classification can be a useful method for authenticating the authorized users based on their ECG signals, thus making the ECG system more secure. One of the advantages of this system is that it employs the same dataset for arrhythmia classification and bio-authentication, thus saving valuable processing time along the way.

## 11.7 CHALLENGES INVOLVED WITH THE PROPOSED SYSTEM

The automated treatment employing various ECG techniques is a popular field; however, it still lacks various aspects in the implementation domain in terms of algorithms and so forth. Therefore, it is important to study more in this field in order to improve it. The necessity of automated ECG analysis system is required with the popularity of remote monitoring technology and long-term ECG recording devices. In order to facilitate a real-time processing of dynamic ECG signals, parameters like complicated, time-consuming algorithms, delayed restriction and the search time of distinguishing wave position window should be kept minimal. The noise of ECG signals should be removed in pre-processing steps and the QRS waves should be detected accurately. Additionally, various cases such as the false positives and missed detection rates can also be determined by the algorithms.

The above-mentioned challenges are faced during the initial phase, but there is a list of challenges that were faced during the implementation part of the system. We have listed the following challenges and how we overcame that during implementation.

- Connecting Analog Sensor to Raspberry Pi-based SoC without using Arduino Module: One of the important parts of the project was to connect the ECG sensor to the Raspberry Pi device. It would not be possible to use Arduino module as the portability is an important aspect for the system; therefore, we used a MCP3008 ADC to connect the sensor.
- Libraries to Access ADC: After we were able to connect the sensor with the board, it was still hard to communicate with the device because the libraries for the communication to ADC are not present in python which was a major programming language used for implementation. Therefore, the connection was designed with processing since it has libraries to communicate directly with the ADC device.
- Understanding the Sensor Signal and Plotting ECG Signal: One of the major challenges involved with our implementation was to understand the signal which was sent by the sensor and also plot it as ECG graph. The signal contains output only in bits and the

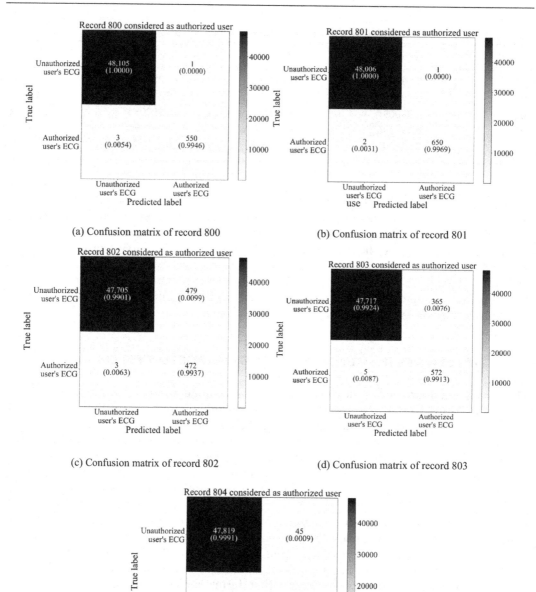

(a) Confusion matrix of record 800

(b) Confusion matrix of record 801

(c) Confusion matrix of record 802

(d) Confusion matrix of record 803

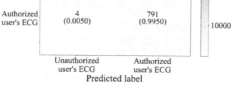

(e) Confusion matrix of record 804

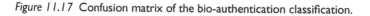

*Figure 11.17* Confusion matrix of the bio-authentication classification.

sensor documentation helped in finding out the formulas for converting the signal to ECG Graph.

- Collecting Live Data for Processing Health Information: The live data collected was to be studied and the QRS component of the data was to be separated from the signal to generate the live dataset from the sensor device. Dividing the signal and saving it into a csv file ignoring the values was the solution we came up with to solve this problem.

- Machine Learning on Raspberry Pi Device: Raspberry Pi is known as a simple compatible device and known for its portability, but we wanted to include machine learning algorithms on our hardware and machine learning to the contrast requires very high-end computing device. Therefore, we used a pre-trained model which was later dumped on the device using 'pickle' to overcome the problem of training the data on the device and saved our times and effort in analyzing the real-time data.

## Limitations

- Noise from the ECG sensor has been a major issue of the system. We were able to reduce some noise by adjusting the resistance to the sensor and ADC. However, complete elimination of the noise was not possible, and this is left as an open research challenge for the future. Admittedly, the noise was responsible to add some missing values in the process.

- The adopted system was tested only on normal cases which achieved an accuracy of 100%, but we were not able to test the system on patients having heart problems.

## 11.8 CONCLUSION AND FUTURE SCOPE

In this chapter, we have presented a prototype of a secured ECG monitoring device with the integration of IoT technology. The proposed model will continuously monitor ECG signals to detect supraventricular arrhythmiaand provide doctors and patient with a more efficient medical service. In this research, the raspberry-pi-based health monitoring system was analyzed through IoT. Heartbeat sensors continuously sense the ECG signals, and the data is transformed through the machine learning algorithm and the prediction is done on edge to determine if the patient is suffering from heart abnormalities or not. There are multiple prediction algorithms used for doing the comparison, and based on best accuracy result the algorithms are further used for prediction. To achieve that, in this chapter, we have applied four different algorithms which are decision tree, Random Forest, ANN and CNN. Random forest performed the best with an accuracy of 97.38% with decision tree being the second best. Therefore, Random Forest was chosen as the most efficient algorithm to be deployed in our system. Some of the benefits of such systems include saving hospital bill, reduce waiting time and long lines in the hospitals. The proposed system provides a lightweight and cheaper alternative to the traditional heavy and costly devices in the hospitals. The system is easily portable, and the patients can be monitored easily from remote places. Hence, this system provides enhanced healthcare services, and is therefore more reliable in cases where the patient is far away from the doctor.

We introduced an ECG-based continuous biometric authentication scheme for all such applications where continuous user monitoring is required. We aim to identify the change from authenticated users to the unauthorized user for user monitoring apps. The proposed Random Forest model analyzes and finds patterns or trends in the user's heart activity by analyzing the ECG wave of each individual. The ECG data will be collected from the user and will be processed locally on an edge device such as Raspberry Pi, adopting AI aided techniques to also monitor if the person's health condition is normal or not. Currently, the supraventricular arrhythmia prediction is done based on QRS complexion from the live data and applying prediction algorithms for fast results. Further this live data that is collected can be used for live authentication purpose which can be used in user monitoring apps such as car insurance companies where ECG signal of each individual is identified and the change from authenticated users to the unauthorized user is identified.

In future, the bio-authentication system can be further developed to be implemented in other scenarios such as car insurance monitoring. For the analysis of pre-processed ECG, the PQRST waves will be used as a pivotal characteristic for the change point detection (CPD). Abrupt variations in time series ECG is considered as change points which can be employed to distinguish among different people's heart activity. Comparing the fundamental differences in the PQRST wave of a person's ECG and studying the behavior of the wave for a particular person we train our system and if there is a change detected in the wave, the system will report it and also find out the point where this change has occurred. Additionally, the ECG of the user will also be monitored using various machine learning algorithms for any possible abnormalities while driving which will ensure some degree of safety for the user while driving. The system model will be trained to find out whether the heart activity of the person is normal or is prone to any sudden cardiovascular abnormalities. Based on the decision, an automated alerting system can be implemented in the system architecture which will alert the user's acquaintances about the user's unusual heart condition. Thus, the system can help several heart patients who are unable to visit the doctor due to their critical condition and get timely treatments and avoid any kind of accidents that might worsen their situation.

## REFERENCES

1. S. B. Baker, W. Xiang, and I. Atkinson, "Internet of things for smart healthcare: Technologies, challenges, and Opportunities," *IEEE Access*, 2017, doi:10.1109/ACCESS.2017.2775180.

2. S. L. Guo, L. N. Han, H. W. Liu, Q. J. Si, D. F. Kong, and F. S. Guo, "The future of remote ECG monitoring systems," *Journal of Geriatric Cardiology*, 2016, doi: 10.11909/j. issn.1671-5411.2016.06.015.

3. A. Bansal et al., "Remote health monitoring system for detecting cardiac disorders," *IET Systems Biology*, 2015, doi:10.1049/iet-syb.2015.0012.

4. J. Son, J. Park, H. Oh, M. Z. A. Bhuiyan, J. Hur, and K. Kang, "Privacy-preserving electrocardiogram monitoring for intelligent arrhythmia detection," *Sensors (Switzerland)*, 2017, doi:10.3390/s17061360.

5. F. J. Martinez-Tabares, Y. J. Costa-Salas, D. Cuesta-Frau, and G. Castellanos-Dominguez, "Multiobjective design of wearable sensor systems for electrocardiogram monitoring," *Journal of Sensors*, 2016, doi:10.1155/2016/2418065.

6. S. Tian, W. Yang, J. M. Le Grange, P. Wang, W. Huang, and Z. Ye, "Smart healthcare: Making medical care more intelligent," *Global Health Journal*, 2019, doi:10.1016/j.glohj.2019.07.001.

7. Y. Yin, Y. Zeng, X. Chen, and Y. Fan, "The internet of things in healthcare: An overview," *Journal of Industrial Information Integration*, 2016, doi:10.1016/j.jii.2016.03.004.

8. S. D. Greenwald, R. S. Patil, and R. G. Mark, "Improved detection and classification of arrhythmias in noise-corrupted electrocardiograms using contextual information within an expert system," *Biomedical Instrumentation and Technology*, 1992.

9. P. P. Ray, "A survey on Internet of Things architectures," *Journal of King Saud University - Computer and Information Sciences*, 2018, doi:10.1016/j.jksuci.2016.10.003.

10. M. S. D. Gupta, V. Patchava, and V. Menezes, "Healthcare based on IoT using Raspberry Pi," 2016, doi:10.1109/ICGCIoT.2015.7380571.

11. R. Kumar and M. Pallikonda Rajasekaran, "An IoT based patient monitoring system using raspberry Pi," 2016, doi:10.1109/ICCTIDE.2016.7725378.

12. S. Jokić, S. Krčo, V. Delić, D. Sakač, I. Jokić, and Z. Lukić, "An efficient ECG modeling for heartbeat classification," 2010, doi:10.1109/NEUREL.2010.5644105.

13. A. Rahman, T. Rahman, N. H. Ghani, S. Hossain, and J. Uddin, "IoT based patient monitoring system using ECG sensor," 2019, doi:10.1109/ICREST.2019.8644065.

14. D. A. M. Budida and R. S. Mangrulkar, "Design and implementation of smart HealthCare system using IoT," 2018, doi:10.1109/ICIIECS.2017.8275903.

15. M. H. Riaz, U. Rashid, M. Ali, and L. Li, "Internet of things based wireless patient body area monitoring network," 2018, doi:10.1109/iThings-GreenCom-CPSCom-SmartData.2017.180.

16. Priyanka Bhoyar and S. S. Sonavane, "Remote patient monitoring using disease detection algorithm," *International Journal of Engineering Research*, vol. V4, no. 09, pp. 307–312, 2015, doi: 10.17577/ijertv4is090445.

17. "Raspberry Pi documentation." https://www.raspberrypi.org/documentation/usage/gpio/.

18. "소리와 불빛이 나는 계단 프로토타입," 2019. https://78project.wordpress.com/author/inkspelloo/.

19. "Heart rate pulse sensor amped introduction." https://microcontrollerslab.com/heart-rate-pulse-sensor/.

20. "MCP3008 8-Channel 10-bit ADC IC." https://components101.com/ics/mcp3008-adc-pinout-equivalent-datasheet.

21. S. Sakib, M. M. Fouda, Z. M. Fadlullah, and N. Nasser, "Migrating intelligence from cloud to ultra-edge smart IoT sensor based on deep learning: An arrhythmia monitoring use-case," 2020, doi:10.1109/IWCMC48107.2020.9148134.

22. H. Leutheuser *et al.*, "Comparison of real-time classification systems for arrhythmia detection on Android-based mobile devices," 2014, doi:10.1109/EMBC.2014.6944177.

23. S. M. Mathews, C. Kambhamettu, and K. E. Barner, "A novel application of deep learning for single-lead ECG classification," *Computers in Biology and Medicine*, 2018, doi:10.1016/j.compbiomed.2018.05.013.

# Section III

# Chapter 12

# Application of Unmanned Aerial Vehicles in Wireless Networks

## Mobile Edge Computing and Caching

*Aniqa Tasnim Oishi, Leeyana Farheen Rahman, Mosarrat Jahan Siddika, and Shahriar Arnab*

Brac University, Bangladesh

*Saifur Rahman Sabuj*

Hanbat National University, South Korea

## CONTENTS

## 12.1 INTRODUCTION

To provide better service for human beings, Unmanned Aerial Vehicles (UAVs), also called drones, are applied in fifth-generation (5G) mobile networks for their versatile functionality. With the use of Mobile Edge Computing (MEC) in the UAVs, data transfer is improved and communication is made more efficient. UAVs work as flying base station (BS) because a static BS cannot be effectively used to serve the mobile users (MUs) when they relocate themselves from the designated coverage range of the BS. In addition, while a MU travels to a new cell, its solicited content might be unavailable at the new BS which leaves the user's request unattended. In such cases, to serve the MU, multiple BSs might be required which will not be efficient. Therefore, we have chosen UAVs to be operated as flying BSs as they can follow the mobility pattern of the users, thereby rightfully serving them. As a result of their high altitude and flexibility, they can set up reliable communication network with the users by diminishing the blockage effect [1].

With UAV as a BS, MEC has been an important part in the 5G network and Internet of Things (IoT). The role of MEC is to provide cloud-like services to its MUs at the network edge. This will in turn allow applications in mobile devices and services from the edge network to function with reduced latency as well as with improved reliability of their communication [2]. Thus, MEC is also responsible for improving the Quality-of-Services (QoS), as well as the Quality-of-Experience (QoE) of the MUs via high-speed communication. It is also implementing the edge computing layer within the UAV-based MEC architecture to further facilitate a traffic free, secure network for real-time applications and machine intelligence [3], along with optimizing computational offloading and resource allocation [4].

A UAV-equipped MEC system which is powered wirelessly has multiple advantages in wireless communication. With effective deployment and operation, drones contribute to a dependable, cost-efficient connection to desired locations. UAV as flying BS (UAV-BS) not only have the potential to modify their altitude as per requirement but are also capable of avoiding obstacles and establishing improved Line-of-Sight (LOS) communications. Apart from mobility and flexibility, they provide enhanced capacity to areas with greater traffic and can be used to deliver coverage to remote areas which do not have proper network access without the need of building an expensive cellular infrastructure [5]. UAVs also act as an energy transmitter which can be used to supply energy to the ground MUs, thereby improving power levels and energy consumption [4]. In addition to UAV's benefits, MEC can further improve the communication by hosting software and applications that can access user traffic and radio network information to help them modify their services for an enhanced user experience [6]. Furthermore, it has the added benefit of not requiring any new consumer technology to enjoy its services [7]. Besides being able to ensure quick responses [8], it has other practical uses which include Augmented Reality (AR), Virtual Reality (VR), autonomous cars and a lot more which will be further explained in [7,8].

### 12.1.1 Chapter Roadmap

Our chapter's contributions can be written in the following manner:

1. To overcome the problems of low-latency and reliability of communication system, the UAV-BS provides better service to the MUs. We will also implement MEC into the system to further improve the efficiency of communication.
2. To provide the advantages and disadvantages of executing MEC and caching at the UAV-BS and explain the different layers of the MEC system and their role in communication.
3. To use NOMA technique in our proposed model, we derive mathematical expression of data rate, transmission delay, time consumption and energy consumption.
4. Simulations are carried out at different signal-to-noise ratio (SNR) for both uplink and downlink communication to compare the relationships with data rate, transmission delay and energy consumption.

The rest of our chapter is written as follows. Literature review is given in Section 12.2. Section 12.3 is comprised of the description, advantages and disadvantages of MEC and caching. Layering of the MEC-based UAV architecture is described in Section12. 4. Our proposed system model is described in Section 12.5. Our simulation results are provided in Section 12.6 and finally Section 12.7 ends this chapter.

## 12.2 LITERATURE REVIEW

A lot of surveys and research have been carried out in the past related to UAV-assisted content caching within MEC. Previous studies discussed the characteristics and requirements of UAV networks, placement of UAVs for effective caching and energy efficient operation. Furthermore, multiple research have been conducted on MEC and its contributions on cybersecurity, UAVs and 5G hierarchical network.

Chen et al. [1] came up with a framework that would grasp user's information to predict his mobility and content demand types in order to find the best suited caching strategy for the UAVs. Mozaffari et al. [5] discussed that the key challenges pertaining to UAVs were its deployment in the three-dimensional space, performance breakdown, channel modeling and energy efficiency, and came up with optimization and design theories to overcome them. Yang et al. [9] proposed a simple algorithm to solve the sum power minimization problem to achieve energy efficiency in UAV-Enabled MEC Networks. Kalinagac et al. [10] explored software-defined UAV Networks to identify where and what to cache and concluded that using UAVs as BSs is preferable as they are capable of providing auxiliary on-demand services in case the existing network gets dismantled due to any catastrophic event. More benefits of caching with UAVs, such as reduced network congestion and interference and increased security, were addressed by Zhao et al. [11]. Sharma et al. [3] proposed the layout of caching enabled MEC architecture that proved to be an efficient transport mechanism to connect end users with Cloud, to ensure low latency and ultra-reliable communication.

Bekkouche et al. in their research paper [2] discussed on how the latency and reliability of the network affect the control on UAVs' flights. Their paper proposed a UTM framework for efficient traffic management since their calculations show that UAVs divert easily from their intended paths leading to packet loss. The work presented in [4] studied a wireless powered MEC system based on UAVs. They presented algorithms to achieve power efficiency which proved to be superior compared to other proposed algorithms in the past which also guaranteed efficiency in terms of convergence. In [8] Ahmed et al. elaborated on the definition of MEC along with its applications and challenges. They also provided an overview of other research papers that was utilized in their survey. The overview was segmented into three parts, cloud computing, MEC and mobile social networks. The architecture, advantages and disadvantages of MEC along with its technological developments were explained in [12]. In addition, security and privacy issues along with their solutions and future research works were also covered. Mao et al. [13] further elaborated on the topic of MEC by including their resource management, mobility management and system deployment. An algorithm comprised of the LSTM-based task prediction algorithm and UAV position optimization algorithm for an offloading strategy was proposed by Wu et al. [14]. The algorithm is programmed based on the delay, UAV height and data size to minimize the energy utilization by the UAV.

Cyber security and message encryption concerns were explored in [15] where Sedjelmaci et al. suggested a hierarchal intrusion detection scheme using both UAV and ground BS to trace any suspicious activity. He merged behavior-based detection with rule-based attack and made UAVs act as supervisors to observe and detect threats. According to his scheme, greater the detection rates, higher will be the security. The work in [16] proposed an authentication algorithm which protected the UAVs from cyber as well as physical attacks by means of an encrypted communication channel. The method allowed the operator to take back control over a UAV that was compromised by using a secondary channel security system. However, in that model, physical security was neglected in case the UAV was preliminarily missing or not used for service. Furthermore, Bai *et al.* [17] proposed an offloading model for UAV-MEC systems while focusing on physical-layer security (PLS) which would protect the system from both active and passive eavesdroppers by taking into account their channel state information and location information. Finally, the work presented in [18] addressed the security issues that came with UAV Edge computing network and how a cyber-defense solution based on a non-cooperative game was useful to guard the network from offloading attacks, while also considering nodes' energy limitations and computation expenses.

## 12.3 DESCRIPTION OF CACHING AND MOBILE EDGE COMPUTING

In this section we will be looking at the overview of caching and MEC as well as present the advantages and disadvantages of implementing these in our UAV-assisted communication system.

### 12.3.1 Overview of Caching

The technique of Caching at network edge is a fresh discovery for the impending 5G mobile network to reduce the backhaul rates during prime hours of communication. In cache-assisted networks, the local caches pre-fetch trending files from the core network during idle times and make them available at the edge nodes to be easily acquired by end users during peak hours. By doing so, traffic at the backhaul can be shifted from the peak time to the off-peak time, and the pressure of backhaul will be significantly relieved. This technique not only brings contents closer to mobile users but also reduces server traffic and makes an efficient use of the existing network bandwidth [1].

Caching is applied at multiple places in flying BSs or UAVs. The content requested by users is fetched from the central server beforehand, in case it is not available at the edge; and then a duplicate of the content is stored for prospective use. In contrast, if this requested data was being retrieved from the core network every time, a notable delay would have been caused by a slow backhaul link [2]. The amount of transmitted data that needs to be processed is reduced as well as the traffic through the network due to these data is brought to a minimum with the use of caching at the MEC server. A higher data transmission rate also ensures an effective use of the bandwidth of the prevailing network. Since we are using UAV for caching, the network must also consider that the fronthaul links that associate the UAVs to the cloud will have finite capacity due to the narrow bandwidth of the UAVs. To solve this problem, we can apply content caching techniques so that the UAVs can preemptively download and cache all the required data during the time of low traffic or after the UAVs have returned to their bases. Caching allows UAVs to channel content to its user who has requested it, thereby narrowing down the traffic load. So with appropriate implementation of the technique, the wireless backhaul overloading of UAVs is remarkably decreased, energy consumption is minimized and better QoE is attained.

#### 12.3.1.1 Advantages

1. Caching reduces network traffic as it allows the user to efficiently access pre-fetched data.
2. Caching helps to improve overall speed and achieve better QoE.
3. It improves data transfer and makes communication more efficient.

4. It saves power by making efficient use of the existing bandwidth.
5. Caching in UAVs enables them to follow the moving pattern of users to effectively serve them.
6. It speeds up loading and minimizes system resources needed to load a content.
7. It also benefits network infrastructure and reduces cost.

### 12.3.1.2 Disadvantages

1. Caching with UAVs lead to greater power consumption as a result of a finite battery life of UAV/drones, if compared to caching at BSs.
2. There is a risk of old data being delivered that is impertinent to the new situation due to rapidly changing content demand.
3. Cache memory can have limited capacity to store content.
4. There is a chance of losing oversight of where data exists leading to high cache-miss rates.
5. Content popularity is complex and non-stationary, so an efficient caching policy needs to be applied [19].

## 12.3.2 Overview of Mobile Edge Computing

The term MEC is created by the European Telecommunications Standards Institute and the Industry Specification Group, and is defined as: MEC offers an information technology infrastructure system and cloud computing technology. It works within the radio access network (RAN) range and in near vicinity to mobile users. MEC also has additional characteristics: MEC can operate independently with the help of the local resources. And with its close proximity with its end user, MEC can analyze and materialize large data with extremely low latency and high bandwidth and also with high quality, all while using low-level signaling for information sharing. Since MEC harbors applications which provide real-time information networks and services, it would be beneficial for businesses and events to implement MEC into their system [12].

### 12.3.2.1 Advantages

1. MEC reduces congestion on mobile networks by managing online traffic and data load [7].
2. It enables application providers to obtain user traffic and radio network information, enabling them to improve user experience by changing their programs and facilities [6].
3. It can house real-time analytics and machine-intelligence software [6].
4. It will not require any new consumer technology to be able to enjoy its services [7].
5. MEC can also serve queries from devices that require response times of below 100 ms [8].
6. Due to MEC's ability to provide speedy, real-time and highly localized feedback, it can have many practical uses, the use cases include [7,8]: AR, VR, Location services, automated cars, IoT, Optimized local content distribution and Data caching.

### 12.3.2.2 Disadvantages

1. It is difficult for application providers to deploy and manage distributed applications across multiple clouds and also coordinate with individual clouds [6].
2. MEC can be prone to system overload or system failures which can result in losing valuable data, however, that problem can be solved by offloading its data to adjacent MECs provided that there are MECs nearby.

3. MUs may change their geographical location and since MECs are decentralized, applications that rely on MEC services have to be mobility-aware and need to fallback to other MEC servers, distant cloud servers or even the UE itself.
4. Since MEC is a cloud-based computing in an edge it raises security issues when it comes to data transfer [8].
5. Implementing MECs is also a challenging task because of the administrative policies [8].

## 12.4 LAYERING OF UAV-BASED MEC ARCHITECTURE

Caching by means of edge layers, particularly for video clients, can lead to high execution and optimization of information acquisition. MEC empowers administrations at the edge of cellular systems by encouraging near-user locales via numerous cloud centers. MEC centers on supporting dependable and low-latency facilities to the clients, for instance, through portable gadgets counting UAVs. Not only does MEC enhance the QoS but also enables communication amid acute situations, like disaster communications, resident monitoring and ad hoc network/communication arrangements. The MEC foundation can further incorporate IoT gadgets for making improvements in QoE to the clients via high-speed communication. MEC decreases the computational separation among the source and the servers by bracing near-user location assessments of information for assisted communications, utilizing caching. Caching allows data to be stored on specific servers so that the latency of transmission is low. But since the layout of the network is hierarchical, sometimes the near-end user can also be affected by overheads which are caused by the maintenance of a continuous connection.

### 12.4.1 Explanation of the Layers

- Mobile computing networks are imagined to consist of three layers as shown in Figure 12.1, that is, cloud, edge and the subscriber service layer. Though the cloud layer is developed and well positioned, a bit of pliancy and indecision is seen in planning the edge layer.
- Service subscriber layer uses the widely available computational assets, e.g., laptops, smart phones and vehicles, superimposed with devoted edge nodes [13].
- The information packets produced by IoT administrations are prepared by the central MEC layer as seen in Figure 12.1. MEC engineering also gives these packets of information some extra features before they reach the core network. The global caching in each drone is part of a specific cluster, which is checked by its top-tier drone, in this way, permitting the arrangement of a multilayer drone network. The drones are equipped with committed caching and the content servers are positioned remotely at the hubs [20].
- For every MEC server, it is necessary to keep storage to cache the data of the most current contents in its cell as well as make use of the fractional storage to make space for the less current ones. Its computation performance is even more upgraded by using other MEC server for cooperative caching. Moreover, by using stochastic geometry, that is, by considering users which are close by as clusters, the performance of big-scale MEC networks equipped with cache can be analyzed.
- In a MEC network which has been enabled with UAV, in accordance with the three-layer offloading strategy, for the transmission of subtask $k$, the $m$ data packets necessary can be divided into two portions, $m = m_1 + m_2$.
  - i. The information packets which are treated by the IoT devices locally are $m_1$.
  - ii. The information packets which are offloaded to the UAV-enabled MEC server for processing are $m_2$ [14].

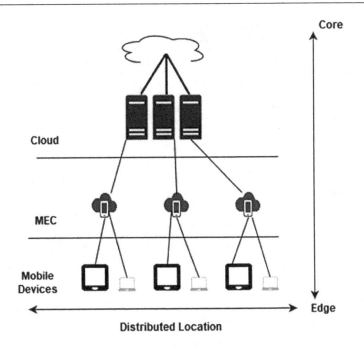

*Figure 12.1* Illustration of MEC and cloud.

## 12.5 SYSTEM MODEL

In Figure 12.2, we assume to use UAV-BS which will have direct communication with the ground MUs. Uplink and downlink communication will be carried out using Non-Orthogonal Multiple Access (NOMA) method. The successive interference cancellation (SIC) of NOMA is employed at the MUs and UAV-BS depending on their channel strength. In the uplink scenario, MUs communicate with the UAV-BS where MUs use the same frequency and time slot but various power levels. In the downlink scenario, UAV-BS communicates with the MUs where UAV-BS use the same frequency and time slot but various power levels.

### 12.5.1 Mathematical Model of NOMA

For uplink NOMA networks, each MU transmits a signal to UAV-BS. Considering that uplink and downlink channels are inverse and the UAV conveys power allocation coefficients to MUs, the received signal at the UAV-BS can be defined as [21]:

$$r_{UB} = \sum_{k=1}^{N} h_k \sqrt{a_k P_{MU} x_k} + N_p \tag{12.1}$$

where $h_k$ is the channel coefficient of the $k^{th}$ MU, $x_k$ is the information of $MU_k$ with unit energy, $P_{MU}$ is the highest transmission power assumed to be common for all MUs, $a_k$ is the power coefficient allocated for MU $k$ subjected to $\sum_{k=1}^{N} a_k = 1$ and $a_1 \geq a_2 \geq \cdots \geq a_N$ since the channel gains are presumed to be ordered as $|h_1|^2 \leq |h_2|^2 \leq \cdots |h_N|^2$ when there is no loss of generality and $N_p$ is the zero mean complex additive Gaussian noise (AWGN) with variance of $\sigma^2$, that is, $N_p \in CN(0, \sigma^2)$.

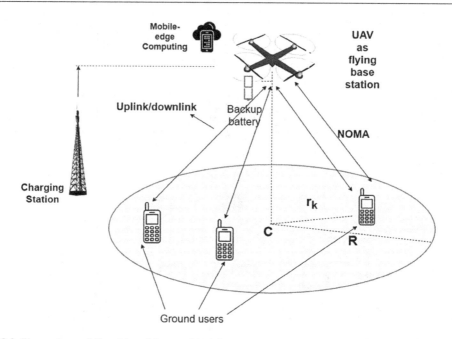

*Figure 12.2* Illustrations of Considered System Model.

From the above expression analysis, the signal-to-interference-plus-noise ratio (SINR) for the $n^{th}$ UAV can be written as:

$$SINR_n = \frac{a_n \gamma |h_n|^2}{\gamma \sum_{k=1}^{n-1} a_k |h_k|^2 + 1} \qquad (12.2)$$

where $\gamma = P_{MU}/\sigma^2$, $\gamma$ represents signal-to-noise ratio (SNR) and for the first MU, we can write

$$SINR_1 = a_1 \gamma |h_1|^2 \qquad (12.3)$$

The sum rate analysis of uplink NOMA network is written for the first UAV and the rest (2 to N) UAVs as a sum and expressed as:

$$R_{sum}^{NOMA-u} = \sum_{n=1}^{N} (1 + SINR_n)$$

$$= \log_2 \left(1 + a_1 \gamma |h_1|^2\right) + \sum_{n=2}^{N} \log_2 \left(1 + \frac{a_n \gamma |h_n|^2}{\gamma \sum_{k=1}^{n-1} a_k |h_k|^2 + 1}\right) \qquad (12.4)$$

$$= \log_2 \left(1 + \gamma \sum_{n=1}^{N} a_n |h_n|^2\right)$$

Now considering downlink NOMA network, the transmitted signal at the UAV-BS is written as:

$$s_{MU} = \sum_{k=1}^{M} \sqrt{a_k P_{UB}} x_k \tag{12.5}$$

where $P_{UB}$ is the transmission power coefficient at the UAV-BS. The received signal at the $m^{th}$ MU can be expressed as:

$$y_m = h_m s_{MU} + N_m = h_m \sum_{k=1}^{M} \sqrt{a_k P_{UB}} x_k + N_m \tag{12.6}$$

where $h_m$ is the channel coefficient of the $m^{th}$ MU and $N_m$ is the zero mean complex AWGN with variance of $\sigma^2$, that is, $N_m \in CN(0, \sigma^2)$.

After SINR analysis of the $m^{th}$ MU to find the $r^{th}$ MU, $r < m$ and $r \neq M$, the SINR can be written as:

$$SINR_{r \to m} = \frac{a_r \gamma |h_m|^2}{\gamma |h_m|^2 \sum_{k=r+1}^{M} a_k + 1} \tag{12.7}$$

where $\gamma = P_{UB}/\sigma^2$ denotes the SNR. If we want to find the required information of the $m^{th}$ MU, SIC will be carried out for the signal of MU $r < m$. So, the SINR of the $m^{th}$ MU is given by:

$$SINR_m = \frac{a_m \gamma |h_m|^2}{\gamma |h_m|^2 \sum_{k=m+1}^{M} a_k + 1} \tag{12.8}$$

The SINR of the $M^{th}$ MU is expressed as:

$$SINR_M = a_M \gamma |h_m|^2 \tag{12.9}$$

Now, we can express the downlink rate of NOMA for the $m^{th}$ MU as:

$$\begin{aligned} R_{sum}^{NOMA-d} &= \log_2 \left( 1 + SINR_m \right) \\ &= \log_2 \left( 1 + \frac{a_m \gamma |h_m|^2}{\gamma |h_m|^2 \sum_{k=m+1}^{M} a_k + 1} \right) \end{aligned} \tag{12.10}$$

Thus, the sum rate for downlink NOMA is written as:

$$\begin{aligned} R_{sum}^{NOMA-d} &= \sum_{m=1}^{N} \left( 1 + SINR_m \right) \\ &= \sum_{m=1}^{M-1} \log_2 \left( 1 + \frac{a_m \gamma |h_m|^2}{\gamma |h_m|^2 \sum_{k=m+1}^{M} a_k + 1} \right) + \log_2 \left( 1 + a_M \gamma |h_M|^2 \right) \\ &= \sum_{m=1}^{M-1} \log_2 \left( 1 + \frac{a_m}{\sum_{k=m+1}^{M} a_k + 1/\gamma |h_m|^2} \right) + \log_2 \left( 1 + a_M \gamma |h_M|^2 \right) \end{aligned} \tag{12.11}$$

### 12.5.2 Path Loss Model

As seen from Figure 12.3, the MU can either have a Line-of-Sight (LOS or a strong Non-Line-of-Sight (NLOS) connection with the UAV-BS based on our preferred Air to Ground (A2G) channel [22,23]. A probabilistic model is obtained which depends on environmental things such as the altitude of buildings, how many buildings there are per unit area and the relative distance between the MU and the UAV-BS. All these factors together determine the elevation angle. In this case we have ignored the effect of small-scale fading because the chance of having frail multi-paths is a lot lower than that of having LOS or strong NLOS connection [24].

For LOS link between the MU and UAV-BS, the probability function is defined by [23]:

$$Pb_i(LOS) = \frac{1}{1 + \lambda \exp(-\mu[\phi_i - \lambda])} \tag{12.12}$$

where the constant values relating to the environmental outline like rural, sub-urban, dense urban etc. are defined by $\lambda$ and $\mu$, respectively. $\varphi_i$ is the elevation angle. For a MU experiencing strong NLOS link with the UAV-BS, the probability function is defined as:

$$Pb_i(NLOS) = 1 - Pb_i(LOS) \tag{12.13}$$

From the Figure 12.3, there are two unique scattering environments with the ground MU and UAV-BS which are low scattering and reflection near the UAV and high scattering because of man-made obstructions near the ground MU. The overall path loss is a sum of the free space path loss and the excessive losses. This is greater for NLOS connections than LOS connections due to excessive loss created by the reflection of transmitted signals and shadowing by objects which are in the coverage area.

The path loss $K_i$ for our A2G channel between the UAV-BS and the $i^{th}$ MU is expressed as [25]:

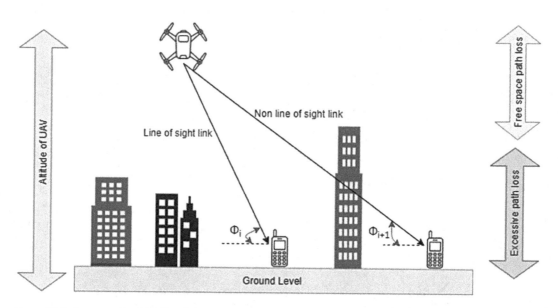

*Figure 12.3* An example of UAV path loss model [22].

$$K_i = \begin{cases} 10\tau \log(Y_i) + y_{LOS}, & LOS\,link \\ 10\tau \log(Y_i) + y_{NLOS}, & NLOS\,link \end{cases} \tag{12.14}$$

where the path loss exponent is defined by $\tau$ and $y_{LOS}$ and $y_{NLOS}$ are the excessive losses for both LOS and NLOS connections affected by shadowing, respectively. Here, both the parts follow normal distribution whose mean and variance are determined by the elevation angle and the environmental dependent constant values. Under normal circumstances, it is not possible to know the type of connection (LOS/NLOS) the MU has with the UAV-BS without having the location of the MU and UAV using a landscape map. $\bar{K}_i(N_b, G)$ is the mean path loss taking into consideration both the probabilities of LOS and NLOS links. This is calculated by:

$$\bar{K}_i(N_b, G) = Pb_i(LOS)K_i(LOS) + Pb_i(NLOS)K_i(NLOS) \tag{12.15}$$

## 12.5.3 Transmission Delay

From (12.4) and (12.11), we can rewrite the uplink and downlink rate equation as:

$$u_{mq,t}(s_{mq,t}) = s_{mq,t} \log_2\left(1 + \gamma \sum_{m=1}^{M} a_m |h_m|^2\right) \tag{12.16}$$

$$d_{mq,t}(s_{mq,t}) = s_{mq,t} \sum_{m=1}^{M-1} \log_2\left(1 + \frac{a_m}{\sum_{k=m+1}^{M} a_k + 1/\gamma |h_m|^2}\right) + \log_2\left(1 + a_M\gamma |h_M|^2\right) \tag{12.17}$$

where $s_{mq,t}$ is the index of the MU. When $s_{mq,t} = 1$, it means that MU $m$ is connected to the UAV-BS $q$ at time $t$, otherwise $s_{mq,t} = 0$. From here we can write the uplink and downlink transmission delay as [26]:

$$\begin{aligned} D_{mq,t}^U &= \frac{\beta_{mq,t} w_{m,t}}{u_{mq,t}(s_{mq,t})} \\ &= \frac{\beta_{mq,t} w_{m,t}}{\log_2\left(1 + \gamma \sum_{m=1}^{M} a_m |h_m|^2\right)} \end{aligned} \tag{12.18}$$

$$\begin{aligned} D_{mq,t}^D &= \frac{\beta_{mq,t} w_{m,t}}{d_{mq,t}(s_{mq,t})} \\ &= \frac{\beta_{mq,t} w_{m,t}}{\sum_{m=1}^{M-1} \log_2\left(1 + \frac{a_m}{\sum_{k=m+1}^{M} a_k + 1/\gamma |h_m|^2}\right) + \log_2\left(1 + a_M\gamma |h_M|\right)} \end{aligned} \tag{12.19}$$

where $\beta_{mq,t} w_{m,t}$ is the part of the task that MU $m$ sends to UAV $q$ for computing at each time instant $t$ where the division parameter is $\beta_{mq,t} \in [0,1]$.

## 12.5.4 Computing Model

Computing model can be separated into two parts: edge computing and local computing. The UAV-BS can cooperatively carry out the task of MU $m$ and this is known as edge computing. Local computing is when the task is processed by the MU itself.

### 12.5.4.1 Edge Computing Model

For a data size of $\beta_{mq,t} w_{m,t}$, which is offloaded by MU $m$ to UAV-BS $q$, the time required by UAV-BS $q$ to compute the task is

$$D_{mq,t}^E \left( \beta_{mq,t} \right) = \frac{\omega \beta_{mq,t} w_{m,t}}{f} \tag{12.20}$$

where the frequency of the central processing unit (CPU) clock of every UAV-BS is $f$ which is assumed to be equal for all UAV-BSs. The number of cycles (per bit) required for processing is $\omega$.

### 12.5.4.2 Local Computing Model

For a data size of $(1 - \beta_{mq,t}) w_{m,t}$, the time taken by MU $m$ to process the task locally is

$$D_{mq,t}^L \left( \beta_{mq,t} \right) = \frac{\omega_m \left( 1 - \beta_{mq,t} \right) w_{m,t}}{f_m} \tag{12.21}$$

where $f_m$ is the frequency of the CPU clock of MU $m$ and the number of cycles (per bit) required for computing the data is $\omega_m$.

## 12.5.5 Time Consumption Model

For our proposed model, the total time needed for a task to be completed is the maximum time between the local computing time and edge computing time since the tasks can be processed by both the MU and the UAV-BS simultaneously. In order to cooperatively carry out the task of MU $m$ by both the MU and the UAV-BS $q$, the total time required can be written as:

$$D_{mq,t} \left( \beta_{mq,t}, s_{mq,t} \right) = \max \left\{ D_{mq,t}^U \left( \beta_{mq,t}, s_{mq,t} \right) + D_{mq,t}^E \left( \beta_{mq,t} \right) + D_{mq,t}^D \left( \beta_{mq,t}, s_{mq,t} \right), D_{mq,t}^L \left( \beta_{mq,t} \right) \right\} \tag{12.22}$$

where $D_{mq,t}^L \left( \beta_{mq,t} \right)$ is the local computing time and $D_{mq,t}^E \left( \beta_{mq,t} \right)$ is the edge computing time.

There will be a wireless access delay as each MU will have to wait for service. For MU $m$ linked with UAV-BS $q$, the access delay is

$$D_{mq,t}^A \left( v_{mq,t} \right) = \sum_{m' \in V_m} D_{m'q,t}^D \left( s_{m'q,t}, \beta_{m'q,t} \right) \tag{12.23}$$

where $|s_{q,t}|$ represents the modulus of $s_{q,t}$ which is the number of MUs that are linked with UAV-BS $q$, $v_{mq,t}$ is the service sequence variable which follows $1 \leq v_{mq,t} \leq |s_{q,t}|$ and $V_m = \{m' | v_{m'q,t} < v_{m,t}\}$ is the group of MUs that are served by UAV $q$ before MU $m$. The total delay for computing a task, which consists of the access delay and the processing delay, is written as:

$$T_{m,t}\left(\beta_{mq,t}, s_{mq,t}, v_{mq,t}\right) = D_{mq,t}^{A}\left(v_{mq,t}\right) + D_{mq,t}\left(\beta_{mq,t}, s_{mq,t}\right) \tag{12.24}$$

## 12.5.6 Energy Consumption Model

Device operating energy consumption, data transmission energy consumption and data computing energy consumption are the three things that make up the total energy consumption of MU. The energy required by the device to operate any application is the device operating energy consumption. For MU $m$, this is written as:

$$E_{m,t}\left(\beta_{mq,t}, s_{mq,t}\right) = C + \varsigma_{m}\left(f_{m}\right)^{2}\left(1 - \beta_{mq,t}\right)w_{m,t} + P_{MU}D_{mq,t}^{U}\left(\beta_{mq,t}, s_{mq,t}\right) \tag{12.25}$$

where $C$ is the energy consumption of device operation, and energy coefficient depending on MU $m$'s device chip is $\varsigma_{m}$. For MU $m$ computing a task of size $(1 - \beta_{mq,t})w_{m,t}$, at its local place, the energy consumption is $\varsigma_{m}(f_{m})^{2}(1 - \beta_{mq,t})w_{m,t}$ and for it to be transmitted to UAV-BS $q$, the energy consumption is $P_{MU}D_{mq,t}^{U}(\beta_{mq,t}, s_{mq,t})$.

In the same way, we can express the energy consumption of each UAV-BS which is

$$E_{q,t}\left(\beta_{mq,t}, s_{mq,t}\right) = C_{q} + \varsigma\left(f\right)^{2}\beta_{mq,t}w_{m,t} + P_{UB}D_{mq,t}^{D}\left(\beta_{mq,t}, s_{mq,t}\right) \tag{12.26}$$

where $C_{q}$ is the energy required for the UAV to hover and the energy consumption coefficient depending on the chip of the UAV-BS is $\varsigma$. For UAV-BS $q$, to compute a task of size $\beta_{mq,t}$ $w_{m,t}$, which has been offloaded by MU $m$, the energy consumption is $\varsigma(f)^{2}\beta_{mq,t}w_{m,t}$. $P_{UB}D_{mq,t}^{D}(\beta_{mq,t}, s_{mq,t})$ is the energy required to transmit the computed task from UAV-BS $q$ to MU $m$.

## 12.6 SIMULATION RESULTS

In this section, we investigate the performance of the proposed system model numerically via simulations. We assume four MUs and they are apart from each other's 100 m, 80 m, 150 m and 50 m. Power coefficients are 0.2, 0.3, 0.3 and 0.2, respectively. The height of UAV-BS is 300m from the ground MUs. The following simulation parameters are considered: $\tau = 2$, $y_{LOS}$ = 1.6 dB, $y_{NLOS}$ = 23 dB, $\lambda$ = 12.087 and $\mu$ = 0.1139.

Figure 12.4 shows the relationship between the data rate and SNR. Here we see that as SNR increases the data rate increases exponentially for both uplink and downlink transmission. Below 30 dB SNR approximately, the data rate is almost zero but beyond that the data rate increases drastically. Also, at a closer look we see that the data rate is slightly higher for downlink transmission than uplink transmission.

The transmission delay versus SNR graph from Figure 12.5 shows a negative relation between the two factors, that is, with increase in SNR the transmission delay decreases linearly for both uplink and downlink transmission even though the decrease is a bit more for downlink transmission.

Figure 12.6 depicts the relationship between the overall delay and the SNR. This too shows a negative linear relationship; with the increase in SNR, the total delay as well as the

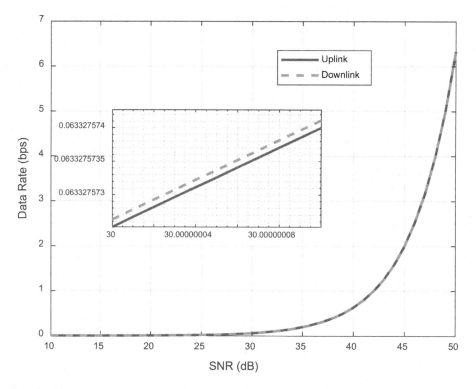

*Figure 12.4* Data Rate (bps) versus SNR (dB).

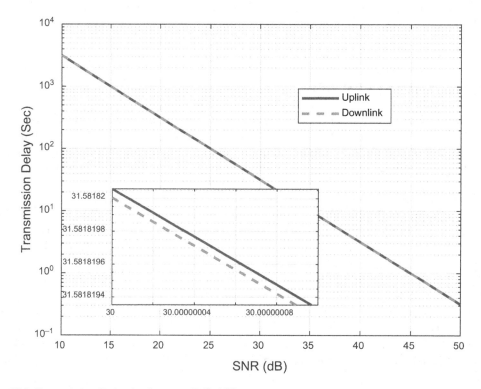

*Figure 12.5* Transmission Delay (sec) versus SNR (dB).

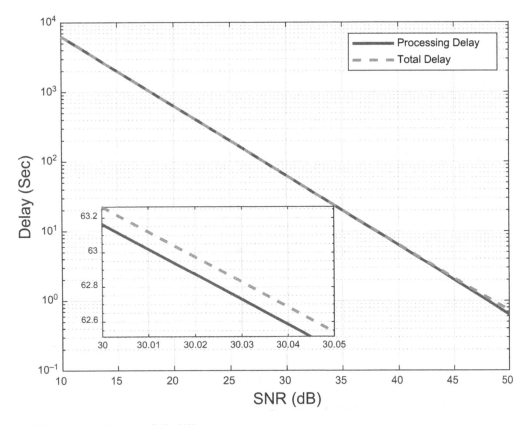

*Figure 12.6* Delay (sec) versus SNR (dB).

processing delay decreases. The total delay is always seen to be greater than the processing delay. At 30 dB SNR, the total delay is 0.16% more than the processing delay.

From Figure 12.7, the effect on energy consumption due to change in SNR is seen. With increase in SNR, the energy consumption for both the MU and the UAV-BS decreases linearly until it levels off at high SNR (approximately 46dB). We also see that the UAV-BS consumes more energy than MU at all SNRs. When compared at 30dB SNR, it is seen that the UAV-BS consumes 90% more energy than the MU.

Lastly, Figure 12.8 shows the effect on energy consumption due to increase in the part of task completed $(\beta_{mq,t})$. Here it can be seen that initially the energy consumption increases very fast then slows down but continues to increase till the entire task is completed and almost levels off. This is true for both MU and UAV-BS, though the energy consumed by the UAV-BS is greater than the MU at all times. At 40% task completion, the energy consumption of the UAV-BS is 90% greater than that of the MU.

## 12.7 CONCLUSION

Using UAV-BS in wireless network communication to improve its effectiveness is slowly becoming inevitable. Along with the use of UAVs, the use of MEC has been implemented in 5G mobile networks to boost reliability and low latency during communication. Data transfer to and from MUs can be done with great efficiency and accuracy with the implementation of MEC in our network architecture. As discussed in the chapter, there are both some benefits

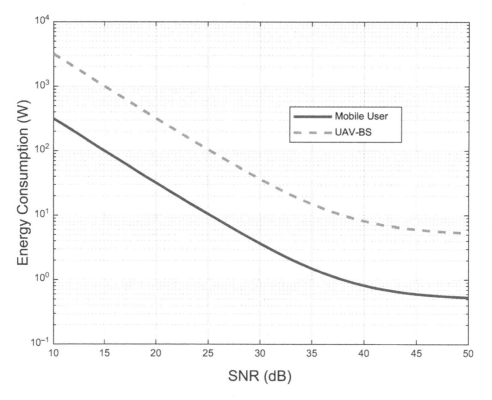

*Figure 12.7* Energy Consumption (W) versus SNR (dB).

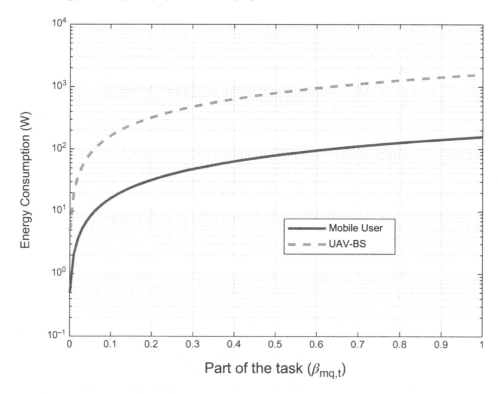

*Figure 12.8* Energy Consumption (W) versus Part of the Task ($\beta_{mq,t}$).

as well as drawbacks of using such a system; however, from numerical results; the benefits outweigh the drawbacks. Our simulation results show that the total delay is 0.16% more than the processing delay at an SNR of 30 dB and the UAV-BS consumes 90% more energy than the MU at 30 dB SNR as well as at 40% task completion. Furthermore, for both uplink and downlink communication, data rate and transmission delay are seen to increase and decrease, respectively, at high SNR when NOMA method is used. This chapter has provided a thorough study on the use of MEC in UAV-BSs and has presented its advantages, disadvantages as well as come up with a proposed system model along with simulation results which can serve as a guideline for further exhaustive research on this topic. In the future we plan to work on energy harvesting [27] and transmit antenna selection [28,29], that is, find a renewable source of energy to power the UAV-BSs. Further, we want to come up with a better model to decrease energy consumption in the UAVs [30], decrease latency and overcome the issues discussed in the chapter involving the use of MEC in UAV-BSs.

## REFERENCES

1. Z. Yang, C. Pan, K. Wang, and M. Shikh-Bahaei, "Energy Efficient Resource Allocation in UAV-Enabled Mobile Edge Computing Networks," *IEEE Transactions on Wireless Communications*, vol. 18, no. 9, pp. 4576–4589, Sept. 2019, doi: 10.1109/TWC.2019.2927313.
2. O. Bekkouche, T. Taleb, and M. Bagaa, *"UAVs Traffic Control Based on Multi-Access Edge Computing,"* 2018 IEEE Global Communications Conference (GLOBECOM), Abu Dhabi, United Arab Emirates, 2018, pp. 1–6.
3. V. Sharma, I. You, D. N. K. Jayakody. D. G. Reina, and K. R. Choo, "Neural-Blockchain-Based Ultrareliable Caching for Edge-Enabled UAV Networks," *IEEE Transactions on Industrial Informatics*, vol. 15, no. 10, pp. 5723–5736, Oct. 2019, doi: 10.1109/TII.2019.2922039.
4. F. Zhou, Y. Wu, H. Sun, and Z. Chu, *"UAV-Enabled Mobile Edge Computing: Offloading Optimization and Trajectory Design,"* 2018 IEEE International Conference on Communications (ICC), Kansas City, MO, 2018, pp. 1–6, doi: 10.1109/ICC.2018.8422277.
5. M. Mozaffari, W. Saad, M. Bennis, Y. Nam, and M. Debbah, "A Tutorial on UAVs for Wireless Networks: Applications, Challenges, and Open Problems," *IEEE Communications Surveys & Tutorials*, vol. 21, no. 3, pp. 2334–2360, thirdquarter 2019, doi: 10.1109/COMST.2019.2902862.
6. L. Gupta, R. Jain, and H. Chan, 2016. "Mobile Edge Computing – An Important Ingredient Of 5G Networks - IEEE Software Defined Networks,". [online] Available at: https://sdn.ieee.org/newsletter/march-2016/mobile-edge-computing-an-important-ingredient-of-5g-networks [Accessed March 27 2020].
7. J. Mundy2019. "What Is Mobile Edge Computing?," [online] 5g.co.uk. Available at: https://5g.co.uk/guides/what-is-mobile-edge-computing/ Accessed March 26 2020.
8. E. Ahmed, and M. H. Rehmani "Mobile Edge Computing: Opportunities Solutions and Challenges," *Future Generation Computer Systems*, vol. 70, pp. 59–63, May 2017.
9. Z. Yang, C. Pan, K. Wang, and M. Shikh-Bahaei, "Energy Efficient Resource Allocation in UAV-Enabled Mobile Edge Computing Networks," *IEEE Transactions on Wireless Communications*, vol. 18, no. 9, pp. 4576–4589, Sept. 2019, doi: 10.1109/TWC.2019.2927313.
10. O. Kalinagac. S. S. Kafiloglu, F. Alagoz, and G. Gur, "Caching and D2D Sharing for Content Delivery in Software-Defined UAV Networks," *2019 IEEE 90th Vehicular Technology Conference (VTC2019-Fall)*, Honolulu, HI, USA, 2019, pp. 1–5, doi: 10.1109/VTCFall.2019.8891497.
11. N. Zhao et al., "Caching UAV Assisted Secure Transmission in Hyper-Dense Networks Based on Interference Alignment," *IEEE Transactions on Communications*, vol. 66, no. 5, pp. 2281–2294, May 2018, doi: 10.1109/TCOMM.2018.2792014.
12. N. Abbas, Y. Zhang, A. Taherkordi, and T. Skeie, "Mobile Edge Computing: A Survey," *IEEE Internet of Things Journal*, vol. 5, no. 1, pp. 450–451, Feb. 2018.
13. Y. Mao, C. You, J. Zhang, K. Huang, and K. B. Letaief, "Mobile Edge Computing: Survey and Research Outlook," *arXiv:1701.01090v3 [cs.IT]*, Apr. 2017. Accessed 26 March 2020 [Online]. Available at: https://arxiv.org/abs/1701.01090v3.

14. G. Wu, Y. Miao, Y. Zang, and A. Barnawi, "Energy Efficient for UAV-Enabled Mobile Edge Computing Networks: Intelligent Task Prediction and Offloading," *Computer Communications*, vol. 150, pp. 556–562, 2019.

15. H. Sedjelmaci, S. M. Senouci, and N. Ansari, "A Hierarchical Detection and Response System to Enhance Security Against Lethal Cyber-Attacks in UAV Networks," *IEEE Transactions on Systems, Man and Cybernetics: Systems*, vol. 48, no. 9, pp. 1594–1606, 2018.

16. K. Yoon, D. Park, Y. Yim, K. Kim, S. K. Yang, and M. Robinson, "Security Authentication System Using Encrypted Channel Using UAV Network," *Proceedings of the first IEEE International Conference on Robotic Computing (IRC)*. IEEE, 2017, pp. 393–398.

17. T. Bai, J. Wang, Y. Ren, and L. Hanzo, "Energy-Efficient Computation Offloading for Secure UAV-Edge-Computing Systems," *IEEE Transactions on Vehicular Technology*, vol. 68, no. 6, pp. 6074–6087.

18. H. Sedjelmaci, A. Boudguiga, I. B. Jemaa, and S. M. Senouci, "An Efficient Cyber Defense Framework for UAV-Edge Computing," *Ad Hoc Networks*, vol. 94, 101970, 2019.

19. W. Jiang, G. Feng, S. Qin, and Y. Liu, "Multi-Agent Reinforcement Learning Based Cooperative Content Caching for Mobile Edge Networks," *IEEE Access*, vol. 7, pp. 61856–61867, 2019.

20. N. Abbas, Y. Zhang, A. Taherkordi, and T. Skeie, "Mobile Edge Computing: A Survey," *IEEE Internet of Things Journal*, vol. 5, no. 1, pp. 4, Feb. 2018.

21. M. Aldababsa, M. Toka, S. Gökçeli, G. K. Kurt, and O. Kucur, "A Tutorial on Nonorthogonal Multiple Access for 5G and Beyond," *Wireless Communications and Mobile Computing*, vol. 2018, 2018. doi: 10.1155/2018/9713450.

22. M. F. Sohail, C. Y. Leow, and S. Won, "Non-Orthogonal Multiple Access for Unmanned Aerial Vehicle Assisted Communication," *IEEE Access*, vol. 6, pp. 22716–22727, 2018.

23. A. Al-Hourani, S. Kandeepan, and A. Jamalipour, "Modeling Air-To-Ground Path Loss for Low Altitude Platforms in Urban Environments," *Proceedings of IEEE Global Communications Conference (GLOBECOM)*, Dec. 2014, pp. 2898–2904.

24. Q. Feng, L. McGeehan, E. K. Tameh, and A.R. Nix, "Path Loss Models for Air-To-Ground Radio Channels in Urban Environments," *Proceedings of IEEE 63rd Vehicular Technology Conference*, vol. 6, May 2006, pp. 2901–2905.

25. M. Mozaffari, W. Saad, M. Bennis, and M. Debbah, "Unmanned Aerial Vehicle with Underlaid Device-to-Device Communications: Performance and Tradeoffs," *IEEE Wireless Communications Letters*, vol. 3, no. 6, pp. 569–572, Dec. 2014.

26. S. Wang, M. Chen, C. Yin, W. Saad, C. S. Hong, S. Cui, and H. V. Poor, "Federated Learning for Task and Resource Allocation in Wireless High Altitude Balloon Networks," *arXiv:2003.09375v1 [eess.SP]*, 19 Mar. 2020. [Online]. Available at: https://arxiv.org/abs/2003.09375 Accessed March 29 2020.

27. S. R. Sabuj and M. Hamamura, "Two-Slope Path-Loss Design of Energy Harvesting in Random Cognitive Radio Networks," *Computer Networks*, vol. 142, pp. 128–141, 2018.

28. S. R. Sabuj and M. Hamamura, "Energy Efficiency Analysis of Cognitive Radio Network Using Stochastic Geometry," *Proceedings of IEEE CSCN*, pp. 245–251, Oct. 2015.

29. M. Khan, M. T. Rahman, and S. R. Sabuj, "Transmit Antenna Selection Technique in Random Cognitive Radio Network," *Proceedings of IEEE Region 10 Conference (TENCON)*, Jeju, Korea, Oct. 2018.

30. A. R. Rahul, S. R. Sabuj, M. S. Akbar, H. Jo, and M. A. Hossain, "An Optimization Based Approach to Enhance the Throughput and Energy Efficiency for Cognitive Unmanned Aerial Vehicle Networks," *Wireless Networks*, 2020. [Online]. Available: https://doi.org/10.1007/s11276-020-02450-9 Accessed on: September 2020.

# Chapter 13

# Vehicular Edge Computing Security

*Mehmet Ali Eken and Pelin Angin*

Middle East Technical University, Turkey

## CONTENTS

## 13.1 INTRODUCTION

The past decade has witnessed immense developments in smart vehicle technologies supported by the advances in vehicular networks and artificial intelligence (AI). Vehicular networks will have a significant role in future Intelligent Transportation Systems (ITS), especially with the rise of advanced wireless networking technologies, including 5G and beyond [1].

These networks promise to provide support for a wide range of mobility-based services, from content-sharing to data aggregation/mining and object recognition.

According to Intel's estimates [2], a smart vehicle should be able to analyze 1 GB of sensor data in a second. Technologies such as autonomous driving and augmented reality require advanced data processing capabilities and high storage capacities. When low latency and reliable communication requirements are considered, conventional cloud computing-based techniques have limited capabilities. The heavy traffic load causes inefficiencies when we take into account the energy consumption and bandwidth usage of conventional cloud computing.

Vehicular Edge Computing (VEC) is a concept that has been introduced to tackle the abovementioned issues in future smart vehicular technologies. In VEC, edge servers (edge nodes) have capabilities of computation and storage deployed in proximity to the vehicles in vehicular networks. Thus, edge computing-enabled vehicular networks are more delay-tolerant and ensure better Quality of Service (QoS) parameters for the vehicles.

The heterogeneous and dynamic topology of vehicular networks makes it challenging to ensure high security among edge nodes. The coexistence of many different types of devices (i.e., high heterogeneity) makes traditional trust and authentication schemes inefficient. Public deployment of edge servers without physical isolation from the environment makes them potentially attractive targets for attackers. Also, as explained in [3], offloading computation tasks from vehicles to edge computing devices may introduce privacy leakage risks, which can lead to tracking, identity tampering, and virtual vehicle hijacking.

This chapter focuses on applications of the edge computing paradigm for vehicular networks and analyzes security threats and state-of-the-art security solutions for VEC. It seeks to answer the question: 'What are the security vulnerabilities of existing VEC systems and how can we provide the best protection without compromising performance and safety in VEC?'. We describe the architecture and the necessity of utilizing edge computing in smart vehicular systems. The potential security issues in edge computing-enabled vehicular networks, including privacy violations for connected vehicles, adversarial actions on edge servers/roadside units (RSUs) and the challenges to adapt security measures are analyzed. The most effective and state-of-the-art solutions are explained in detail.

### 13.1.1 Chapter Roadmap

The rest of the chapter is structured as follows. Section 13.2 reviews VEC concepts, architecture and enabling technologies for future vehicular networks. Section 13.3 covers potential security issues and mitigation challenges in VEC. Section 13.4 presents state-of-the-art solutions for ensuring security of VEC in detail, which are categorized as Identity Preservation, Authentication and Trust Management, Secure Data Management, Secure Distributed Computation, RSU and Vehicle Anomaly Detection, Attack Detection and Mitigation Systems. In Section 13.5, the overall summary of the chapter is provided with a discussion of the limitations of existing VEC security approaches. Section 13.6 concludes the chapter with future work directions and recommendations for achieving high security in future VEC.

## 13.2 VEHICULAR EDGE COMPUTING OVERVIEW

In the previous generation of smart vehicle technologies, cloud computing was used as the promising platform for high storage and computation requirements of a variety of vehicular applications, by performing offloaded computation tasks the vehicles themselves are not capable of achieving in real time. As the number of connected devices (vehicles) has been increasing rapidly, these systems will not be able to satisfy the QoS requirements of the future real-time ITS applications in highly congested and mobile scenarios [4]. The distance of cloud servers from vehicles introduces latencies unfit for the real-time nature of vehicular applications, which will become even more pronounced with the widespread availability of autonomous vehicles relying on a variety of real-time computation tasks for safe navigation. Edge computing, which involves the utilization of computing resources at the edge of the network instead of the remote clouds, has recently gained significant attention from both academia and industry as the promising technology to satisfy these increasing requirements. Edge computing plays the role of an intermediary between the cloud and vehicles, supporting services ranging from infotainment to traffic efficiency and road safety. The next-generation smart vehicles will also be supported significantly by new networking technologies to increase the flexibility, control and efficiency of these heterogeneous networks [4], including Software-Defined Networking (SDN), Network Function Virtualization (NFV) and 5G radio access [5].

In the following subsections, the architecture, enabling technologies, applications and the challenges of VEC are explained in detail.

## 13.2.1 VEC Architecture and Provided Services

At a high level, VEC has a three-layered architecture consisting of the cloud layer, edge cloud layer and the vehicle layer [6–8] as shown in Figure 13.1.

- **Cloud Layer:** Due to its extensive storage and high computation capabilities, the cloud can process massive amounts of data and perform complex computations very fast. This layer is used for centralized data aggregation and storage, optimization and complex computations on data. The collected data, which do not need real-time computation, could be sent to the cloud layer through edge nodes for computation or permanent storage. The cloud layer has a global view of the whole system, so it handles global level management and control over the network to optimize the whole system.
- **Edge Cloud Layer:** The purpose of this layer is to extend cloud computing capabilities to the edge of the network. Also, the connection between the cloud layer and the vehicle layer is provided by the edge cloud layer. The edge nodes are commonly deployed at RSUs, which are in proximity to the vehicles. They are equipped with massive storage and decent computation capabilities compared to a smart vehicle. This way, low latency, location awareness, emergency management, caching, content discovery, decent computation and improved QoS are ensured.
- **Vehicle Layer:** This layer consists of a group of smart vehicles, which share on-board services and storage, and communicate with other vehicles. The vehicles continuously collect data from their surroundings via sensors, including RADAR, LIDAR, GPS, etc. However, they lack sufficient computation and storage capabilities. Thus, the collected data need to be processed with the cooperation of either other vehicles or RSUs.

The edge cloud layer provides a variety of services to the vehicles [4], including but not limited to the following:

- *Infotainment services* provide information about events like emergencies (flood, landslide or avalanche on the road) and digital entertainment products like videos, games or music. The intention is to improve the safety and quality of user experience.
- *Network services* enable vehicles to connect with other vehicles for valuable information sharing over RSUs.

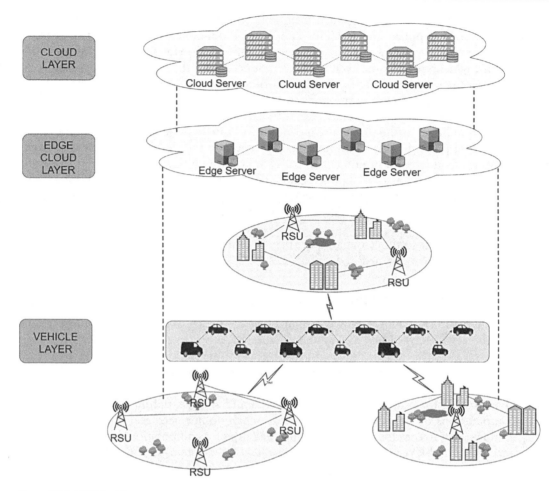

*Figure 13.1* VEC Architecture.

- *Computation services* provide resource cooperation between vehicles, which can provide access to unused resources to accomplish intensive computation tasks.
- *Storage services* provide extra storage for the vehicles when their running applications need substantial storage capacities. Edge servers are capable of supplying the extra needed storage in such cases.

Figure 13.2 provides a list of smart vehicular applications supported by VEC.

## 13.2.2 Enabling Technologies: 5G, SDN, NFV, AI, Blockchain

To achieve high performance and provide enhanced safety and security in VEC, collaborative utilization of advanced technologies including AI, SDN, NFV and blockchain besides edge computing has gained attention in the literature.

Blockchain technology has shown a significant potential for facilitating secure authentication and data management in VEC. Recent studies reveal that the blockchain technology has gained growing attention for application to vehicular network communications because of its provisioning of anonymity, trust and its decentralized structure [9]. Blockchain is a fitting solution for ensuring secure data sharing by enabling better infrastructure and resource usage.

*Figure 13.2* Applications of Vehicular Edge Computing.

AI is one of the enabling technologies for enhancing the cognition and intelligence of the network and ensuring optimal resource allocation [10, 11] in addition to forming the basis of a variety of services such as object recognition, traffic intelligence, etc. The dynamic communication topology of vehicular networks leads to challenges in efficient and reliable data transmission in the VEC environment. Also, wireless channel conditions, content popularity and other key factors are time-varying, and they are tough to be analyzed [10]. AI is a promising technology to tackle those challenges and to optimize system performance. For instance, approaches utilizing deep learning algorithms to optimize resource allocation and increase cost-efficiency have been demonstrated to be promising solutions in the context of VEC [12].

SDN and NFV are two key technologies that have arisen in the past decade to especially support networks of dynamic nature, such as vehicular networks, by enabling flexible network optimization and management [13]. In SDN, the data plane and logical plane are separated from each other so that a more flexible and efficient network management can be achieved. The data plane consists of all the data forwarding devices in the network (switches, routers, gateways), and the control plane manages the decision tasks related to data forwarding and allocation of network resources to achieve high performance. NFV is the virtualization of the functions of network nodes into functional segment blocks [14]. Its purpose is to virtualize the abilities and applications of the networking hardware (routing, security, policy, caching, etc.). NFV enables abstraction of the hardware capabilities, which leads to a more convenient way of controlling the network functionalities.

The recent developments in cellular networks, including 5G and beyond, are also promising to support future intelligent transportation systems, including providing the necessary infrastructure for achieving high-performance, agile VEC [15]. 5G is augmented with technologies like millimeter-wave multiple-input multiple-output (MIMO) radio communications, SDN,

NFV and other state-of-the-art technologies, thus increased spectrum efficiency, energy efficiency and better throughputs can be achieved.

In Section 13.4, a detailed review of security solutions based on these technologies is provided.

### 13.2.3 Overview of Challenges

As illustrated in the previous sections of the chapter, the close proximity infrastructure and decentralized architecture of edge computing provides benefits for vehicular networks, including low latency, improved throughput and reduced energy consumption. However, VEC frameworks still face many challenges, such as efficient task offloading, flexible management, high-performance caching, data management, and security and privacy [4, 16]. Below we provide an overview of these challenges.

#### 13.2.3.1 Task Offloading

Vehicles lack powerful computation resources, hence need to offload their computational tasks to cloud-like infrastructures. Conventional cloud services are inefficient for delay-sensitive applications because they are deployed at long distances from vehicles. Therefore, an efficient task offloading may be achieved in two ways in a VEC environment: using server-based task offloading and cooperative task offloading [16]. Edge servers (e.g., RSUs) are the primary options of the vehicles for server-based task offloading. They can decrease cost and response time of computational tasks by task offloading services, without the help of cloud systems in most of the cases. However, edge servers have limited resources compared to conventional cloud servers [4]. Due to the deployment cost and high load of the resources in edge servers, for offloading the computational tasks, the unused resources of other vehicles can be utilized. Through the aggregation of idle and rich resources of parked vehicles, cooperative task offloading can be accomplished. Also, some of the vehicles on the road may have unused resources, and utilization of these resources are valuable to achieve cooperative task offloading. Since vehicles are extremely mobile devices and RSUs have small coverage areas, the offloaded task could be finished after the vehicle leaves the coverage of the corresponding RSU. Therefore, mobility-aware task migration is a major requirement to accomplish task offloading. The result or the rest of the task should be directed to the new RSU in the coverage area of the vehicle. Because of the high density of smart vehicles in the system, task offloading can be an issue for VEC. There are many studies in the literature addressing the computation offloading issue, including game-theoretic server-based techniques [17], idle vehicle resource aggregation [18] and AI-based techniques [19].

#### 13.2.3.2 Network Management

VEC faces significant challenges in effectively managing the limited resources in the network [16]. Due to the high demand for resources from vehicles, the edge servers can quickly become overloaded. Therefore, advanced network monitoring and management techniques are needed. SDN is a sophisticated and crucial technology to manage the future's highly loaded heterogeneous networks like vehicular networks [4]. With the help of SDN, flexible and dynamic network management can be achieved. SDN increases network efficiency and reduces the management cost by separating data and control planes. Also, SDN-based approaches can be used to guide efficient handover strategies. On the other hand, sophisticated AI-based techniques can be used for enhancing network management and optimization.

### 13.2.3.3 Caching

Due to the increasing number of data-consuming applications in vehicular networks, the load on wireless networks has been growing. This increasing demand results in significant latency and bandwidth problems. Edge caching schemes are needed to tackle these issues such that frequently used content can be cached, and the traffic load can be eliminated [16]. There are three critical issues in designing such schemes: caching location (RSUs, vehicles), caching contents and caching policies. RSUs (edge servers) are considered as the primary caching option to decrease the latency of the frequently used popular content in the system due to their proximity to the vehicles. Relative to conventional cloud systems, the low capacity and limited range of RSUs makes determining an optimum strategy more challenging. For achieving an optimal strategy to cache the data in RSUs, AI-based schemes could provide promising solutions [16]. As in the task offloading problem, caching through using the idle resources of other vehicles could help solve caching optimization and efficiency problems. However, smart vehicles also suffer from low storage capacities and extreme mobility of vehicles.

### 13.2.3.4 Data Management

Vehicles are equipped with complex sensors such as LIDAR, RADAR, GPS, camera and several other sensors, which generate large sizes of data, and vehicles may share those data with the network or other vehicles for extra processing and storage. Also, vehicles may need real-time information from other vehicles for safe and effective driving. Exponential growth in the volume of data gathered and processed by smart vehicular systems leads to significant response time and bandwidth challenges. Thus, reliable data management, aggregation, analysis, processing and dissemination techniques are needed. Efficient edge computing-based data collection and processing schemes can help satisfy these requirements [20]. Also, context-based data dissemination strategies are needed, especially for safety messages to be forwarded quickly [16]. On the other hand, as vehicles are not obligated to share data with other vehicles, they may behave selfishly. This makes it important to create data sharing schemes that provide incentives for the participating vehicles [21].

### 13.2.3.5 Security and Privacy

Due to the high mobility of vehicles and the flexible and heterogeneous nature of VEC, there are many security and privacy challenges surrounding the real-world, widespread deployment of VEC systems. Among these challenges are identity preservation, data storage and sharing, as well as secure task offloading. The details of these issues are investigated in Section 13.3, and advanced state-of-the-art solutions addressing the stated challenges are provided in Section 13.4.

## 13.3 SECURITY THREATS AND ANALYSIS OF POTENTIAL SECURITY CHALLENGES

The highly heterogeneous structure of VEC and the many safety-critical tasks that need to be performed in a vehicular network make security a prime requirement in VEC. When the highly frequent usage of edge resources due to the processing requirements of vehicular applications and dynamic topology changes are considered, it is obvious that edge nodes will be increasingly vulnerable to intrusions, unauthorized access and attacks breaching the

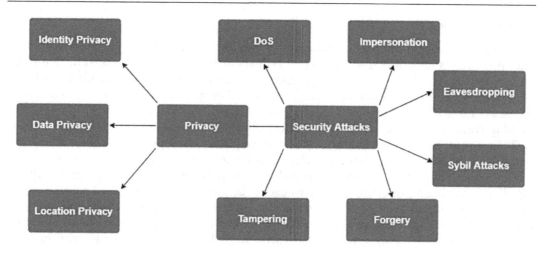

*Figure 13.3* Security and privacy threats in VEC.

security of the whole vehicular network infrastructure [22]. Figure 13.3 provides an overview of the common privacy and security threats in VEC.

The privacy of personal data is another important concern in a VEC framework. Privacy preservation, especially location information preservation, has become more and more critical in vehicular networks in recent years [16]. Vehicles have to share their driving information (location, speed, identity) with the surrounding devices for safe driving and location-based applications. As in other edge computing-based IoT applications, privacy can be investigated under three primary categories for vehicular networks: identity privacy, data privacy and location privacy [8].

- **Identity Privacy:** The vehicle's identity may include the name, phone number, credit card information, driving license and public-key certificate of the user, among other personal information. In a VEC scenario, the identity of the vehicle or vehicle owner can be leaked by the information that the vehicle provides to the edge servers.
- **Data Privacy:** Untrusted parties can disclose the data in the edge servers provided by vehicles. The disclosure of the data can be exploited to obtain private information of vehicle owners such as frequently visited restaurants, health status or addresses among a wealth of other relevant data collected by the edge servers.
- **Location Privacy:** The location-based services comprise a significant portion of smart vehicular applications in VEC. Vehicles continuously share location information with surrounding vehicles or the edge servers. From the aggregated information, an attacker can obtain the trajectory of the vehicle; that is, vehicles become vulnerable to tracking by adversaries. Location information correlated with vehicle identities can also be used by data mining algorithms to discover certain patterns about vehicle owners, which could be exploited for other malicious attacks by adversaries. Leakage of private information makes the vehicle vulnerable to other kinds of attacks as well.

An adversary can launch the following attacks to prevent proper functioning of edge nodes, vehicles and the end-to-end system in VEC [8]:

- **Denial-of-Service (DoS):** DoS attacks prevent the utilization of the edge nodes' services by their legitimate users. This is an active attack that consumes the edge servers' resources by sending a flood of malicious requests, causing the resources to become unreachable by the legitimate vehicles that need to use them. The vulnerability of an edge server is much higher compared to that of a cloud server due to its relatively limited resources.

- **Impersonation:** In impersonation attacks, an adversary acts like a legitimate user to consume the services provided by edge servers or acts as an edge server to provide fake services to the vehicles. Especially in the case of a fake edge server, relying on the bogus results provided can have devastating consequences, particularly for safety-critical applications.

- **Eavesdropping:** Eavesdropping is a passive attack, where an adversary captures transmitted data packets and can access their content in the case that they are not encrypted, by listening on the communication channel. The captured packets can contain sensitive information, resulting in privacy violations.

- **Sybil Attacks:** In Sybil attacks, an attacker manipulates fake identities or pseudonyms to compromise functionalities of edge servers. They can generate misleading reports (e.g., related to road conditions). Also, the attacker can compromise the private information of a vehicle.

- **Forgery:** Attackers can forge their own identity and generate incorrect information to mislead other vehicles, as well as the whole system. They can also use forgery to consume network resources in a manner that cannot be detected easily by intrusion detection systems (IDSs).

- **Tampering:** Attackers can drop, delay or modify the data transmitted to decrease the performance of edge computing. The detection of these attacks is not easy because transmission delays and failures frequently occur in a vehicular system. They can also modify the contents of safety-critical data packets to mislead the vehicles, disrupting the correct operation of important functions in the vehicular network.

In the rest of this section, the security and privacy issues in VEC are investigated under four main topics: (1) Access Control and Trust Management, (2) Data Sharing, (3) Computation Offloading and (4) Intrusions and Anomaly Detection. A summary of security and privacy issues and related limitations of the solutions is illustrated in Table 13.1.

## 13.3.1 Access Control and Trust Management

A VEC framework consists of various entities including edge servers, vehicles and cloud servers. At any point in time, it is difficult to ensure that all the entities involved are trusted. This requires each vehicle to be authenticated before they are granted access to services in order to prevent adversarial actions targeting the resources of the services. Otherwise, for an attacker, it would be trivial to imitate one of the legitimate users to access services without being detected by IDSs

Traditional centralized authentication schemes would be inefficient in a vehicular network setting due to latency issues, especially when we consider the high mobility and increasing number of vehicles involved. On the other hand, since each vehicle connects to many edge nodes during its travel along the road, independent authentications to each edge node may introduce a delay in the system. Therefore, cooperative authentication schemes have been gaining increasing attention for eliminating the redundant authentication processes, where edge nodes perform authentication cooperatively. Efficiently designed cooperative authentication schemes are required for ensuring tolerable delay and authentication overhead [8]. Also, during the authentication procedure, the identities of the vehicles should not be disclosed; since the disclosure of identity may cause location privacy leakage concerns. There are several anonymity techniques addressing this issue [23], including usage of pseudonyms [24],

Table 13.1 Security and Privacy Issues and Related Limitations of VEC.

| Problems | Solutions | Limitations |
| --- | --- | --- |
| Access Control & Trust Management | Pseudonym [24] Group Signatures [25] K-anonymity [26] Access Control with ABE [27] Reputation Management [28] | Since VEC is a heterogeneous and decentralized environment, aggregating and managing the behavior information and trust evaluations of the vehicles and generating an access policy for the system is challenging. |
| Data Management | Data Possession Protocols [29] Blockchain [30] | Edge servers are vulnerable to attacks, and because of their limited capacities, vital data may be discarded frequently. On the other hand, data encryption complicates data searching and finding. |
| Decentralized Computation | Task Recomposition [31] Secure Big Data Analytics [32] | The result verification of the offloaded tasks is challenging due to the decentralized computation architecture. Also, vehicles share their private information with edge computing servers when they offload tasks which possess risks for private information leakage. |
| Intrusion & Anomaly Detection | RSU misbehavior Detection [42] Vehicle Anomaly Detection [43] RL empowered IDPS [44] | The increasing number of network elements makes monitoring the system more complicated. Performing latency-sensitive intrusion and anomaly detection is a must. Performing accurate and latency-sensitive intrusion detection is a challenging issue for high mobility and heterogeneous systems. |

group signatures [25] and k-anonymity [26]. Their purpose is to disguise the link between vehicle identity and authentication information [8].

The privileges to access particular services in VEC differ among entities (i.e., vehicles, edge nodes/servers, cloud servers). Efficient authorization techniques are required for preventing unauthorized adversaries from gaining access to the network in a way that will allow them to manipulate the services. Therefore, fine-grain access control policies should be generated for different entities (e.g., vehicles, edge nodes/servers), and administrators should enforce the policies in each domain [8]. While generating the policy, various factors should be considered, such as the trustworthiness of the entities. One of the widely used access control policy schemes is attribute-based access control [27], based on attribute-based encryption (ABE). In this scheme, vehicles have the right to access the system' services if their attributes satisfy the predefined system policies. In VEC, unlike conventional methods, a decentralized and distributed access control model is needed to define access control policies, since VEC is a fully distributed system.

Although authentication mechanisms and access control policies can prevent some misbehaving vehicles or nodes from gaining access to a VEC system, there is still need for mechanisms to guarantee that all entities in the system are trusted [23]. A vehicle can get service from various edge nodes, and an edge node has many options for selecting others to cooperate with. Some nodes may not be able to meet the vehicle's QoS requirements because of their heavy loads or low resource capacities, in which case the node cannot be trusted for cooperation. Therefore, selecting nodes with the desired cooperation capabilities creates the need for a trust management mechanism [8]. Reputation management is one of the promising trust management techniques such that vehicles periodically deliver their experiences of interactions with the neighboring vehicles to locally authorized (LA) entities. Each LA calculates a reputation value based on the recent opinions about a vehicle and shares it with the other entities in the system. Before a vehicle communicates with another, it requests the reputation value of it and makes a decision to start the communication according to the reputation information obtained from the LA [28]. However, because of the decentralized nature of VEC, aggregating and managing the behavior information to evaluate entities' trustworthiness is challenging. Thus, a scalable, consistent and decentralized trust management mechanism is needed in VEC.

### 13.3.2 Data Management

The data generated by vehicles can be stored or distributed with the aid of edge nodes in VEC. Although local storage reduces data management complexity, some security concerns arise due to the risk of compromised edge nodes. In most cases, an attacker can compromise the data transmitted or stored in edge nodes more trivially than it can for a cloud storage server. Therefore, data integrity protection, secure data sharing and secure data querying concepts are critical to avoid security and privacy threats for vehicle data [8]. Also, lightweight cryptography becomes prominent, especially for real-time applications in order to prevent communication delays in time-critical applications. In environments like VEC, which provides non-latency-sensitive applications and has limited computation and storage capabilities, satisfying low latency is a critical issue, and lightweight cryptography is a promising technology with low-cost and fast data encryption capabilities to satisfy those requirements [8].

When the data is stored in edge or cloud servers, vehicles lose their supreme control on their data. Vehicles may hesitate to share their data with edge nodes because an attacker can delete, modify or exploit the data in the edge node. Also, the edge node can discard infrequently accessed data to reclaim the storage space without the permission of the data owner. Therefore, robust data integrity protection mechanisms are needed to encourage the use of edge computing [8]. Some data possession protocols based on cloud computing exist in the literature [29]; however, they cannot be adapted directly to the VEC setting. Since the storage capacities of edge servers are limited, the data is stored temporarily. It is either discarded sometime after it is stored, or it can be sent to the cloud servers for permanent storage. Also, the vehicle data is not stored in a single edge server. Many edge servers may have the data which is owned by a single vehicle, so checking the data availability and integrity for all edge servers is inefficient. Therefore, an efficient protocol is necessary to protect data integrity.

Data sharing is a frequently performed operation in data storage and computation systems, especially in cloud-aided or edge-aided systems as in VEC, where vehicles transmit various types of sensor data to the edge servers for storage and computation purposes. The transmitted data is encrypted before being uploaded to the edge computing servers due to security measures. However, when the data is encrypted, it becomes impossible to read the content of the data for other entities. This makes sharing data with other entities challenging for the data provider, as data cannot be read by the requestors unless the decryption key is provided. Obviously, sharing the private key for the data generated by a vehicle creates other security concerns. Widely investigated approaches to solve the problem of secure data sharing in the challenging decentralized environment of VEC include ABE techniques and blockchain technology [8].

On the other hand, data search is another challenge for the data requestor vehicle. The data stored in the servers may be encrypted, as previously discussed. Since the data is encrypted, it is challenging for a vehicle to search in the data store and retrieve the sought information. This requires the building of an index for the uploaded data by the data owner. The development of a secure searching request and index matching mechanism is critical in a VEC framework. In order to address the issue, blockchain is a promising technology for data sharing and searching systems in IoT networks because of its support for anonymity and decentralized nature [30].

### 13.3.3 Decentralized Computation

Vehicles may offload some tasks to edge servers for running computation-intensive vehicular applications, and edge nodes may perform some additional computational tasks for locally managing network operations. However, due to the prevalence of security threats, not only the processing or storage of data but also the computation results are under risk, such that the results can be controlled or modified by an adversary. Therefore, besides data privacy and security, the validity and security of computational results must be ensured in VEC.

In VEC, vehicles offload some tasks to the edge servers and retrieve the computation results from them. This process can happen very quickly because the tasks are offloaded to edge servers that are one or two hops away in the network most of the time. However, verifying the correctness of the retrieved results is a challenging task, since the vehicle itself will not be able to perform the computation itself due to its limited computation capabilities. Also, in edge computing environments, edge nodes may cooperatively perform the task in a distributed way. Therefore, the computational error that arose in one edge node can propagate through all of the other nodes, which affects the final result; that is, not only the final result, but the intermediate results should be verified. For those reasons, verifying computational results and composition of the tasks [31] is a challenging issue.

In the big data era, various types of user data are stored in cloud or edge servers. The analysis of these data using data mining and machine learning algorithms possess risks in terms of users' privacy [32] since the algorithms can exploit private user information from different datasets. This makes secure big data analytics a challenging issue in edge computing systems. In order to prevent any privacy leakage, robust decentralized big data analysis techniques are fundamental in VEC frameworks.

### 13.3.4 Intrusion and Anomaly Detection

VEC architecture is vulnerable to a variety of attacks as detailed at the beginning of this section. Edge servers and vehicles are most vulnerable to attacks since in most cases, they do not have complex protection mechanisms like cloud platforms due to their lack of high-performance computation capabilities. The compromised devices may imitate a legitimate node or vehicle. Detection of those rogue nodes is not an easy task, because trust management schemes may differ among different edge nodes and vehicle clusters, which introduces additional complexities to the system [8]. Also, the distributed topology of VEC makes it challenging to keep track of the list of rogue edge nodes and vehicles. Therefore, more sophisticated rogue node detection systems need to be developed.

Due to the vulnerabilities of edge computing, a successful attack can compromise the whole VEC system slowly. The advantage of edge computing is that the intrusion effects are most probably constrained in a local area. However, local services can be controlled, and the attack can cause significant damages to the users of those services. Therefore, VEC needs robust collaborative IDSs. Possible cyber-attacks should be analyzed, and the architecture of VEC should be understood carefully. A collaborative intrusion detection hierarchy should be designed for protection from the local to the global.

## 13.4 STATE-OF-THE-ART SOLUTIONS FOR SECURITY ISSUES IN VEC

VEC has many security and privacy issues, as discussed in Section 13.3. Without proper countermeasures against those issues, deployment of edge computing in vehicular networks (i.e. VEC) could have disastrous consequences. In the scope of this section, the state-of-the-art solutions in the literature addressing some of those issues are reviewed. The classification of the solutions is illustrated in Figure 13.4.

### 13.4.1 Identity Preservation, Trust Management and Authentication

As discussed above, decentralized authentication and trust management are essential in a VEC framework. While doing that, preserving vehicle identity is also necessary to prevent exploitation by adversaries. Recent promising techniques for identity and trust management in VEC include usage of pseudonyms, distributed reputation management systems and blockchain-aided authentication schemes. Below we provide an overview of each of these techniques.

#### 13.4.1.1 Pseudonym Management Scheme for Identity Preservation

In a VEC environment, vehicles periodically share safety messages with the surrounding vehicles and RSUs. These messages include the current location and speed of the vehicles, which can be exploited to get information about the trajectory of the vehicles; in other words, location privacy can be breached. In order to prevent data leakage, the real identities of the vehicles are replaced with pseudonyms [33]. Conventionally, vehicles change their pseudonyms periodically to decrease traceability risk, but when an extremely large number of vehicles is considered, this is not a feasible approach. Also, pseudonym management, namely, generation, distribution and revocation of pseudonyms, is challenging in VEC due to its decentralized and heterogeneous nature.

Kang and Yu proposed a decentralized pseudonym management architecture addressing this issue [34]. A three-layer architecture including (1) cloud layer, (2) fog layer and (3) vehicle

*Figure 13.4* The classification of the state-of-the-art security solutions in VEC.

layer was used. In the cloud layer, a central authority (CA) is deployed, which is undertaken by the ITS department of a government. CA is responsible for generation and distribution of identity-related information (consisting of public, private keys and digital certificates) of the vehicles. The system includes a registration database for storing that information. Also, the global pseudonym usage information of vehicles is updated periodically in this database. There is also an event database, which records violation events of vehicles. The fog layer, which can also be considered as the edge cloud layer, has four components: (1) pseudonym pool, (2) fog/edge devices, (3) Local Authority (LA) and (4) event data recorder. The pseudonym pool is responsible for pseudonym generation and storage, and the LA is responsible for distributing these pseudonyms to vehicles. Also, local pseudonym usage records of the corresponding vehicles are stored in LA. Finally, the event data recorder keeps track of local events and communicates with adjacent fog/edge nodes for synchronization purposes. The blacklist (revocation list of vehicles) is periodically uploaded to the central event database for revealing misbehaving vehicles. In the vehicle layer, vehicles are equipped with pseudonym storage units to store pseudonyms issued by LA. The advantages of this architecture are (1) privacy breach risk is reduced due to local pseudonym management and (2) the LA can quickly revoke the pseudonym of a misbehaving vehicle owing to being in close proximity.

In the proposed scheme, there are three fundamental interactions between fog/edge nodes and vehicles. Firstly, a vehicle periodically requests a new pseudonym from the LA to decrease the risk of traceability. If LA verifies the legitimacy of the vehicle and admits the request, it supplies the vehicle with a new pseudonym. Then LA updates the database with the new pseudonym of the vehicle. Secondly, when a vehicle crosses a new region, it requests a new pseudonym from the LA responsible for that region. The LA communicates with the previous one to validate the information of the vehicle. After that, total responsibility and the information (previously used pseudonyms, safety messages, other records) of the vehicle are transferred to the new LA. Finally, if any violation of a vehicle is detected by neighboring vehicles or by fog/edge nodes, the responsible LA is informed. LA checks the validity of the report and stores it to the event data recorder. After that, the report is sent to the CA. If CA also verifies it, CA broadcasts the true identity of the vehicle and adds the vehicle's information to the blacklist. The blacklist is periodically broadcast to the nearby devices of the revoked vehicle.

### 13.4.1.2 Ensuring Trust with Distributed Reputation Management

Vehicles may perform selfish or malicious activities in vehicular networks. The growing number of vehicles in the system increases the probability of encountering these malicious activities. Reputation evaluation is a useful approach for eliminating those vehicles and assuring mutual trust in the network. However, in central reputation management systems, reputation querying, calculating and responding operations are inefficient due to heavy backbone loads on the network. Also, the distributed architecture of VEC makes reputation management more challenging. Therefore, a distributed reputation management system is required for a VEC framework.

Huang et al. [28] proposed a distributed reputation management system (abbreviated as DREAMS) to enhance trustworthiness in VEC. As in the proposed scheme for pseudonym management, most of the operations are handled by Local Authorities (LA) in the network. LA is responsible for collecting reputation segments consisting of the opinions of a vehicle based on previous interactions of other vehicles or RSUs. This information is recorded with the pseudonyms of the providers. LA is the trusted local authority such that a vehicle can query it for a neighboring vehicle's reputation value for safe further interactions. Reputation segment generation about the interacting vehicles is based on subjective logic. The segments consist of belief, disbelief, uncertainty and base rate parameters. Belief is the parameter corresponding to the good opinions about the interactions with a specific vehicle, and disbelief is just the opposite. The uncertainty parameter corresponds to confidence related to the opinion of the segment provider. Also, the base rate constant reflects the willingness for the interaction of the segment provider. The reputation segments are aggregated by LA. After that, LA weights the aggregated reputation segments by interaction quality of the provider and the subjected vehicle, as well as freshness and the certainty of the opinion. This way, the quality of the segments is evaluated, and more accurate reputation calculations can be achieved. The calculated value is combined with the last updated reputation value of the subject, and a new reputation value is formed. If the vehicle is new in that region, and there is not any local information about that vehicle, LA queries the reputation value from the global reputation database. Finally, the most recently generated reputation value is updated in the global reputation database. When a vehicle needs to interact with other vehicles, it can query the corresponding reputation value from LA and can make a decision.

### 13.4.1.3 Blockchain-Aided Cooperative Authentication

Identity authentication is one of the most prominent countermeasures against malicious activities in VEC. Instead of conventional authentication schemes, cooperative authentication is more efficient for avoiding redundant individual authentications to each edge node.

Liu et al. [35] proposed a blockchain-aided cooperative authentication scheme to enhance security and privacy preservation in VEC. In the proposed scheme, cooperative authentication is based on a secret-sharing procedure, and trust management is accomplished by blockchain technology. The architecture consists of (1) trusted authority (TA), (2) driving vehicles, (3) proxy vehicles and (4) RSUs. TA is responsible for initialization work, completion operations of the registrations of the devices (vehicles, RSUs), and generation and distribution of public parameters and keys. Driving vehicles move dynamically on their routes, and they can deliver their route to transfer stations (RSUs or micro base stations) to ensure they are on the correct route. Proxy vehicles are the edge nodes on the road. They are bounded by only one RSU, and they can be considered as RSU agents for driving vehicles' route information collection and identity authentication. RSUs are the transfer stations deployed by service providers. They perform computation operations and receive authentication results of driving vehicles, which are aggregated and uploaded by proxy vehicles. One or more RSUs form road segments. One RSU is responsible for multiple proxy vehicles. This way, mobility and flexibility is ensured.

In the distributed authentication model, as in Figure 13.5, RSU and proxy vehicles check their validity by mutual authentication to construct an entrusted relationship. The validity is ensured by cryptographic algorithms. After that, in order to select its proxy members, RSU generates a secret $s$ and divides it to the number of proxy vehicles in the system and distributes the sub-secret parts of $s$ to them. When a driving vehicle enters the regions of a road segment, it communicates with proxy vehicles. The driving vehicle provides the information to proxy vehicles, including the identification information of the previous RSU and the next RSU at the transfer station where it will arrive (i.e., routing path information). After mutual validation of the driving vehicle's and proxy vehicles' legality, each proxy vehicle broadcasts the result of their validation procedure to others.

Each of these keeps a list including the authentication results of other proxy vehicles for the same driving vehicle. At this stage, a miner is selected. Most probably, the proxy vehicle with the highest trust value, namely the vehicle with the highest reputation value, is selected as the miner. This is because, if the reputation value of a proxy vehicle is higher, finding an appropriate nonce to calculate the cryptographic hash value gets easier. Due to the incentive purposes, the miner is rewarded with a trust-coin, which can be used to increase reputation.

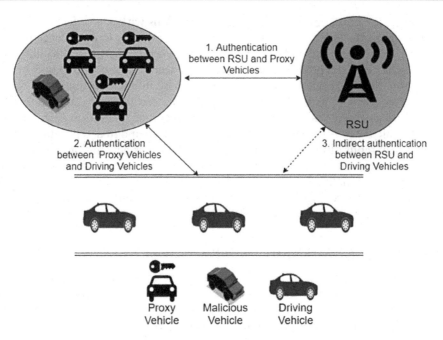

*Figure 13.5* Blockchain-aided Cooperative Authentication Model for VEC.

The miner forms a block for proxy vehicles' reputation values, and this block is added to the blockchain. Afterward, the proxy vehicle uploads the final authentication results to the RSU. Then, the RSU checks the miner's trust value stored in the blockchain to validate the authentication result. If the legality of the driving vehicle is verified, mutual identity authentication between RSU and the driving vehicle is, indirectly, accomplished. In this way, a self-organizing and decentralized authentication scheme is established.

### 13.4.2 Blockchain-Based Secure Data Management

In VEC, vehicles may hesitate to upload their data to the edge servers (RSUs), because edge nodes are distributed all over the roads without robust security measures, unlike cloud servers. Peer-to-peer (P2P) data sharing among vehicles is another concern due to security risks. Also, encrypting data before transmission is not efficient because it makes data search challenging for a vehicle that needs the data. In order to solve these issues, some data indexes (metadata) must be provided by the uploader to enable any legitimate requestor to find the data. Attribute-based data sharing schemes and verifiable data querying schemes have been investigated widely in the literature [36, 37]. Also, blockchain-based data sharing and querying schemes addressing the issues have been investigated in the context of vehicular network security [38].

Kang et al. [38] proposed a data sharing and querying scheme based on blockchain to address the issues explained above. Due to the high cost of establishing blockchain and low storage capacities of the vehicles, P2P data sharing is not feasible. Therefore, the authors exploited the consortium blockchain method [39] in which preselected edge nodes (RSUs) establish the blockchain procedures instead of actual peers sharing the data (vehicles). A three-layer architecture is maintained as shown in Figure 13.6. The vehicular blockchain system consists of data requestors, data providers, edge nodes (RSUs), a data storage smart contract (DSSC) and an information-sharing smart contract (ISSC).

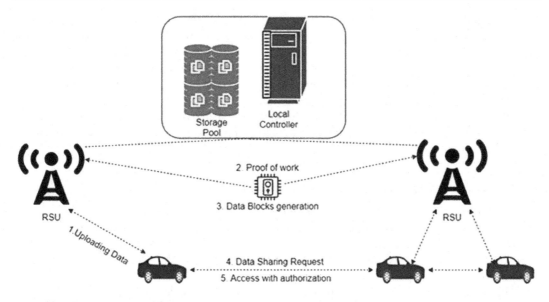

*Figure 13.6* Blockchain-Based Secure Data Management Model for VEC.

Vehicles could play two roles in the system: The data providers collect information related to the surroundings and share their data for getting rewards, and the data requestors demand the data stored in the edge nodes by applying to the providers. A certain number of edge nodes (RSUs) form a vehicular edge cluster. A local controller and a storage pool are allocated for each cluster in the network. The local controllers manage data requests from data requestor vehicles, and the storage pool stores the data provided by vehicles (data providers). The RSUs perform data aggregation operations in DSSC and act as miners in ISSC. DSSC is a process for distributed data storage and consists of raw data and data blocks. The raw data collected by data providers is encrypted with their pseudonyms and uploaded to the RSUs for storage. The RSUs integrate the raw data into a data block and broadcast to the other RSUs in the edge cluster for verification, for establishing consensus among the cluster through a proof-of-storage procedure. The RSU with the most contribution of storage in the cluster is rewarded with a vehicle coin by the local controller, namely a proof-of-storage reward. Also, the local controller of the cluster generates an address list of the raw data for data providers to enable them to search for and read the data afterward. For decentralized data sharing, the ISSC method is used. A data provider generates an index for the raw data before uploading. The index includes the information of the provider's pseudonym, a storage address, features of the data and reputation segments related to other vehicles. Also, a sharing record is generated and with the metadata for each raw data, and they are integrated into a block and uploaded to edge nodes for a proof-of-work procedure. Each edge node periodically broadcasts its metadata blocks to other nodes, and they compete for finding a proper cryptographic hash value for it. The node with the fastest solution adds the block to the vehicular blockchain and gets its reward as a vehicle coin.

For the data requesting procedure, a vehicle (a data requestor) first downloads the latest information of blocks in the vehicular blockchain from the RSUs. Then it searches for information of interest by using information indexes. When it finds the data of interest and selects the optimal provider according to the reputation value of providers, it applies with a request message to the provider. After the request is received and the identity of the requestor is verified, the provider sends the information related to the performed communication and the requested data to the nearest RSU. Then, the RSU searches the data from the vehicular blockchain with the information provided. After finding it, RSU encrypts the data with the public key of the requestor and sends the data. As soon as the requestor gets the data, it pays the provider with some amount of vehicle coin and integrates the data sharing event to a block to be added to the vehicular blockchain by the RSU. In the proposed model, every vehicle has a wallet account to manage their vehicle coins.

In the proposed model, a consortium blockchain is utilized to establish security and distributed data management. Secure data storage and reputation-based secure data sharing are ensured by smart contracts.

### 13.4.3 Secure Distributed Computation Techniques

Offloading computation tasks to edge servers is a must for the vehicles in VEC, due to the lack of sufficient computation and storage resources [40]. However, the offloading process can be disrupted by malicious activities, which add extra burden to the network.

Sedjelmaci et al. [41] proposed a model to detect attacks in task offloading links for secure computation offloading. The authors mainly focused on spoofing and jamming attacks, and their model consists of four components: (1) Vehicle, (2) Attacker, (3) Distributed Security Agent (DSA) and (4) Cyber Defense Center (CDC). A vehicle can offload computational tasks to edge servers via the cellular network infrastructure (i.e., eNodeB) or 802.11p, either directly using network access points on the road or with the help of other vehicles to reach that access node. An attacker tries to compromise those operational links between the vehicles and edge servers. A DSA is a machine learning-based embedded protection module, which is deployed in each vehicle and edge server, to detect malicious activities of devices. The CDC is a centralized agent creating intrusion alerts according to the information collected from DSAs.

In order to achieve distributed and cooperative intrusion prediction and decision-making in a VEC environment, a game-theoretic approach is adopted. The proposed model has a cooperative game model. The intention is to model the behaviors of the vehicles and other devices in the system. The Nash Equilibrium concept is used to ensure that the components of the models take their best strategies. First, the payoffs of each element in the model are calculated. The payoff of the vehicle is determined by successful offloading rate, probability of a successful attack and offloading cost rate. DSA's payoff is calculated by the success rate of attack detection, the damage caused by the attacks and the cost of attack monitoring and detection. Calculating the payoff of CDC is very similar to DSA. After that, the cooperative payoff is calculated by adding all the payoffs together. Higher values of cooperative payoff indicate more successful task offloading and misbehavior detection. Finally, the attacker payoff consists of the cooperative payoff and the cost of the attack that would be performed. After the calculation process of payoffs, each device in the game ends up with a strategy to optimize the offloading process and protect their links. This way, designing a cooperative and distributed attack detection in offloading links can be achieved. Also, offloading performance can be optimized.

### 13.4.4 RSU Misbehavior and Vehicle Anomaly Detection

The edge nodes, namely RSUs, mostly suffer from a lack of hardware protection measures or are incapable of software-based security measures [42]. Thus, communication through edge nodes possesses risks against some attacks (e.g., eavesdropping, man-in-the-middle, jamming, etc.) Also, vehicle vulnerabilities have been gaining significant attention, especially with the developments in autonomous vehicles. These attacks target Electronic Control Units (ECUs), and through accessing the Controller Area Network (CAN) bus, they inject instructions inside vehicles to gain control over them [43]. In order to address these issues, two methods are investigated in this section: (1) IDS for Detecting RSU Misbehavior [42] and (2) Vehicle Anomaly Detection through exploiting sensor data fusion [43].

Abhishek et al. [42] proposed an RSU misbehavior detection method, where an attack model is assumed with the attacker gaining root access to the RSU and imitating the transmission link between vehicles and the RSU. By doing that, a continuous load is introduced in the network, and the resources are kept busy. Also, the compromised RSU could be used for many attacks targeting the vehicles. The authors specifically focused on a selective modification attack. The attack intentionally disrupts the physical layer payload of a packet during the transmission to vehicles. The vehicle drops the failed packet and requests re-transmission, and these redundant transmissions result in an increased delay in the system. Although the channel quality is low, the signal-to-noise ratio (SNR) is not affected, which makes detection of these attacks difficult. The authors proposed an IDS with the help of trust management to solve the issue. Firstly, vehicles calculate the trust level of the RSU. The calculated trust values are periodically aggregated and combined at a central server. If the value is below a threshold, the RSU is considered malicious. The trust values are calculated according to the packet drop probabilities during transmission.

Guo et al. [43] proposed an Edge Computing-based Vehicle Anomaly Detection (EVAD) system, which utilizes vehicles' sensor data properties in time and frequency domain to detect vehicle anomalies; that is, sensor results are correlated due to common physical parameters of the readings (speed, acceleration, location). An undesired correlation change of those readings in the time domain can be considered as a vehicle anomaly. Also, the comparison of the current and previous correlation results in the frequency domain can be used to detect anomalies. In the proposed technique, a ring architecture is used to combine data from as many sensors as possible to increase the accuracy and the robustness of the detection operation. The detection operation is performed in the edge servers to increase the pace of detection by aggregating sensor data in the edge servers. A vehicle contains many ECUs and a CAN, which connect all the ECUs with a central bus. Therefore, the information of sensors can be collected from the CAN-bus structure. The procedure works as follows: First, EVAD connects to the vehicle through CAN-bus for monitoring and transferring messages. Then EVAD selects sensor pairs based on previously collected data. The purpose is to model the correlation ring of sensors and the threshold for determining anomalies. For anomaly detection, the sensor data is analyzed in time and frequency domains by calculating the correlation of variables in the correlation ring. EVAD compares the results with the previous ones for the same variable, and if the result is above the predefined threshold, the detection is approved. In the time-domain analysis, the utilized parameter to detect anomalies is the Pearson Correlation Coefficient (PCC), and in the frequency domain, it is Power Spectral Density (PSD). Briefly, significant deviations in the measured or calculated values of PCC and PDS indicate an anomaly for the vehicle.

On the other hand, Xiong et al. [44] proposed a reinforcement learning (RL) empowered intrusion detection and prevention system (IDPS) for VEC. The study aims to apply RL algorithms in the VEC system to make accurate and latency-aware decisions for intrusion detection. In the proposed framework, IDPS functions can be divided into virtual network functions (VNFs), and those VNFs can be orchestrated to involve in a specific IDPS task, forming a service function chain (SFC). The authors separated the framework into four layers including IDPS decision-making, IDPS VNF scheduling, vehicle communication management, and vehicle localization and mobility management layers. In the vehicle localization and mobility management layer, the objective of RL is to learn and reveal the relation of vehicle behaviors and communication patterns that will be helpful for misbehaving vehicle detection. In the vehicle communication layer, RL is trained according to channel transmission features (transmission request rate, traffic amount, data transmission success) and vehicle localization information (collected from the bottom layer). In the IDPS virtual function scheduling layer, SFCs are organized, and VNF placement is arranged. In this layer, RL is trained to deploy VNFs optimally at edge servers and organize SFCs efficiently. Finally, in the IDPS decision-making layer, RL is trained to make proper decisions when an intrusion is detected and select mitigation methods according to the state of the network.

## 13.5 DISCUSSION

VEC is expected to significantly shape the future of intelligent transportation systems with the many use cases it will make possible, especially for autonomous vehicles. Despite the fast developments in VEC, research on its security and privacy is still at a premature state. Important security problems that need to be solved for widespread adoption include secure computation offloading and distributed computation, distributed vehicle and edge server identity management, secure data sharing and privacy-preserving data communication/storage among others. The security solutions built upon technologies like blockchain and AI, which have been adapted to a VEC setting, require much more rigorous testing and evaluation under conditions closely mimicking real-world VEC settings of high complexity and heterogeneity. The solutions also need to expand upon their focus on the real-time requirements of VEC and energy consumption, as these are difficult-to-achieve yet indispensable requirements for VEC, which involve challenging trade-offs when complex security architectures involving AI and blockchain are utilized.

Next-generation security architectures for VEC will need to make better use of advances in networking technologies including SDN and NFV to implement intrusion detection and reputation management systems that provide a wider visibility of the network as compared to the local solutions deployed at edge servers. SDN, through its capacity to observe important network parameters in the global vehicular network and update packet forwarding rules based on fine-grain security policies will provide immense opportunities for achieving quick detection and isolation of malicious entities in a VEC setting. This needs to be complemented with machine learning techniques for detecting anomalous behavior of edge nodes and vehicles to make more effective decisions regarding reputation management. Ensuring the correctness of computation results received after offloading tasks to edge servers is one of the difficult problems, remaining mostly unsolved for VEC. Remote attestation techniques for ensuring faithful execution of the offloaded tasks on the edge platform, gleaned from execution flow tracing and cryptographic integrity assurance techniques applied in mobile-cloud computing settings [45] can be applied to VEC as well. In order to ensure dissemination of vehicle-generated data according to the principle of least privilege, where all parties have access to only the portion of the data they need to complete their task, techniques that make data an active entity capable of enforcing its own security policies [46] can be applied.

## 13.6 CONCLUSION

In the scope of this chapter, a survey of existing work on the security and privacy issues and solutions for VEC is presented. For this purpose, an overview of background information on VEC including its architecture, provided services and enabling technologies has been provided. Existing challenges for edge computing enabled vehicular networks, including task offloading, network management, caching and data management have been discussed. Further, analysis of security and privacy problems in VEC has been presented in detail. The issues are categorized under four main topics: Authentication and Trust Management, Secure Data Management, Secure Distributed Computation, RSU and Vehicle Anomaly Detection. State-of-the-art solutions for each of these security and privacy issues have been discussed in detail.

VEC is a fast-growing field, where advances in smart vehicular systems will bring along many more computation problems and associated security vulnerabilities. Despite the growing research and development efforts, much work remains to be done to provide real-time, cost-efficient security and privacy preservation approaches for these safety-critical systems. In addition to the flexibility and agility provided by SDN and NFV, future security solutions will need to benefit maximally from lightweight authentication algorithms and cryptography at edge servers and smart vehicles. Also, they should consider different networking architectures such as those offered by network slicing to achieve more isolated and fine-grain traffic management for enhanced security.

## REFERENCES

1. Agiwal, M., Roy, A., & Saxena, N. (2016). Next generation 5G wireless networks: A comprehensive survey. *IEEE Communications Surveys & Tutorials*, 18(3), 1617–1655.
2. Technology and requirements for self-driving cars, https://www.intel.com/content/www/us/en/automotive/driving-safetyadvanced-driver-assistance-systems-self-driving-technologypaper.html/.
3. Xu, X., Xue, Y., Qi, L., Yuan, Y., Zhang, X., Umer, T., & Wan, S. (2019). An edge computing-enabled computation offloading method with privacy preservation for internet of connected vehicles. *Future Generation Computer Systems*, 96, 89–100.
4. Raza, S., Wang, S., Ahmed, M., & Anwar, M. R. (2019). A survey on vehicular edge computing: Architecture, applications, technical issues, and future directions. *Wireless Communications and Mobile Computing*, 2019, 3159762:1–3159762:19.
5. Huang, X., Yu, R., Kang, J., He, Y., & Zhang, Y. (2017). Exploring mobile edge computing for 5G-enabled software defined vehicular networks. *IEEE Wireless Communications*, 24(6), 55–63.
6. Huang, C., Lu, R., & Choo, K. K. R. (2017). Vehicular fog computing: Architecture, use case, and security and forensic challenges. *IEEE Communications Magazine*, 55(11), 105–111.
7. Mendiboure, L., Chalouf, M. A., & Krief, F. (2019). Edge computing based applications in vehicular environments: Comparative study and main issues. *Journal of Computer Science and Technology*, 34(4), 869–886.
8. Ni, J., Zhang, K., Lin, X., & Shen, X. S. (2017). Securing fog computing for internet of things applications: Challenges and solutions. *IEEE Communications Surveys & Tutorials*, 20(1), 601–628.
9. Sharma, P. K., Moon, S. Y., & Park, J. H. (2017). Block-VN: A distributed Blockchain based vehicular network architecture in smart city. *Journal of information processing systems*, 13(1), 184–195.
10. Dai, Y., Xu, D., Maharjan, S., Qiao, G., & Zhang, Y. (2019). Artificial intelligence empowered edge computing and caching for internet of vehicles. *IEEE Wireless Communications*, 26(3), 12–18.
11. Wang, X., Li, X., & Leung, V. C. (2015). Artificial intelligence-based techniques for emerging heterogeneous network: State of the arts, opportunities, and challenges. *IEEE Access*, 3, 1379–1391.
12. Peng, Y., Liu, L., Zhou, Y., Shi, J., & Li, J. (2019, December). *Deep reinforcement learning-based dynamic service migration in vehicular networks*. In *2019 IEEE Global Communications Conference (GLOBECOM)* (pp. 1–6). IEEE.
13. Ge, X., Li, Z., & Li, S. (2017). 5G software defined vehicular networks. *IEEE Communications Magazine*, 55(7), 87–93.
14. Wang, K., Yin, H., Quan, W., & Min, G. (2018). Enabling collaborative edge computing for software defined vehicular networks. *IEEE Network*, 32(5), 112–117.

15. Khan, A. A., Abolhasan, M., & Ni, W. (2018, January). 5G next generation VANETs using SDN and fog computing framework. In *2018 15th IEEE Annual Consumer Communications & Networking Conference (CCNC)* (pp. 1–6). IEEE.

16. Liu, L., Chen, C., Pei, Q., Maharjan, S., & Zhang, Y. (2020). Vehicular edge computing and networking: A survey. *Mobile Networks and Applications*, 1–24.

17. Liu, Y., Wang, S., Huang, J., & Yang, F. (2018, May). A computation offloading algorithm based on game theory for vehicular edge networks. In *2018 IEEE International Conference on Communications (ICC)* (pp. 1–6). IEEE.

18. Hou, X., Li, Y., Chen, M., Wu, D., Jin, D., & Chen, S. (2016). Vehicular fog computing: A viewpoint of vehicles as the infrastructures. *IEEE Transactions on Vehicular Technology*, 65(6), 3860–3873.

19. He, Y., Zhao, N., & Yin, H. (2017). Integrated networking, caching, and computing for connected vehicles: A deep reinforcement learning approach. *IEEE Transactions on Vehicular Technology*, 67(1), 44–55.

20. Zhang, Y., Zhang, H., Long, K., Zheng, Q., & Xie, X. (2018). Software-defined and fog-computing-based next generation vehicular networks. *IEEE Communications Magazine*, 56(9), 34–41.

21. Hui, Y., Su, Z., Luan, T. H., & Cai, J. (2018). Content in motion: An edge computing based relay scheme for content dissemination in urban vehicular networks. *IEEE Transactions on Intelligent Transportation Systems*, 20(8), 3115–3128.

22. Khan, W. Z., Ahmed, E., Hakak, S., Yaqoob, I., & Ahmed, A. (2019). Edge computing: A survey. *Future Generation Computer Systems*, 97, 219–235.

23. Onieva, J. A., Rios, R., Roman, R., & Lopez, J. (2019). Edge-assisted vehicular networks security. *IEEE Internet of Things Journal*, 6(5), 8038–8045.

24. Lu, R., Lin, X., Luan, T. H., Liang, X., & Shen, X. (2011). Pseudonym changing at social spots: An effective strategy for location privacy in VANETs. *IEEE Transactions on Vehicular Technology*, 61(1), 86–96.

25. Pointcheval, D., & Sanders, O. (2016, February). Short randomizable signatures. In *Cryptographers' Track at the RSA Conference* (pp. 111–126). Springer, Cham.

26. LeFevre, K., DeWitt, D. J., & Ramakrishnan, R. (2005, June). Incognito: Efficient full-domain k-anonymity. In *Proceedings of the 2005 ACM SIGMOD international conference on Management of data* (pp. 49–60).

27. Gupta, M., Benson, J., Patwa, F., & Sandhu, R. (2019, March). Dynamic groups and attribute-based access control for next-generation smart cars. In *Proceedings of the Ninth ACM Conference on Data and Application Security and Privacy* (pp. 61–72).

28. Huang, X., Yu, R., Kang, J., & Zhang, Y. (2017). Distributed reputation management for secure and efficient vehicular edge computing and networks. *IEEE Access*, 5, 25408–25420.

29. Yu, Y., Au, M. H., Ateniese, G., Huang, X., Susilo, W., Dai, Y., & Min, G. (2016). Identity-based remote data integrity checking with perfect data privacy preserving for cloud storage. *IEEE Transactions on Information Forensics and Security*, 12(4), 767–778.

30. Mistry, I., Tanwar, S., Tyagi, S., & Kumar, N. (2020). Blockchain for 5G-enabled IoT for industrial automation: A systematic review, solutions, and challenges. *Mechanical Systems and Signal Processing*, 135, 106382.

31. Wang, B., Chang, Z., Zhou, Z., & Ristaniemi, T. (2018, June). Reliable and privacy-preserving task recomposition for crowdsensing in vehicular fog computing. In *2018 IEEE 87th Vehicular Technology Conference (VTC Spring)* (pp. 1–6). IEEE.

32. Darwish, T. S., & Bakar, K. A. (2018). Fog based intelligent transportation big data analytics in the internet of vehicles environment: motivations, architecture, challenges, and critical issues. *IEEE Access*, 6, 15679–15701.

33. Petit, J., Schaub, F., Feiri, M., & Kargl, F. (2014). Pseudonym schemes in vehicular networks: A survey. *IEEE Communications Surveys & Tutorials*, 17(1), 228–255.

34. Kang, J., Yu, R., Huang, X., & Zhang, Y. (2017). Privacy-preserved pseudonym scheme for fog computing supported internet of vehicles. *IEEE Transactions on Intelligent Transportation Systems*, 19(8), 2627–2637.

35. Liu, H., Zhang, P., Pu, G., Yang, T., Maharjan, S., & Zhang, Y. (2020). Blockchain empowered cooperative authentication with data traceability in vehicular edge computing. *IEEE Transactions on Vehicular Technology*, 69(4), 4221–4232.

36. Fan, K., Wang, J., Wang, X., Li, H., & Yang, Y. (2018). Secure, efficient and revocable data sharing scheme for vehicular fogs. *Peer-to-Peer Networking and Applications*, 11(4), 766–777.

37. Kong, Q., Lu, R., Ma, M., & Bao, H. (2018). A privacy-preserving and verifiable querying scheme in vehicular fog data dissemination. *IEEE Transactions on Vehicular Technology*, 68(2), 1877–1887.

38. Kang, J., Yu, R., Huang, X., Wu, M., Maharjan, S., Xie, S., & Zhang, Y. (2018). Blockchain for secure and efficient data sharing in vehicular edge computing and networks. *IEEE Internet of Things Journal*, 6(3), 4660–4670.

39. Li, Z., Kang, J., Yu, R., Ye, D., Deng, Q., & Zhang, Y. (2017). Consortium blockchain for secure energy trading in industrial internet of things. *IEEE Transactions on Industrial Informatics*, 14(8), 3690–3700.

40. Xu, X., Xue, Y., Qi, L., Yuan, Y., Zhang, X., Umer, T., & Wan, S. (2019). An edge computing-enabled computation offloading method with privacy preservation for internet of connected vehicles. *Future Generation Computer Systems*, 96, 89–100.

41. Sedjelmaci, H., Jemaa, I. B., Hadji, M., & Kaiser, A. (2018, December). Security framework for vehicular edge computing network based on behavioral game. In *2018 IEEE Global Communications Conference (GLOBECOM)* (pp. 1–6). IEEE.

42. Abhishek, N. V., Lim, T. J., Sikdar, B., & Liang, B. (2019, August). Detecting RSU misbehavior in vehicular edge computing. In *2019 IEEE/CIC International Conference on Communications in China (ICCC)* (pp. 42–47). IEEE.

43. Guo, F., Wang, Z., Du, S., Li, H., Zhu, H., Pei, Q., … & Zhao, J. (2019). Detecting vehicle anomaly in the edge via sensor consistency and frequency characteristic. *IEEE Transactions on Vehicular Technology*, 68(6), 5618–5628.

44. Xiong, M., Li, Y., Gu, L., Pan, S., Zeng, D., & Li, P. (2020). Reinforcement learning empowered IDPS for vehicular networks in edge computing. *IEEE Network*, 34(3), 57–63.

45. Angin, P., Bhargava, B., & Ranchal, R. (2018). A self-protecting agents based model for high-performance mobile-cloud computing. *Computers & Security*, 77, 380–396.

46. Ranchal, R., Bhargava, B., Angin, P., & ben Othmane, L. (2018). Epics: A framework for enforcing security policies in composite web services. *IEEE Transactions on Services Computing*, 12(3), 415–428.

# Section IV

# Chapter 14

# On Exploiting Blockchain Technology to Approach toward Secured, Sliced and Edge Deployed Virtual Network Functions for Improvised IoT Services

*Mahzabeen Emu and Salimur Choudhury*

Lakehead University, Canada

## CONTENTS

## 14.1 INTRODUCTION

The era of Software-Defined Networking (SDN) has encouraged the transition from a hardware-dependent network system to virtualized services that has been a revolutionary step in telecommunications. Network Functions Virtualization (NFV) [2] is an architecture where the communication services of the network are virtualized with software-based infrastructures for ensuring privacy preservation, cost-effectiveness, scalability, efficiency and resiliency. Virtual Network Function (VNF) [2, 3] deployments are highly beneficial for reducing hardware-related, initial setup, and regulatory maintenance costs for Internet Service Provider (ISP) companies. The traffic in the network and usage of Internet of Things (IoT) devices are on the verge of increasing by a significant factor every day. The virtualization of services has allowed adding new users or services to the endpoints with the least effort and hassle. Nevertheless, the massive connection of IoT devices (i.e., attaching possible intrusion points) extends the threat surface of a network system, thereby raising the overall security risk. It becomes even more prominent when the services in future networks (6G) are expecting to be controlled and managed by fully automated orchestration techniques. Based on the notion of Multi-Access Edge Computing (MEC) [2], storing, computing and processing are executed at nearby edge devices rather than on shared cloud data centers. The presence of the cloud in the core network does not disappear though. The revolutionary twist is to use neighboring endpoints (router, devices and gateways) that complete operations on the data and execute services. In the NFV context, VNFs can be deployed at neighboring devices instead of cloud for privacy-sensitive service components (e.g., augmented reality, autonomous vehicles, tele-surgery, mobile health services and collaborative computing) [3, 4]. This idea can eliminate the obligation of personal data being unnecessary traversed through public clouds and core networks [4].

One of the primary concerns of IoT services is powering personalized data (e.g., through wearable devices like Fitbits, remote health monitoring devices and Google glass or IoT sensors) [3]. Thus, the risks of breaching several security terms, such as identity theft, device manipulation, data falsification through different kinds of attacks and malicious nodes arise in the ad hoc wireless networks. Therefore, the edge-based VNF orchestration scheme must guarantee a secured and decentralized VNF deployment strategy to prevent messing up with the private and sensitive IoT data and services.

Blockchain [5, 6] is a distributed security approach usually known for secure and immutable transactions verified by the blockchain database itself in the distributed ledger that can be employed for secured VNF services. If a malicious VNF gets introduced to the service chain anyhow, the application's complete behavior may be irregular. The most disturbing fact is that most of the time, the central service manager remains unknown to this matter and the destructive activities go on undetected for a long time. Sometimes the attackers make their way directly to the central registration database of VNF information, which may lead to deceptive data updates and mishandling reports for orchestrator. Undoubtedly, incorporating blockchain technology to the orchestration system adds the extra computational burden of locally verifying each VNF transaction. Yet, the computation cost trade-off with the highly secured transaction is remarkable according to the application domain's nature. Blockchain employs previously popular security enforcement technologies in the context of security, specifically public-key cryptography, hashing and digital sign or endorsement. Communication is performed utilizing two public or private digital signatures. All of the blockchain members or nodes in the network system are identified using the public key. The digital signature of each node to verify a VNF transaction is employed through leveraging the private key. All the digitally signed transactions are routed over the network and connected to the service chain only after being proven as valid. To ensure validity, a consensus protocol is imposed. Thus, all the blockchain members provide to maintain the VNF transactions and services' transparency and validity. The forge of a VNF update is only possible after the brute force recomputation of hash functions. Therefore, it is difficult for malicious users to revise the data contents of the blockchain database.

Therefore, employing a blockchain architecture that serves different network slices separately, such as, massive IoT, critical communication, low latency and real-time performance demanding slices, etc. [8] is considered as the main goal. The network slicing [9] technology offers customizable and ultra-reliable, high-performing IoT services according to the adaptive needs of various IoT scenarios. The isolation among various network slices is a common approach to avoid and prevent attacks in shared network infrastructure. Service providers' accountability becomes a critical issue in the multi-tenants (tenants from one single slice sharing the same infrastructure) in a multi-domain environment (VNF executing in competing providers domains), primarily during faulty events. In such case, employing blockchain nodes in a slice can be applicable that is imperceptible to anyone outside the slice. Furthermore, the VNF orchestrator or selected blockchain manager designated in charge needs to record all the VNF transactions regarding deployment, relocation or other activities. This way, transparency and local verification of VNF updates can be done through the registered blockchain database. Every operation is signed by the edge node or the orchestrator that requested the VNF configuration update. Only upon the reception of approval and signature by each blockchain member, the corresponding VNF deployment or relocation can be accepted by the system to take place.

The blockchain architectural design is expected to follow the specifications of various network slices. According to the functionalities of network slices, the linked lists of transactions, encryption interoperability cryptographic algorithms and the fault-tolerance technique can be chosen. The Hyperledger blockchain tool [7] offers privilege to develop, implement and evaluate various blockchain prototype architectures. In this chapter's context, the prototype implementation needs to include two smart contracts for the security of network slice administration and VNF configuration updates. Hyperledger chain code can facilitate the security purpose of network slices by utilizing some particular transaction format. Each hyperledger channel allows to run individual network slices in an isolated manner [10]. However, along with secured slice construction, the optimization of data structures matters for the scaling purpose of transactions intended by each network slice. Thus, efficient blockchain-powered network slices emerge the necessity to accurately locate vulnerabilities and prevent detrimental unwanted users that disrupts regular flow and activities concerning the VNFs and quality of service for IoT applications in unprotected and exposed network domain with surge of traffic and growing demand for privacy-preserving data [11].

The remainder of this chapter has been structured as follows. We describe the literature review of the subject of our interest in Section 14.2. Section 14.3 includes the explanation of creating blockchain-empowered network slices. Blockchain architecture and attacker paradigms are discussed in Section 14.4. Section 14.5 covers the discussion of Hyperledger Fabric inspired prototype and its performance explanation. Finally, Section 14.6 concludes the chapter.

## 14.2 LITERATURE REVIEW

Various literatures investigate the use of different kinds of blockchain employed to improvise the security aspects of service orchestration and network management systems [8, 12–18]. They emphasize the idea of locally verified and digitally signed entities containing blockchain data regarding related network operations. Every historical transaction is verified, approved and recorded with digitally verified encryption techniques. The implementation of blockchain in ad hoc networks has been suggested and proven to be effective for ensuring security for mobile devices in the literature [12, 13]. It has been claimed that even with extra computation costs, blockchain can ensure secured for confidential and ultra-low latency required services. Thuemler et al. address the importance of future telecommunication in telehealth sectors [14, 15]. As there are personalized and private data involved to e-Health industries, communication must be fully secured and authenticated. Blockchain can play a significant role in making privacy-aware IoT health applications and secured telehealth cases specified in these papers through the validation and integrity checking of health data utilizing encryption, hash functions and agreement protocols in the Internet domain.

To maintain confidentiality and validation among Internet companies' different operations, blockchain has been proposed to build a core interface for network management system [14]. The general procedure to design the blockchain architecture for different network models and applications has been discussed in [8]. Moreover, edge cache based blockchain design for IoT devices to reduce the private data traffic to be routed on the public domain has also been encouraged [16]. The harmony among blockchain entities and edge IoT devices can reduce data traversal and extra computational expense with personalized security level. This chapter rather provides a blockchain-based network slicing taxonomy that incorporates and infers all earlier mentioned blockchain applicability in sliced and secured environment.

Other existing literatures study different security concerns emerging in the shared and virtualized network domain models and applications [11, 19]. Most of the studies explain that trust and security among cloud providers are unpredictable. Moreover, they emphasize that jeopardizing a single VNF at the system core threatens the complete end-to-end network function services. Zaowat et al. came up with SECure Application Provenance (SECAP) that is built on blockchain tool for saving and forming an origin tree for cloud infrastructures and applications [17]. The framework shields the phase transitions of all application block entities. An introduction to integrate a blockchain-based policy for effectively promoting the virtual machines' different phases in network orchestrator has been suggested [20]. The main idea is to use local databases inside blockchain entities to store all the operations and service update transactions. In the case of the IoT ecosystem, the quasi-random representation technique emerges to be implemented for maintaining security inside and outside of network slices and evolved node B (eNodeB) [9]. Hence, this proposal basically concerns network slicing security. Khettab et al. recommends employing virtualized service orchestration mechanisms for achieving security by initiating secured software functions (e.g., packet filtering for network protection) [21]. All the mentioned studies, nevertheless, ignore the need to approach for securing the network upon the exposure of service orchestrator itself to various intruders. Furthermore, few studies recommend the blockchain-inspired applications to build on security in intermediary entities of the network.

Findings from an article suggest various benefits of using blockchain architectures in prospective network applications [5]. Overall, many research studies have shown to inspire blockchain tools or architectures for different network settings for integrity and validation [22]. To the best of our knowledge, the blockchain-inspired architecture or tool employed in a sliced network environment for VNF orchestration has not been studied thoroughly yet. The motivation of this study and research endeavors can ensure privacy-preserving data and services in different network arrangements (e.g., medical domain, collaborative computing).

## 14.3 BLOCKCHAIN-POWERED SECURED SLICING

Among various security computing techniques, blockchain can be commonly used for distributed systems that include a record of transactions stored in a replicated data structure. Thus, this can guarantee the security and individual service execution in shared system disregarding centralized supervision. Usually, some cryptographic hash functions perform as algorithm in blockchain technology to achieve the so-called avalanche effect. It generates an enciphered value that indicates an individual block containing information about transactions occurring in a specific timeline and identifier about the preceding block. Figure 14.1 illustrates a typical blockchain structure.

Every node of the blockchain structure has access to the decentralized data blocks containing transaction details from the very beginning. As the most recent time-stamped data is the same for every blockchain member, the authenticity and confidentiality features are ensured

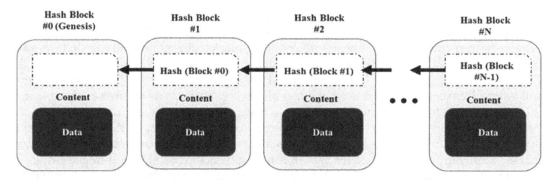

*Figure 14.1* Blockchain structure with linked hash blocks containing data for verification.

since all transactions are digitally verified, validated and acknowledged. Besides, all the nodes apply their public cryptographic key imposed like credentials. In a distributed system context, blockchain can play an important role by eliminating the requirement for a centralized administration that deals with all sensitive network services. The virtual cloud service orchestration in the multiple data centers can be significantly affected upon the occurrences of the following events:

- A single intruder VNF can disrupt the service function leading the whole system to be irregular and unaware of the facts, causes and threats concerning security violation.
- The manipulation in the central register system of service orchestration can forge and deceive the system and its users by different vulnerable means.

Due to verified transactions administered locally by each node, the blockchain mechanism can ensure integrity and nonrepudiation. However, it is needless to say that this process involves significant extra processing for secured VNF orchestration.

Blockchain Attacks: These types of attacks strive to cause a failure for a valid block or transaction when some malicious entities are added as blocks. In such attacks, usually the intruder requires to regulate major share of the environment for falsification of agreement protocols. Policy embedded in the fault-tolerant algorithms can help to mitigate the after-effects of the attack. Attacks that prompt transaction record manipulation and un-authorization are unlikely to occur when every transaction carries its corresponding signed hash.

VNF or Tenant Attack: Impersonation of the target is the main motive of these attacks by obtaining configuration information. If every transaction is signed by the issuer and then appended to the blockchain, the possibilities of personification threats can be reduced by a significant amount. Private information with a highly efficient encryption technique can mitigate attacks that attempt to acquire configuration data, for example, the secret key of the targeted receiver. However, the key hijacking invasion case to compromise a VNF or tenant goes beyond the scope of the attacker model [23] considered in this chapter. The considered architecture in this chapter, however, records the nonexistence of any active listening service in a VNF and manages a terminal device in read-only mode, therefore alleviating attack vectors. Additionally, the architecture supports auditing of every preceding transaction as required. Thus, if an intruder seeks to alter the blockchain applying stolen key combinations, the system will log the attempt. Upon detection of such an event, the tenant can promptly replace the seized key pairs, restoring protection and blocking additional damage.

Network Isolation Attack: The attackers attempt to detach a single VNF entity or multiple entities from the system, hence restricting the network from completing transactions or rendering information from the blockchain. These types of classical attacks can be prevented to some extent by introducing redundant routes among the VNF, tenants and the blockchain. Thus, it becomes difficult for the attacker to target a single entity without being in its neighboring network. It is obvious to say that absolute mitigation of attack in the network is practically impossible. The architecture in this chapter primarily focuses on blockchain and transaction attacks. Anyway, with the ability to eliminate VNF listening services, the model can abolish the denial-of-service (DoS) attack [24] in the application layers. DoS attacks are a frequent threat in shared and distributed cloud settings.

Storage Host Substitution Attack: The malicious entity causes the orchestrator to disregard data storage placement strategies, to expose data storage with exploitable vulnerabilities. In the case of a successful attack, the adversary can derive private and sensitive information from the cached or stored data.

**Resource Parasite Attack:** The attacker convinces the service orchestrator to remodel the infrastructure configuration demanded by some tenants. In case of the successful attempt of the attack, the malicious entity can perform hidden parasite procedures (e.g., cryptocurrency mining) on the infrastructure of the tenant.

**Placement Bias Attack:** The malicious agent causes the orchestrator to neglect placement policies in the distributed federated cloud deployments to favor a deployment target. In case of the successful attempt of the attack, the adversary can raise the utilization and inevitably the profit of a particular infrastructure service provider.

## 14.4 THE BLOCKCHAIN-INSPIRED ARCHITECTURE FOR NETWORK SLICING

Network slicing [9] is a process for dividing network resources for particular applications. This may maintain capacity for specific traffic flows (e.g., in traffic engineering), or it may assist in keeping traffic from various users isolated, as is the situation with virtual routing and forwarding (VRF), including layer three type virtual private networks (L3VPN) [21, 25]. In consideration of the provision for diverse services, network slicing can be a valuable resource administration tool. For example, it can be utilized to assemble a virtual network that can be managed by a service provider's client as though it was a genuine and private network. On the other hand, a network service operator may utilize network slicing for shielding resources and assigning them to the facilitation of a range of applications, services or customers.

Therefore, a network slice might be formed to support the required bandwidth, low latency, security and resiliency for a variety of services or a particular user. This feature has been gaining a lot of attention in the setting of 5G networking and beyond [26]. The slicing technique to ensure isolation is an essential demand that supports enforcing the center notion of network slicing regarding the contemporary coexistence of various slices sharing the identical infrastructure. This feature is obtained by inflicting that an individual slice's performance must not affect the other slice's administration. The advantage of this scheme preference is that it intensifies the network slice structure in two main perspectives [27]:

- **Secured Slice:** Cyber-attacks or blunder phenomena concern only the target slice of the attacker and have a restricted influence on the life-cycle concerning other existing slices.
- **Privacy-Preserving Slice:** Private data associated with each slice (e.g., user or service statistics, orchestration business model) remain protected from being shared among other slices.

Several use cases demand particular functionalities and provoke various blockchain properties for any network slice. Thus, the strategy can be employing a group of blockchains that fit numerous use cases, instead of attempting to provide for various use cases individually. Hence, a simplistic blockchain taxonomy can offer and promote diverse range of slice creations suited for different application communities:

i. **Individual master slice:** The particular kind effectively suits scenarios where complete slice of network is administrated and controlled from an individual endpoint acting as master. In such cases, blockchain tool can mimic simply as a collection of multiple local databases and the full control remains in the hands of a master slice for any kind of

VNF deployment of relocation to happen as transaction. For example, in case of non-public and individualistic settings, such a single master slicing technique is appropriate.

ii. **Crash-resistive fault-tolerant slices:** This mechanism can provide for use cases where single nodes in the system could collapse for various attacks, although the network remains eventually protected from the malicious act. This kind of slicing renders high competence for multi-domain distributed conditions that guarantee network security through contact-dependent plans. Moreover, this is suitable for systems with up to ten administrators. For example, the fitted scenarios can include parallel agreement and communication among Software-Defined Networking (SDN) controllers to execute a service, where several administrators are involved in a decentralized manner. This sort of slice can be powered by confederated and collective blockchains practicing various protocols, such as PAXOS or RAFT [28].

iii. **Byzantine-resistive fault-tolerant slices:** In a byzantine fault, a component such as a network function server orchestrator or VNF node can inconsistently seem both failed and adequately functioning to the failure-detection systems, exhibiting various symptoms to separate observers [29]. It is challenging for the other servers or components to indicate it abandoned and evacuate it out of the system, as they primarily require to reach a consent concerning which component has failed in the first place. This slicing mechanism practices byzantine fault-tolerant (BFT) agreement protocols to shield the network from threats. BFT protocols can ensure relatively high capability for environments with over a few hundred classified nodes. Such settings can involve multi-domain and multi-tenant NFV-enabled conditions that orchestrate and execute end-to-end services. These slicing methods can be managed by the consortium blockchains to guarantee security and robustness against various threats and malicious attacks.

iv. **Entirely distributed non-private slices:** The particular category promotes the massive usage of IoT edge devices by trading off performance and throughput [8]. Such a slicing mechanism relies on proof-based agreement protocols that define the global truth over ultimate consent. Proof-based protocols with network slicing can ensure efficient performance in such a case, as there is no requirement to comprehend with every node in the network, rather just the consensus matters. Hence, this type of slicing can be employed on massive IoT network slices.

Thus, the idea is to employ a blockchain architecture where each kind of blockchain slice covers a wide range of 6G use cases, building detached networks by protection, trust and security. Figure 14.2 portrays an outline utilizing blockchain-driven slices according to domain context: i) wireless cellular, ii) vehicular ad hoc network slice and iii) an Industry 4.0 slice. To secure legitimacy in consensus, each service orchestrator in the data center cannot host multiple blockchain entities inside a single functional network slice. The verified and appended blocks inside a secured segment cannot be seen or tracked by nodes from other slices. Furthermore, the intention is to equip the individual entities for authenticated fabrication along with administration, while storing and registering all the VNF transactions in the blockchain.

The authority of blockchain records orchestration services regarding generation or alternation upon the execution of each VNF transaction inside a particular slice. All the transactions are endorsed and digitally authenticated from service users or hosting devices, who asked for intended VNF operation. Before executing a transaction, all the participating members of a blockchain have to validate every single operation using consensus protocol with an irrefutable signed proof to acknowledge the acceptance of the transaction [30]. The signed and verified request, in combination with the permanent database managed using the blockchain, guarantees that malicious activities are traceable.

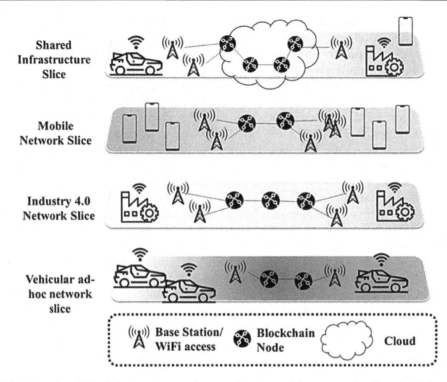

*Figure 14.2* Isolated and blockchain-empowered secured segments/slices over distributed wireless network environment. Every segment gets accustomed according to perspective of network domain applications.

Therefore, the administration blockchain architecture secures creation provenance, liability and determination of vulnerable entities for distributed environment, especially in the IoT context. Smart contacts from blockchain are significant as they ensure conflict-free VNF transactions among all the system intermediaries. The fact that all the members get involved over the software infrastructure, the transaction process does not require manual intervention and is completely authenticated. The communication protocol ensures appropriate transaction practices to be followed by all blockchain members connected among different network slices. Again, service execution process and updates are accessible by all nodes in the network at any time.

Figure 14.3 depicts a blockchain architecture that includes four principal components that are mentioned in the following:

- NFV management and placement segment [31]
- Blockchain computing management segment
- Blockchain building server module
- User interface

Various modules are basically comprised of the Global Manager module [31] in charge of finding and combining appropriate offered services for clients. In the considered design, user interface gathers all up-to-date and related VNF deployment or relocation information to ensure segregation and protection among network slices.

According to the requirements and preferences set by users, the VNFs are rearranged in different sliced chains. An artificial embedded user interface can thoroughly predict and

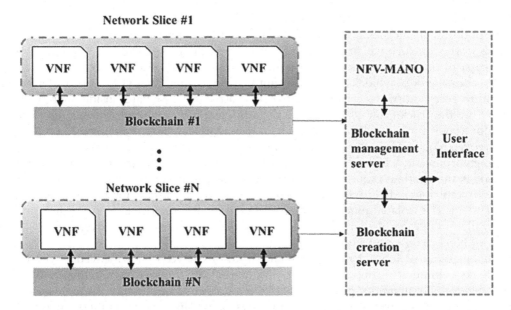

*Figure 14.3* The architectural design of blockchain ensures secured VNF transaction for each slice. User interface provides the abilities to disperse authenticated transaction over entire network domain. Depending upon users' preferences, all the VNFs are mapped into their respective blockchain for deployment and relocation operations completion.

complete the mapping of varying VNF services to various blockchain entities. Upon the validation of VNF operations, the system manager loops through all kinds of already authenticated transactions. Finally, the centralized manager approves and admits the transaction to the system. Upon successfully executing VNF operations, the approval messages are sent to the clients' system interface to preview the detailed logs.

## 14.5 THE HYPERLEDGER FABRIC-DRIVEN PROTOTYPE

Hyperledger Fabric [32] platform is publicly available tool to make software infrastructure for different types of blockchain architecture. Hyperledger Fabric allows building with segments, for example, consensus and agreement services, to be plug-and-play. Its versatile and modular design can provide for a wide range of industry and network-specific use cases. This IBM tool guarantees integrity and security by implementing blockchains in different network domains in segregation. The entire system maintains and manages model that are responsible for the insertion or update of immutable records in the blockchain. Before appending anything to the blockchain, the consensus protocol has to be issued and followed by all the members. This compact tool enables central manager to maintain different VNF operations intended for different slices supporting blockchain-powered abilities in isolation and collectively. For this platform, blockchains can have pluggable agreement protocol support that promotes customization abilities to provide for specific trust models and use cases. Developers can set customizable operation authorizations for building confederated, confidential and isolated IoT slices.

The blockchain tool developed by IBM implements partnership identification of function services by operating identification numbers, verifying participating members into system for facilitating authenticated and transparent environment. Device topological arrangements are very significant fundamental notion concerning blockchain authentication tools. Entities can be of different categories, which are associates or partners, clients and service requestors. Entities in the network which take part in processing the transactions or maintain a replicated copy of the ledger are known as nodes. Consumers propose VNF operation transactions to the neighboring blocks for seeking authentication, and finally, the approval messages are sent to every entity present in the network as a record. Associates inside the blockchain context are the crucial role players, since the administration and performance for verifying and admitting records into central blockchain managing database are registered by them.

Moreover, blockchain associates initiate and manage smart contracts including the overall system environment, which is basically a concise overview of the most recent ledger state. The nodes that initiate requests altogether compose the ordering service are generally in charge of applying and verifying agreement protocols and synthesizing the service management system. The isolated modules enhance effectivity and performance since they support the parallel processing of each stage. These modules also improve concurrent computation power of blockchain architecture.

Different types of blockchain-directed organizations have been portrayed in the Figure 14.4. Every community group considers and validates VNF transaction individually. All functional network communities possess a service request, ensuring legality through agreement and validation rules. Various communication ways, named links or preferably channels, separate the blockchains. The Hyperledger Fabric channel acts as a separate (private) subnetwork for interaction among a subset of distinct network nodes for the cause of supporting confidentiality and secrecy regarding operations.

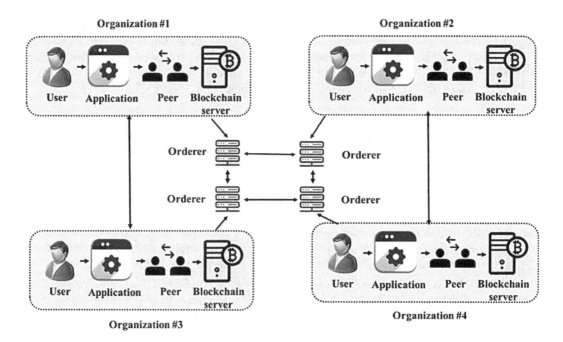

*Figure 14.4* Blockchain architecture consists of different application domains and organizations connected to several blockchain servers. Local organizations forward their request to the centralized manager to validate their suggested VNF transaction and append the block's authenticated request. Upon the successful agreement protocols, the central database registers the transaction information as records.

Every packet transferred through the network, transaction data, association updates and channel-related information, and network parameters remain hidden for all participating block entities. Outcomes of functional services equip the concern for allowing customizable parametric settings for different application domains. Network administrators are in charges of final validation of blockchain entities. Therefore, the utilization of prolonged linked slices of different domains is authenticated with the aid of customization according to the needs and preferences blockchains. Transaction-related setup configuration information is known as chain code in blockchain-development tools. The implementation are dependent on the programming languages Go, Node.js or Java.

Various blockchain architectures have been considered for the administration blockchain to guard the security purposes of a network slice. The blockchain model ensures the privacy of VNF deployment and relocation inside IoT slices while recording configurations settings and information embedded in blocks. Multiapplication based communities manage different blockchain designs by orchestrating service requestor in harmony through simultaneous updates in blockchain records. Prototypical models can employ Kafka consensus protocol available on the Hyperledger Fabric platform to consent to global transaction order [33]. Every individual group of application in charge manages single centrally authorized entity that grants validation and disperses the authorization notification in the entire environment system.

Various organizations are expected to receive dynamic transactions requested from different nodes existing in the system model. Privacy and separation features are usually offered through the communication links of blockchain tools that are channeled through TLS embedded into each transferred packet. A machine configured with Intel Core i7 processor, including 32 GB memory and 3.2 GHz clock, generates simulated collection of network entities that can together act as Docker containers [7]. These Docker [1] containers form various separate application layers by supporting the resource optimization of the interface concerning the intended blockchain. The development and implementation of one from the considered smart contracts can be designed using appropriate programming language (e.g., Go.dev) and executed in all entities of the simulated environment by the machine.

```
1.Struct transactionInstruction
2.{
3.string command
4.string nameOfTransaction
5.string typeOfTransaction
6.string issuer
7.}
8.Initialize a Queue
9.initializeInstruction (instruction < nameOfTransaction, command,
  issuer>)
10.{
11.if (instruction does not follow proper formatting or well-formed or is
   not unique):
12.return error
13.save the state using nameOfTransaction and other instruction
   information
14.put the transaction ID in the Queue
15.notify the service orchestrator
16.return success
17.}
```

Listing 1 Partial pseudocode explaining how the smart contract issues VNF operations. Then, the NFV manager is expected to execute the command for initializing requested transactions. The First In First Out (FIFO) data structure holds all the requests that have been verified but not admitted to the system yet by service orchestration handler.

Firstly, one of the two considered smart contracts, partially represented in Listing 1, automatically supervises VNF administration and orchestration through a set of instructions and responses regarding transactions [7]. As soon as a user proposes transaction request execution, the central system manager admits the request and issues command as a flag notification. Usually, smart contracts are responsible for placing the instruction transaction in a queue that includes all the pending instruction transactions. Then, a success message or packet can be routed through the blockchain issued by the central service orchestrator that initiates the acceptance of queued VNF transactions existing in the central service line of not admitted requests. Finally, the termination indicating packet including corresponding identifier numbers for each VNF deployment or relocation are routed through the network system linking blockchains.

The combined transparency power of each contract represented in Listing 2 is concerned with instantiation of VNF deployment and relocation events [7]. A user yields VNF placement and events in the appropriate IoT or wireless functioning slice. All the event records include detailed textual description concerning related information regarding VNF orchestration and service relocation paths. The considered prototype utilizes Hyperledger Fabric certification authorities (CA) to create and maintain each node's digital records inside network system employing blockchain. Authentication mechanisms guarantee transparency to admit and append already authorized and verified VNFs. These validated transactions can be executed inside blockchain environment leading to identification of unwanted service existence or activities.

```
1.struct transactionConfiguration
2.{
3.string configuration
4.string description
5.string configurationID
6.string versionID
7.string nameOfTransaction
8.string typeOfTransaction
9.string issuer
10.}
11.initializeConfiguration (configuration < description, configuration,
   nameOfTransaction, issuer>)
12.{
13.if (configuration does not follow proper formatting or well-formed or
   is not unique):
14.return error
15.save the state using configuration name and other configuration
   information
16.return success
}
```

Listing 2 Partial pseudocode explaining how the configuration transactions are being issued. The configurationID variable includes an individual unique identifier for each configuration.

The prototype employs all the components of blockchain interface tools in a particular machine and other neighboring ones allowing parallel processing. Performances are justified by recording the processing time service transactions issued from progressively growing users

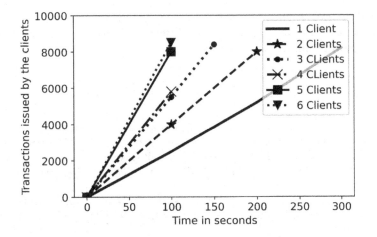

*Figure 14.5* The total running and processing time taken by blockchain manager to operate on the issued transaction with the growing number of users and requests. Findings suggest the incremental differences in timing caused by significant upgrade in the number of clients and transaction requests.

by an increasing rate. The findings on the mentioned performance metric have been mentioned in the Figure 14.5 [7]. The issued VNF request transaction for performance evaluation inside the considered wireless slice approaches as high as around 72 transactions per unit of time considering the user or requestor side. In the considered experiment, one core per client has been deployed, and hence, the parallelization enhances the throughput. The configuration of the block generation on settings was set according to how the former benchmarks performed in Hyperledger Fabric. The selected size of the new block was set to 99 MB, excluding the header. The highest number of transactions was allowed to 10 in a block.

The timeout period was defined as 2 seconds to execute a single round of consensus [7]. In case one of the requirements is satisfied, the requestor initiates newly initiated agreement iteration and conveys unique mechanism for blockchains as a whole. Following the successful agreement protocol achievement, the participant VNFs get attached to the service chain of corresponding model.

## 14.6 CONCLUSION

Isolated network mechanisms can offer customizable applications through generating chains of VNFs among distributed and massive IoT environment exposed to various kinds of vulnerabilities. With a progressively increasing programmable abilities due to the virtualization of network services, the possible number of threats for traffic increases as well. Hence, it becomes essential to determine and locate failures precisely. Moreover, it is essential to identify the malicious entities that can misuse network services. These malicious objects may jeopardize the overall performance rate for a vast number of users. A blockchain-inspired architecture can ensure the security for different personalized mobile and IoT slices. Wide ranging features are expected from different functional slices considering the application domain's environment settings. In this chapter, a proof of concept-based prototypical model has been discussed utilizing multiple designed blockchains promoting privacy-preserving virtual service governance. A blockchain tool, named as Hyperledger fabric, can assist instantiation and management of several secured service chains in various links. In this research aspect, to aid and improve the rate of transactions, throughput and consensus protocols, the research focus should be drawn toward optimizing the data structure. The efficient optimization of data structures can make a significant difference in the virtual network performance using the blockchain technology.

## REFERENCES

1. S. Sun, M. Kadoch, L. Gong, and B. Rong, "Integrating network function virtualization with SDR and SDN for 4G/5G networks," *IEEE Netw.*, vol. 29, no. 3, pp. 54–59, 2015.
2. G. Miotto, M. C. Luizelli, W. L. da Cordeiro, and L. P. Gaspary, "Adaptive placement & chaining of virtual network functions with NFV-PEAR," *J. Internet Serv. Appl.*, vol. 10, no. 1, pp. 1–19, 2019.
3. S. Kim, S. Park, Y. Kim, S. Kim, and K. Lee, "VNF-EQ: Dynamic placement of virtual network functions for energy efficiency and QoS guarantee in NFV," *Cluster Comput.*, vol. 20, no. 3, pp. 2107–2117, 2017.
4. L. Zhang, Y. C. Liang, and D. Niyato, "6G Visions: Mobile ultra-broadband, super internet-of-things, and artificial intelligence," *China Commun.*, vol. 16, no. 8, pp. 1–14, 2019.
5. K. Valtanen, J. Backman, and S. Yrjola, "Creating value through blockchain powered resource configurations: Analysis of 5G network slice brokering case," *2018 IEEE Wirel. Commun. Netw. Conf. Work. WCNCW 2018*, pp. 185–190, 2018.
6. A. Nag, A. Kalla, and M. Liyanage, "Blockchain-over-optical networks: A trusted virtual network function (VNF) management proposition for 5G optical networks," *Opt. InfoBase Conf. Pap.*, vol. Part F138, pp. 2019–2021, 2019.
7. G. A. F. Rebello et al., "Providing a sliced, secure, and isolated software infrastructure of virtual functions through blockchain technology," *IEEE Int. Conf. High Perform. Switch. Routing, HPSR*, vol. 2019-May, pp. 0–5, 2019.
8. R. Rosa and C. E. Rothenberg, "Blockchain-based decentralized applications for multiple administrative domain networking," *IEEE Commun. Stand. Mag.*, vol. 2, no. 3, pp. 29–37, 2018.
9. B. Bordel, A. B. Orue, R. Alcarria, and D. Sanchez-De-Rivera, "An intra-slice security solution for emerging 5G networks based on pseudo-random number generators," *IEEE Access*, vol. 6, pp. 16149–16164, 2018.
10. M. Li et al., "Swiftfabric: Optimizing fabric private data transaction flow TPS," *Proc. – 2019 IEEE Intl Conf Parallel Distrib. Process. with Appl. Big Data Cloud Comput. Sustain. Comput. Commun. Soc. Comput. Networking, ISPA/BDCloud/SustainCom/SocialCom 2019*, pp. 308–315, 2019.
11. N. Paladi, A. Michalas, and H. Van Dang, "Towards secure cloud orchestration for multi-cloud deployments," *CrossCloud 2018 - 5th Work. CrossCloud Infrastructures Platforms, Coloca. with EuroSys 2018*, 2018.
12. Y. Yahiatene and A. Rachedi, "Towards a blockchain and software-defined vehicular networks approaches to secure vehicular social network," *2018 IEEE Conf. Stand. Commun. Networking, CSCN 2018*, 2018.
13. V. Ortega, F. B, and J. F. Monserrat, "Trusted 5G vehicular networks," *IEEE Veh. Technol. Mag.*, vol. 13, no. 2, pp. 2–8, 2018.
14. C. Thuemmler, C. Rolffs, A. Bollmann, G. Hindricks, and W. Buchanan, "Requirements for 5G based telemetric cardiac monitoring," *Int. Conf. Wirel. Mob. Comput. Netw. Commun.*, vol. 2018-Octob, pp. 1–4, 2018.
15. A. Capossele, A. Gaglione, M. Nati, M. Conti, R. Lazzeretti, and P. Missier, "Leveraging blockchain to enable smart-health applications," *IEEE 4th Int. Forum Res. Technol. Soc. Ind. RTSI 2018 – Proc.*, 2018.
16. D. B. Rawat and A. Alshaikhi, "Leveraging distributed blockchain-based scheme for wireless network virtualization with security and QoS constraints," *2018 Int. Conf. Comput. Netw. Commun. ICNC 2018*, pp. 332–336, 2018.
17. S. Zawoad and R. Hasan, "SECAP: Towards securing application provenance in the cloud," *IEEE Int. Conf. Cloud Comput. CLOUD*, pp. 900–903, 2017.

18. I. D. Alvarenga, G. A. F. Rebello, and O. C. M. B. Duarte, "Securing configuration management and migration of virtual network functions using blockchain," *IEEE/IFIP Netw. Oper. Manag. Symp. Cogn. Manag. Cyber World, NOMS 2018*, pp. 1–9, 2018.

19. M. Pattaranantakul, R. He, Q. Song, Z. Zhang, and A. Meddahi, "NFV security survey: From use case driven threat analysis to state-of-the-art countermeasures," *IEEE Commun. Surv. Tutorials*, vol. 20, no. 4, pp. 3330–3368, 2018.

20. N. Bozic, G. Pujolle, and S. Secci, "Securing virtual machine orchestration with blockchains," *2017 1st Cyber Secur. Netw. Conf. CSNet 2017*, vol. 2017-Janua, pp. 1–8, 2017.

21. Y. Khettab, M. Bagaa, D. L. C. Dutra, T. Taleb, and N. Toumi, "Virtual security as a service for 5G verticals," *IEEE Wirel. Commun. Netw. Conf. WCNC*, vol. 2018-April, pp. 1–6, 2018.

22. J. Backman, S. Yrjola, K. Valtanen, and O. Mammela, "Blockchain network slice broker in 5G: Slice leasing in factory of the future use case," *Jt. 13th CTTE 10th C. Conf. Internet Things - Bus. Model. Users, Networks*, vol. 2018-Janua, pp. 1–8, 2017.

23. I. Cervesato, "The Dolev-Yao intruder is the most powerful attacker," *Lics*, vol. 1, pp. 5–6, 2001.

24. R. Wutthikarn and Y. G. Hui, "Prototype of blockchain in dental care service application based on hyperledger composer in hyperledger fabric framework," *2018 22nd Int. Comput. Sci. Eng. Conf. ICSEC 2018*, pp. 2018–2021, 2018.

25. C. Song *et al.*, "Hierarchical edge cloud enabling network slicing for 5G optical fronthaul," *J. Opt. Commun. Netw.*, vol. 11, no. 4, pp. B60–B70, 2019.

26. X. Foukas, G. Patounas, A. Elmokashfi, and M. K. Marina, "Network slicing in 5G: Survey and challenges," *IEEE Commun. Mag.*, vol. 55, no. 5, pp. 94–100, 2017.

27. P. Schneider, C. Mannweiler, and S. Kerboeuf, "Providing strong 5G mobile network slice isolation for highly sensitive third-party services," *IEEE Wirel. Commun. Netw. Conf. WCNC*, vol. 2018-April, pp. 1–6, 2018.

28. P. Massonet, S. Dupont, A. Michot, A. Levin, and M. Villari, "An architecture for securing federated cloud networks with Service Function Chaining," *Proc. – IEEE Symp. Comput. Commun.*, vol. 2016-Augus, pp. 38–43, 2016.

29. L. Zhang, G. Ding, Q. Wu, Y. Zou, Z. Han, and J. Wang, "Byzantine attack and defense in cognitive radio networks: A survey," *IEEE Commun. Surv. Tutorials*, vol. 17, no. 3, pp. 1342–1363, 2015.

30. V. S. Rathina, B. Rebekka, N. Gunavathi, and B. Malarkodi, "Novel NFV entities managing scheme for telecom providers using proof of concept blockchain," *Proc. 2019 TEQIP – III Spons. Int. Conf. Microw. Integr. Circuits, Photonics Wirel. Networks, IMICPW 2019*, pp. 288–292, 2019.

31. G. A. F. Rebello, I. D. Alvarenga, I. J. Sanz, and O. C. M. B. Duarte, "BSec-NFVO: A blockchain-based security for network function virtualization orchestration," *IEEE Int. Conf. Commun.*, vol. 2019-May, 2019.

32. O. Vtxduhv, S. U. Re, D. Frqwuro, O. T. J. Frqwuro, and W. Olqhdu, "# AWV , w " B A + w 6 5WAWV, + , w," no. July, pp. 1–4, 1997.

33. H. Javaid, C. Hu, and G. Brebner, "Optimizing validation phase of hyperledger fabric," *Proc. – IEEE Comput. Soc. Annu. Int. Symp. Model. Anal. Simul. Comput. Telecommun. Syst. MASCOTS*, vol. 2019-Octob, pp. 269–275, 2019.

Chapter 15

# Usage of Blockchain for Edge Computing

*A B M Mehedi Hasan and Md Shamsur Rahim*
Australian Institute of Higher Education, Australia

*Sabbir Ahmed*
University of South Australia, Australia

*Dr Andrew Levula*
Sydney International School of Technology and Commerce, Australia

## CONTENTS

## 15.1 INTRODUCTION

The rapid technological advancements in the period of IoT and cloud framework-based applications has led to the introduction of edge computing, which is an extension of cloud computing at the peripheral of the network. In the ICT sector, edge computing is synonymous with other names such as virtual computing, mobile computing or fog computing. Edge computing connects billions of endpoint devices in the network to aid cloud computation. Since the computation and data storage is closer to the source of where it is needed, the applications get faster responses from the edge level server and access to the cloud server. This distributed architecture of edge computing has brought numerous benefits such as speed, scalability and versatility at the edge of the system. However, it raises questions about preserving security and privacy of data that is being transmitted at the edge and the security of the edge devices.

Blockchain is an emerging technology that has often been associated with the world of digital cryptocurrency technology. However, Blockchain is a growing list of records known as blocks that are linked using cryptography. The decentralized approach, while maintaining the distributed ledger, includes validation and synchronization performed by different users which can be located at various locations across the world as long as they have Internet access. Blockchain is a technology that transfers centralized processing to decentralized processing, whereby information can be shared based on consensus. In this decentralized paradigm, Blockchain technology ensures transparency, confidentiality, security and immutability. Since Blockchain technology can address the security and privacy gaps that are prevalent with edge computing, it becomes a naturalistic approach to incorporate Blockchain with edge computing technologies in a system. Computation of the countless numbers of edge servers, controlling the whole network and providing trustworthy retrieval of information is feasible for a system that is integrated with Blockchain.

Moreover, it can strengthen the total system network security and improve the data manipulation and validation process. Since edge nodes have limited power resources, they would also have the energy provisions needed for storing and executing computation. Additionally, the edge network, which includes the distributed processing would generate scalable processes through Blockchain.

Edge computing integrated with Blockchain offers vast opportunities to overcome the limitations of both technologies. Few studies have been conducted until now on integrating Blockchain in edge computing [1–4]. These studies have proposed different architectures and/or frameworks for integrating Blockchain in edge computing. One of the primary goals of this chapter is to inform researchers and practitioners on recent trends of this topic. A summary of selected research on this topic has been presented in this chapter. Also, several requirements need to be fulfilled before one can meaningfully integrate Blockchain with edge computing such as authentication, adaptability, network security, data integrity and low latency. This chapter will also cover their requirements and critical challenges of integrating Blockchain and edge computing systems such as security, scalability, consensus optimization, resource management and intrusion detection. This will be followed by future research directions which will introduce emerging topics on Blockchain and edge computing.

The residual of the chapter is sorted as follows. The applications and benefits of edge computing are described in Section 15.2. Section 15.3 provides an overview of the issues due to implementing edge computing. Section 15.4 addresses how Blockchain can deal with the issues in edge computing, the challenges and existing approaches associated with Blockchain and edge computing. This section also addresses the details about requirements to integrate Blockchain in edge computing and finally proposes the frameworks. The future research directions and the challenges are covered by Section 15.5. Section 15.6 concludes the chapter and provides an overview of the chapter.

## 15.2 APPLICATIONS AND BENEFITS OF EDGE COMPUTING

### 15.2.1 Identify the Benefits of Using Edge Computing from Different Perspectives

When studying edge computing and its applications, one cannot do so without understanding the opportunities and challenges that it presents to the issue of having centralized ICT solutions. A significant number of studies have highlighted motivations, benefits and challenges of edge computing [5–9]. Figure 15.1 demonstrates the motivations in edge computing which can be rendered as potential benefits of edge computing [5]:

Edge computing is critical for the Internet of Things (IoT) because of the added benefits that it can present to an IoT appliance. The IoT is defined as a system characterized by many interconnected objects that contain unique addressing scheme and sensors that are

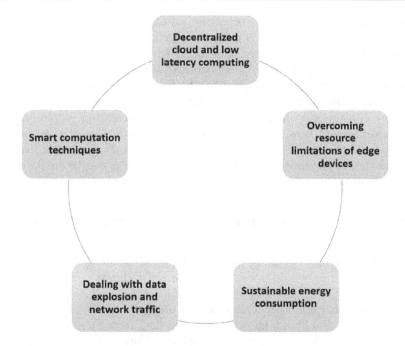

*Figure 15.1* Motivations in edge computing extracted from Varghese et al. [5].

dynamically linked over a distributed network [6]. Edge devices that are dependent on the IoT include Amazon Alexa, Google Home, Google Assistant and all connected home appliances and devices. On the one hand, competitors might be racing for a low-latency processed data delivery system. On the other hand, consumers are expecting quick responses to their queries through their devices. Cloud-dependent services are challenged when it comes to low-latency computing. At this point, edge computing brings light to the problem of low-latency computing. Computing at the edge nodes is expected to be helpful to decrease dependency on the centralized cloud computing servers. There is a significant advantage of using edge nodes nearest to the edge devices to overcome network delays [5].

Edge devices can capture data from different sources. Data that are transmitted over the Internet to cloud computing servers for analyzing and analyzed outcome are transmitted back to the edge devices. In this type of condition, edge devices may experience high latency. Hardware and middleware limitations in edge devices may lead to failure while performing analytics which is complex in nature [7]. However, edge computing could be a beneficial solution to overcome resource limitations of edge devices, if a small proportion of data can be analyzed at edge nodes. Edge nodes can be used as unoccupied computational resources for analyzing or filtering data [5].

The benefits of edge computing also encompass a potential reduction of energy consumption at data centers and reduce the processing load of data centers. Energy consumption by data centers is projected to become three times greater than what is consumed nowadays [8], and energy-efficient approaches are profoundly required to diminish the consumption of energy [9]. Edge nodes within the edge networks can take a possible number of loads offloaded by cloud-based data centers according to capacity. According to Varghese et al. [5], consolidation of power management policy can be helpful to mitigate the challenge of energy consumption when edge nodes next to data sources can be used to handle some of the analytical tasks. Additionally, this may help reduce overloading problems of data centers.

It is obvious that edge devices are increasing rapidly. From mobile phones to wearable devices, a significant amount of data is being collected, which is increasing over time exponentially. Edge computing can be beneficial against increasing amount of data generated every day by a growing number of edge devices. An enormous amount of data which different devices generally generate is required to be handled in this world of interconnected networks. This situation triggers a need for data center expansion and raises a concern of increased energy consumption. Additionally, there is an increasing volume of traffic being forwarded to cloud-based servers which is another concern. Use of edge nodes could be potentially beneficial to reduce loads of cloud-based servers. Probable use of edge nodes to support some parts of computations of devices or data centers can be an advantage to cope with the surge of data and network traffic [5].

## 15.2.2 Identify the Applications of Edge Computing in Different Fields

Researchers show different types of applications of edge computing. According to the following studies, edge computing would open the door of possibilities:

A. Artificial Intelligence and Face Recognition Systems
   There are concerns of high-latency issues when data from face recognition systems are transmitted to the cloud for analyses purposes. A study was conducted by Zeng, Li et al. [10] where a face recognition system was developed to study the capabilities of Artificial Intelligence (AI) when applied to edge devices. A complete system had been built to prove the effectiveness of the proposed framework using the cloud server, rk3288 development platform and webcam [11].

B. Gaming
   Numerous computer or mobile phone users are playing video games, especially users with smart devices. Google has kept its promise to support gamers by launching Google Stadia in 2019, and now it is available in many countries. Although it has been reviewed as a technical and conceptual disaster, this is just a start. Google is rendering video games in their cloud servers and streaming videos to any devices at the user end. There is a major challenge for Google to overcome high-latency and bandwidth issues. Zhang, Chen et al. [12], proposed a framework to improve cloud gaming with the help of edge resources. Rendering part of edge games which requires demanding computation resources can be offloaded to edge devices helping to alleviate latency and consumption of bandwidth [12].

C. Healthcare
   Healthcare industry generates a large volume of data, especially emergency departments. Healthcare systems can be combined with edge computing technologies to increase their efficiency. A smart healthcare framework based on edge computing is proposed by Oueida et al. (2018). According to them, hospital emergencies deal with real-time systems which have complicated and dynamic structure, and the proposed framework offers the application of different key performance indicators optimized for a particular user group [13] (Figure 15.2).

   According to the framework stated above, all databases and healthcare-related software are deployed on the cloud where data is closer to the workflow of Smart HealthCare. Smart devices used in healthcare are edge devices. When assigned tasks are complete, a status notification containing the availability of resources in the pool is sent to the cloud servers with the help of edge nodes [13].

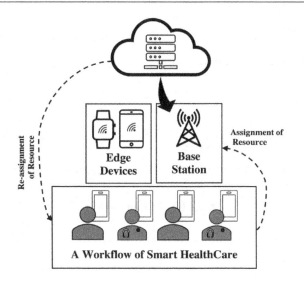

*Figure 15.2* A smart healthcare framework based on edge computing.

D. Oil and Gas Industry

Oil and gas industry is expanding due to high demand for petroleum. Petroleum extraction plants use different types of sensors for extraction operations. According to Hussain, Salehi et al. [14], sensors for measuring pipeline pressure, gas leakage, air pollution and many more are used in extraction sites, and data is sent to the cloud servers for processing and high-latency satellite communications are used. All the latency-prone tasks or processes can be potentially handled with the help of edge computing [14].

E. Manufacturing

In smart manufacturing plants, different types of tools, robots, machines, computers and devices relate to sensors to measure pressure, humidity and heat. In smart manufacturing, data is processed on the cloud servers, and factors like high latency, bandwidth issue and Internet unavailability affect the manufacturing process. Edge computing can be beneficial to reduce the issues stated above (Figure 15.3).

According to Qi and Tao [15], edge computing responds to the issues mentioned above. The capacity of data computation, networking and data storing are extended by edge computing. Therefore, edge computing can be beneficial to manufacturing processes.

## 15.3 ISSUES IN EDGE COMPUTING

### 15.3.1 Issues in Security and Privacy

Cloud data center tasks are offloaded through edge computing with its own storage and evaluation in the edge network. Hence, performing the computation in edge network-level mainly raises the concern of providing data security and privacy. Information privacy and security have turned into fundamental prerequisites to ensure that clients in e-commerce businesses, financial and operational data are not compromised. This is a pressing issue with edge computing, and it provides an opportunity where Blockchain can play an integral part in addressing this limitation in edge computing. Additionally, when addressing privacy and security related to edge computing strategies need to be put in place for each tier of the

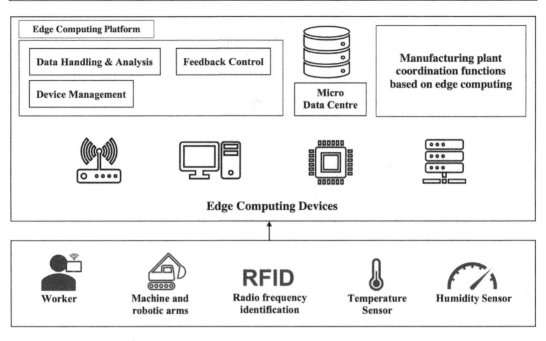

*Figure 15.3* Edge computing-based manufacturing interaction and control.

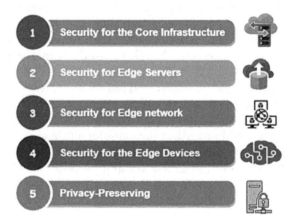

*Figure 15.4* Issues in security and privacy with edge computation.

edge processing frameworks. In the subsection that follows, embryonic privacy and security challenges dependent on the different tier engineering of edge computing will be covered. Figure 15.4 demonstrates the issues related to privacy and security in terms of edge computing.

A. Security for the core Infrastructure

The core infrastructure of cloud storage and administration supports the edge paradigm. Different cloud service providers may be included inside of the core infrastructure to support the different edge layers. The core architecture will be supported by suppliers or any other provider (e.g. mobile network operators). Hence, privacy leakage, information altering, denial of service (DoS) attacks and administration control types of severe difficulties would arise due to semi-trusted or unsecured infrastructure.

Edge devices will transmit different information in the main cloud storage through the edge data centers. The data that is transmitted would contain personal and confidential user information generated from different endpoint edge devices. Intruders might be able to tamper with the data or bypass the data processing while the edge data center is communicating with the core architecture. This highlights the issues of privacy leakages and information altering that exists with edge computing.

Additionally, a malignant virtual machine can attempt to drain the assets where it is executing, and for this reason, it can also hamper computational processing, network stability and storage assets. According to Zhang, Chen et al. [16], there is a severe threat as most edge data servers will not have the information which can be accessed by other cloud frameworks. Inside of the distributed and decentralized architecture, a hijacked or jammed core infrastructure network can provide or exchange false information due to insufficient service privileges [16]. This prevents unauthorized access to sensitive data. Figure 15.5 enlisted the categorization of privacy and security challenges in an edge computing architecture.

B. Security for Edge Servers

Different virtualized services and management of services are executed through edge servers. Like the multi-cloud server scenario, the edge server performs its activities in a specific geographical location. Considering the case, here, both external and internal parties can access or alter the private data which are processed by the server. Accessing sensitive data or false data injection attacks may happen due to a lack of privacy within the system. Consequently, the server activities can be manipulated by intruders if it has breakable access privileges. The full access can make the edge data server a rogue data center as in extreme cases; it will control the whole infrastructure. Another threat includes a physical attack of the actual edge data center. Even though the edge servers require a specific data center storage location, to be identified, however, these, servers

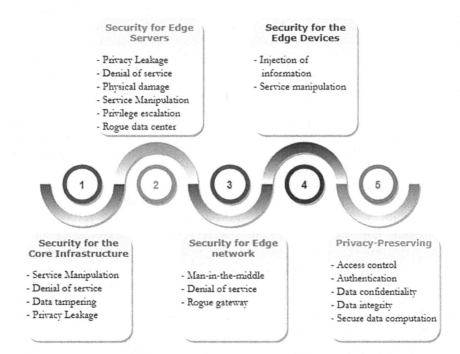

*Figure 15.5* Categorization of privacy and security challenges in an edge computing architecture.

may be physically damaged and/or stolen [17]. It is worth noting that attacks are restricted to certain locations because of the decentralized nature of edge computing.

C. Security for Edge network

According to the paradigm of edge computing, it will reduce the possibilities of severe attacks in the network, such as the distributed denial of service (DDoS) and DoS attacks. Malicious activities may hamper the network through attacks like eavesdropping and traffic injection. There are also high chances of a man-in-the-middle attack where a hacker can hijack the streaming information of the network. Malicious activities may be launched through the rogue gateway, which can have a similar effect to that of a man-in-the-middle on the whole infrastructure [16]. In such cases, the network infrastructure is compromised, and hackers can easily gain access to sensitive information that is transmitted over the network.

D. Security for the Edge Devices

With IoT, devices are interconnected with each other over multiple communication networks such as wireless networks, Internet and mobile core networks. In edge computing architecture, there are numerous IoT-related gadgets at each compositional layer. These devices are inclined to actively interact with each other at the edge ecosystem, and these could be constrained by a central malignant framework. The attack brought about by malware comes in numerous shapes and types. Malware can capture data and sensitive information from smart devices such as debit and credit card user information. Further, malware can obstruct the elements of physical savvy hardware which can have a severe impact [18].

E. Privacy-Preserving

The multi-layered architecture of the edge computing framework creates the possibilities of cybersecurity and privacy issues. Such issues can be adequately addressed using state-of-the-art systems for access control that would use sophisticated algorithms and cryptography at the edge of the network to restrict unauthorized user access. The traditional access control system will not be compatible with these more dynamic and agile environments of the edge paradigm. The aforementioned different malicious activities can be controlled through a sophisticated access control system.

Edge computing paradigm includes services, for instance, data storage, virtual machine, and the total infrastructure encapsulates edge devices, edge data center, and core infrastructure. Multiple functional roles are executed by end-users, service providers and infrastructure providers in the edge architecture [16]. In the complex situation of the edge environment, it is not only about assigning every component in one trust area but also about the need to let the elements commonly confirm each other among various trust areas. Thinking about the high versatility of the edge gadgets, the handover confirmation innovation is likewise a significant examination point in the validation convention. Secure lightweight multi-factor authentication protocols are a more realistic solution for edge framework to preserve privacy [19, 20].

Additionally, an enormous security transformation is occurring because IoT devices are normally not providing built-in security mechanisms. This gives intruders easy access to the system. Because getting remote access to the edge layer much of the time breaks confidentiality. One of the significant issues is data integrity for the security of the edge network. As the client information is transmitted to the servers of the edge network, the information trustworthiness could be undermined executing this procedure. In the data transmission procedure, the owner should check the integrity and accessibility of the information to ensure that there are no undetected alterations of information by any unapproved user. The protected information search is the preferred test which implies the client needs to tackle the issue of the keyword search over the encrypted information records [20–22].

## 15.3.2 Issues in Decentralized Architecture

In decentralized conditions, where any client can turn into a supplier and assets might be heterogeneous, contrasting equipment and network execution is essential. The optimal test for decentralized cloud arrangements is confirmation of the calculation, which is expected to keep away from malevolent activities by suppliers and customers. End-user information can be overseen by decentralized cloud systems. It is essential that solutions to resolve information security are thoroughly considered, and that necessary actions are taken to mitigate such hazards. In this case, probably the verification process is a vital challenge for decentralized edge computing with the cloud server. The targeted approach to resolve this issue would be to restrict the different malicious activities performed by customers and service providers [23, 24].

In a distributed architecture the network has heavy traffic congestion as endpoint devices transmitting data to the cloud server. Consider the performance of a system; it might be affected by the remoteness of the communication between the endpoint devices with the main server. Moreover, the volume of data being transferred between different applications such as live audio streaming, video streaming or e-commerce would be dependent on the location of the main cloud server. With the use of edge servers, edge computing can decrease the transmission latency by sieving and managing the data. This ensures that less bandwidth is used, and it improves the energy efficiency of the system. Hence, when applied to smart applications, data processing would be faster and more efficient through edge computing in a decentralized framework [25].

## 15.4 INTEGRATING BLOCKCHAIN IN EDGE COMPUTING: THE MISSING PIECE OF THE PUZZLE?

### 15.4.1 Blockchain: Beyond Cryptocurrency

Blockchain is a rapidly emerging technology that involves a distributed chain of blocks or transactions that provides publicly available immutable records for the participants (e.g. human, device) [26]. In the Blockchain, the existing records cannot be modified or erased as each block is connected using a cryptographic hash of another block, along with a timestamp and transaction data. New blocks are appended only at the end. Therefore, Blockchain is also known as the immutable data storehouse [22]. Though the history of the application of Blockchain starts with cryptocurrency (e.g. bitcoin), nowadays it is not limited in cryptocurrency but applicable across different industry and sectors within the economy and society as a whole. Due to the benefits of Blockchain technology, it has become a widely used technology in many sectors, especially in the smart grid and IoT [27]. Figure 15.6 illustrates the key application areas of Blockchain.

### 15.4.2 Advantages of Blockchain

There are several reasons behind the wide adaptation of Blockchain technology in different fields. Blockchain technology has the ability to ensure integrity, transparency, high security, simplicity, faster processing power and above all, decentralization.

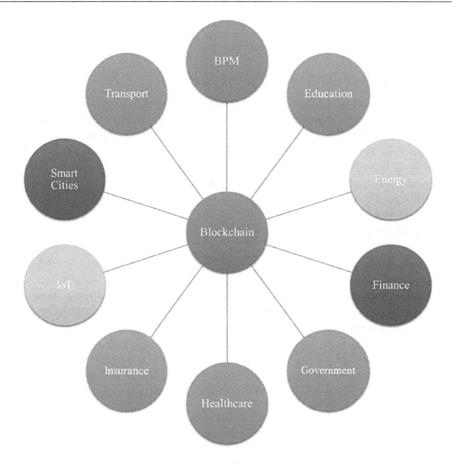

*Figure 15.6* Key application areas of Blockchain.

A. Decentralization

The main advantage of Blockchain technology is its decentralized architecture. Instead of storing valuable data at a central location, Blockchain technology stores data across its peer-to-peer network, and it reduces the risk of storing data at a central location by eliminating numerous threats. In this decentralized environment, it is more difficult for intruders or hackers to infiltrate any vulnerabilities in the network.

B. Process Integrity and Transparency

Process integrity and transparency are two of the advantages of Blockchain technology. The technology is designed in such a way so that each record or transaction is added to the Blockchain and the data of these entries are available to the participants who were involved in the transaction. Once these transactions or blocks are added to the chains, then it cannot be modified, which results in a high level of process integrity in Blockchain compared with other approaches [28–30]. Additionally, transparency is attained by copying the transactions to all the computers connected to the Blockchain network. Hence, the participant can access all the public transactions, which cannot be modified [31].

C. Security

Ensuring better security is another great advantage of Blockchain. When a user enters the Blockchain network, the user is given a unique identity that is linked to his/her account. This identity ensures that the transaction is performed by the owner of that account. In addition, the use of a cryptographic hash enhances the security of this technology further where the cryptographic hash of the previous block is held by the newly created block that leads to creating the chain. This hash is created automatically that consists of a type, ID number of the block, time of creation, previous hash's value, miner's level and Merkle root [30]. This enables higher security levels to be maintained in Blockchain. Furthermore, the combination of the Blockchain hashing process and cryptography leads to immutability that can be defined as the ability of a Blockchain ledger to remain unchanged.

D. Simplification

Blockchain offers a simplified ecosystem of transaction over the existing multiple ledger system. In the existing system, multiple ledgers result in disorder and difficulties to the parties involved with the system. By offering a single public ledge to store all the transactions, Blockchain is a simplification of the ecosystem [30].

E. Faster Processing

Another advantage of Blockchain is increased speed in processing. In a conventional approach, a transaction would take up to 3 days in processing and authorization. However, using the Blockchain technology, it takes a few minutes as Blockchain helps to reduce time through secured digital signature [30].

F. Privacy

The risk of a data breach has increased with the wide adaptation of technology in recent years. Such data breaches pose a threat to violate the privacy of the customers/ users as these data may contain delicate private data such as the name of a person, identification number, banking details and their residential or work address. Traditionally, a provider such as a bank or a hospital would be responsible for creating the data and storing it in their corporate database. However, this creates several security and privacy concerns that require immediate attention [32]. Blockchain technology has the ability to address these problems to ensure high security and privacy due to its decentralized structure which ensures that sensitive information can be better protected [32, 33].

## 15.4.3 How Blockchain Will Complement Edge Computing

Based on earlier discussions, the main challenges of edge computing are distributed control, ensuring security and preserving privacy. This highlights a clear gap in current edge computing approaches and the need for a more secure form of a transaction at the edge of the network. This is where Blockchain technology can be advantages because of its decentralized nature and its ability to ensure security and privacy preservation. Delivering cloud resources and services at the edge of the network is the main motivation behind edge computing. However, there are many limitations that need careful considerations to ensure that the costs do not outweigh the benefits [4]. Yang and et al. [4] observed that integrating Blockchain with edge computing would allow distributed control over numerous edge nodes. Moreover, Blockchain technology can maintain the accuracy, consistency and data validation on a large number of nodes throughout their life cycle [4, 34]. It also ensures privacy by storing data locally or among multiple parties as small fragments which reduces the risk of disclosing large amounts of information due to the coordination of information via its ledge system. This challenge can be overcome with the help of Blockchain technology as it offers complete privacy through manageable keys to each user for accessing and controlling data and coordination without revealing any metadata to the peers on the network. It is highly likely to maintain privacy by integrating Blockchain technology with edge computing. Figure 15.7 portrays the advantages of Blockchain technology and disadvantages of edge computing.

| Blockchain | Edge Computing |
| --- | --- |
| Decentralisation | Distributed control |
| Assured Security | Security Concerns |
| Assured Data Privacy | Privacy Concerns |

*Figure 15.7* Advantages of Blockchain and disadvantages of edge computing.

## 15.4.4 How Blockchain Can be Integrated with Edge Computing

Integrating Blockchain with edge computing has several benefits. Several architectures or frameworks are proposed in the existing studies. However, before integrating Blockchain with edge computing, there are some requirements that need to be fulfilled. In this section, these requirements are discussed followed by the summary of the concepts, frameworks and challenges covered in this section.

### 15.4.4.1 Requirements: Integrated Blockchain and Edge Computing

Several studies have highlighted the requirements needed to ensure that Blockchain can be integrated with edge computing [4, 35–38]. The concepts identified in these studies will be further discussed in this section.

i. Authentication: The authentication of several entities such as service providers, infrastructures and services in the edge computing environments is necessary to establish and maintain secure communication channels. While these entities are signing smart contracts after reaching an agreement, Blockchain records the privileges and requirements of these entities at the contract establishing stage.

ii. Adaptability: The number of edge devices and the complexity of the services are increasing overtime where the resources are limited to the devices. Therefore, the integrated system of edge computing and Blockchain should be flexible enough to adapt so that it can support the changing number of users and the complexity of the tasks. Furthermore, the system should have the competence where objects or nodes can join or disconnect to the network freely.

iii. Network security: The integrated system should be able to offer a secured network by replacing the heavy key management in several communication protocols. In addition, for the immense-scale distributed edge servers, the system should deliver easy access for maintenance and facilitates easier monitoring to prevent malicious attachments.

iv. Data integrity: Maintaining and assuring the accuracy of the data is a pivotal process, and it is known as data integrity. In such integrated decentralized system, a reliable data integrity verification process is mandatory to ensure that data integrity violations do not happen.

v. Low latency: In general, there can be two types of latency of a system: computational latency and transmission latency. Computational latency means the amount of time required in data processing and mining. The computational latency largely depends on the computational power of the devices, and this latency decreases from edge nodes to cloud servers as cloud servers are more powerful than edge nodes. However, moving toward the cloud also causes significant transmission latency. Therefore, the integrated system should have the ability to map what computation will be performed to minimize issues associated with latency.

### 15.4.4.2 Overview on Existing Frameworks

A limited number of studies have been conducted that cover the emerging topic of integrated systems of Blockchain and edge computing. This section provides a brief description of some of the notable approaches. A distributed cloud architecture based on Blockchain and edge computing is facilitated by a software-defined network (SDN) [1]. This architecture can be categorized into three layers: device layer, fog layer and cloud layer. The device layer performs the transmission of the filtered data to the fog layer after collecting the raw data. The SDN-enabled fog layer performs data analytics in real-time and delivers services to the local devices in a group. In this proposed approach, Blockchain technology was integrated to connect the SDN controllers in a distributed way. A fog node informs the distributed cloud regarding the processed data. When necessary, the device layers can access the cloud to enable application services, and when computing resources are insufficient, the device layer transfers computational tasks to the cloud. This architecture has proposed a consensus protocol Proof-of-Stake (PoS) that uses the 2-hop mechanism for integrating PoS and Proof-of-Work (PoW) methods. This integration allows to approve contributions in performance of computing, transferring and storing data within Blockchain.

Another study highlighted a multi-layered IoT-enabled Blockchain network [2]. The model was split into two parts: the edge layer and high-level layer. The edge layer consists of a certain number of objects in a local area network. Moreover, it also ensures that all the objects are managed by a central node. In contrast, the high-level layer appears as a combination of fog nodes and aggregation nodes that are similar to each other [1].

In addition, a decentralized IoT based on the Blockchain is known as an Autonomous Decentralized Peer-to-Peer Telemetry (ADEPT) which was jointly developed by IBM and Samsung Electronics [3, 39]. This proposed approach provides greater autonomy to the devices and makes a point of transactions in Blockchain by shifting the power from the center to the edges of the network. In the Alpha version of this approach, Ethereum protocol was chosen with three peers: light peers, standard peers and peer exchange. Messaging, preserving a light wallet that consists of Blockchain addresses and balances are performed by light peers with minimal sharing of files. On the other hand, standard peers are responsible for maintaining a section of the Blockchain and supporting the light peers. The peer exchanges act as possible repositories for copying the complete Blockchain and delivering analytic services.

Yang, Yu et al. [4] highlighted the integrated frameworks of edge computing and Blockchain as three general level structures: A) Private Blockchain-based local network, B) Blockchain-based P2P network of edge servers and C) Blockchain-based distributed cloud. The private Blockchain-based local network consists of End nodes (devices) and End servers (Fog) where the devices communicate to the central server. Expensive consensus mechanisms and economic incentives are not required in the local network because of the controllable access and clear identity. In the case of Blockchain-based P2P network of edge servers, they have the capabilities to communicate with each other in order to replicate data, sharing data, computing coordinately, etc. Finally, the Blockchain-based distributed cloud provides vast computation and storage capabilities.

Based on the previous studies, we summarize that research on integrating Blockchain in edge computing is quite new and broad. There are many challenges that need to be addressed for successful integrated Blockchain and edge computing systems. In the next section, we have discussed some of these key challenges and provided future research directions.

## 15.5 CHALLENGES AND FUTURE SCOPE FOR INCORPORATING BLOCKCHAIN TO EDGE COMPUTING

Though the integration of Blockchain and edge computing provides valuable prospects, however, there exist some research challenges that need to be addressed. This section briefly outlines some of the challenges of trying to integrate Blockchain with edge computing.

A. Security

Though Blockchain can improve the security of edge computing, yet, Blockchain has some security issues in that it is exposed to several attacks like DoS attack, Sybil attack and man-in-the-middle attack.

Another important challenge is protecting the data in devices and servers. Due to the limited resources in these devices, it is difficult to install improved security cryptographic software. Other security challenges include ensuring security in communication and protecting the privacy of devices [40]. These factors need to be examined further in future studies.

B. Scalability

Scalability is another challenge for integrated systems of Blockchain and edge computing. Blockchain suffers from scalability issues such as low throughput, higher latency and resource-hungry systems [4]. In edge computing, it becomes a major challenge, as the IoT devices offer minimum storage and processing power.

Even though it is possible to transfer the transactions and data generated by the edge devices to servers, the increased number of devices provide the much-needed platform to conduct a large volume of transactions between participants. This is why the scalability of the IoT networks is restricted as it is challenging to increase the effectiveness of the network [40]. Future studies will need to investigate these points in future to determine approaches that would enhance the scalability of the network within the existing edge computing ecosystem.

C. Consensus Optimization

In the existing consensus mechanisms, to complete the mining, the verifications of most of the participating nodes are required. However, this leads to higher network latency. In addition, light servers with limited resources are missing the current consensus techniques like PoS and PoW. These lead to be further studied to identify new consensus mechanisms that would be able to improve the latency in the network.

D. Resource Management

Resource management is another challenge for integrated edge computing and Blockchain systems. Alone in the edge computing, there are several challenges in resource management such as: adapting to dynamic environments, optimizing the larger collaborations of edge servers. In integrated systems, these issues are significant and hence further studies are required to determine workable solutions.

E. Intrusion Detection:

To protect a system from cyber-attacks intrusion detection system embedded with other security systems are mandatory. The intrusion detection system works through different encryption techniques that are focused on access control and user authentication.

Data mining and machine learning mechanisms can be applied in this context because they can be used to detect unusual and abnormal activities in a system. The challenge that is presented here is to determine which machine learning technique would be appropriate among the different types, such as supervised or unsupervised or reinforcement learning.

## 15.6 CONCLUSION

This chapter addresses a gap in the literature on understanding how two emerging technologies can be integrated together to strengthen their applications. After considering the cloud administrations and data transmissions from IoT, edge computing network is used to processes information at the edge of a network through edge servers. The target of edge processing is to ensure the low cost and fast processing of distributed frameworks. Edge computing also enhances the cloud server performance rather than making it slow and overloaded as the requests are processed at the edge level. However, challenges associated with privacy and security, scalability and intrusion detection issues are associated with the edge computing paradigm. Moreover, different approaches and techniques are proposed and applied to ensure the smooth manipulation of activities performed in edge architecture.

Blockchain is a rapidly emerging technology. It is a technology that is having widespread influence across all sectors because it has a distributed architecture and ensures that a system is not easily compromised. The decentralized architecture of edge computing is suffering from major issues such as privacy and security. These can be minimized by the integration of Blockchain and edge computing which are technologies that would continue to grow as their applications continue to increase.

In conclusion, this proposes a framework for understanding the link between Blockchain and edge computing and how these technologies can be integrated together to offer a solution that addresses the existing limitations with edge computing. Moreover, when addressing the integration of Blockchain with edge computing, it is important to take note of requirements such as authentication, adaptation, network security and data integrity that need to be met to ensure the integrity of the data and that the systems are not compromised. This chapter also discussed the key challenges and future research directions of integrated Blockchain and edge computing systems which include, but are not limited to, security, scalability, consensus optimization, resource management and intrusion detection.

## REFERENCES

1. P. K. Sharma, M.-Y. Chen, and J. H. Park, "A software defined fog node based distributed blockchain cloud architecture for IoT," *IEEE Access*, vol. 6, pp. 115–124, 2017.
2. C. Li and L.-J. Zhang, "A blockchain based new secure multi-layer network model for Internet of Things," in *2017 IEEE International Congress on Internet of Things (ICIOT)*, 2017, pp. 33–41: IEEE.
3. S. Panikkar, S. Nair, P. Brody, and V. Pureswaran, "Adept: An iot practitioner perspective," *Draft Copy for Advance Review, IBM*, 2015.
4. R. Yang, F. R. Yu, P. Si, Z. Yang, and Y. Zhang, "Integrated blockchain and edge computing systems: A survey, some research issues and challenges," *IEEE Communications Surveys & Tutorials*, vol. 21, no. 2, pp. 1508–1532, 2019.
5. B. Varghese, N. Wang, S. Barbhuiya, P. Kilpatrick, and D. S. Nikolopoulos, "Challenges and opportunities in edge computing," in *2016 IEEE International Conference on Smart Cloud (SmartCloud)*, 2016, pp. 20–26: IEEE.
6. D. Miorandi, S. Sicari, F. De Pellegrini, and I. Chlamtac, "Internet of things: Vision, applications and research challenges," *Ad HOC Networks*, vol. 10, no. 7, pp. 1497–1516, 2012.
7. D. Damopoulos, G. Kambourakis, and G. Portokalidis, "The best of both worlds: A framework for the synergistic operation of host and cloud anomaly-based IDS for smartphones," in *Proceedings of the seventh European workshop on system security*, 2014, pp. 1–6.
8. T. Bawden, "Global warming: Data centres to consume three times as much energy in next decade, experts warn," *The Independent*, vol. 23, 2016.

9. P. Thibodeau, "Data centers are the new polluters," *Computer World*, 2014.

10. J. Zeng, C. Li, and L.-J. Zhang, "*A face recognition system based on cloud computing and AI edge for IOT*," in *International Conference on Edge Computing*, 2018, pp. 91–98: Springer.

11. A. H. Shehab and S. Al-Janabi, "Edge computing: Review and future directions (Computación de Borde: Revisión y Direcciones Futuras)," *REVISTA AUS Journal*, no. 26–2, pp. 368–380, 2019.

12. X. Zhang et al., "Improving cloud gaming experience through mobile edge computing," *IEEE Wireless Communications*, vol. 26, no. 4, pp. 178–183, 2019.

13. S. Oueida, Y. Kotb, M. Aloqaily, Y. Jararweh, and T. Baker, "An edge computing based smart healthcare framework for resource management," *Sensors*, vol. 18, no. 12, p. 4307, 2018.

14. R. F. Hussain, M. A. Salehi, and O. Semiari, "Serverless edge computing for green oil and gas industry," in *2019 IEEE Green Technologies Conference (GreenTech)*, 2019, pp. 1–4: IEEE.

15. Q. Qi and F. Tao, "A smart manufacturing service system based on edge computing, fog computing, and cloud computing," *IEEE Access*, vol. 7, pp. 86769–86777, 2019.

16. J. Zhang, B. Chen, Y. Zhao, X. Cheng, and F. Hu, "Data security and privacy-preserving in edge computing paradigm: Survey and open issues," *IEEE Access*, vol. 6, pp. 18209–18237, 2018.

17. R. Roman, J. Lopez, and M. Mambo, "Mobile edge computing, fog et al.: A survey and analysis of security threats and challenges," *Future Generation Computer Systems*, vol. 78, pp. 680–698, 2018.

18. N. Hassan, S. Gillani, E. Ahmed, I. Yaqoob, and M. Imran, "The role of edge computing in internet of things," *IEEE Communications Magazine*, vol. 56, no. 11, pp. 110–115, 2018.

19. A. Alrawais, A. Alhothaily, C. Hu, and X. Cheng, :Fog computing for the internet of things: Security and privacy issues," *IEEE Internet Computing*, vol. 21, no. 2, pp. 34–42, 2017.

20. M. Mukherjee et al., "Security and privacy in fog computing: Challenges," *IEEE Access*, vol. 5, pp. 19293–19304, 2017.

21. W. Z. Khan, E. Ahmed, S. Hakak, I. Yaqoob, and A. Ahmed, "Edge computing: A survey," *Future Generation Computer Systems*, vol. 97, pp. 219–235, 2019.

22. S. Ahmed and R. H. Khan "Blockchain and industry 4.0," in *Blockchain in Data Analytics*, Mohiuddin Ahmed, Ed. UK: Cambridge Scholars Publishing, p. 52, 2020.

23. G. F. Elkabbany and M. Rasslan, "Security issues in distributed computing system models," in *Cyber Security and Threats: Concepts, Methodologies, Tools, and Applications*, IGI Global, 2018, pp. 381–418.

24. I. Psaras, "Decentralised edge-computing and IoT through distributed trust," in *Proceedings of the 16th Annual International Conference on Mobile Systems, Applications, and Services*, 2018, pp. 505–507.

25. H. El-Sayed et al., "Edge of things: The big picture on the integration of edge, IoT and the cloud in a distributed computing environment," *IEEE Access*, vol. 6, pp. 1706–1717, 2017.

26. A. Narayanan, J. Bonneau, E. Felten, A. Miller, and S. Goldfeder, *Bitcoin and Cryptocurrency Technologies: A Comprehensive Introduction*. Princeton University Press, 2016.

27. K. Christidis and M. Devetsikiotis, "Blockchains and smart contracts for the internet of things," *IEEE Access*, vol. 4, pp. 2292–2303, 2016.

28. A. Bahga and V. Madisetti, *Internet of Things: A hands-on approach*. Vpt, 2014.

29. A. Bahga and V. K. Madisetti, "Blockchain platform for industrial internet of things," *Journal of Software Engineering and Applications*, vol. 9, no. 10, pp. 533–546, 2016.

30. J. Golosova and A. Romanovs, "The advantages and disadvantages of the blockchain technology," in *2018 IEEE 6th Workshop on Advances in Information, Electronic and Electrical Engineering (AIEEE)*, 2018, pp. 1–6: IEEE.

31. A. Songara and L. Chouhan, "Blockchain: A decentralised technique for securing Internet of Things," in *Conference on Emerging Trends in Engineering Innovations & Technology Management (ICET: EITM-2017)*, 2017.

32. G. G. Dagher, J. Mohler, M. Milojkovic, and P. B. Marella, "Ancile: Privacy-preserving framework for access control and interoperability of electronic health records using blockchain technology," *Sustainable Cities and Society*, vol. 39, pp. 283–297, 2018.

33. N. Kshetri, "Blockchain's roles in strengthening cybersecurity and protecting privacy," *Telecommunications Policy*, vol. 41, no. 10, pp. 1027–1038, 2017.

34. P. De Filippi, "The interplay between decentralisation and privacy: The case of blockchain technologies," *Journal of Peer Production*, vol. 7, no. 7, 2016.

35. R. Kumaresan and I. Bentov, "How to use bitcoin to incentivise correct computations," in *Proceedings of the 2014 ACM SIGSAC Conference on Computer and Communications Security*, 2014, pp. 30–41.

36. M. Conoscenti, A. Vetro, and J. C. De Martin, "Blockchain for the Internet of Things: A systematic literature review," in *2016 IEEE/ACS 13th International Conference of Computer Systems and Applications (AICCSA)*, 2016, pp. 1–6: IEEE.

37. E. Gaetani, L. Aniello, R. Baldoni, F. Lombardi, A. Margheri, and V. Sassone, "Blockchain-based database to ensure data integrity in cloud computing environments," in *Italian Conference on Cybersecurity*, Italy. 17–20 Jan 2017. 10 pp.

38. M. A. Salahuddin, A. Al-Fuqaha, M. Guizani, K. Shuaib, and F. Sallabi, "Softwarization of internet of things infrastructure for secure and smart healthcare," *Computer*, vol. 50, no. 7, pp. 74–79, 2017, doi: 10.1109/MC.2017.195.

39. P. Veena, S. Panikkar, S. Nair, and P. Brody, "Empowering the edge-practical insights on a decentralised internet of things," *IBM Institute for Business Value*, vol. 17, 2015.

40. C. Luo, L. Xu, D. Li, and W. Wu, "Edge computing integrated with blockchain technologies," in *Complexity and Approximation: Lecture Notes in Computer Science*, vol. 12000. Springer, 2020, pp. 268–288.

# Index

Page numbers in *Italics* refer to figures.